TRUE VAMPIRES

True Vampires © 2004 by Sondra London and Feral House

ISBN 0-922915-93-8
ALL RIGHTS RESERVED.

FERAL HOUSE
PO BOX 39910
LOS ANGELES, CA 90039

WWW.FERALHOUSE.COM
INFO@FERALHOUSE.COM

DESIGNED BY HEDI EL KHOLTI

TRUE VAMPIRES

Sondra London

Experts Are Saying

"Vampires ought not to exist—that is a statement with which every sensible person will agree. Yet the research of Sondra London has revealed that on this matter, common sense is mistaken. Her account, which is destined to become a classic of the literature, ranges from Hungary in the 17th century to America in our own time, leaving no doubt that vampirism is more than a superstition—more, even, than a rare psychological illness: it is a reality that deserves to be taken into account by all students of paranormal research. The author, best known as a fine criminologist, here reveals herself as a remarkable historian."

+ Colin Wilson, author, *The Outsider* and *The Occult*

"Prodigious research and compelling prose make *True Vampires* Sondra London's most impressive work to date. If you believe bloodsuckers dwell only in myths and movies, think again. This is the ultimate insider's view of a ghastly subculture as real—and as deadly—as it is difficult for 'civilized' minds to conceive. London rips the lid off, and you won't like what you find inside, which makes it all the more imperative to face the grisly truth."

+ Michael Newton, author, *The Encyclopedia of Serial Killers*

"Far from the sensual, seductive image of the vampire made popular in romantic fiction and motion pictures, there lies a dark and dangerous being, monstrously human, rather than preternatural. We are fortunate to have such a guide as Sondra London through a world that is all the more frightening because this book is not merely the creation of an imaginative author, but the product of a darn good investigative journalist."

+ Brad Steiger, author of *The Werewolf Book: An Encyclopedia of Shapeshifting Beings*

"If you've ever wondered if vampires really exist in human form, Sondra London has written the book for you, and it is an absolutely absorbing read."

+ Clifford Linedecker, author, *Blood in the Sand*

"Did a contemporary Cambodian vampire drink his victims' blood to cure himself of AIDS? Is one of Japan's foremost writers guilty of once having killed and devoured a college coed in Paris? Was the Russian monster known as "Iron Teeth" fond of human-flesh stews? These are among the myriad intriguing questions answered in Sondra London's masterpiece, *True Vampires*, a genuine work of high scholarship on this sanguinary subject. This book carries my highest commendation!"

+ Dr. Franklin Ruehl, Host/Producer of *Mysteries From Beyond The Other Dominion*

Thanks

to Dr. Dale & Dr. Ann, to Mr. Jack & Mr. Jay,
& those I can't name who have helped along the way.

Artwork by Nicolas Claux

CONTENTS

Part 1

THE UNDEAD ZONE

The vampire is the undead, living and dying on the border between life and death, the messenger of death to the world of the living. Vampires represent the transformation of a world of victims and victimizers into a world of the living and the dead. Only in this world the dead have won.

+C. Fred Alford, *What Evil Means to Us*

VAMPIRES AMONG US

Rod Ferrell's long nails were painted the color of a vampire's shriveled soul and his hair, dyed to match, was worn in a Mohawk—shoulder-length in back and shorn to the scalp along the sides. Given to wearing black cowboy boots, black shirts and pants, and a long black trench coat, Ferrell often wielded a wooden staff and boasted of his immortality.

Dean Wride was becoming a vampire. He had already drunk the blood of two humans from syringes to hasten the transition, but he wouldn't become a full-fledged vampire until he drank the blood of the third one. He needed a victim who was prepared to give more than just blood.

David Harker was becoming a cannibal. The 24-year-old skateboarding skinhead sporting menacing tattoos on his scalp reading "Subhuman" and "Disorder," eagerly boasted to at least 25 people of turning his lover into a yummy casserole of sautèed thigh with macaroni and cheese, but none of them took his outrageous claims seriously enough to report them to police.

Daniel Ruda was looking for a bride. "Raven-black Vampire seeks Princess of Darkness who hates everybody and everything," read his lonely-hearts ad. In dreams Satan told Daniel to marry the Dark Princess Manuela and then a month later, to sacrifice a victim, carve him up with a pentagram, drink his blood, and leave his mutilated body next to the coffin in the living room.

Serial slasher **Joshua Rudiger**, 24, told San Francisco police he was a 2,000-year-old vampire with "special psychic powers" who had lived all over the world, and had sucked the blood of all of his victims after slashing their throats.

Psychotic slayer **Richard Chase** believed he suffered from "soap-dish poisoning" that was turning his own blood to powder. The 28-year-old started out injecting rabbit's blood into his veins and biting the heads off birds, but soon he had to replace it by drinking the fresh blood of human victims.

Nicolas Claux, a 22-year-old Parisian mortician covered with occult tattoos, confessed to one murder, then went on to describe in nauseating detail the pleasure he derived from eating the flesh of a corpse on the slab. Declared a "nearly psychotic sadist," he was dubbed by the tabloids "The Vampire of Paris."

"Somewhere along the line, my dad had developed a real need for human blood," recalls **Kathleen Sullivan**, a survivor of satanic ritual abuse. "He really believed drinking it would extend his life span and would give him energy. He particularly preferred the blood of infants."

From blood fetishists to serial slashers, role-playing lifestylers to ritual abusers, they are all true vampires. Where do they get these ideas? What is the significance of their behavior? And is it just harmless eccentricity—or is it a crime?

VAMPIRE MYSTIQUE

Perhaps we're not altogether human after all. Perhaps there is something about us that can be transformed into something subhuman or even superhuman.

We have an ancient way to deal with the darkness, destruction, and wild passion that shadows the bright path of those who bask untroubled in the Light. We all know it's there, the domain of the Shadow. But it takes a real monster—a werewolf, perhaps, or a vampire—to identify with the darkness, to seek to become one with it.

The myth shapes the impulse, and so the pathology of the conditioned mind readily follows the imagery at hand which is most resonant with the inner chaos experienced.

The 1998 edition of *Webster's Revised Unabridged Dictionary* tells us that the vampire is "a blood-sucking ghost; a soul of a dead person superstitiously believed to come from the grave and wander about by night sucking the blood of persons asleep, thus causing their death."

The vampire has traditionally been understood as a mythical creature, a human being who has been dead and buried; who yet returns, revivified and intact, to travel about at night, attacking people and drinking the blood required to lend animation to its undead corpse. Legends from all over the world report fantastical creatures of a similar inclination, with regional variations.

Legends of vampire-like creatures are found in places as diverse as Greece and Scotland, Mexico, Brazil and China. While the Brazilian vampire might slip silently through the night on plush slippers, the Chinese vampire was more likely to practice funerary *feng shui* by drawing down the power of the moon and stabbing victims with dagger-like porcelain nails.

In *Mr. Vampire*, a 1985 Chinese film by Lau Cheng Wei, contemporary Chinese vampires not only wield the full component of martial arts skills, they are also distinguished by a tendency to hop, rather than skulk or glide, and they come with detachable flying heads.

The origins of the modern vampire are shrouded in the mists from the mediæval castles of the Balkan and Carpathian mountains of eastern Europe. Many of the distinguishing characteristics of the creature originally known as the *wampyr* are still found in film, fiction and folkloric games.

Emaciated and foul-mouthed, the Transylvanian vampire had lush red lips, long sharp claws, hairy palms, and a piercing gaze. The Bulgarian vampire was remarkable for having only one nostril, while his Bavarian cousin slept with one eye open. The Russian vampire had a violaceous face, and openly cursed the Church. European vampires were often called witches, and were known for their black or red hair. Many had fangs; some had either a harelip or a persistent snarl.

The fearsome, cautionary phantasm the vampire presents is symbolic of the chaos that may befall the careless wayfarer. Most who hear these tales will be chastened into more low-risk behavior like staying out of graveyards at midnight. But then there are always the ones who want to know what it's like to be as feared and powerful as these mythic creatures. The allure of becoming a vampire is the Mephistophelian promise of attaining superhuman powers, passing through solid walls, changing shapes, fleeing the noisome horde, frightening the horses, enjoying intense intimacy, and remaining forever young.

Of course there is more to it. The vampire myth is based on our most primordial fears. The paradigm of the psychic vampire is evident amongst the living. Psychic vampirism speaks of hungry ghosts, unsatisfied revenants looming up from the shadows to demand their due, attaching themselves to those filled with vitality, and sapping the vital substance of the soul to sustain their own morbid existence.

Then there are the real creatures whose passionate bloodthirst carries them once and for all beyond the pale. They were born human, but because of what they have chosen to do with their lives, they have become vampires. Their behavior is monstrous, and the root of the word *monster* tells us that this is a type of creature who heralds a warning. The warning implicit in the legend of the vampire relies on the subconscious awareness of the possibility of a breakthrough of raw passion and criminality that is inhibited by our social conditioning.

Vampires, cannibals, witches and ritual slayers of long ago and far away come to us shrouded in layer upon layer of glamorizing mythos, but the tight focus we have on our modern vampire killers strips us of our own delusions of their grandeur. True vampires show no interest in making a fashion statement at the annual Vampire Ball, in cape and whiteface, sporting elegant custom-made silver fangs and spooky contact lenses.

Vampire kind that seem dashing when cloaked in the romanticism of myth and legend, quite often seem simply depraved when encountered up close and in person, their glamorous mystique dispersed like a fetid miasma in the clear light of day.

> Vampires are living parts of our humanity that people in a technological age have ignored. They have to do with the darkness and magic that is not given its due. If we ignore the unconscious, it becomes avaricious, voracious... the vampire is another side of our culture that needs a voice.
> + Stephen Martin

CLINICAL VAMPIRISM

In his 1992 book, *Vampires, Werewolves, & Demons: Twentieth Century Reports in the Psychiatric Literature*, Richard Noll proposes that a cluster of vampiric symptoms be classified as a recognized syndrome:

> It is proposed that the sexual blood-fetish syndrome defined here as clinical vampirism should bear a new eponymous label in future psychiatric treatments and be renamed Renfield's syndrome in honor of the character in Bram Stoker's *Dracula* who bore many of the classic signs and symptoms of the disorder.
>
> The following are the proposed characteristics of Renfield's syndrome: A pivotal event often leads to the development of vampirism (blood drinking). This usually occurs in childhood, and the experience of bleeding or the taste of blood is found to be "exciting." After puberty, this excitement associated with blood is experienced as sexual arousal.
>
> The progression of Renfield's syndrome follows a typical course in many cases: Autovampirism is generally developed first, usually in childhood, by initially self-inducing scrapes or cuts in the skin to produce blood, which is then ingested, to later learning how to open major blood vessels (veins, arteries) in order to drink a steady stream of warm blood

more directly. The blood may then be ingested at the time of the opening, or may be saved in jars or other containers for later imbibing or for other reasons. Masturbation often accompanies autovampiristic practices.

Zoophagia (literally the eating of living creatures, but more specifically the drinking of their blood) may develop prior to autovampirism in some cases, but usually is the next to develop. Persons with Renfield's syndrome may themselves catch and eat or drink the blood of living creatures such as insects, cats, dogs, or birds. The blood of other species may be obtained at places such as slaughterhouses and then ingested. Sexual activity may or may not accompany these functions.

Vampirism in its true form is the next stage to develop—procuring and drinking the blood of living human beings. This may be done by stealing blood from hospitals, laboratories, and so forth, or by attempting to drink the blood directly from others. Usually this involves some sort of consensual sexual activity, but in lust-murder type cases and in other non-lethal violent crimes, the sexual activity and vampirism may not be consensual. The compulsion to drink blood almost always has a strong sexual component associated with it.

Noll based his conclusions in part on the research of Herschel Prins, who has shown that since the 19th century, the term "vampire" has been used within the psychiatric profession to describe numerous different behavior patterns, including not only love of blood or phlebophilia, but also necrophilia, necrophagia, and even necrosadism—extreme pleasures involving interference with the dead.

It will be noted, however, that the proposed terminology, "Renfield's syndrome," has not found acceptance in the medical lexicon, and remains merely a fanciful construct of popular culture.

VAMPIRE VIRUS

Even though there is officially no such thing as Renfield's syndrome, there are recognized genetic anomalies, chemical deficiencies and psychiatric disorders that can cause human nature to manifest strange distortions. A rare disorder in the synthesis of blood called porphyria causes many of the same symptoms that have traditionally been associated with the vampire.

There are eight different varieties of this genetic anomaly that cause severe abdominal pain, eruptions of the skin, sensitivity to light, difficulty breathing, and a transformation of the appearance. More than 50,000 Americans suffer from one of the eight variations of porphyria.

In May of 1985, David Dolphin, Ph.D., a chemistry professor at the University of British Columbia, made quite a controversial suggestion in his presentation to the American Association for the Advancement of Modern Science. "It is our contention that blood-drinking vampires were in fact victims of porphyria trying to alleviate the symptoms of their dreadful disease."

The modern therapy for porphyria includes injections of heme, which is a component of blood. Dr. Dolphin speculated that since refinement of blood was impossible in the remote past, porphyria patients might have instinctively tried to treat their disorder by drinking blood.

In discussing the stereotype of fangs, he pointed out that while the teeth do not become enlarged, the lips and gums are drawn back, creating an illusion of elongation of the teeth.

Dr. Dolphin speculated that garlic exacerbates the symptoms of porphyria, thus explaining the famous aversion to its vapors. He points out that its active ingredient, dialkyl disulfide, is known to destroy heme.

However, his imaginative thesis was not well received. Many experts called it far-fetched. "Dr. Dolphin's assumption that blood-derived heme might benefit these patients is as wrong as his connotation of harm from garlic," said Dr. Claus A. Pierach of Abbot Northwestern Hospital in Minneapolis, Minnesota. "There is no evidence heme is gut-absorbed, and patients may eat garlic with impunity."

"One might understand how a myth might have arisen, but this has nothing to do with scientific reality," said Jerome Marmorstein, M.D. of Santa Barbara, California. "As for the claim that ingestion of blood might relieve the pain of porphyria attacks, there is no scientific basis for this at all."

Writing in *New Scientist*, R.S. Day, a South African electron microscopist, rushed to the defense of much-maligned porphyria patients, and assured the public that they are not "predisposed to blood-sucking, sadomasochism, assault or murder, and that garlic will not poison them."

Porphyria is not the only diagnosis which has been evaluated in explaining the origins of vampire legend. In a 1998 interview with Reuters, a Spanish neurologist explained his theory that the origin of the modern vampire myth was an actual epidemic of the rabies virus that swept through Europe in the eighteenth century.

"Sometimes things that are apparently bizarre and senseless can have a logical explanation," said Dr. Juan Gomez-Alonso of Xeral Hospital in Vigo, Spain. His rabid vampire thesis appeared in the September, 1998 issue of the journal *Neurology*.

He began his line of inquiry after watching the original film *Dracula*. He began to notice how many similarities there were between the vampire imagery and the reality of rabies, "such as aggressiveness and hypersexuality."

Gomez-Alonso found that 25 percent of rabid men "have a tendency to bite others."

He correlated the timing of the old tales of vampires with known rabies outbreaks, focusing on an especially virulent epidemic in Hungary from 1721 through 1728.

He noted the famed hypersensitivity to light, mirrors and garlic, had a sound biological basis.

"Men with rabies react to stimuli such as water, light, odors or mirrors with spasms of the facial and vocal muscles that can cause hoarse sounds, bared teeth and frothing at the mouth of bloody fluid," he said.

"Hypersexuality may be a striking manifestation of rabies," Gomez-Alonso wrote in his article, adding that "the literature reports cases of rabid patients who practiced intercourse up to 30 times in a day."

He pointed out how bats and wolves often carry rabies, and their snarling visage is like that of an infected human.

"It would be imaginable that men and beasts with identical ferocious and bizarre behavior might have been seen as similar malign beings," Gomez-Alonso said.

The vampire's fatal bite is also common in rabies victims.

"Man has a tendency to bite, both in fighting and in sexual activities," Gomez-Alonso says. "The intensification of such tendency by rabies increases the risk of transmission, as the virus is in saliva and other body secretions."

The traditional vampire diet of blood would most likely make their fangs fall out, said the German Professor Thomas Crozier, who is researching vampire legends in Eastern Europe—unless oranges were somehow added to their diet. "Otherwise they risked losing their teeth due to scurvy which, to a vampire, would have meant death by starvation," he told *Frankfurter Rundschau*.

There is absolutely no medical basis for the idea that drinking blood can be nutritious, much less addictive. Blood is, in fact, most likely to be nauseating when taken orally, as it is metabolized by gastric juices into indigestible caustic compounds. When blood is accidentally swallowed, if vomiting does not expel it immediately, "it should be eliminated as promptly as possible with enemas and cathartics," reads *The Merck Manual*, "and the GI tract should be sterilized with nonabsorbable antibiotics to prevent the breakdown of blood and the absorption of ammonia."

Though a mythic vampire may have some magical way of metabolizing blood, human beings who behave like vampires do not. Taking blood from an animal or human poses considerable health risks. Besides the immediate nausea upon swallowing blood, there are diseases to consider: AIDS, hepatitis, heartworm, salmonella, trichinosis, and a host of unknown bacteria and viruses. Since blood has no nutritive value, and the impulse to drink it is not a physiological one, it is best understood as a maladaptive psychological aberration.

The urge to eat human flesh has been with us since earliest times, but anthropological research suggests it causes a fatal degenerative disease. Creutzfield-Jakob Disease is known as *kuru* among the Fore people of Papua, New Guinea. Starting with tremors and dementia, *kuru* makes holes throughout the brain and is fatal within two years. Transmitted by a prion, or deviant protein, it is related to mad-cow disease. The Fore started a tradition of dining on the flesh of their dead in the early 1900s, and by 1950, they had been decimated by the disease.

GOTHS WITH FANGS

The Medium shows its People what life is, what people are, and its People believe it: expect people to be that, try themselves to be that. Seeing is believing: and if what you see in Life is different from what you see in life, which of the two are you to believe? For many people it is what you see in Life (and in the movies, over television, on the radio) that is real life; and everyday existence, mere local or personal variation, is not real in the same sense.

+ Douglas Rushkoff, *Media Virus: Hidden Agendas in Popular Culture*

Nocturnal fashion statements accessorized in a palette restricted to the colors of midnight and moonlight—the gaunt pallor, the studied, nonchalant languor and flatness of affect, the ubiquitous silver jewelry—are emblematic of magical thinking and a fascination with fantasy, all too often leading to incipient depression, delusions of grandeur and acute alienation, a morbid obsession with death, decay, misery and an 18th century-style romanticism worthy of *The Sorrows of Werther*. Beyond the mystique held in common with the modern Goth, we see in the vampire a willful denial of the aging process combined with an obsession with feeding on the blood or élan vital of others.

But modern vampires are more than just "Goths with fangs." The drinking of blood is an act both palpable and symbolic. The symbolic aspect involves the ingestion of the essence of a living soul. The sensual aspect involves an intimacy that provides a pansexual and cryptosexual fetishistic thrill, and supports the exploration of the subtleties of transgenderal expression.

THE SATANIC BIBLE

In the constant interplay between the myths we teach ourselves and the forms those myths take in our lives, the real actions of real people provide the constellation of attributes that comprise the monstrous mythos.

When those struggling with chaotic impulses become aware of the details of these documented cases, they may develop parallel ideas about how the stress of their own chaos may be relieved, either by acting out the same paradigm, or inversely, by defending themselves against allowing this to happen. It's by incorporating fantasized roles that we become what we will, and so by stepping through that looking glass, a mundane creature becomes a mythical one.

Though some are just in it for the fun, many vampires take their dark identity seriously indeed, and a significant number of those who have been apprehended committing crimes claim to be satanists. Anton LaVey's *Satanic Bible* has been found on more than one true vampire. Although this ubiquitous volume does not contain instructions on transformation into a vampire, LaVey did publish instructions on how to become a werewolf in a later volume. The lycanthropic ritual calls for summoning up the feral spirit from the atavistic reservoir of the unconscious mind. After becoming a wild beast, one would be unbounded, one would move about hungry and strong, willful and bold in the night—as much like a vampire as a wolf.

 Anton LaVey

"The cult that I was raised in used a number of satanic mythologies for their ritual abuse," says Johanna C. in her memoir, *Wolf Girl Declassified*. "They worshipped the sun god and they believed they turned into werewolves. Werewolves, like vampires, appear human by day, but by night they turn into wolf-like creatures that live on blood they drain from the necks or bodies of humans."

Johanna describes how she was shown vampire and werewolf movies, so that when she began to recall the rituals, her emerging memories would be dismissed as she would be told that it was only her imagination and she must have been watching too many scary movies. "Perhaps this was also to create some allure about the werewolf rituals so that I would not resist so much. My cautious opinion is that werewolves are shape-shifters, dwelling in another dimension that is demonic. People can convince themselves that they turn into other creatures if they are strongly enough hypnotized, have believed this in their family line for generations, and have been exposed to extreme evil."

Whether or not any of the killer vampires have actually adhered to the beliefs and practices described in the books they owned, their behavior nevertheless contains many similarities to the significance of the formalized rituals. And the simple facts place satanic writings within the ambit of the investigation into their motivations. But although the lifestyles of the killers may show some influence of the occult, the crimes that have come to light are rarely undertaken in any ritual manner, but more often occur as mindless brutality. Yet paradoxically, that same kind of uninformed chaos is exactly what is summoned up in the rituals of transformation.

THE NECRONOMICON

In the magical world of the modern role-playing vampire, *The Necronomicon* is often used ceremonially. While it may be used with an occult intent, its nature and origin are not, however, quite the same as those of an authentic grimoire. With this volume, we move from the world of occult tradition into the world of occult fantasy.

Weird Tales was founded in 1923, and the short stories of H.P. Lovecraft darkened its pages throughout the Twenties. In a series of 13 stories, he conjured up a charming and magical world "long ago and far away" that recalled when Cthulhu and the Old Ones were worshipped, and the words were often quoted of a mad Iraqi poet named Abdul Al-Hazred, whose ancient wisdom had been passed down since 700 A.D. in a book of Arabic chants, spells and curses called *Al-Azif*.

Lovecraft explained that in English this fabled tome was called *The Necronomicon*, and he employed references to its contents as a recurring plot device. His stories so impressed his peers that a number of other *Weird Tales* authors also began to incorporate the poet and his ravings into their own stories.

To date, Lovecraft's vision of a mythic book of powerful rituals has given rise to at least a half-dozen different volumes all entitled *The Necronomicon*. Thus this still-viable literary tradition has wrought its progeny.

In time, a new generation of readers, heedless of the context of Lovecraftian fiction, have become so persuaded by the ubiquity of the references to the antiquity of this onomatopoetic gibberish, they give its authenticity enough credit to incorporate its spells into their rituals.

Even knowing that it is an interactive fictional motif of a literary movement, comparable to *The Principia Discordia*, there are law-abiding eclectic practitioners who find its invocations as efficacious as those gleaned from historical sources and stylized for modern audiences by Anton LaVey. And there are those who say of the rituals, quite simply, "they work." And so, perhaps, does homegrown glossolalia. If so, the power surely comes from within the human mind itself rather than the tones and rhythms used to heighten and focus that power.

If its function is to induce a trance, allowing the reader to cross that line between the conscious and unconscious, channeling human psychic energy and intention, then these verses do serve that function. For the credulous, *The Necronomicon* can serve as a portal, providing a passage out of the limitations of mundane reality and into the vast possibilities of an alluring magical world, where it's easy to believe one may work one's evil will by channeling malice and rage.

Besides being a portal for the mind, *The Necronomicon* also provides a pretext for those of like mind to come together to chant and sing. Nothing sinister about a group ritual; all worship services involve rituals. But these rituals do not invoke mercy or kindness, peace or patience. In chanting the curses of *The Necronomicon*, the powers invoked by any name are those of rage, revenge, and the enforcement of rampant will.

In a couple of very similar crimes by teenage vampire clans, investigation revealed that *The Necronomicon* had been used. It is safe to say there were no supernatural phenomena, no spirits summoned up, no powers of flight or invisibility granted. But the animus aroused in those rituals was so powerful it overcame all individual inclinations towards common courtesy and restraint. These disaffected, intoxicated teenagers were chanting their way toward violent crime, and would have to wake up from their vampire dreams in prison.

Interestingly enough, H.P. Lovecraft apparently was exposed to authentic occult literature, although he denied being a practitioner himself, and spurned the legions of followers who asked if the fanciful tales he told were true. "I am forced to say that most of them are purely imaginary," he wrote in a 1936 letter. "There never was any Abdul Al-Hazred or *Necronomicon*, for I invented these names myself."

Among true vampires, only a minority take any interest in fantasy or ceremonial magic at all. But among those who do partake of the vampire mystique, *The Necronomicon* is at least as popular as *The Satanic Bible*, if not more. This volume of chants and rituals is neither an ancient tome nor an occult fraud; it was offered as sheer entertainment.

The Necronomicon is well within the established traditions of both literature and ceremonial magic as an exemplar of creative embellishment. The book itself, and the literary movement that spawned it, dare you to accept them in the same spirit of ongoing improvisation.

> And if I do not finish this task, take what is here and discover the rest, for time is short and mankind does not know or understand the evil that awaits it from every side, from every open gate, from every broken barrier, from every mindless acolyte at the altars of madness.
> + Abdul Al-Hazred, *The Necronomicon*

THE CAMARILLA

Nobody perpetuates the vampire mystique better than White Wolf, the publisher of *Vampire: The Masquerade*, a book laying out the structure of an interactive role-playing game in which each player assumes the identity of a vampire, and becomes involved in an ongoing worldwide improvisational theater. Since 1991, they have helped players enact "modern stories of tragedy and personal horror." Arbitrated by a Storyteller, players rely on rolling dice to determine the success of the dramatic intrigues they dream up.

White Wolf provides a revisionist world history in which acknowledged facts are interwoven with a somber fantasy involving a long-secret conspiracy by vampire elders commanding from the shadows, manipulating mortals and other vampires alike, using our leaders, cultures, nations and armies as pawns in their secret war.

In the Gospel according to White Wolf, it all started with Caine, the same one previously known as Cain in the Bible. But in this new version, Caine consorts with Adam's first wife Lilith, otherwise known as the Original Vampire, and it is their licentious and rebellious childer who become the Thirteen Original Vampire Clans.

After enduring the horrors of the Inquisition, or so the story goes, the Childer of Caine held a council in the Fifteenth Century, and seven of the clans agreed to join the Camarilla (Spanish for "small chamber"). Members of the Camarilla established a hierarchy and protocol at that time, and agreed that from thence forth, they would operate covertly; this game they would play with society, then, was to be The Masquerade.

Vampires who decide to join one of the Camarilla clans today agree to participate under its terms. Depending upon their personal affinities, they decide whether to identify themselves as Brujah, Gangrel, Malkavian, Nosferatu, Toreador, Tremere, or the aristocratic Ventrue. The White Wolf mythology even welcomes vampires who want to play but do not want to be bound by the obligations of the Camarilla. The Sabbat vampires are the Camarilla's outright enemies. Then for vampires who find even this outlaw sect too restrictive, they can still play along as Anarchs.

In time the Vampire game has become a worldwide phenomenon, moving from the make-believe world of books and dice to Live Action Role Playing, known as LARP. Instead of relying on dice, a simple system of hand signs has evolved, denoting challenges, time-outs and special powers, such as invisibility. The rules, as played recreationally, are unambiguous: Don't touch. No weapons. And no biting. It's not about sucking blood. It's about using your mind to win a game.

Storytellers are offering it as an entertaining alternative to gangbanging and drugs, and thousands are playing it just for fun in San Francisco, New Orleans, and New York—not to mention London, Paris, Helsinki and Sydney.

There are several conventions sponsored by White Wolf every year, and events are always being held at a local level as well, so there is plenty of material to feed the imagination of the lost souls who hope to find themselves among vampires.

Interactive participation in vampire virtual reality is offered via yet another dimension in a series of White Wolf video games that can be played on or offline. The press release of *Vampire: The Masquerade—Bloodlines* crows: "In addition to vampire skills and powers, gamers will be able to call upon a devastating arsenal of weapons including stake guns, shotguns, flamethrowers, submachine guns and sniper rifles, to name a few. Once players arm themselves to the teeth they will be ready to tackle the host of human vampire hunters, ghouls, werewolves, and enemy vampires that inhabit the City of Angels after nightfall."

SO YOU WANT TO BE A VAMPIRE

From Bram Stoker's Drac through Nosferatu on to the immortal Bela Lugosi, as vampires of fiction and drama have elaborated on the ancient myth of vampire kind, the image of the vampire has shifted and changed as a reflection of the times. Perhaps the vampire's face cannot be caught in a mirror, because the reflection cast is always that of our own timeless fears and secret desires, which we are not fated to see.

For Stoker, Dracula was Darwinism run amuck, a foul, smelly mixture of man and beast, complete with fangs and hairy palms. He was man's prehistoric nature, crawling from regions beyond England's empire, to challenge a rational and modern scientific world. To Germany of the 1920s, still reeling from the devastation of the First World War, the Dracula seen in F.W. Murnau's *Nosferatu* was pestilence incarnate: a hideous force of nature that implacably plodded forward, like war, disease, and grim death. And so on.

Dracula's redemption started in the warm and fuzzy 1970s, and he returned to the fold of brooding, doomed, sympathetic vampires that were in vogue before Stoker's masterwork. It is this complex Dracula, both predator and victim, that is still with us today in the current atmosphere of New Ageism, recovery programs, and cloudy morality.

+ Bob Madison, *Dracula: The First Hundred Years*

The popular television shows *Dark Shadows* and *Forever Knight* had their fans like any other shows, but not until the millennial years did the modern vampire come to life as a full-blown media virus.

Anne Rice's *Vampire Lestat* grafted the ancient paradigm of the Undead onto that of the rock icon, at a time when rock personalities had progressed from Alice Cooper and Kiss with their good-natured whiteface mugging, through Ozzy Osbourne biting off the heads of small animals and G.G. Allin with his scatological terrorist art, culminating with Marilyn Manson cutting himself and letting it bleed on stage.

Over 600 vampire films have been made to date. In one of the most impressive, *Shadow of a Vampire*, Willem Dafoe portrays Max Schreck as a homicidal vampire cast in the role of the original Nosferatu, giving the effect of passing through a series of inter-reflective mirrors, an extra dimension intertwining fact and fiction in a way that is reminiscent of Rice's fictional Parisian theater where true vampires pretend to be human as they play the roles of vampires, blood feasting and hamming it up onstage.

And now Sir Elton John is taking *The Vampire Lestat* to Broadway. "I think that the book is so beautifully written, and there's so many different areas—in Paris, in New Orleans, whatever—the different scenarios at the opera," rhapsodized Sir Elton at a press conference in May of 2003. "It is a very visual book. It screams out for me that this is a very good subject matter for music." He stressed that the theatrical production would not be a "rock opera," but instead would have a classical feel. "This will be dark, sexy and scary, but that doesn't mean it has to be cliché. This is serious, not a parody."

Anne Rice describes the vampire as a "romantic, enthralling" character, "a person who never dies... takes a blood sacrifice in order to live, and exerts a charm over people... a handsome, alluring, seductive person who captivates us, then drains the life out of us so that he or she can live." The mystique thus promoted is overwhelmingly attractive to those who know themselves to fall somewhat short of enthralling, and who yearn to gain power and self-esteem from participating in this romantic paradigm in some way.

"The vampire is everything we love about sex and the night and the dark dream-side of ourselves," says Poppy Z. Brite in her novel *Love in Vein*, "adventure on the edge of pain, the thrill to be had from breaking taboos."

"Vampires are tragic; they are not pure evil. They have a conscience, they suffer loneliness," Rice enthuses. "The vampire is a cerebral image that transcends gender. In Bram Stoker's *Dracula*, they're presented as close to animals, but I always saw them as angels going in another direction... finely tuned imitations of human beings imbued with this evil spirit."

"Vampires are snappy dressers," astutely observes Suzy McKee Charnas in *The Vampire Tapestry*. "Think what a zombie or a mummy wears. That's why vampires are so popular."

The marketing of *Buffy the Vampire Slayer* is a study in the mining of anxieties, concerns and desires prevalent in the youth market. "They're trying to shortcut having to do adult things, like get a job or go to school," executive producer Marti Noxon said in a 2002 interview with *Sci-Fi Wire*. "So really the whole thing is either about evading or accepting responsibility, which is sort of what the 20s are all about, baby! The faster you run, the worse it gets."

> Media viruses spread through the datasphere the same way biological ones spread through the body or a community. But instead of traveling along an organic circulatory system, a media virus travels through the networks of the mediaspace.... Like real genetic material, these memes infiltrate the way we do business, educate ourselves, interact with one another—even the way we perceive reality.
>
> + Douglas Rushkoff, *Media Virus: Hidden Agendas in Popular Culture*

Buffy provides prima facie evidence of a well-defined media virus, with symptoms and side effects that extend beyond the virtual, a virus replete with -isms and -ologies, proliferating through books, movies, TV shows, comic books, fashion boutiques and social clubs.

Then you have the all-inclusive packages; *The Little Vampire*, for example, is billed as "a movie the whole family can sink their teeth into." The DVD product includes the following features, designed to provide a bridge between fantasy and reality: script-to-screen screenplay, an original website, a coloring book, easy-to-make recipes for "spooky snacks"; vampire and monster jokes that will tickle your funny bone, a "cool" flying vampire cow screensaver, a deck of trading cards, and three interactive games—*Graveyard Golf*, *Find the Amulet*, and *Mix & Match*—all for just $19.98.

Once your interest in vampire lore has been piqued by such primetime media packages, perhaps you'd like to go to the next level and become a vampire yourself. Couldn't be easier: just log on to the World

Wide Web and with a simple search you can step right into the Vampire Church, Vampire Crypt or Vampire Coven of your choice.

The Temple of the Vampire, out of Lacey, Washington, has published a slim tome called *The Vampire Bible*, including an injunction against committing violent crimes, an apocalyptic prophecy of the Final Harvest of Humankind, and a "true magic ritual, The Calling of the Undead Gods." It can be purchased from their website for only 30 dollars, including shipping and handling.

As you sink your new fangs into *The Vampire Bible*, and memorize the Vampire Creed, why not get in the mood with some vampire music? The opera *Der Vampyr* by Heinrich Marschner was peformed in 1828, but never recorded. It's unlikely you could arrange a private concerto from the score, but until Sir Elton graces the stage, perhaps you could get by with recordings of a couple of Broadway musicals. *Camilla* appeared in 1970, and *Possessed* in 1989. More contemporary would be "Surprise! You're Dead!" by Faith No More, but metalheads still prefer "Fiend for Blood" by Autopsy, "Waltz of the Vampire" by Motorhead, or perhaps "Nosferatu" by Coroner.

You could tune in to Vampire Radio for some Spooky Tooth or Cannibal Corpse while you download Japanese *Vampire Hunter D* anime and *Vampire Miyu* manga. You could send virtual vampire postcards to friend and foe alike, and seek your fortune in the Vampire Tarot.

After you've taken your Vampire Oath and sworn away your soul to become a true vampire, if your friends don't care for your *nouveau vampirismo*, no need to lurk lonely and forlorn in your dank tenement. Get back on the Web and find yourself some new running partners whose hearts are as black as your own. Venture into vampiric venues like Sanguinarius, the Vampire Connection, and VampireFreaks.com. Troll Usenet groups like alt.vampyres, and log on to vampire chatrooms. It won't take long to get in touch with kindred all over the world.

While you're becoming a vampire, sooner or later you need to step out and make the vampire scene. Even if you don't have a dungeon boutique in your hometown, you can find all the vampire accoutrements your benighted little heart desires, at commercial websites flogging vampire cosmetics, contact lenses, capes and fangs, vampire wine, even vampire condoms.

DRACULA LAND

If you reside in an A-List city, you can make the scene simply by tossing on the old cape, painting your face and hitting the streets, but if you are stuck out in the provinces, yearning to join in the social scene with like-minded vampires, to hasten your transition you might book a vampire cruise or a vampire tour. To fully cross over into the lifestyle, it may become necessary to do as so many American vampires have done: ditch your old hometown and head out for the City That Time Forgot—where Endless Night Productions sponsors an annual Vampire Ball on Halloween, and for the $50 price of admission, you get to take home your own special pendant hand-crafted by a real vampire.

Once you arrive in America's premier vampire venue, which also plays host to the Dark Cotillion and the Vampire Lestat Fan Club Party, why not have a vampire tour-guide show you the sights? The author of *Journey Into Darkness: Ghosts & Vampires of New Orleans* explained to *Playboy* for their Mardi Gras 2001 special why the French Quarter has been the timeless destination of choice for aspiring vampires.

"One of the reasons is because it is believed New Orleans was settled on ancient burial ground," Katherine Smith of Haunted History Tours. "The native Indians warned the French not to build a city here. After the city was built, it was destroyed a couple of times by major fires, several hurricanes and a number of wars. So there's been death on top of death on a very small concentrated area; the original City of New Orleans was just the French Quarter, which is only 12 blocks long.

"Plus, you've got voodoo here," added the Elvira look-alike. "Voodoo came here in the late 1700s. It's a religion that's based on spiritualism, calling the spirits up. It believes that the spirits are all around us, so I think that energy right there has kept things going on that esoteric level."

The Haunted History Tour winds up at the Big Easy's first mortuary, which is now a vampire hangout called the Babylon Club, where you can taste a Vampire's Kiss in the form of vodka, cranberry juice, raspberry schnapps and a "secret ingredient," as you listen to Katherine Smith tell you why it's only natural for vampires to congregate there:

New Orleans has an above-ground cemetery system, and when people were dying by the thousands with yellow fever, they were literally running out of tombs to put them in, and they had to store the bodies here in the mortuary and then eventually start burying them along the sides of the street. So this is a very highly concentrated area for hauntings, and we do have some active ghosts in the Babylon Club. And it's a known hangout for people who live in what we call the 'vampire reality.' A lot of people live the vampire lifestyle, and this is one of the places they enjoy hanging out.

"*National Geographic* has called New Orleans the most vampirically active city in the country," caped tour-guide Brett Thomas told *Playboy*, and surely it provides the most sympathetic environment in the United States to develop your identity as a vampire, but if you are the traveling kind, your ultimate destination will be a province nestled deep in the Carpathian Mountains of Romania called Transylvania. Should you aspire to walk in the steps of the original Dracula, you might find yourself joining the hundreds of vampires and their fans who travel from all over the world in the spring of every year to a mediæval Romanian castle, to confer with one another at the World Dracula Congress.

"Romania is the spiritual home for people interested in ghosts, vampires and the paranormal," said Alan Murdie, head of England's Ghost Club at the 2002 Congress. Scholars, artists and fans gather to enjoy film screenings, book launchings, lectures and debates, along with red wine tastings and indulgence in garlic-heavy Transylvanian cuisine.

"In the dark world of the occult there is no more terrifying figure than the vampire," intoned Murdie, whose 2003 presentation was titled *Scared to Death: the Power of Fear to Injure and Kill*. "Two of the most important drives are the sex drive and the fear of death, and the vampire is a symbol for both," he told Reuters, explaining the pervasive allure that has proven to be such a powerful draw for Romania.

There are even plans for a mad, macabre theme park called Dracula Land. Noting that every year about a quarter million tourists visit Bran Castle in Transylvania, in September of 2001 the Romanian government announced their intention to create some 3,000 jobs and draw a million new visitors to the region every year. They announced it would be located in the "jewel of Transylvania," the city of Sighisoara, where Vlad "The Impaler" Tepes was born, and Dracula Land would encompass not only sight-seeing tours and seminars for the elders attending the vampirology institute, but creepy entertainment for the kiddies—thrill rides through a castle of horror and catacombs flowing with blood.

As soon as the official plans were announced, however, Romania's established church criticized the Dracula Land project as glorifying paganism and the "dark arts." The Patriarchal Bishop of Bucharest, Vincentiu Ploiesteanu, said he was disturbed because "Romanians are known abroad as the people living in the vampire's country."

To counter this unflattering publicity and to convince tour operators to organize trips to the new theme park, the Romanian state tourism commission released a 12-minute promotional video called *Dracula and The Good Lord*, featuring Romania's most famous monasteries. At Berlin's Tourism Fair, Tourism Minister Dan Matei-Agathon said, "We're trying to convince foreign tourists to come to the land of Dracula in order to find God."

Then in December of 2001, the Bucharest dreamers where shocked to find out they did not have the right to use the world-famous image of Dracula. Blood-suckers in the form of Hollywood lawyers came calling to extract royalties for Universal Studios, where seven Dracula films had been made between 1930 and 1960. Although Vlad Tepes provided the inspiration for the Dracula myth, it was the Universal films that contributed the visuals: the iconic black cape, ominous gaze, deathly pale skin and fangs. The nation of Romania could not use any images derived from the films without cutting Hollywood in on the deal.

The Romanians, however, refused to cough it up, and instead announced a contest among schoolchildren to come up with a new, home-grown copyright-free image of Dracula. "Universal Studios is asking for money if we use an image from their old Dracula films," Matei-Agathon told *Ananova*. "But maybe we can make a new concept and make Dracula Romanian and then I won't need to buy any copyright. I think that would be better. We'll see."

In June of 1993, a poltergeist, or perhaps the ghost of Dracula, intervened in an apparent effort to demonstrate his disapproval of the Dracula Land project. A Transylvanian ghostbuster was called in to investigate reports of a restless revenant wandering the streets of Sighisoara, vandalizing property and terrorizing the tourists.

"If I find that the reports are correct and it is Dracula who has been terrorizing people in Sighisoara, then I intend to link up the cameras to the internet so that the world can see his ghost for themselves," Damian Ioan Cusleaga told *Ananova*, somberly confirming that there was "definitely some activity" in the area.

Next to complain was Greenpeace. They condemned the planned

construction on the grounds that it would damage a nature preserve forested with oak trees that had been living there for over seven hundred years, while the fortunes of dramatic interlopers like Vlad Tepes waxed and waned. Since the mediæval citadel at Sighisoara is a world heritage site funded by UNESCO, the international organization also came out against the park. After England's Prince Charles visited the site and joined the growing opposition, the Ministry of Tourism decided it would be best after all to relocate Dracula Land closer to the Bucharest airport, and its debut date was pushed back to 2005.

Despite delays, spooky spinoffs have already popped up to catch the tourist overflow from Dracula Land. A Dracula Workshop has an extended engagement in nearby Bacau. Your Transylvanian host Constatin Talpau will welcome you into a ghoulish cave decorated with skeletons, seat you in a coffin, and paint your portrait on goat skin with your own blood.

Meanwhile in Germany, an antique dealer named Ottomar Rudolphe Vlad Dracul Kretzulesco, better known simply as "Count Dracula," the last known relative of Vlad the Impaler, has turned his home into a vampire museum, featuring scores of bats, "Blood Red" wine, a hearse and a coffin collection.

In May of 2002, the 61-year-old retired banker announced that in his home town of Schenkendorf, a hamlet of 1200 living souls, the elected officials were supporting him in their bid to secede from Germany, and form the Kingdom of Dracula, destined to become a more responsive and less bureaucratic utopia.

"In the Kingdom of Dracula, you'll find that tax collecting is much less of a pain in the neck," the Count told Buck Wolf. "I want a maximum tax of no more than 20 percent."

"We could change 'I come to suck your blood' to 'I come to collect your taxes!'"

The childless Count also announced that he was desperately seeking new blood for the House of Dracula, and invited European nobility to send him letters, enclosing photos. With arch insouciance, he told the *Independent*, "I would be pleased to hear from practically any prince or princess. We would like to adopt, but a real prince or princess. I cannot just take anyone from the street."

"It would probably be easier if it were to be a German," the discriminating Count stipulated, but on second thought, lowered the bar. "I would also be very happy for a British aristocrat to come and be adopted."

 Dracula

VAMPIRE RESEARCH

The Queen of Vampire Literature has conjured up a fantastical world so seductive that many of her fans actually try to climb through the looking glass and move in bag and baggage, leaving cloven hoofprints on the lady's carpet. But when she is not crooning the tune of her deathless prose, when spell-binding time is over, the true beliefs of this author might come as quite a shock to vampire lifestylers and fans alike. "I don't believe in vampires at all and I don't believe in blood-drinking," Anne Rice told the student reporters at the *Loyola Maroon* for their Halloween 2000 special issue. "Vampires don't exist."

And yet some go on behaving very much as if they do.

"You know you're a vampire instinctively," says one of the New Orleans tour-guides, as reported by the *Loyola Maroon*. "It's like learning how to crawl or walk. It just happens." While vampires are just "wannabes," as a *vampyre* (pronounced *vom-PEER* in French), Vlad Tepes Knight claims that he only consumes blood out of necessity.

"I do drink blood, by consent only and from people like you; normal people," Vlad insists. "I don't go around sucking peoples' blood unless they consent."

In New York City, Dr. Stephen Kaplan, who has been the founder and director of the Vampire Research Center since 1972, compiled the only "vampire census" ever taken, first in 1981, then again in 1989. "There are about 500 vampires worldwide," he announced in 1989, "and we've heard from several vampires in Australia." In 1994, he claimed the known population had grown to upwards of 850 vampires. The self-proclaimed vampirologist has also developed a questionnaire that is used to assess the VQ, or vampire quotient.

An article in *American Demographics* quotes Kaplan on the characteristics of true vampires. According to Kaplan's research, the average woman vampire has green eyes, blonde hair, weighs 118 pounds, stands about 5'8" and appears to be about 20. The average male vampire is 5'10", 150 pounds and looks about 21.

As paraphrased from his 1984 book, *Vampires Are*, traits of the modern vampire include:

+ Both physical and psychological needs.

+ A need to drink human blood every day.

+ Being very body-conscious, usually nice-looking, well-groomed, and looking younger than their age.

+ Believing that drinking human blood is going to extend their lives while keeping them young-looking.

+ Believing that if they stop drinking human blood they will age and possibly die.

+ Having strong personalities; typically taking charge in a conversation, demonstrating an ability to get people to do things their way, yet are generally genial, intelligent and good conversationalists.

+ Being "night people," preferring to work at night and sleep during the day.

+ Never having been married, or had any children.

"Real vampires have a physiological need to drink a few ounces of blood several times a week," Kaplan told *Omni* in 1994, downgrading the average frequency from his 1984 figures. "They rarely kill, and most are nice. Unlike their fictional counterparts, real vampires can tolerate daylight if they wear a sunscreen, and they don't leave fang marks, rather, they bite very gently or use cutting devices."

Katherine Ramsland, in her book *The Science of Vampires*, references a study of American vampires that was conducted in 1999:

> At the end of the decade, Dr. Jeanne Keyes Youngson sent out a survey to assess the situation of the vampire in our culture. In her abridged report on the results, she tabulated the data based on the 713 returned questionnaires out of the 933 distributed. One part was directed to those who considered themselves vampires and the other was for people simply interested in the vampire genre. A vast majority were Caucasian and one-third participated in the vampire lifestyle. There were more females than males in the mix. Of those who believed they were vampires, most kept it secret and most claimed to wear fangs and drink blood. Interestingly, few thought that they would have a longer life span than nonvampires. Three-fourths admitted to having been abused as children. Of their favorite vampire movies, first on nearly every list was *Dracula*, starring Bela Lugosi. Old vampires die hard.

In *American Vampires: Fans, Victims, and Practitioners*, folklorist Norine Dresser reported that 27% of 574 high school and college students admitted that they thought vampires actually might exist. Of course, that *was* in California, but still, literally millions of people the world over enjoy vampire lore recreationally. Pretending to be a vampire is all in fun, and it's perfectly harmless. Or is it?

The most essential personality characteristic of the modern vampire is a profound form of rebellion. There is a willful unleashing of the most primitive instincts as the *daemon* within is conjured up, and summoned to overwhelm and transform all more subtle impulses. The urge to bite, to snarl and tear, to suckle and throttle is indulged without inhibition by a true vampire. But long before it reaches that crescendo, the nascent vampire knows himself as an Outsider.

"When the Outsider is in his earliest stages—when he does not know himself or understand why he is 'out of harmony' with the rest of humankind—his hatred for men and the world makes him an unbalanced misfit, a man full of spite and envy, neurotic, cowardly, shrinking and wincing," says Colin Wilson, in *Religion and the Rebel*. "What all Outsiders have in common is a desire to escape the endless confusion of the outer world and retreat deep into themselves. Truth is subjectivity, and is therefore to be achieved by becoming concentrated in oneself."

Avatars of the modern vampire communities officially disavow violence amongst vampire kind, and prefer to stress the metaphorical aspects of the roles they choose to play in the Theater of the Real.

"This idea of people coming back from the dead is simply myth," says Beverly Richardson, a vampirologist who studies and lectures about the mythic vampires of film and fiction. "If vampires did exist, I probably wouldn't be interested in reading about them. For instance, I'm not interested in serial killers, because their existence is all too true and there is nothing particularly enjoyable or fun about that."

Those who indulge recreationally in the mythos and mystique surrounding the modern vampire hope to do so without being tainted by association with despicable crimes. There is nothing particularly fun about being the kind of creatures who by their crimes, might be described variously as vampires, cannibals, necrophiles or ghouls. Our focus is on what happens after the fun stops, after the darkness swallows the sun. We are looking into the darkest side of the vampire's shadow, the domain of pure unmitigated evil incarnate.

> Evil is an intense relationship that wants all the other person has to offer, without the fearsome bother of having the other person around. So you try to take what they have and kill them, or throw them away, use them up. Suck them try, and throw the empty husk away.
>   + C. Fred Alford, *What Evil Means to Us*

Evil is always present, exactly like a pathogen. Just as the physical body resists infection by virus or bacteria, the psychic body resists infestation by frank evil—so long as the psychic immune system is robust and functioning. Factors bolstering up psychic health include a social network of love, respect, and reciprocal benefit; spiritual texts, teachings and fellowship; a body free of biological toxins; exercise and meaningful, vigorous work; a fully functioning sex life; cultivation of plants and animals; musical and artistic enrichment.

Factors that contribute to breaking down the immunity to evil include intimate personal abuse, which consists of the victim having the pernicious evil of the abuser demonstrated and enacted as an object lesson and model, enforcing the pain, fear and rage of victimization while simultaneously providing a close look at the power and dominion represented by the abuser; rhetoric, artwork, and music specifically intended to incite and enjoin the audience in conscious practice of organized evil, promising fulfillment of desires which are otherwise frustrated; economic degradation combined with lack of education or opportunity to improve circumstances; voluntary or involuntary intoxication via substance abuse and industrial pollution; physical illness, infirmities and inadequacies, especially those perceived as socially unattractive.

Each individual organism is inherently healthy by default; this is the essence of the gift of life. Ambient evil can and often does coexist without infecting/infesting the psyche. Evil is everywhere, and people do encounter it, handle it, and work with it, without having it enter into their own soul, occupy it, and drive out the original healthy soul. As the factors contributing to vulnerability accrue, the psyche becomes more likely to succumb to evil, just as factors providing resistance can strengthen the psyche and prevent an infection.

Rhetoric, songs and visual arts, slogans and symbols—all have the ability to influence the human mind. So does human behavior—personal interactions as well as more far-reaching performance art, political and socioreligious acts that serve as models for millions.

A contagious idea can operate exactly like a virus. It can be carried from one mind to another, invading the very core of a person, and transforming their psyche into that foreign substance, which in turn becomes infectious with that same essence to the next mind and the next. And that same form of transmission occurs in the forced transaction between predator and prey.

A healthy person, regarding an evil one, may have a sense that what they are seeing is sick or insane. But someone who is thoroughly infected with the essence of evil is not sick in the medical or even psychiatric sense, because there are no drugs or therapies which are known to provide a cure.

The only way the damage that evil does to the soul can be mitigated is by immersion in every variety of therapeutic influence. This is neither quick, cheap nor simple. A quantity of fortifying influences simply may not be available. This may account for the pervasiveness of evil in circumstances in which pathogenic factors are prevalent.

There is no use protesting that vampires are "only" imaginary creatures who do not "actually" exist. The history of malignant transformation has provided a body of texts, images, and *dramatis personae*. There has been widespread word-of-mouth propagation of the idea of the healthy human mind crossing over into the penumbra of evil, pursuant to the perennial promise of power through conscious cruelty.

Thus the fabled vampire becomes a modern reality, taking the form of the fevered mind driven by fear and superstition layered over dark currents of narcissistic rage. As the cloacal emotional miasma at the core of the broken soul creates a pressure that requires an outlet to express its primal urges, so the vampire rises up from our cosmic consciousness.

The vampire lives only in darkness and curses the light, sucks vital substance from living souls, strikes out in fear, spite and cruelty. A person may become a vampire in fact, whether or not they see themselves as such. Sometimes the entire fatal drama is enacted entirely unconsciously, as the blood predator descends to a primitive level of consuming human essence without having any idea of what they are doing or why. Others are more organized. Insofar as they are conscious of the direness of their dilemma, they require the contrival or adoption of a conceptual frame of reference that will support their mode of antithesis.

That's where vampire literature, role-playing games, movies, books, comics, songs and websites come in. They provide the script for the disaffected soul who is seeking a way to vent their own personal *angst*.

Sure, connoisseurs might delight in a recreational *frisson* of fright, just as one might toss a dash of hot sauce on the eggs. But there are those who are disturbed enough and vulnerable enough and otherwise predisposed enough that the entertainment comes together with their malaise like nitro and glycerine.

Instead of being at the mercy of wild beasts, earthquakes, landslides, and inundations, modern man is battered by the elemental forces of his own psyche. This is the World Power that vastly exceeds all other powers on earth. The Age of Enlightenment, which stripped nature and human institutions of gods, overlooked the God of Terror who dwells in the human soul.

+ Carl Jung

 Voracious

MORE THAN MAKE-BELIEVE

"Medical science recognizes a vampire psychosis wherein troubled individuals may become convinced that their life depends upon drawing fresh blood from human victims," writes Brad Steiger in *The Werewolf Book: The Encyclopedia of Shape-Shifting Beings*. "The persons suffering from such a psychosis may, in extreme cases, actually believe themselves to be dead."

However, it is important to note that a thorough search of the *Diagnostic & Statistical Manual*, the bible of psychopathology, reveals no such malady as a "vampire psychosis," and none of the modern vampires who have been subjected to psychiatric scrutiny have been diagnosed as such. A psychosis, or condition of being out of touch with reality, is a symptom, not a disease, and while such bloodthirsty delusional beliefs may exist within the context of several medically recognized mental illnesses, they do not comprise the illness itself, but rather contribute to the overall complex of symptoms that are defined by a diagnosis that also pertains to people without these specific symptoms.

The sensation of undergoing a transformation and emerging as a different sort of creature is essential to vampire lore. In the perennially popular 1927 novel *Steppenwolf*, Hermann Hesse explores his character's psychic transformation into a beastly dimension as he rhapsodizes about a victim:

> The lovely creature I would so treasure,
> And feast myself deep on her tender thigh,
> I would drink of her red blood full measure,
> Then howl till the night went by.

A ritual, rich with symbols, texts and music, and a character to enact with costume, makeup and accessories, may be just make-believe for most of the participants, but among the group there may be those for whom it triggers a more profound shift in identity. In some cases, a psychic transformation into a bloodthirsty primitive predator may be as dramatic as if they had suddenly sprouted fangs and glow-in-the-dark eyes like Michael Jackson in *Thriller*.

In November of 2001, an Australian study was published in the *Journal of Trauma and Dissociation* that suggests that those who are predisposed towards dissociation may be doing more than acting when the spirit of vampirism animates them. There may actually be more than one person present in their mind.

What used to be called multiple personality disorder is now more accurately styled dissociative identity disorder. But under either name, it is a condition that allows the mind to slip into a different mode of being.

Recent research reveals that these personality changes are associated with distinct physiological changes such as rapidly appearing and disappearing rashes, welts, scars, switches in handwriting and handedness, allergies, addictions, vision changes and even color blindness.

By no means do all DID patients have alter personalities who are violent criminals, but our inquiry here concerns those individuals who behave so monstrously that behaviorally, they may actually become vampires, werewolves, ghouls, or cannibals. Now that criminal defendants are commonly subjected to psychiatric scrutiny, we do find a tendency toward dissociation or personality shift in case after case of these ghoulish criminals. Perhaps in years past, a similar phenomenon gave rise to some aspects of vampire mythology as well.

Dr. Joseph Ciorciari conducted a study at Swinburne University in Melbourne, Australia, performing coherence analysis on electroencephalograms of brain activity in identity-shifting DID patients.

> DID patients were compared with professional actors who role-played on the basis of age and gender corresponding to each DID host and alter personality.
> The significant differences in EEG coherence between the host and alter personalities but not between the actors' hosts and alter personalities provides physiological evidence for the authenticity of DID.

Dr. John Spensley and psychiatric nurse Gillian Johnson from the Jamillon Centre, where the study was done, hailed it as an important step in gaining a better understanding of DID.

> The results clearly show there is something different about people with DID. DID patients have usually suffered severe trauma during their childhood. Some people have questioned the authenticity of the alter personalities or suggested they are induced by therapists. Taken in conjunction with other scientific evidence the study's findings suggest that there is more to DID than these explanations.

The mind that is capable of housing multiple personalities is often confused with the diseased mind of schizophrenia. While it is possible for someone to have both disorders, it is unlikely, because their etiology and treatment are completely different. Dissociative identity disorder cannot be treated with medication; a true schizophrenia is responsive to drug therapy in over 70 percent of cases.

Schizophrenics often suffer hallucinations and delusions, and these may explain the more grotesque elements of their crimes. Many of those who either believe themselves to be vampires or who act the part have been diagnosed at one time or another with schizophrenia, and this may explain why their role-playing behavior goes beyond a harmless form of make-believe.

In the remote past, when the ancient impressions of vampires were formed, some of the primitive crimes that became legendary could have stemmed from schizophrenia, dissociative identity disorder, or any of a half-dozen other psychiatric and neurologic disorders, including brain damage.

A recent study of Vietnam veterans showed that those who had sustained frontal-lobe damage were two to six times as violent and aggressive as veterans who had suffered other types of head injuries. Neurological or organic, rage is aggression experienced as explosive and uncontrollable. With frontal brain damage the ability to control impulsive behavior is lost, and unreasoning violence is often the dire result.

Jonathan H. Pincus is chief of neurology at the Veteran's Administration Hospital, Washington, DC, and professor of neurology at Georgetown University School of Medicine. Along with professor of psychology Dorothy Otnow Lewis, he has interviewed and examined over 150 murderers. In his book, *Base Instincts: What Makes Killers Kill*, he reports that neurological deficits, mental illness resulting in paranoia, and a history of being abused are the most important factors. Two-thirds of the murderers he examined have all three, and the remainder have two of the three.

Each of these factors may be overcome without violence, but when they combine, the urge to kill can become irresistible. Irritants that could have been easily tolerated instead trigger escalation of stress, along with a deterioration of the ability to moderate or inhibit impulses. Other factors, such as genetic predisposition to violence and low concentrations of brain serotonin, also play a role as contributing factors, but Pincus stresses the primacy of the fatal triad as precursors of violent crime.

Pincus examined cannibal killer Arthur Shawcross, who had sustained several serious head injuries during a childhood pervaded by physical abuse, being hit on the head with a sledgehammer at one time and a discus at another. Later, he fell onto his head from the top of a 40-foot ladder. On examination by computerized electroencephalogram, he was found to have a cyst pressing on one temporal lobe and scarring in both frontal lobes.

Before being institutionalized, Shawcross had demonstrated peculiar signs of neurological damage by what he called "walking cross-lots," in absolutely straight lines, plowing through puddles and over barbed-wire fencing instead of using a nearby gate. This odd habit provides the very image of behavior that used to be called psychopathic, and would now be diagnosed as proceeding from "antisocial personality disorder." It seems to reveal a callous disregard for the laws of common sense, and speaks of a sense of entitlement along with an unwillingness to mitigate the will.

Prosecutors overwhelmingly favor this diagnosis in criminal cases, Pincus points out, because it justifies punishment rather than treatment. Noting that all of the death row inmates he and his colleagues have examined have received this diagnosis, he demurs that they also "have suffered from a combination of other diagnosable neurologic and psychiatric diseases." For such prisoners, Pincus says, "execution is not an acceptable treatment... though restraint in a prison or hospital is." Pincus argues that "the diagnosis of antisocial personality is inappropriate for brain-damaged and/or psychotic individuals, even for those who have committed antisocial acts."

Antisocial personality disorder "is not a proper medical diagnosis at all," Pincus says, because it suggests that no actual disease exists, and that the crimes should be judged and treated morally rather than medically. But Pincus shows that brain damage "clearly characterizes the extremely violent," and cites PET and MRI scans, neurological and psychological tests that inexorably link violence to brain damage. He believes that reducing brain injury would be the most rational social response to crime. "This is likely to be more successful in reducing violence in America than increasing the number of prison beds or increasing the certainty and frequency of executions."

In a *Salon* interview, Pincus addresses the so-called "homicidal triad"—cruelty to animals, fire setting, bed-wetting. It has been known for some time that these behaviors in a child tend to correspond with the development of criminal violence later on. "What hasn't been known is that they are indicators of abuse," says the neurologist. "You show me a kid who's set fire to his bed or his parents' bed and I'll show you a kid who's been sexually abused. With cruelty to animals—things like setting a cat on fire, really awful things—he's trying to enact what's happened to him on something weaker than him."

PART 2

VAMPIRE CRIME

True vampires are far more fearsome than their fictional counterparts. They are the dread and terror of the night, the fear of death, and the helplessness in the face of the unknown. They are the evil of hell and the dark side of the universe.

+Rosemary Ellen Guiley,
The Complete Vampire Companion

SATANIC SACRIFICE

How many girls would answer a personal ad like the one that ran in the fall of 2000 in *Metal-Hammer*, a German *okkulte* magazine: "Raven-black Vampire seeks Princess of Darkness who hates everybody and everything"? It only took one Vampiress to make the fatal match, and that one was Manuela Bartel.

At 21, she was already a veteran dominatrix who had sworn her soul to Satan— the same Satan who appeared in a dream to 24-year-old Daniel Ruda, commanding him to marry Manuela on the sixth day of the sixth month of 2001. As Daniel's satanic instructions continued, he was ordered to sacrifice a human soul on the sixth day of the seventh month, and then to culminate the satanic rites with a murder-suicide that would give them both the supernatural powers of the vampire, allowing them to fly, and to live forever in Hell's Kingdom. "Kill, sacrifice, bring souls," was how Daniel summed up Satan's commands.

"We had to kill," said Manuela. "We couldn't go to hell unless we did." The purpose of the marriage was not love, or even lust. It was so that they could be united in death.

On the ninth day of the seventh month, Manuela's parents received a letter from their daughter, bidding them a final farewell, and enclosing a Last Will and Testament, in which the young vampire asked to be buried in her own casket, by which she meant the silk-lined casket in which she slept at home. "I am not of this world," she said. "I must liberate my soul from the mortal flesh."

Unable to contact their disturbed daughter by phone, the alarmed parents called the police in Witten, Germany, and accompanied them to Manuela's apartment. The first thing they saw, in dripping blood-red paint on the window, was the ominous phrase in English, "When Satan Lives!"

Fearing the worst, the Bartels waited outside while police entered the front door, which had been left unlocked. Behind the darkened windows was more darkness. There were no lamps. The carpet was black, the walls a dingy gray or dark blood-red, hung with swastikas and upside-down crosses, and defaced with satanic slogans and inverted pentagrams. Handcuffs hung by a chain from the ceiling; a whip, a metal collar and rivet belts were on display; candles, pieces of stone ransacked from graveyards and former concentration camps, a human mask bearing the horns of an animal, cemetery lights and imitation skulls set the ghoulish scene.

Blood spattered the walls and pooled in quantity on the floor, where next to the open casket sprawled an unidentifiable corpse, disfigured by 66 wounds. A scalpel was lodged in his stomach and a pentagram cut into the skin of his chest.

Near the fearsome arsenal of knives, axes and machetes the couple had collected over the years, was found a death list of 15 more intended victims.

Though Manuela now says she has no memories of her childhood, by all accounts she was the well-kept only child of a stable working-class married couple—a railway clerk and his wife, who had stayed home with the child since her difficult birth, complicated by having the cord around the baby's neck.

Manuela was affectionately educated, but also strictly. "I was not allowed everything, but I had good parents," she wrote in a letter to one of her friends. "They never struck me. Those were always there for me."

Father Franz Josef Hagemann remembers preparing Manuela for her First Communion at the age of ten. Shy and reserved, completely inconspicuous, she attended church regularly and believed in God. She loved animals, and had many pets: birds, hamsters, guinea pigs, a rabbit and a dog; she even had a pony. She often played alone, but as a single child, that was only natural.

Even with her sheltered upbringing, Manuela told psychiatrists that it was about that time she first had the feeling that she was "different than others" in an unspecified way, or that she was in a false body, and not of this world. Though it's not uncommon for children going through puberty to feel awkward and out-of-place, this early depersonalization was perhaps the first unrecognized and untreated symptom of an actual mental illness. Though Manuela tried therapy once briefly, she abruptly broke it off, because she was afraid if she let anyone know what was really going on in her mind, they would have locked her up.

By the age of 13, she was ditching class to hang out by the bus station with older kids, and shocking her parents with her first punk hairstyle. Wearing torn jeans and T-shirts, with safety pins in her face, she joined the other punk rockers smoking pot, drinking beer and listening to The Damned by the Wittener town center.

She still managed to do well enough at school to be selected to attend gymnasium, the German equivalent of a grammar school intended to groom its pupils for university. But she dropped out at the age of 14, and about the same time tried to kill herself with an overdose of heroin.

At 15, Manuela visited a Renaissance Fair, and there amidst the fantasies enhanced by antique costumes and courtly manners, she felt as if a light clicked on in her head, and she told a friend, "I was at home. It was there I truly lived. There, everything was beautiful. There, I belonged." Years later, she would weep, says her friend, when she saw anything about the Middle

Ages on TV, sighing that it made her feel homesick.

Her quest for exotica took her from Witten to the nearby big city of Hanover, and by the time she was 16 in the summer of 1996, she found a part-time job as a chambermaid in a hotel in the Scottish Highlands, where her yearnings for solitude were fueled by the bleak surroundings and frequent visits to cemeteries.

When the hotel closed for the winter season, she went to live briefly in a cave on the Isle of Skye with a 62-year-old Scotsman known as Tom Leppard, for the leopardskin tattoos that cover his entire body. An amiable eccentric, he was a devout Catholic with no occult background who had lived in his solitary grotto for 12 years, after retiring from a lifetime of military service.

"She expressed an interest in me and told me she wanted to come and visit," he told *The Observer*. He arranged for the manager of a local youth hostel to bring the girl to his den. "She seemed like an ordinary teenager," he said. "I thought her much like any other teenager. Hundreds of people have passed through here. Backpackers from Australia, Canada, and Germany. I speak to many of them and there really was nothing so different about her."

When the rigors of the winter bearing down on the cave became more than Manuela could bear, she got a job at a Gothic club in the north London district of Islington. "That was my apprenticeship," she said. It was there that she first met satanists and went with them to "bite parties."

In her testimony at the murder trial, she revealed her emerging attitude as a Lady of the Night: "Men were always trotting after me in London. I made them pay for their affections — with their blood. That's all I wanted from them — to drink their blood. They were my blood donors."

"I met ordinary people and I met vampires," she told the Court. "At night we visited cemeteries, ruins and woods. We drank blood from willing donors. We learned which veins to bite so it wasn't an artery we drank from. Later I filed down my teeth to razor sharpness... We slept on graves. One time we dug a grave and slept in that to feel how it was."

Back in Witten and nearby Bochum, Germany, Manuela cut a distinctive enough figure on the S&M scene to be featured in leather, lacquer and latex, dragging a love-slave on a dog-chain through a cemetery, in a 1997 article on youth culture in *Stern* that quoted her brazen boast: "I will gladly whip and bind you!"

During this period besides cultivating a social life based on the domination of slaves, she was "studying chaos magic" in between stints as a waitress and a bakery assistant. She could no longer talk to her family about the parallel universe she inhabited, and their relations grew strained.

Manuela painted her rooms black and quoted from Aleister Crowley. She dressed only in black and wore her face corpse-white. She plucked out her eyebrows and stenciled on geometric designs in their place.

The morbid chic soon became more than just a masquerade. She had her lips pierced and her skin tattooed with satanic symbols. She had her eye-teeth removed, and animal fangs implanted, to enhance her vampiric transformation. She avoided the daylight, saying she could not bear it. She began hearing the voices of the undead—generally it was benign murmurs such as "Take care," but there were times she heard the summons of the same voice that had called her at the age of 14.

She began to speak of herself as "Allegra," saying she was taking the name after the daughter of Lord Byron, who was said to have been sacrificed to Satan.

Allegra demanded blood, human blood. She would cut her willing donors, whom she met at discos or through the internet, bite them with her animal fangs, and drink their blood. As often as not she would cut herself and drink her own blood. The self-mutilation left her with scars on her arms, face, neck, and legs. She learned to carry her scars as decorations.

In 1999, to celebrate the satanic high holy day of Samhain, which coincides with Halloween, Manuela swore a solemn blood oath signing over her soul to Satan. And it was that year she met Daniel Ruda.

The following autumn, when she answered the provocative personal ad, she wrote of "the beauty of the night, expired ruins of cemeteries illuminated by the full moon" and assured her prospective soul-mate that she "hates mankind and abhors the light." She signed off, "Allegra."

Unbeknownst to Manuela, Dani had just returned from his own pilgrimage to the British Isles, and was under Satan's orders to find the other half of his empty soul.

The meeting place for their first rendezvous was the ancient cemetery in Recklinghausen. The two vampires instantly felt a "harmony of souls." In Dani's Opel Vectra "Grave Beauty" with the Pentagram and Dachau bumper stickers, they would cruise through the cemeteries in the district, and open their hearts to one another.

They became acquainted with other vampires and satanists over the internet, talking on the phone and meeting by arrangement at cemeteries or clubs like Easy and Matrix. They drank each other's blood, and sacrificed goats and chickens in woodlands. They traveled to England together.

But, according to Daniel Ruda's sworn affidavit, even after they were married, the odd couple rejected the "terrestrial lust" of sexual relations.

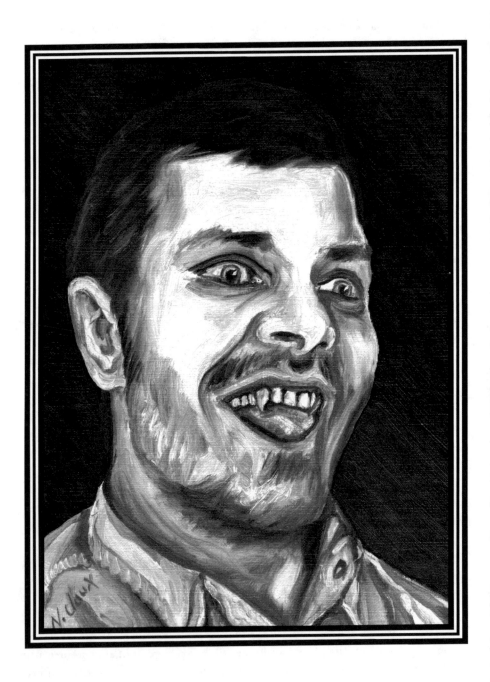

 Daniel Ruda

Like Manuela, Daniel came from a solid working-class family; his father worked in a chemical plant and his mother stayed home to watch the kids. He never felt close to his sisters, and always craved the spotlight.

Though he excelled in grade school, by high school he was testing well intellectually, but refusing to perform intellectually, instead spending more and more time withdrawn into a morbid world of his own.

From the age of 12, Dani had felt a "lust for blood, the metallic salty taste." He confessed that he had realized at an early age that he was meant to be Satan's Messenger of Death.

He had always hated people; caresses and embraces disgusted him. After a vision of a powerful satanic spirit called Samiel at the age of 14, he began to explore the dark side of his soul, his "bloody dreams" and slaughterous visions.

His earliest fantasies were of being a monstrous creature who snapped off the heads of humans and gorged on them. This primitive daydream developed over the years into a frequent impulse to commit mass murder—but he said he would only do such a thing after his parents were dead, to avoid bringing dishonor to their name. He admitted to being particularly fascinated with the criminal legacy of Charles Manson, and wanted to emulate it himself.

As his interest in the occult progressed, he read *The Satanic Bible* and mutilated himself to drink his own blood. He began to answer to the name "Sundown."

In March of 2001, Dani had another vision in which Samiel ordered him to marry his soul-mate Manu on the symbolic date of 6/6, and to enjoin her in a murder-suicide on 6/7.

The date was important, Dani reminded Frank Hackerts several times, and he was to be the guest of honor. The occasion was to be a farewell party. Dani had been drawing fire from management and employees alike for flashing his fangs at work, showing off his self-inflicted wounds and the sadomasochistic photos he took with his spouse. He knew the end was coming, so he planned to quit before they could fire him, and he wanted to celebrate.

"Hacki," as they called him, was a Beatles fan with a sunny disposition. At 33, he was still single, and he took his Christianity seriously enough to consider joining a monastery at one time. At the auto-parts dealership where they worked, he was well-liked by everyone, and was, in fact, the only person who would have anything to do with Dani. He realized Dani was a little freaky, but he was broad-minded enough to accept the differences in personal style.

Hacki represented everything that Dani was not and could not be in this life. He was trusted, generous, popular and happy. He had everything to live for, and that was why he was chosen for the ritual sacrifice. "He was so funny," Manuela explained with diabolical logic. "We thought he would be the perfect court jester for Satan."

According to Daniel Ruda's written confession, he was already dissociated when he arrived at Manuela's apartment in Witten, just east of Bochum, early in the afternoon of the appointed day. Neither drugs nor alcohol were involved, he stated, but "his perceptions seemed distant" because Satan had taken over his body. While he does not deny committing the crime, he remembers nothing except sitting on the floor gazing at the pentagram carved into the victim's chest.

Manuela's memory of the murder is more detailed. They spent most of the day "just hanging out," she told the court. She took a short nap in her coffin before they sat down to write their farewell letters. At 6 p.m., they took the Grave Beauty to pick up their intended sacrificial victim.

As soon as the three of them arrived back at the apartment, Manuela sensed the presence of a "strange force" and "other beings."

"We were sitting on the couch the whole time, then my husband stood up," she told the court in a soft voice. "He had terrible, glowing eyes, and he hit out with the hammer. Frank stood up and said something, or wanted to say something. The knife was glowing and a voice told me: 'Stab him in the heart!'

"He then sank down. I saw a light flickering around him. That was the sign that his soul had departed for the underworld. We said a prayer to Satan. We were empowered and alone."

Before they were done, the two vampires dealt their blameless victim 66 blows with a sledgehammer, machete, scalpel, and knife; carved a pentagram in his chest; drained his blood into a bowl and ceremonially drank a toast to their Dark Lord.

Manuela remembered being disappointed that the ritual had not turned her into a vampire, "because as a vampire I would not have needed the streets."

"We were exhausted, and we wanted to die ourselves. But the visitation was too short," she said. "We could no longer kill ourselves."

Detective Franz Sobolewski gave the court a slightly different interpretation of the couple's actions. He was the officer who interrogated the Rudas upon arrest, and they both told him that Frank Hackerts had been killed with a single blow of the hammer, and that the stabbings were a spontaneous act performed after he was already dead. Manuela told him they sliced open the victim's forearms as a rehearsal of their own suicides.

"Suddenly, they realized that killing someone is not that simple, that it was monstrous and brutal," the detective testified. "They didn't want to repeat that with themselves. They just didn't have the courage."

Their original plan had been to slash their wrists and bleed to death at the scene of the murder, but regardless of whether it be from a flagging sense of support from the Dark Kingdom, or from a simple failure of nerve, they didn't do the deed.

Without clear instructions from Satan or his minions, they threw a few things in the car and headed east. They slept together in a bed that night in a hotel in Magdeburg, and for the first time, the married couple actually had sexual intercourse.

The next day they withdrew some cash from a instant teller, had the brakes checked, changed the tires, and instead of traversing death's other kingdom, they drove the Grave Beauty aimlessly across Germany while debating the pros and cons of plans to drive to Denmark, buy a gun and shoot themselves, or fill up the trunk with gas containers and ram the Beauty into a truck.

Finally on July 12, the fugitives were captured in Jena, a city in the eastern state of Thuringia. They had been trying to find a cemetery where a 15-year-old boy had been sacrificed in a Black Mass in 1993 by Hendrik Moebius and two other self-professed "Children of Satan." Since his conviction, Moebius had become a dark folk hero, releasing a CD mocking his victim and proudly promoting white supremacist and satanic rhetoric on worldwide websites, so the Rudas thought that would be an appropriate site for a double suicide. But they couldn't locate the satanic hot spot. So they kept riding.

Despite his status as a much-wanted fugitive, Dani decided to visit a department store to purchase a chainsaw, saying he did not want to be caught empty-handed if his demons decided to issue him new orders. He was recognized and reported, and shortly the distinctive Vectra was stopped at a roadblock, and the two vampires were taken into custody without further ado.

Both of the Rudas promptly confessed to police, and were incarcerated for 192 days before they came to trial. During this time they were allowed no personal contact except through letters. Their correspondence was monitored and censored; inverted crosses and pentagrams and other satanic slogans were not allowed.

Manuela was a well-behaved prisoner, but for his own protection, Daniel had to be placed in a special isolation cell like the one seen in *Silence of the Lambs*, with walls of bulletproof glass, after sharpening his nails like razors, slashing his flesh and drinking his own blood.

On January 10, 2002, the trial began, and what a trial it would be. The judge allowed in more than 100 photographers and cameramen, and the galleries were overflowing with ghouls, skinheads, and curiosity-seekers. The flamboyant vampires turned the somber proceedings into an outrageous fashion show, and took every opportunity to cut a jape, laughing and grimacing, sticking out their tongues, flashing their fangs and rolling their eyes, openly flashing obscene and satanic hand-signs for the cameras.

Daniel made his grand entrance the first day with fresh lacerations on his lips, sporting a *Nosferatu* T-shirt and a menacing snarl. Strutting down the ramp into the courtroom as if he were a runway model, he fully extended both arms and flashed satanic signs. "My people!" he cried as he caught sight of the Gothic garb in the gallery.

The satanic murderer cut quite a theatrical figure, but the diabolical diva made it clear that she was the real star of the show: her long black hair had been shorn on both sides, throwing into stark relief an inverted cross on the right side of her scalp and a target on the left. She was up at four every morning to prepare, and it showed. Every day her look sported a new twist. She painted her long, flashy nails by turns blood red, ghoul green, and death black. Her whiteface makeup was as stylized as a Japanese Noh mask, never the same face twice. She showed off plenty of flesh in her black leather pumps and leggings, and her midriff-skimming, off-the-shoulder, see-through black tops, playing peek-a-boo with the satanic tattoos on her shoulders.

The second day of the trial, the Rudas' attorney Siegmund Benecken petitioned the court on Manuela's behalf, asking that the courtroom lights be turned down and the windows blacked out. "She cannot stand the light. She sleeps all day and comes out only at night," he said. He made his case that suffering the light would put a strain on the accused, giving her a headache and causing her to sustain undue duress. The uncommonly tolerant judge dismissed the request, but allowed the vampiress to wear dark glasses for the duration. Thereafter she would slouch her way through the trial behind her shades, smacking away at her gum, pouting and grinning by turns.

 Manuela Ruda

The couple entered pleas of not guilty to murder. Although conceding that they had in fact committed the crime, their defense was based on diminished responsibility, because they had been simply obeying orders—the Devil's orders.

In his written statement, Daniel Ruda compared himself to a vehicle involved in a fatal accident. "If I kill a person with my car and half his bloody head is left on my bumpers, it is not the car that goes to jail," he said. "It is the driver who is evil, not the car. I have nothing to repent, because I did nothing."

Manuela described the killing for the court, and then her attorney asked, "What do you say about the prosecution's accusation that you committed an act of murder?"

"It was not murder. We are not murderers," she testified in a soft voice. "It wasn't meant in a bad way. We wanted to release his soul from the hateful flesh, so that he could serve Satan. It was in his own best interest. We were only following orders. We wanted to make sure that the victim suffered well."

She insisted that she and her husband liked their victim, and that his killing was nothing personal. "Hacki is still here," she said, although she admitted he was no longer visible.

The victim's family members attended the whole trial. His mother Doris, her eyes moist with tears, said, "I came here each day to try to find some kind of remorse or sorrow in their eyes. I found nothing."

The victim's father, Hermann Hackerts, said, "At the beginning I did not want to go to the trial but now I'm glad that we sat eye to eye. Now I understand that they are bad people, but people—not devils, and absolutely unsound of mind."

The Rudas were examined by three psychiatric consultants including one of the most outstanding forensic psychiatrists of the republic, Professor Norbert Leygraf. They were unanimous in diagnosing both of the Rudas with severe narcissistic personality disorder, which is better understood as a character defect than an illness. Professor Leygraf estimated that therapy sufficient to render them harmless would take more than ten years, but he could not exclude the complete failure of his therapy, noting the pair's shared inability to develop guilt feelings.

Michael Emde, the attorney representing Hackerts, was skeptical about how disturbed the Rudas really were. "I was told that the defendants behaved quite normally outside the court," he told *Stern*. "This strong make-up, the cruel haircut, showing these signs of the Devil with their fingers and making faces, all this has been instigated and supported by this massive media presence."

Prosecutor Dieter Justinsky summed up the State's case: "I have never, ever seen such a picture of cruelty and depravity before. They simply had a lust for murder."

On February 1, 2001, both defendants sat quietly for their sentencing, Daniel staring at his victim's mother, Manuela chewing her gum and yawning.

Before passing sentence, Judge Arno Kersting-Tombroke said, "This case was not about satanism. It was about a crime committed by two people with severe disorders. Nothing mystical or cult-like happened here; just simple, base murder."

Despite the prosecution's request that they should serve their time in maximum security prisons, the Rudas were both sentenced to serve time in secure mental facilities—Manuela for 13 years and Daniel for 15 years.

The judge said the Rudas were not insane and were fit for trial, but he allowed that their psychiatric disorders were sufficient to prevent him from handing down life sentences—the standard punishment for premeditated murder.

The judge also said so much fan mail had been sent to the Rudas during the case that he was worried about the "limitless stupidity" of many members of the public.

Dear Sondra,

I thank you for getting in touch with me. I wasn't quite sure whether to reply to you or not. To be honest, I'm not really pleased about the appearance of Nico's portrait of me and the press accounts in your book.

Actually, I got fed up of all the show. Some people out there call me a hero just because of that fucked-up story. Believe me, I'm not proud of what I've done, and now I know I've been wrong all the time. I'm not that fucking weirdo you might have expected to meet.

Yeah, maybe there's something I'd have to say, I'll think it over. Unfortunately I can't get on the internet, but I'm gonna tell a friend to check your pages. That's it for now. My best regards to Nico.

laters,

ANOTHER PERSON INSIDE ME

There is an old French saying: "There is no way to account for taste except by taste." And thus the discriminating gourmand who develops a taste for taboo finds himself dreaming of a partner who will enjoy the forbidden feasting as much as he will.

Armin Meiwes grew up in the middle of Germany as the son of a policeman, and he was gripped at an early age by a morbid fascination for Hansel and Gretel—especially the part where the witch fattens up the boy in anticipation of harvesting his flesh. The nightmarish old fairy tale stimulated his childish fantasies in a way he later explained to mystified investigators: "I got a kick out of the idea of having another person inside me."

Since the age of 12, he had dreamed of eating a human being, and cultivated an elaborate fantasy of impaling a classmate on a kebab "and slowly roasting him."

In the mid-Seventies, when Armin was 16, his family moved into a sprawling seventeenth-century manor house in the picturesque Hessian village of Rotenburg, near the town of Kassel. However, the family soon broke up and his father and two stepbrothers moved out. Though most of the 47 rooms in the ramshackle mansion were stone-cold and empty, Armin remained there with his mother, staying on even after her death in 1999.

"He was a mama's boy," said a neighbor. "He was totally fixated on his mother, whom he said never let him date girls."

Living in a neighboring estate was a self-professed practicing satanist named Ulla von Bernus, who published occult treatises and boasted to the media of her powers at casting death spells "with 90 percent reliability," according to *Der Tagesspiegel*, altlhough her practice hit the headlines in the early Eighties, when she was sued by a woman who had paid her 3,000 marks to curse her husband to death, and complained that the old man was not dead yet. Von Bernus was found guilty of an "illusory crime exempt from punishment" and ordered to give the customer back her money. A reporter for *Der Tagesspiegel* who interviewed the mediagenic witch in the Eighties recalled being introduced to her "best friend," who happened to be Fraulein Meiwes, Armin's mother.

According to *Bild*, Armin himself was "in and out of Ulla's house all the time," until her death in 1998 at age 86. There is no direct connection between her beliefs and practices and those that made Armin famous. Still in terms of contributing factors, it is worth noting that during his formative years, this impressionable youth with the longstanding fairy-tale fascination moved into a castle in the woods right next to a bona fide witch.

As youth became manhood, Armin spent 12 years in the German armed forces as a non-commissioned officer, where he was described as "amiable and conscientious." A former childhood friend who also spent time with Armin during his military duty told a local television news team that his friend was "always good-natured and considerate."

After completing his military tour of duty in 1991, Armin accepted a job as a computer technician with a software firm in Karlsruhe, a Rhine Valley town a half-hour's commute south of Rotenburg.

He performed well at work, and though his neighbors found him on the reclusive side, by and large they described him as a polite and pleasant gentleman who kept to himself. Neighbor Joerg Paulusen told Reuters TV, "It was sort of clear to us that he had a different perspective on life than we did, but he was a normal person, to speak to him, drink a glass of beer with him—just like you and me."

The "different perspective" was that Armin was openly gay, and he was also a bit of a wirehead. Though he spent all day with computers at work, he couldn't get enough of that wild wild web, and as the Nineties progressed, so did Armin's reliance on the internet to enhance his social life and broaden his opportunities to contact people who shared a sexual kink that is fortunately still uncommon.

In December of 2002 he was calling himself Franky as he trolled chatrooms like Cannibal Café, Gourmet, and Eaten Up, where had placed over 80 ads for "young, well-built men 18-30 to slaughter." In his ads and email correspondence, he had been explicit about his desire to accommodate a man who wished to have his penis cut off and be forced to eat it, before being stabbed to death. A curious student from Innsbruck, Austria, responded, and when the boy learned that Franky was drop-dead serious, he took the ads and emails to police.

It took authorities two months to track Armin to his baronial digs, but once they took him into custody, he cooperated freely, authorizing them to search the property, confessing, and producing copious evidence of indulgence in criminal appetites so recherché that investigating officers had to go into psychiatric counseling after their exposure to the grisly details.

On searching the Rotenburg estate, police found 15 pounds of frozen human flesh in the freezer. And on Armin's bookshelves, next to his collection of Walt Disney videos, were cookbooks listing such recipes as Penis in Red Wine and Breaded Young Man's Liver. Perhaps in another context, such fetishistic fictions could be regarded as light-hearted tongue-in-cheek satires, like the short story by sci-fi writer Sprague de Camp based on an old Twilight Zone episode, "To Serve Man." However, in this case, criminal investigators wisely inventoried them as a highly specialized form of pornography.

Remarkably, the investigation revealed that Armin had developed over 400 email contacts. Interested parties from Kassel, Essen and Frankfurt had visited the castle to meet Armin. Investigators interviewed a 31-year-old hotel cook named Jörg, who had come from Füssen. He enjoyed fantasizing about his own murder, and was aroused as Armin described out which tender bits he would especially savor. Jörg was a freak all right, but when it came down to the reality of actually ending his own life, he chickened out. Armin, to his credit, did not force the issue.

One Londoner flew to Germany to participate in a death fantasy with Armin. He was placed naked in a wooden cage in a customized room Armin called his "butchery," then taken out and wrapped in cellophane. Armin taped notes to his body, labelling them "rump," "steak," "fillet" and "bacon." The Brit was enjoying the fantasy until Armin began to sharpen his weapons for the slaughter. He must have thought about England, because suddenly he was ready to go home, and ever the gracious host, Armin let him go.

"I need a *REAL* victim!" he lamented to one and all on the internet in February of 2001, and indeed the frustrated fantasist did not have long to wait.

Bernd "Jürgen" Brandes was a trim, bespectacled developer of computer chips for Siemens, who lived in a lavish Berlin penthouse apartment with his partner, Rene. Unbeknownst to Rene, Jürgen nurtured a morbid obsession to be eaten alive. It was early in the spring of 2001 when he responded to one of Franky's ads, using the name Cator.

Aburptly Jürgen sold his Porsche, and on the morning of Friday, March 9, 2001, he drafted a new will, leaving the penthouse and over 50,000 marks worth of computer equipment to Rene. He called Siemens and told his boss he had to take the day off "to attend to some personal matters." Taking several thousand marks in cash, his laptop and his passport, the 43-year-old gay yuppie headed for the subway station, where he was seen by a couple of co-workers wearing faded jeans, a green jacket and navy blue running shoes.

According to *Berliner Morgenpost*, that was the last time Jürgen was seen in Berlin. Four hours later, when he stepped off the train in Kassel, he said to Armin: "I am your flesh."

As Armin drove his guest home, he elaborated on his desire to slaughter and eat him. And Jürgen confided that he had become fascinated with being eaten since watching Anthony Hopkins in *Silence of the Lambs*.

However, after a few drinks at the estate in Rotenburg, Jürgen had second thoughts and demurred. He agreed to have sex with Armin, but asked him to take him back to the train station afterwards. Armin graciously agreed with the change of plan, and drove his guest to Kassel, where Jürgen bought a ticket for Berlin—and then changed his mind again. This time Jürgen decided to go along with the proposed slaughter, and returned to Rotenburg with Armin.

"The victim appeared to be fully aware of the situation," an investigator said at a press conference. "Videotape material definitely shows him and the suspect engaged in eating his own flesh prior to his death."

Armin had set up lights and video equipment to record hours upon hours of the remarkable ritual and its aftermath, so that it would be meticulously documented for his own viewing pleasure—apparently without concern for how such explicit evidence might also be equally useful in making a criminal case against him.

With Bernd fully conscious and participating willingly, the camera's unflinching eye stared incuriously at Armin as he sliced off the man's penis and tied off its bleeding stump, then sautéed the sweetmeat with garlic, salt and pepper in a frying pan. He later admitted to being a bit disappointed to find that unlike a Ballpark Frank, Jürgen's sausage did not plump when he cooked it, but in fact, shriveled. Dashing it with liqueur, the chef ignited it to serve flambé.

Both men tasted the seared flesh, then mused that it needed a little more... *something*. Concluding the severed member had not been cooked thoroughly enough to tenderize it properly, Armin returned it to the pan and gave it another go, adjusting the seasoning, before joining his wounded companion in downing his own refried manhood.

After their macabre Last Supper, the cameras kept right on rolling as Armin helped Jürgen to the bathroom, where he reclined in a tub of warm water and peacefully exsanguinated, while Armin rested nearby, idly turning the pages of a Star Trek novel. Jürgen's last request was for Armin to wait until he was unconscious from loss of blood before finalizing the slaughter, but sadly, the record reveals that his wish was not honored.

At 4:30 a.m., Armin dragged the dazed Jürgen from the bath into the "butchery" and moved the video camera to record the next scene. Jürgen suddenly "became emotional," and Armin looked into his eyes and whispered, "I must do this," before he slaughtered the man by a flurry of deep hacking cuts to the chest and neck with a 12-inch butcher knife. "It was an indescribable feeling for me," he told police. "Hate, love, happiness, power. My life's dream had come true."

After savoring this transcendent moment, he selected Judy Garland's "Over The Rainbow" to put him in the mood to start butchering 65 pounds of fresh freak. The careful cannibal wrapped the prime cuts in greaseproof paper, bagged them in dinner-sized portions and labeled them for freezer storage. One of Jürgen's arms was spiced and slowly dried out in the oven, so Armin could hang it from the eaves, thinking it would be like the air-dried hams of Parma in Italy. Even the intestines were turned into tiny *chipolata* sausages, perfect for a high-protein snack.

Armin later swooned with perverse delight as he described to police the first meal he served out in his private garden, barbecuing a thigh steak marinated in Muscat wine with garlic, and having it with fried potato balls and steamed Brussels sprouts. Hoisting a glass of rare South African cabernet in a toast to dear Jürgen, Armin enjoyed him intimately. "The flesh tasted so much like pork, I just can't tell you," he rhapsodized.

As for the inedible portions, the skull, bones and teeth were ceremonially interred in the garden. "I gave them a proper burial. I recited the 23rd Psalm, The Lord is my Shepherd, I shall not want. Then I said the Lord's Prayer."

"It seems his practice was to take the flesh out as and when he felt hungry over the course of the next couple of years," the prosecutor said on December 11, 2002, as he charged Armin Meiwes with murder, while lamenting the fact that in Germany, cannibalism is still not a crime.

The blithe cannibal filed a not-guilty plea, claiming that his victim had died willingly in pursuit of his own fantasy of being consumed, and he regarded his future lightly. "I think I will be out after four or five years. It isn't as if I killed anyone against their will."

In July of 2003, Herr Meiwes told *Stern* that killing Herr Brandes had made him feel "fulfilled—like I was married or something."

THE GENTLEMAN GHOUL OF JAPAN

Towards midnight on a warm June night in 1981, a slight, shy Japanese grad student at the Sorbonne in Paris was caught trying to dispose of a blood-soaked suitcase containing the inedible remains of a fellow student.

Issei Sagawa, 31, had been given the cold shoulder by most of his youthful classmates, but Renèe Hartevelt, an attractive 25-year-old Dutch student, was more sympathetic to the awkward foreigner than the xenophobic French girls were. One night she agreed to help him with a translation, and accompanied him to his apartment. He prepared tea, spiking it with whiskey and serving it to her as he eyed her admiringly.

Then he shot her in the head and cut up her body with an electric carving knife. Over the next two days, he dined upon her flesh, later raving that it "melted in my mouth like raw tuna. Nothing was so delicious."

From his confessions, as translated from an article in the defunct French magazine, *L'écho des savanes*:

I am amazed. She's the most beautiful woman I've ever seen. Tall, blonde, with pure white skin, she astonishes me with her grace. I invited her to my home for a Japanese dinner. She accepts. After the meal I asked her to read my favorite German Expressionist poem. As she reads I can't keep my eyes off her. After she leaves I can still smell her body on the bed sheet where she sat reading the poem. I lick the chopsticks and dishes she used. I can taste her lips. My passion is so great, I want to eat her. If I do she will be mine forever. There is no escape from this desire.

I arrange for her to read the poem for me once more. I lie to her. I tell her I want to record the poem on tape for my Japanese teacher. She believes. I prepare everything. The cassette recorder for the poem, the rifle for the sacrifice. She arrives on time. After drinking tea and whiskey, she speaks. She smiles at me. But I know inside that I'm the strangest one of all. Her yellow sleeveless top shows off her beautiful white arms. I can smell her body.

I turn on the recorder. She starts to read. She speaks in perfect German. I reach for the rifle hidden beside the chest of drawers. I stand slowly and aim the rifle at the back of her head. I cannot stop myself.

There is a loud sound and her body falls from the chair onto the floor. It is like she is watching me. I see her cheeks, her eyes, her nose and mouth, the blood pouring from her head. I try to talk to her, but she no longer answers. There is blood all over the floor. I try to wipe it up, but I realize I cannot stop the flow of blood from her head. It is very quiet here. There is only the silence of death.

I start to take off her clothes. It is hard to take the clothes off a dead body. Finally it is done. Her beautiful white body is before me. I've waited so long this day and now it is here. I touch her ass. It is so very smooth. I wonder where I should bite first. I decide to bite the top of her butt. My nose is covered with her cold white skin. I try to bite down hard, but I can't. I suddenly have a horrible headache. I get a knife from the kitchen and stab it deeply into her skin.

Suddenly a lot of sallow fat oozes from the wound. It reminds me of Indian corn. It continues to ooze. It is strange. Finally I find the red meat under the sallow fat. I scoop it out and put it in my mouth. I chew. It has no smell and no taste. It melts in my mouth like a perfect piece of tuna. I look in her eyes and say: "You are delicious."

I cut her body and lift the meat to my mouth again and again. Then I take a photograph of her white corpse with its deep wounds. I have sex with her body. When I hug her she lets out a breath. I'm frightened, she seems alive. I kiss her and tell her I love her. Then I drag her body to the bathroom. By now I am exhausted, but I cut into her hip and put the meat in a roasting pan. After it is cooked I sit at the table using her underwear as a napkin. They still smell of her body.

Then I turn on the tape of her reading the German poem and eat. There is not enough taste. I use some salt and some mustard and it is delicious, very high quality meat. Then I go back to the bathroom and cut off her breast and bake it. It swells while it cooks. I serve the breast on the table and eat it with a fork and knife. It isn't very good. Too greasy. I try to cut into another part of her body. Her thighs were wonderful. Finally she is in my stomach. Finally she is mine. It is the best dinner I've ever had...

I put her underwear beside the dish. I sniff it and look at a nude woman in a magazine. I try to remember which part of her is in my mouth, but it is difficult to connect the meat with a body. It just seems like a piece of meat. I continue to eat her body until I am caught. Each day the meat becomes more tender, each day the taste is more sweet and delicious.

Sagawa was found guilty but insane, and hospitalized in France for the next three years. His influential father had him repatriated to Japan in 1984, by agreeing to have him confined to a hospital there. After 15 months, he was released. In the nation of sushi-eaters, this connoisseur of human flesh was found to be perfectly sane, after all.

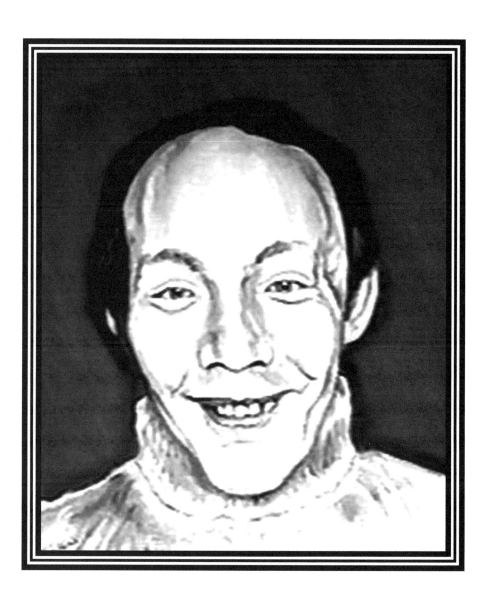

 Issei Sagawa

The gentleman ghoul went on to distinguish himself in literary, dramatic and artistic circles. His six books have all been bestsellers, and he has directed and appeared in several motion pictures. An art student since the age of five, his paintings are much in demand.

The artsy gourmet has become a restaurant critic for *Spa* magazine, written a newspaper column, and made celebrity guest appearances on television. His "Parisian affair" was parodied in the Rolling Stones song, "Too Much Blood."

In 1994, he presented a seminar called *Sagawa's World*, where he debuted an erotic film called *The Desire To Be Eaten*.

From personal correspondence:

I am a romantic living in an age whose heart has gone dry.

It has been said that because I loved my victim, I confessed my feelings for her, she laughed at me, and I lost control of myself and killed her. That is completely false.

It was only one month after I met my victim that the accident occurred. Renèe was a very beautiful girl, but we were just friends. I am a very short, ugly, yellow monkey man. I admired the tall, beautiful white girls, and I wanted to taste them. I strongly wanted to eat their meat. I felt I could never fulfill myself unless I did it.

I was very lonely in Paris. French people are generally racist, and I felt a big distance between myself and the French girls. On the other hand, most Dutch people are gentle and friendly, and my victim was Dutch.

Renèe was such a gentle girl. But unfortunately at that time, I could not understand her friendship was from the heart. She was a good friend. But I saw her as just an appetizing bowl of meat.

Because I thought I could not have such a beautiful white girl for a lover, I decided to eat her. But when I realized my fantasy, I was frightened by the power of the realism: the blood, the silence. I was nauseated by what I did.

I didn't want to kill Renèe, I just wanted to taste her meat. I regret terribly killing her. That's why I have not repeated my cannibal crime. I still enjoy my fantasy of eating human flesh, but I will never kill again.

My cannibal fantasy is a sexual fetish, not philosophical or spiritual. For me, sex involves eating, and any sexual pose reminds me of cannibalism. I do enjoy drinking my lover's urine or milk instead of eating her meat, though.

I have met a lot of girls who want to be eaten. But when they ask me to eat them, I have to tell them no, because I don't want to be a bad influence on other people.

I could never kill again, but if someone could cook a part of a beautiful white girl without killing her, I would still be glad to eat it, because the meat of a young girl is so delicious!

Eating and being eaten are the same to me. I am always dreaming of being eaten by a beautiful white woman. Because I prefer white women, Japanese women are jealous. They ask, "Why not Japanese girls?"

The question remains why cannibalism must be taboo. According to the Marquis de Sade, 'It is wrong to think of cannibalism as a debasement of character. Eating people is as simple a matter as eating beef. Once the destruction is carried out, does it matter whether we bury the dismembered remains in the ground or feed them to our stomachs?' In this I see not rhetoric or irony, but a highly realistic pronouncement offered to mankind. It takes more than ordinary sentimentalism to argue with this.

Sincerely,

Issei Sagawa

✦✦✦✦

JUST A GIGOLO

He was just a gigolo, as they say, albeit a very attractive one—tall, dark and handsome, and popular with the clientèle he discreetly serviced through the Cloud Nine Escort Agency in Melbourne, Australia.

Going by the *nom d'amour* of Simon, he specialized in roughing up men and women, and carried a black valise with whips, restraints and other sado-masochistic toys to use on about a dozen clients a week, at a going rate of $300 an hour.

Shane Chartres-Abbott had been summoned to meet with a 30-year-old Thai woman at her home several times since July, 2002, and he was pleased to meet her again on August 16 at the Hotel Saville, in South Yarra, a suburb 40 miles east of Melbourne.

He had told her that he was a vampire who was older than the city of Melbourne, and required blood to survive. This fanciful line of pillow talk had apparently given her ideas, as she told him about her plans to cast him in a pornographic film. But unbeknownst to the star, as soon as he demonstrated his sexual prowess, the script called for him to be murdered on camera.

This plot point was the subject of a loud and rancorous discussion between the woman and an unidentified man in the hotel room, which was overheard by the gigolo as he stood outside, hesitant to knock. He stepped away for a moment, then after the other man left he approached the room again, knocked and entered.

The woman admitted the plan for using him in a snuff film, but assured him that she had vetoed it because she liked him too much to lose him.

Accounts vary about what happened next; the gigolo said he simply serviced the woman's sexual needs until 5 a.m. and then went home. However, according to the woman, it was he who was responsible for her condition when she was found unconscious in the shower by hotel staff at 11:15 a.m. She was nude and blood-soaked, with battered genitals, black eyes, and a swollen and bruised neck. Most of her tongue had been torn out, and a large bite had been taken out of her thigh.

Chartres-Abbott was charged with rape and, according to prosecutor George Slim, the infliction of "brutal and life-threatening personal violence."

As trial commenced on May 29, 2003, the defense attorney petitioned the Court to seal the defendant's home address. Apparently someone was a bit nervous about the sex secrets kept by the gigolo, because he had been threatened that he would be killed if he testified, and he was concerned about protecting his personal privacy.

Upon hearing this testimony, the judge ordered the documents to be redacted before being given to the jury, but during legal arguments the address was recited in open court, thus placing it in the public record.

Five days into the trial, on the morning of June 4, 2003, the accused vampire rapist was shot dead while leaving his suburban home on his way to court, by two men who attacked him in his front yard before two witnesses. The hitmen fled the scene and vanished.

Judge Bill White discharged the jurors without a verdict, and thanked them "on behalf of the community on what has been a very unusual trial."

PEOPLE... YOU KILL 'EM

I had bought a little house on Border Lane in Shakhty. I was planning to fix the place up and put in a garden.... I don't remember the exact date, but it was an evening at the end of December, 1978. I got off at the Grushevka Bridge streetcar stop, the one nearest the house on Border Lane. It was late in the day and getting dark. I started heading toward my house. To my surprise, I noticed a girl of about eleven or twelve with a school case who was walking in the same direction I was. For a little while, we walked side by side down the dark, unlit street by the river. I struck up a conversation with the girl. I remember she said she was going to see a friend.

When we came near the tall reeds that grow by the river and were a distance from the nearest houses, an irresistible urge to have sexual relations with that girl came over me. I don't know what happened to me, but I literally began shaking. I stopped the girl and threw her down into the reeds. She tried to struggle free, but I was literally in a state of animal frenzy, I couldn't stop myself. I pulled off her pants and began thrusting my hands into her sexual organs. At the same time, to keep her quiet, I began squeezing her throat as I began ripping at her sexual organs. I had an orgasm while lying on top of her and tearing at her sexual organs. I did not have intercourse as such with her. The sperm either went between her legs or on her stomach.

When I realized the girl was dead, I dressed her and threw her body in the river. Then I threw her school case in too. I washed my hands and put my clothes in order. Then I returned to the streetcar stop, and went home...

This was my first crime and I sincerely regretted it... What happened that night made a very strong impression on me. I can even say that I don't remember the moment when I ejaculated. All I remember clearly is that tearing at her sexual organs caused me a tremendous sensation. I can't describe it any more precisely, but it was real. I was in some kind of frenzy, ruled by some sort of bestial passion. It was only when I had regained some calm that I realized she was dead. A few days later I was called in for questioning. The police asked me where I was on the night of the murder. I said I had been home and my wife verified this. I was aware that someone else was arrested for this crime.

After that first murder I think my psyche underwent certain definite changes. I was haunted by the image of my hands tearing the girl's organs apart. I couldn't get it out of my mind.

 Andrei Chikatilo

Thus began the confessions of Andrei Chikatilo, who murdered 55 people, mostly schoolchildren, between 1978 and 1990, drinking their blood and cannibalizing them.

"I felt a kind of madness and ungovernability in perverted sexual acts," Chikatilo wrote in a letter addressed to the Prosecutor General of Russia. "I couldn't control my actions, because from childhood I was unable to realize myself as a real man and a complete human being."

"He tortured his victims while they were alive by biting out their tongues, tearing away their sexual organs, and cutting their bellies open," read the guilty verdict, written by Judge Leonid Akubzhanov, who went on to sentence Chikatilo to death by a gunshot to the head.

"I liked to nibble on a uterus, they're so pink and springy," said the man who called himself "a mistake of nature, a mad beast."

He was nondescript and harmless-looking, a nearsighted and slope-shouldered grandfather who actually assisted in the manhunt for the predator who had snatched his victims from train stations and public areas, starting in the hamlet of Shakhty, progressing to nearby Rostov, and then expanding his reach to encompass the eastern half of the Russian Republic.

Born on October 16, 1936, as a child Chikatilo was often told that before his birth, an older brother named Stepan had been kidnapped and cannibalized, as were many others during the Ukrainian famine. No record has ever been found of the birth or death of his brother, but the vivid imagery of his mother's anguished and hysterical stories shaped the imagination of the shy, retiring child.

Chikatelo would later say that he was born blind and impotent. It was not literally so, but his vision was poor and he spent his youth in a haze, afraid to worsen the mockery of his peers by wearing glasses. His sexual inadequacy was equally profound in shaping his psyche. While he did marry and father two children, he was unable to attain a satisfactory level of erection, until he discovered that sexual violence provided enough stimulation for him to achieve what he once called "a poor imitation of sexual intercourse."

The signature of his murders involved the victims' eyes and sexual organs, which were excised and either mutilated or eaten.

"I gave myself to my work, my studies, my family, my children, and my grandchildren," wrote the man who described himself as "the perfect husband" in a confession. "But when I found myself in a different setting, I became a different person, uncontrollable, as if some evil force were controlling me against my will. And I could not resist."

 Andrei Chikatilo

Another stunningly prolific Ukrainian serial killer who started his seven-year criminal career in 1989, before Chikatilo was quite done with his, confessed to murdering 52 people, and was likewise tried, convicted, and summarily executed.

More articulate and less abashed than his predecessor, 32-year-old Anatoly Onoprienko openly boasted of his crimes and eloquently elaborated on his uncanny compulsion. In a selection of statements he gave to the press and the courtroom, he sounds like either a schizophrenic or a mind-controlled assassin, programmed to "stand anything and forget everything":

People... you kill 'em and that's the way it is.

The first time I killed, I shot down a deer in the woods. I was in my early twenties and I recall feeling very upset when I saw it dead. I couldn't explain why I had done it, and I felt sorry for the deer. I never had that feeling again.

Rage at God and Satan had driven me to start killing in 1989.

To me it was like hunting. Hunting people down. I would be sitting, bored, with nothing to do. And then suddenly this idea would get into my head. I would do everything to get it out of my mind, but I couldn't. It was stronger than me. So I would get in the car or catch a train and go out to kill.

To me killing people is like ripping up a duvet. Men, women, old people, children, they are all the same. I have never felt sorry for those I killed. No love, no hatred, just blind indifference. I don't see them as individuals, but just as masses.

I knew what I was doing. I didn't just set off blindly for the sake of a piece of sausage. I can't say I did it with some mercenary goal in mind. It was a game.

I just shot them. It's not that it gave me pleasure, but I felt this urge. From then on, it was almost like some game from outer space.

I've robbed and killed, but I'm a robot, I don't feel anything. I've been close to death so many times that it's even interesting for me now to venture into the afterworld, to see what is there, after this death.

Naturally, I would prefer the death penalty. I have absolutely no interest in relations with people. I have betrayed them.

After the last murder I tried to commit suicide. I put a gun to my temple but it seemed that the bullet would only wound me and not kill me.

If I could, I would go to Germany and kill hundreds of people in an even more crueler way. I have no remorse and no excuse to offer.

It was foretold that I would kill, let's say 360 people in Germany, give or take 10, after I'd killed 40 in Ukraine. I would be ready to do it even right this minute.

If I am ever let out, I will start killing again. But this time it will be worse, 10 times worse. The urge is there. Seize this chance because I am being groomed to serve Satan. After what I have learnt out there, I have no competitors in my field. And if I am not killed I will escape from this jail and the first thing I'll do is find [Ukrainian President] Kuchma and hang him from a tree by his testicles.

I would kill today in spite of anything. Today I am a Beast of Satan. You are not able to take me as I am. You do not see all the good I am going to do, and you will never understand me.

This is a great force that controls this hall as well. You will never understand this. Maybe only your grandchildren will understand.

People don't appreciate life. To be more sensitive they have to see horrors. I'm the horror who forces people to try to live differently.

I perceive it all as a kind of experiment. There can be no answer in this experiment to what you're trying to learn.

I'm not a maniac. If I were, I would have thrown myself onto you and killed you right here. No, it's not that simple. I have been taken over by a higher force, something telepathic or cosmic, which drove me. For instance, I wanted to kill my brother's first wife, because I hated her. I really wanted to kill her, but I couldn't because I had not received the order. I waited for it all the time, but it did not come. I am like a rabbit in a laboratory. A part of an experiment to prove that man is capable of murdering and learning to live with his crimes. To show that I can cope, that I can stand anything, forget everything.

I think it was a very strong psychological experiment and I would fit this role so well, that I still think of myself as some kind of administrator of some serious tasks. To kill your own son when you know it was you that gave him life is easy. To kill an innocent child is very hard.

In 1995 I was forced to kill again by outside forces. I was ordered not to realize what I was doing and in the process I saw it wasn't me carrying out the killings.

I couldn't see the point of killing just for a few pennies, because I know plenty of stupid people I could kill with joy. There is only one thing I can tell people and that is that they suffered.

There is no better killer in the world than me. Anyone who wants to measure up to me can always try... I have no regrets, no remorse and I would do it again if I could. I was accomplishing a mission. I don't believe in God but in a supreme force. There is a devil sitting inside me which controls everything.

IRON TEETH

Nikolai Dzhumagalayev got the nickname "Iron Teeth" after most of his teeth were replaced with steel caps. Born to a Russian mother and a Kazakh father, he was first arrested in 1981, when one of his friends complained to police after being fed human flesh in a stew by this former officer of the Red Army. He escaped from prison, and continued his predations until 1991, when he was tried and convicted of multiple murders. Upon arrest, he boasted to authorities that he had killed as many as a 100 women, and used 47 of his victims to make ethnic dishes for his neighbors. He went on to say that two women could provide enough delicate meat to keep him going for a week. Police claimed he killed 21. But unlike Chikatilo and Onoprienko, Dzhumagalayev was found not guilty by reason of insanity. Sentenced to three years in a mental institution, he later claimed the best psychiatrists from all over the world had come to see him. After his release, he was questioned at a homeless shelter by the French magazine *Interview*, in 1995.

Q: How many people did you kill?

A: I killed seven women, not twenty-one, like the police claim. These women were attracted to me. They were the ones who came to have a drink in my house. I let them get drunk before cutting them to pieces with a kitchen knife.

Q: Since when and why do you hate women so much?

A: It started twenty years ago, in 1974. At the time, I was sent to a place in USSR where all women were hookers. I stayed three years over there. Some of them really disgusted me. Real whores—drinking and swearing all the time! When I came back to my hometown, Yzun Agal, I couldn't believe that women could behave in such a bad way. Unluckily, they were all prostitutes, so I decided to kill them!

Q: Why did you attack only blonde, European type of women?

A: They are the root of all evil! Most of them are prostitutes. I remember well the first woman that I killed. She was named Volkova. I picked her up because she seemed so pure. A really nice virgin. I stabbed her and cut her body in pieces before salting the whole mess.

Q: What did you do to the other ones?

A: The second one was called Anna. She was 30, 35 years old. I followed her from church to her home. She seemed respectable. She invited me inside. I stabbed her too, then I cut off her breasts and her calves.

Q: Why breasts and calves?

A: Breasts and calves are the best parts of the human body. I'm a hunter. So I can tell you that girl meat tastes like hog. Once, I even served dinner, ravioli stuffed with human flesh, to some friends. Then I showed them pieces of the corpse. They turned me in to the police. I escaped from the mental institution. I don't always eat the meat from women I kill. The third time, for example, I didn't drink her blood because she was too drunk.

Q: Could you achieve normal sexual relationships with your victims?

A: Only with the last one, in 1991. I raped her before killing her. Then, when she was dead, I raped her again. Then after dismembering her, I drank the blood from her throat because I've read that human blood purifies the soul. I poured the last liters in a bucket, then I ate the flesh. When I showed her decapitated head to several friends, one of them called the police. I went to hide in a hunting cabin, but a week after, they found me. They had launched a real manhunt all over the area.

Q: What did you feel while committing a murder?

A: I never felt anything sexual while killing them. I was only doing my duty by purifying the world from these whores!

 Nikolai "Iron Teeth" Dzhumagalayev

RUSSIAN CUTLETS

In 1996, there were ten people charged with killing and eating other people in the Soviet Union. In March, 1996, for example, police were called to investigate a murder in Sebastopol. When they entered the home of a 33-year-old former convict, in the kitchen investigators found the internal organs of two victims in saucepans, and nearby laid out on a plate, they found a freshly roasted piece of human flesh. The owner of the apartment had been stabbed to death, along with her mother and her boyfriend, and their bodies neatly butchered by the killer.

In the winter of 1996, 38-year-old Vladimir Nikolayev, who ten years before had been denounced as a particularly dangerous criminal, was arrested in his apartment in the town of Novocheboksary, in Russia's Chuvash Autonomous Republic, where police found a pan of roasted human meat on the stove and another cannibal dish in the oven. He had stored more body parts outside, packed into the snow on his balcony. Investigators who questioned Nikolayev said he had asked them to prepare a dinner for him, using the human meat he had stocked. Just a little joke.

Also in 1996, in the Siberian town of Kemerovo, rag-pickers scavenging through a garbage dump discovered a severed human head. This grisly find led police to arrest a man who confessed to killing and cutting up his friend, then using the flesh to make a filling for a Russian ravioli called *pelmeni*, which, coincidentally, is the putative vampire Boris Yeltsin's favorite dish. After discarding the useless parts like the head, the killer had minced up the human being, baked him, and sold him at cut-rate prices in the local market.

In Russia's second-largest city, St. Petersburg, big-city cannibal Ilshat Kuzikov preferred his meat marinated with onions. Upon his arrest in 1996, there were several choice cuts marinating in a plastic bag hung outside his window. Police found Pepsi bottles full of human blood and dried human ears tacked on the wall. The hospitable 37-year-old cannibal offered the arresting officers some fresh marinated meat and vodka, if they would let him go. On March 19, 1997, he was found guilty of killing three of his vodka-drinking buddies and eating them. After sating his appetite on the tastiest and most nutritious internal organs, Kuzikov had dismembered his friends and tossed their cumbersome limbs in a garbage dump. He readily confessed to his crimes, and told police he had killed his first victim in

1992, after inviting a stranger to his flat for a nightcap. The rationale he gave for his behavior was strictly pragmatic: he couldn't buy enough to eat on his $20 monthly pension.

Russian specialists have said that "people meat" has a distinctive taste. "The taste of a victim," says the Main Criminal Investigations Administration of the Ministry of Internal Affairs, "depends on the victim himself: if he drank or smoked a lot, whether he liked sweets or salt." Police estimate that at least 30 Russians were eaten in 1996, but charges could not always be brought because of lack of evidence. Thus the only ones who were prosecuted were the ones where there were grisly remains.

In July of 1998, a serial rapist in St. Petersburg crossed the bloody line for the tenth and final time. Sergei Shipin invited a 19-year-old woman over to his house, where he bound, brutalized, and raped her, and finally beat her to death when she tried to escape. After dismembering her corpse in the bathtub, he made soup from her remains. In November of 1999, investigators announced that after months of grilling in a Moscow medical facility, the 24-year-old former security guard had confessed to a dozen rapes and ten murders, as well as dining upon the corpses of his victims.

Less than a week later, a gang of Russian cannibals were sentenced in the western Russian town of Pskov. After killing one of their own friends in a drunken brawl, they had butchered and boiled him and sold his flesh as stewed meat. The Pskov City Court gave the four killers sentences ranging from five-and-a-half to 18 years. One woman who had bought the meat to do a bit of canning was released for lack of evidence that she knew the meat was from a man she considered a friend.

On March 5, 1999, in Bishkek, the capital city of the Russian nation of Kyrgyzstan, Paval Gorobets was sentenced to die for murdering his tenant, Viktor Grekhovodov, in December of 1977, and then his girlfriend, Valentina Kashina, in March of 1998. He confessed to dismembering their bodies and eating "meat cutlets" of their flesh, and then scattering their less appetizing remains about the neighborhood.

"The ruling has been pronounced—the death sentence," Judge Marat Osmonkulov told Reuters. "The case of cannibalism was proved."

While cannibalism itself is not a crime in Kyrgyzstan, Gorobets was officially sentenced for double murder, cutting up the bodies and using the organs and flesh from the corpses. Even without proof of cannibalism, the two murders would still carry the death sentence, explained the judge. Kyrgyzstan had a moratorium on the death penalty, but if the moratorium were not extended, Gorobets would be put to death.

Although he had admitted making cutlets of his friend and tenant, in a final statement before sentencing, Gorobets pulled his punches and claimed he never actually ate the cutlets himself. He just fed them to his friends.

In Kiev, three men were convicted of an occult murder on August 3, 1999. Dmitry Dyomin was sentenced to death, and his accomplices, Valentin Chelyshev and Alexei Andreyev were sentenced to prison terms of 13 and eight years, respectively. Dyomin admitted to belonging to a satanic cult under whose auspices he enjoined the others in slaying a 15-year-old girl, ceremonially excising her tongue, boiling and eating it. Dyomin severed the girl's head with a kitchen knife, cleaned and lacquered the skull, and kept it with him in his bedroom as a grisly memento. Besides the skull of his victim, inverted crucifixes and books on satanism were found during a search of his house.

In April of 2001, police in the former Soviet republic of Tajikistan announced that a vampire-style murderer had been discovered. Toyr Khamidov killed two men, cut their bodies into pieces, poured the blood into a glass, and drank it. Police believed that the 22-year-old man posed as a harmless shepherd before killing the men and vampirizing their remains.

On June 28, 2001 *Pravda* reported that a killer had stayed in his victim's apartment for a week, dining upon his rotting flesh. The generosity of the host had been returned by the grossest of indignities. The victim had offered to let a stranger stay in his apartment when he found out he was homeless. In an argument over vodka and money, the host's head was beaten in with a metal rod. Then since the hapless killer had no cash and no place to live, he decided to just stay in the flat and eat the resident.

On July 17, 2002, Ukrainian police arrested a gang of three men and a woman, accusing them of murder. They had lured their victim into a forest about a 100 miles south of Kiev near Zhytomyr, on June 26, intending to steal her keys and use them to rob her house, according to Serhiy Nesterchuk, chief of Zhytomyr police. But when she could not produce her house keys, they stabbed her to death, dismembered her, and dished her up for supper. They even fed some of her stewed remains to a four-year-old child, according to Interfax. Police were summoned to the home of the victim's elderly parents when the brazen ghouls showed up in person, demanding $3,000 ransom for return of the daughter they had already disposed of. They were promptly taken into custody, and investigation soon revealed they had been implicated in another five murders and two dozen robberies and assaults.

THE RIDDLE OF THE HUNGRY BOY

There have been a number of cases recently where people have been murdered in Russia and turned into their equivalent of ravioli. It's simply because of poverty. We spoke to one man who served his son human flesh. He didn't know it was human—they thought it was a stray dog. It's a cautionary tale. Our façade of civilization can slip very easily.

+ Dr. Timothy Taylor

While dining on our human friends creates an instinctive shudder of revulsion, the oral consumption of our close animal companions must be just as intuitively repugnant. Yet the significance of the act all depends upon the situation.

Take Robert Radu from Comanesti, Romania for example. This four-year-old boy strangled his pet cat, then went on to strip off the meat and eat it raw. The cat was nothing but bones and fur when the boy was caught. Doctors refused to believe his mother's account of the cat's demise, until they found cat hair in the tot's mouth and ordered his stomach pumped, to reveal the disgusting remains of the friendly family feline.

Was little Robert demented, degenerate or possessed to do such a thing? Or was he just a healthy growing boy in the throes of a powerful hunger? And the cat, was she a kindred spirit whose very being was entwined with Robert's forever? Or was she just a snack?

On the other hand, in April of 1999, another hungry boy turned the same dilemma the opposite way. A 16-year-old boy was arrested in Moscow after he had become frustrated with his father's drunken abuse and murdered him with a meat axe, said *Moskovsky Komsomolet*. He boiled up the old curmudgeon into a juicy stew to feed himself and his cats. Police called to the scene found dozens of cats gnawing on dishes of boiled meat, and prime pieces of stewed man-thigh piled high on a plate in the fridge.

NOTHING THEY WON'T DO

War, at times, can be even worse than hell. Sometimes the rigors of war distort behavior beyond the range considered human. True cases of war horrors could be related *ad nauseam*, but a few details from behind the lines of Nazi Germany should suffice to set a benchmark. This, then, is from *The Scourge of the Swastika*, by Lord Russell of Liverpool (1954):

> There were no gas chambers in Belsen, but thousands were nevertheless exterminated by disease and starvation. During the last few months of the camp's existence the shortage of food was so acute that the prisoners (the camp staff were still well fed) resorted to cannibalism, and one former British internee gave evidence at the trial of the Commandant and some of his staff that when engaged in clearing away dead bodies, as many as one in ten had a piece cut from the thigh or other part of the body, which had been taken and eaten, and that he had seen people in the act of doing this. To such lengths had they been brought by the pangs of hunger.

In addition to starving and degrading prisoners, war also encourages individuals who have just been waiting for an excuse to run amok.

Atrocities carried out by the Serbians on a massive scale have desensitized all involved, but an evil Serb policeman who not only tortured hapless Kosovars, but actually ate them, sparked a wave of revulsion.

An investigation was ordered by the British Royal Military Police upon the discovery of human arms, legs, and organs in his Pristina apartment on June 28, 1999, but they refuse to comment on whether the "Cannibal of Kosovo" was keeping the parts as wartime provisions, or simply as ghoulish trophies of his crimes. War crimes investigators believe the full extent of the horrors carried out by the Serbs may never be known.

Meanwhile, ethnic Albanians in the neighborhood gathered around the apartment building where the officer kept his grisly stash. "He was a cannibal," said one. "Why else does he want parts of bodies in his fridge and freezer?"

One woman called the stench "disgusting," since the power had been off for several days. "It was unbearable. It looked like hell in there."

"There is nothing these Serbs would not do."

Archaeologist Timothy Taylor has studied both ancient and modern cannibalism, and reminds us how close we are to our most primitive instincts. "I think the fact we live near supermarkets and are allowed to live a life of luxury makes us think cannibalism is horrific. But it doesn't take much—a serious food shortage or a crisis—to bring the instinct to survive back to the surface."

CAMBODIAN CURES

In February of 1999, police in Phnom Penh, Cambodia, announced they might have a cannibal at work there. Body parts found at the city dump were suggestive that this one had a taste for the exotic young female variety. "We're not sure whether she was foreign or Cambodian, as we found some reddish hair along with the bones," said Prach Nhat.

First found by scavengers were a pair of feet and a few bones wrapped in plastic. A police investigation produced a lung, a leg bone and three ribs. All of the bones bore knife marks.

"If it was just a killing why do they need to cut the flesh from the body?" asked senior criminal investigator, Ek Kreth. "We're investigating the possibility she might have been killed for making soup."

Other known crimes in the same area would suggest that rather than this crime being just a matter of a dietary supplement to stave off base hunger, elements of occult ritualism served up by local witch doctors may provide a more persuasive motive for a range of crimes including sacrificial murder.

On November 4, 1999, a former Khmer Rouge guerrilla was charged with murdering his traditional healer to dine upon his liver. "The soldier had been on a human rights course, but he still didn't understand the concept," said General Bun Seng of Cambodia.

"He killed the magic doctor and cut out and cooked his liver because he was very angry after his two children died and his sister got sick," said the senior military official of the western Battambang province. "He believed the magic doctor was to blame." Seng announced that three other people had also been charged with conspiracy to murder.

On December 15, 1999, a Cambodian man described as a vampire by local villagers was accused of killing people and drinking their blood. According to the *Koh Santepheap* newspaper, Pheach Phen, 20, had been arrested a week earlier in the eastern province of Kompong Cham after slashing a 5-year-old boy to death with a machete and sucking his blood.

Though initially only charged with one murder, Pheach Phen is a suspect in four others. One of an estimated 200,000 Cambodians infected with the HIV virus, the captured vampire told police that he had been instructed to kill by his traditional healer in order to cure the AIDS so he could live forever.

Although other indigenous AIDS cures call for having sex with virgins and drinking the blood of dogs and other slaughtered creatures, still, crossing that bloody line by attacking and consuming one's own kind does inspire a certain visceral revulsion that transcends even the most generous cultural relativism.

INDIAN VAMPIRES

"I want blood, it energizes me," admitted Arulraj Subbiah. "The very smell of blood gives me pleasure." From his prison cell in Palayamkottai, India, the 24-year-old serial killer confessed to drinking the blood of his victims.

Neighbors remembered him as a sensitive and reserved child who did well at school, until the sudden death of his father when he was 14, when the pleasant child quit school and turned quarrelsome.

He went to live with his elder sister Indira, who took him along with her when she married a man named Shanker. When marital problems drove Indira to suicide, Arulraj blamed his brother-in-law, and in November 1998, he stabbed Shanker to death. He told police he licked the knife clean.

He was out on bail six months later, and he found a job, and in November of 1999, he got in a drunken argument and hit a co-worker named Durai on the head with a stone. This time, police caught Arulraj drinking liquor mixed with Durai's blood.

Once again, Indian authorities found it appropriate to release this bloodthirsty killer on bail, and in November of 2001, he sought out a man named Kutty, who was one of the witnesses in the Durai murder case. He urged Kutty not to testify against him, and when Kutty refused, Arulraj knifed him to death. He confessed to having drunk Kutty's blood.

Arulraj's mother insisted that her son is not mentally ill. "It is his vengeful attitude and uncontrollable temper," she demurred. As most mothers would, she suspected her son had confessed under duress.

But there was no duress when news magazine *The Week* interviewed him in prison. While Arulraj remained silent throughout a steady stream of questions, he acknowledged the most salient point with an enigmatic smile: "Yes, I want blood."

In downtown Calcutta in July of 2001, more than 500 human skulls and bones were found in the home of 50-year-old Viresh Arora, who was accused of selling body parts for use in rituals. Environment official Javed Khan discovered the ghoulish respository after he responded to complaints about the smell.

"When we raided the house, we saw a number of skulls scattered on the roof for drying," Khan told *The Times Of India*. "Consignment letters say that he was engaged in shipping bones to Karachi and New York."

The Hindu Mother Goddess rules death and destruction. The iconic image of Kali depicts her as a naked black woman with four arms, brandishing a sword and the head of a slain demon with two, while beckoning with the other two. Festooned with a necklace of skulls and earrings of dead bodies, at her waist is a belt fashioned from human hands. Her eyes are red, her teeth are sharp like fangs, her hair is wild about her head and her breasts are smeared with blood. A long red tongue lolls from her mouth as she stands on top of her husband, Shiva, who has thrown himself before her in an effort to satisfy her. There are those who interpret this horrifying image as inspirational and symbolic of higher spiritual truths. For example, there are the Binderwurs of central India who eat their own elderly and infirm, in good faith that this is what Kali wants.

INDONESIAN SORCERY

On May 2, 1997, a Sumatran sorcerer confessed to 42 ritual murders dating back to 1986. Datuk Maringgi, who was known by the single name Suradji, specialized in love potions. According to his confessions, the victims, all women aged 12 to 30, had contracted with the sorcerer to cast spells to ensure the faithfulness of their husbands or lovers.

After being paid $200 to $500, he would take each woman to a sugar plantation adjacent to his house in the outskirts of Medan on the island of Sumatra, about 875 miles northwest of Jakarta. There he would tell her that his ritual required her to be buried in the ground up to her waist. As soon as the victim was thus immobilized, the sorcerer would strangle her to death with electrical cable.

He would then perform a magical ritual—not to bind his client's errant lover to her, but rather to heighten his own powers. Suradji believed that if he imbibed the victim's saliva, undressed her corpse, and buried it with the head pointing towards his home, this would give him the supernatural power that was the purpose of his fraudulent enterprise. He claimed that the idea for this magical working came to him in a dream.

"I just wanted to improve my ability in healing. That's all," the querulous magician told *The Jakarta Post*. "I've killed 42," he allowed, while claiming that his target was 70.

"I am ready to accept whatever punishment is given me, even the death penalty," he told *Kompas*, and Indonesian authorities obliged. Suradji was sentenced to death in April of 1998.

In January of 2003, another Indonesian sorcerer known as Sumanto was arrested and charged with murder. He admitted eating the flesh of three bodies, on the belief that if he could consume the flesh of seven human beings he would attain supernatural powers.

"I feel guilty. I'm asking for mercy," the 32-year-old farmer told Elshinta radio before his trial in April, 2003.

Neighbors searching for a missing 81-year-old woman were drawn to his shack by the vile smell. Inside were found skulls and bones, and body parts prepared for eating. Although he committed his crimes with a magical purpose, Sumanto was also pragmatic enough to make a human stew and serve it up to his elderly father for dinner.

During the trial, the publicity apparently triggered a copycat cannibal, who was caught robbing the grave of an infant in a village to the northwest of Jakarta, saying that voices were directing him. "I felt like something was moving my feet," he told police.

After Sumanto was found guilty and given the maximum sentence of seven years in prison, the Indonesian movie studio Starvision Plus paid him five million rupiah to secure exclusive film rights to his story.

PROUD CANNIBAL

For magnificence, for variety of form and color, for profusion of brilliant life—plant, bird, insect, reptile, beast—for vast scale... Uganda is truly the Pearl of Africa.
+ Winston Churchill

When Uganda was liberated from British colonial rule in 1962, its people were plunged into years of horror at the hands of unscrupulous despots. In 1966, when Milton Obote seized power, he declared a monstrous soldier who had been serving in the King's African Rifles to be his Chief of Staff. During Idi Amin's years of service, he plotted to overthrow Obote, and in a 1971 *coup d'état*, he seized power, taking Obote's vanquished supporters as prisoners. His first orders were for them to be decapitated live on television.

"They must wear white to make it easy to see the blood," Amin instructed. With the grimacing heads looking on, he made sure everyone absorbed the lesson, as he bit into their flesh.

He described himself coyly as a "reluctant cannibal," demurring that human flesh was actually a bit salty for his taste. Reluctant or not, he murdered his wife, dismembered her, and dined upon her flesh in the raw. He even cannibalized his own son.

The illiterate and syphilitic head of state would force his aides to play soccer with him, then if anyone blocked him from scoring, he would have them executed. He once sent Queen Elizabeth II a telegram, calling her "Liz" and inviting her to be his guest in Uganda "if she wanted to meet a real man."

Proclaiming himself "Lord of All Beasts of the Earth and Fishes of the Sea and Conqueror of the British Empire in Africa in General and Uganda in Particular," the grandiose leader showed no respect for African traditions. A strict Muslim, he ordered all Jews and Asians out of the country, after seizing their assets. Upon his orders, Christians were slaughtered, and he personally executed many Catholic priests. During the eight years of his reign, 300,000 Ugandans lost their lives, and the battered nation was not sorry to see him go in 1979, when Milton Obote made a comeback, leaving Amin to retire to a life of ease in Saudi Arabia, where he reportedly was noshing 40 oranges a day to keep up his "sex power," until July of 2003, when he fell into a coma. Idi Amin died in his late 70s on August 16, 2003.

But in the Pearl of Africa, not only the Lords of All Beasts have a taste for human flesh. In March of 2001, a man-eater of modest means was arrested in Luweero, about 60 miles north of the capital city of Kampala. Ssande Sserwadda, a 23-year-old factory worker, appeared in court to answer charges of trespassing on a burial site.

"I'm proud to be a cannibal," he told Chief Magistrate Isaac Muwata, according to *New Vision*. "My brother is a cannibal, and my father is a cannibal. His father was a cannibal, as was his father's father. We are a family of cannibals, we always have been, and I feel queasy if I go too long without tasting human meat. But just because we like to eat human flesh, does that mean we're bad people?

"None of us has ever killed anybody, that would be immoral," he smiled, all charm. "But we like our human flesh, and we don't see anything wrong in digging up corpses and eating them, after they've been buried. We don't like to see the meat going to waste. And we always wait at least a week after the funeral, out of respect to the relatives, and also because the meat tastes much better once it's matured. I have personally eaten parts of seven corpses in the past year, but my brother is the really greedy one. He's eaten dozens."

Convicted and sentenced to three years imprisonment, he picked his teeth as he eyeballed the judge, and asked if he could take the human leg bone in evidence with him. "It's still got plenty of meat on it," he pointed out. "It's a shame to let it go to waste."

In the Lugazi area along the Nile, people still remember the two cannibals who ate a 13-year-old girl back in the colonial days, and were sentenced to death for it. In October of 2002, *New Vision* published an interview with another Lugazi cannibal. He had been caught roasting meat out in the bush, by villagers who had suspected he had been behind the recent theft of livestock. As they approached him, they recognized the bush game hunter from a nearby village as 26-year-old Benedict Sseruwu.

"What do you want with me?" he growled, as Aloni Musoke approached, backed by the other villagers. There was no answer. The men kept walking closer.

"I caught my animal and killed it. You have no business intruding in my private affairs!"

"Why do you eat game meat in the bush?" Musoke asked.

"No one tells me where I should have my *muchomo*," Sseruwu replied, then as the villagers stepped closer, he suddenly leapt up and dashed off into the forest. The villagers examined the roasting game.

Expecting a pig or a goat, they were shocked to recognize the partially roasted body of a 3-year-old girl who had recently died of natural causes.

Their hopes that this was a one-off were dashed three days later when Sseruwu was caught in the act of digging up a body. As soon as the cannibal was taken into custody and charged with "disturbing the tranquility or peace of the dead," the *New Vision* reporter was down at the Lugazi police station requesting an interview.

Sseruwu has unkempt hair and rarely washes his clothes. His feet and fingers have been colonised by jiggers. His clothes are yawning for the next pint of water.

"Do you eat human bodies?" I asked.

"Yes," he answered. He kept quiet for a while, before adding, "It is not a crime to eat something that has been thrown away." He equated dead bodies to scrap. "If you cannot use it, I can," he said.

"For how long have you eaten dead bodies?"

He craned his head and smiled momentarily. His teeth were black, uncleaned for years perhaps.

He then answered: "Ten years," kept quiet for a moment and added, "It is not a crime."

"What attracts you to dead human beings?"

I expected a clear answer. Instead, he asked: "What attracts you to dead animals like cows?"

"Cows and other animals are edible. Everyone knows it," I answered.

He grinned at me, the only time he did it, then answered, "When a person dies, he changes from human to something else, he or she is meat that should be eaten. It is not a crime," Sseruwu added. "Other animals eat each other, why not us," he defended himself. "There is no crime," he added.

"How did you learn to eat dead bodies?"

"I do not remember, but it is not a crime," he insisted. "I don't want people who waste things. Once you throw away such meat, I can't allow it to happen," he answered.

"Will you be happy if your body is eaten when you die?"

"I will be dead and useless," he answered.

Sseruwu said that there are many other people eating dead bodies in his village, and that the villagers are just jealous because he always beats them to the nice meat.

"This is hatred. They hate me because I conquer all the good meat. They should seek advice from me, instead of putting me in prison," he lambasted.

VAMPIRE CULT

Africa's most populous nation, with more than 110 million people, is Nigeria, where society is permeated to the highest levels by a murderous vampire cult known as the Ogboni.

In April of 2001, a Nigerian man sought asylum in Canada as a defector. In an affidavit, Bolaji Oloyede described how his father had initiated him to the cult when he was eight years old, in a ritual leaving him with distinctive scars on his left cheek and left arm.

"My father joined this organization on the belief it was a business group... but it is much more than that."

He described cult rituals he attended that involved slashing a victim to death and spilling his blood on an altar strewn with skulls and human remains. While still beating, his heart would be cut out and eaten by all of the cult members.

Oloyede tolerated it for years. His father had risen to the rank of chief priest, and when he died in April of 1999, cult members demanded that Oloyede succeed him. He rebelled, and "that was the beginning of my problems with the cult."

Two months later, two armed cult members came to get him, and when he refused to join them, they shot his mother dead. His car was bombed and his family's butcher shop was burned to the ground.

Oloyede moved his daughters and their mother from their home in Abeokuta to Lagos, Nigeria, and thence to Canada.

"I am seriously scared to go back to Nigeria now," he told Reuters from Toronto, where as a husband, a father, and a practicing Christian, he worked as a meat packer.

To substantiate his claim, Oloyede filed an autopsy report attributing his mother's death to gunshot wounds, and a letter from a Nigerian attorney who confirmed that his life was indeed in danger from the cult. Expert opinions and previous findings confirming the existence of such cults were also filed, along with recent rulings granting asylum to Nigerian applicants based on their fear they may be forced to participate in cannibalistic rituals.

The report by the Canadian Immigration and Refugee Board substantiated his claim and explained why Oloyede could not expect any help from the Nigerian authorities:

Documentary evidence supports his contention that the cult is a powerful organization whose membership gives it the ability in some instances to co-opt the judicial system for its own ends. The Ogboni cult is described as 'pervasive in Nigerian society.' The same source reports that the membership is drawn from those with 'political influence and links to the political power base' and that 'some leading army and police commanders from the western part of Nigeria and Benin city are influenced by the Ogboni cult.'

Professor Emeritus Peter Morton-Williams of the University of Ulster provided a report to the Research Directorate that confirmed that Ogboni rituals include "forced suicide, poisoning, human sacrifice and cannibalism." Another student of Nigerian culture, Maureen Eke, Associate Outreach Coordinator of African Studies Center at Michigan State University, filed a report stating that "the main purpose of any society like the Obgoni claiming the use of rituals involving human sacrifice and cannibalism is to deter inquiries into their affairs; to promote a sense of mysticism and of the occult; and to build themselves up in the eyes of the impressionable in order to keep some sense of influence and control over the people."

"Eating human flesh was a tradition of warriors pertaining to the ethnic group of the Fang, which lives in Equatorial Guinea, Nigeria, Gabon and Cameroon," a Spanish journalist and ethnographer told *Deutsche Presse-Agentur*. Jose Manuel Novoa, who has conducted investigations in Equatorial Guinea since 1979 and has written two books about cannibalism, spoke in an April 5, 1998 interview: "As they conquered new territories, Fang warriors ate parts of their victims to absorb desirable qualities such as youth and strength... human organs are eaten by members of secret brotherhoods which practice sorcery in forests at night. New members are initiated in ceremonies which invoke spirits... bodies are obtained through murder and robbing them from cemeteries..."

The Board found Oloyede's accounts of the cannibalistic cult credible enough, and agreed that the group threatened his safety. But they rejected his immigration bid under the terms of the Geneva Convention because they declared the violent attacks sustained by his family were common crimes rather than a form of religious persecution for his refusal to join the notorious vampire cult.

THE BLOOD THAT CRIED

Many Nigerians still believe that using human body parts in rituals can make them wealthy, sexy and powerful, and even give them invisibility. Every now and then someone gets caught but ties to the wealthy and powerful clientèle are rarely investigated, with the notorious "Otokoto affair" being the most notable exception.

On September 11, 1996, an 11-year-old Nigerian street urchin named Ikechukwu Okonkwo, who gathered groundnuts and sold them in Owerri, the capital city of Imo State, was lured to the upscale Otokoto Hotel, where he was decapitated. When his headless corpse was found, the community was profoundly shaken. Those who were suspected of involvement in the occult were hounded out of town. The local piano store was torched, as were the Chibet Hotel, the Overcomers Church, and the Otokoto Hotel itself.

In the midst of the rioting, police nabbed Innocent Ekeanyanwu, who worked at the Otokoto Hotel, in possession of the head of the boy, with the tracks of his blood and tears still visible on the face. Upon interrogation, the suspect named the owner of the hotel as his direct handler, then dropped a bombshell by naming Chief Leonard Unaogu, the wealthy and prominent elder brother of a cabinet minister, as the one who had demanded the fresh head. After promising to name more names the next day, he was taken to his cell—and murdered.

All seven police officers on duty that night were charged with his murder and incarcerated pending trial, while the investigation into the murder of Ikechukwu Okonkwo commenced. The first to be sentenced were six flunkies and fall guys including the son of the owner of the Otokoto Hotel. They were executed by firing squad in 1997.

In 2001, seven policemen were tried for the murder of Innocent Ekeanyanwu; four were found guilty and hanged; three were released.

Prosecution of those at the higher levels of the cult, including the owner of the hotel, Chief Vincent Duru, and the cult leader, Chief Unaogu, was more problematic, with two witnesses being murdered in custody and four journalists being assaulted for investigating the case.

In October of 2002, final arguments were concluded at the trial of the final seven defendants in the murder of Ikechukwu Okonkwo. On January 23, 2003, trial judge Chioma Nwosu-Iheme ascended to the bench before a packed courtroom, and resplendent in her ceremonial red regalia, announced her conclusions.

"This is a case where a circumstantial evidence has proved a case of murder with the accuracy surpassing that of mathematics," she intoned. "It has left no one in doubt of the connection between one accused person and others. It is to me a syndicated arrangement with clear division of labor."

The judge described Chief Duru as "a hardened and unrepentant murderer," but she reserved the heaviest burden of guilt for Chief Unaogu, calling him "an intelligent but highly sophisticated criminal," and declaring that he was "the actor who orders for the heads of human beings as if he is ordering for goat heads."

"It is indeed an unfortunate case, a very intelligent man who chose to channel his intelligence the wrong way," she said. "The blood of Ikechukwu Okonkwo must be a very strong and powerful one that cried to God in high heavens."

"It is indeed condemnable, even God Himself condemned it when he said in Ezekiel, Chapter 8 Verse 20, that 'the soul that sinneth shall die.' The accused have demonstrated a species of wickedness surpassing those of Jezebel. The law is very clear on the consequences of these acts and the perpetrators will go in for it."

Judge Nwosu-Iheme sentenced all seven defendants to death by hanging, bringing the total convicted of these occult crimes to 16, and the total executed for them to ten.

A DATE WITH A MAN-EATER

Underneath a bridge on the Airport Road in Lagos was the lair of a couple of bloodthirsty, sex-crazed trolls, who were arrested the first week of February in 1999, after a young woman's cries were heard as she was being slaughtered. When police arrived at the scene, human limbs were found roasting on the grill.

"Some of the limbs and feet on the man's grill are believed to be those of a young woman, going by the size of the feet and the long black permed hair," sources at the scene told the *Guardian*. "The rest of the body was said to have been eaten up before the arrest."

The trolls specialized in attacking "young, fine girls with long hairs," as one of them later put it.

Another young woman, traumatized and unconscious, was rescued from the "house of horror," which immediately became a ghastly tourist attraction.

Working-class acquaintances of Clifford Orji had long suspected him and his inscrutable sidekick, Ali Dahiru, of murdering wayfarers along the road to sell their body parts for ritual sacrifices, but apparently were not concerned enough to report the suspicious activity.

The day of his arrest, Orji said in a formal confessional statement, "I just look unto the forehead of any woman, blow the air from my mouth as directed by the spirit, then the woman will follow me. When I get to the underbridge, I will have sexual affair with her to a state of unconsciousness before we slaughter her and roast. I am not alone, I have between four to ten people. They take their own parts and go while I wait again for another meat."

By the next day, word spread throughout Nigeria of the grisly crime scene, and a massive traffic jam developed as thousands of curious observers tried to catch a glimpse of the pitiful remains of their victims.

Lagos State Police Commissioner Sunday Aghedo called a press conference, and had the two suspects brought out. The Commissioner was explaining how they would dig a hole and cover it with branches, and then when a victim fell in the hole, they would pounce, when Orji interrupted, making an urgent fashion statement: "We wanted to stop women from wearing wigs."

Though Orji claimed to be from Enugu State, inexplicably he never uttered a word in the Enugu native tongue of Igbo. In an oddly broken English, he said, "We came from America... We use in ourselves human being to sexually satisfy ourselves."

Orji's sidekick Dahiru, on the other hand, had nothing to say, except to deny that he knew Orji. But Orji spoke up to claim that he only went out to hunt for their victims, but it was Dahiru who actually butchered them.

The speech Orji made, as transcribed by the attentive press, resembled a word salad: "That is that man... Ijeoma... Abraka Chichi Cho, we will distributed... All that you are talking in this reference... We will eat in ourselves human beings that we may enjoy sex in the opportunity and the right woman."

Then in a singsong rhythm suggesting a mockery of the Nigerian national anthem, he broke into a little soft-shoe: "Danso, Ranso, Ransang, just like that," he sang as they hustled him offstage and back to his cell.

Though their hideous hovel was still piled high with charred human remains, both defendants were charged with only one count of murder in the slaying of young Hauwa'u Lawal.

At his arraignment, Orji told the Court, "I killed them at Oshodi, I ate their flesh like potatoes."

Magistrate Bajulaiye inquired, "How did you get the flesh discovered with you?"

He replied: "I did not kill them, Sir. Well, I killed them at Oshodi then ate the flesh like potatoes."

Just to clarify that he was hearing correctly, the magistrate asked him again, "You mean you ate human beings like you are eating potatoes?"

"Yes, sir."

The two suspects were held at the Makinde Police Station for two months, then transported to the Psychiatric Hospital at Yaba for a six-month evaluation. Orji and Dahiru were separated and placed in solitary confinement in the state prison at Ikoyi to await trial.

On September 7, 1999, *The News* in Lagos published a sensational exclusive interview, under the irresistible headline, *A Date With a Man-Eater.*

> His disposition to the fairer sex necessitated the decision to send two crack female reporters to draw him out in prison. But first, Lara Owo-eye-Wyse and Nkiru Nwokediuko had to get close enough to the dreaded beings. They devised the ingenious method of posing as sisters of the man-eaters. What they found was beyond the reporters' wildest expectations. One of them fell in love, almost, with Clifford!

Nkiru Nwokediuko told prison authorities she was Clifford Orji's sister, and he was brought in to meet her, and asked by the guards if he recognized her. With a savvy gleam of intelligence, he immediately claimed her as his sister, and the contact visit commenced.

She had been prepared for the nasty, bedraggled mumbling maniac she had seen in the press conference. Instead here was a clean and trim attractive man with broad, manly shoulders and a deep voice. He sat next to her on a bench and stroked her arm as they spoke.

The 'man-eater' had skin-piercing eyes, a nice smile, nicely shaped ears and luscious thick lips. He looked as someone who had just stepped out of the pages of a romantic novel. The reporter barely resisted the urge to wrap him in a warm embrace.

"Nkiru," he crooned, "I like this your name. It suits a beautiful girl like you. Since I came to this prison, I have never had a visitor, but when I was told I had a visitor and your name was mentioned to be my sister, I know I didn't know you, but I believed you were God-sent to help me. Immediately, I set my eyes on you, I had a feeling we were meant for each other. The same blood runs through our veins. In fact, if I get out of this place, I won't hesitate making you my queen, my only woman. I will shower you with the whole love I have and make sure you lack nothing. Who could ever be as daring as you Nkiru? For you to have thought of visiting me is enough for me to like you."

His words and the manner he spoke could send shivers down any lady's spine. In fact, it struck a cord in the reporter's spine. Then he touched her. It was simply electrifying.

His keepers described their prize catch as a friendly, outgoing prisoner. "In fact, he gives us a lot of rib-cracking jokes here," one of the guards told *The News*. "We don't see him as one who is mentally unbalanced, we relate with him as a normal human being."

Clifford described himself to the curious reporter as well-adjusted and sociable, hardly a mental case. "I relate freely with everybody here, they are all my friends. Recently, I was moved from ward B, single cell that was occupied by seven of us to a cell that houses about 73 people. Though I don't like that place as it is not as conducive as the other cell, I still prefer it as I am in the midst of many."

And when Nkiru asked him the hard questions about his crimes, the wily con beguiled her with a diversion, shifting blame while admitting to being the fall guy for an organization, yet still being loyal to his clientèle by refusing to incriminate any of them.

"No, it is my business associates who set me up. They didn't want to pay me my own share of the deal I got them connected to, so they put me in this state. They are owing me close to N700,000. I became frustrated and packed my things to live under the bridge. I don't eat human beings. How can I eat a fellow human being? What people saw in my 'kitchen' were remains of a pussy cat."

Sensing the reporter's disappointment, he followed this by playing both sides of the game at once, courting her with ingratiating intimacies while proffering an oblique confession. "I saw a piece of human flesh on the expressway. I picked it up and roasted it, but when I tasted it, I didn't like it, so I spat it out and threw away the remaining. Nkiru, you know I like you, so I won't lie to you as I have done to other people. Please, believe me."

When the guard told them their time was up, the infamous cannibal begged the reporter for money "for soap." When she told him soap was in the package she had brought him, he insisted, "No, now! At least, money to buy other things."

The journalist gave in and forked over the cash. The cannibal beamed. She had her scoop. Everybody was happy.

The attempt to interview Dahiru employing the same ruse was productive only of an hilarious dialogue in which the prisoner refused to pretend to recognize the reporter, angrily denounced her, and rejected her gifts.

Reporter: Dahiru, so you don't want what I brought for you?

Dahiru: Me I no say me I no want. You no be my sister.

From the beginning there were doubts about the official rationale that these were savage maniacs, and to a country still reeling from the Otokoto trials, the more the public learned about the man-eating trolls, the more they seemed like savvy spare parts dealers serving the occult trade. Reporters quoted sources claiming to know Clifford "very well," who charged that large sums of cash had been seized at the scene, along with two cellphones. If law enforcement were involved in covering up a lucrative trade in human flesh, that would explain why no such evidence was reported. Witnesses told reporters they had often seen upscale vehicles stopped under the bridge, but their testimony was not taken by investigators.

The News reported in November of 1999 that Police Commissioner Aghedo had been transferred out of Lagos, and his successor, Mike Okiro, claimed that no mention had been made of the Clifford Orji case in the notes handed over to him. "I'm not a casemonger to start looking for cases to prosecute."

"I think the case is over," Okiro told *The News*, "because since I came, I've never heard anything about Clifford Orji."

Despite all efforts to make the Clifford Orji case file disappear, in November of 2000, the Lagos State Ministry of Justice finally brought the suspect before the Court to face formal charges on three counts of murder and cannibalism. The Ministry of Justice blamed the delay on police, accusing them of dragging their feet in the investigation. Informed sources suspected pressure from influential Nigerians.

A month later on December 17, 2000 the Court ruled that based upon testimony by a state-paid psychiatrist, the defendant was not competent to stand trial.

Over a year later in February of 2002, Police Commissioner Okiro said in an television interview that Clifford Orji had been confined to the psychiatric hospital because he was mentally unstable, and that the case file had been turned over to the Lagos State Director of Public Prosecution.

The Solicitor General angrily denied it. "We have immediate access to records and nothing of such is here."

Public hopes for a just resolution of the troubling case plummeted as reporters from *The News* determined that rather than Orji and Dahiru being hospitalized at Yaba, they both were still in Ikoyi Prison.

And on March 14, 2003, Dr. Reuben Abati discussed the implications of the still-unresolved case with the *Guardian*:

> The other year, a cannibal was arrested right inside Lagos, one Clifford Orji. He confessed to being a dealer in fresh human body parts. According to him, many of his customers are rich Nigerians who buy the body parts for ritual purposes. Whatever he is unable to sell, he eats. The police found skulls and bones at his hideout. To date, no rich man has been arrested in connection with the Clifford Orji case. While the case grabbed the headlines, journalists were more interested in asking the accused person about how human flesh tastes, as if they too were planning to have a taste of the special delicacy.

Allegations of ritual consumption of human flesh persist throughout Nigeria, but have proven very difficult to prosecute, because law enforcement, corrections and the entire justice system are infiltrated by these deadly, powerful and secretive cults. The guy who takes a fall for being caught, corpse in hand, is left mugging for the cameras and talking gibberish in a bid to appear incompetent and plead for leniency with the court, meanwhile remaining silent about his powerful criminal clientèle, who could easily have him eliminated, even in "protective" custody, if he dare mention their names.

SOMETIME MY HEAD WILL JUST TURN

On February 20, 2002, a 23-year-old Nigerian man settled a dispute over his wages by slaughtering his boss and chopping her up into a pepper soup. Reuters reported that Salifu Ojo, who worked on a farm in southwest Ondo State, took a machete to his boss, Christiana Elijah, a 40-year-old mother of four who had refused his demands for payment. Christiana's internal organs were used as ingredients for his soup, while the head and limbs were reserved for customers who later bought them.

But Ojo would not feast on his stomach-churning revenge in peace; when the bosslady/pepper soup would not stay down, he gave up and confessed to his fellow laborers, who asked him for a piece of the meat, and then when he brought it to them, forcibly restrained him, tying him up until police arrived to take him into custody.

"We recovered the trunk of the woman's body and some uncooked parts on the farm," said Ondo State Commissioner of Police Paul Ochonu. He told Reuters that his men were on the trail of the gang buying human parts, adding that the suspected cannibal was cooperating with police.

Two weeks later on March 7, 2002, *Tempo* of Lagos published an exclusive interview with the cannibal. He was described by reporter Dele Oyewale as unkempt, with "a forlorn and faraway look in his eyes."

Q: Why are you in police custody?

A: One day, my father house where I dey stay, na so water dey beat us for inside, that's why I say make I go outside go find work to do am, make I carry my wife and pikin, make we dey there, from there, na in problem come happen to me like this.

Q: What problem?

A: By that time, I no well, they carry me for somewhere, my mother go treat me, as I come well small, na in I say make I come do work.

Q: This is a police station. You were arrested for doing something. What was that thing you did?

A: Na problem sir.

Q: What problem brought you here?

A: The problem is that, he get one woman, she gave me work do, I do am, as I do am, one day, if I cook soup for inside the house, I will go farm, I will come back, if I chop the soup, I will get problem.

Q: You see, something brought you here.

A: Yes sir.

Q: Tell me that particular thing.

A: Okay, dey say I get problem, one woman died and dey say I killed am, but it's a mistake, it is not my mind.

Q: It was alleged you killed her. Did you?

A: I killed am but it's not my mind, na confusion na in make me go do like that.

Q: What confusion?

A: The time when I do the thing, I no know but when I do am, na in my face come clear and I say make I come report myself for police.

Q: You turned yourself in?

A: Na me carry myself dey come, when I come tell my town people and they come report me to the police.

Q: Now, I want you to tell me how you killed the woman?

A: Ehen, the woman give me work, I dey do am, as I dey do am, sometime, all my body, my head will just turn.

Q: I want you to tell me the truth, how did you kill the woman?

A: It's not in my mind to kill am.

Q: But you said that earlier, how did you kill her?

A: Na hand I take knack am, she fall for ground.

Q: You didn't use any weapon?

A: Na hand I use, I no hold any weapon but as I go house come, na in I come carry cutlass, I come dey do am.

Q: What did you do?

A: I dey pieces her body with cutlass.

Q: Which part did you cut first?

A: Armpit, later her backside.

Q: What of her head?

A: I no cut am.

Q: What of the trunk?

A: I no carry am.

Q: The one you carried, what did you do with it?

A: I cooked am.

Q: Why?

A: I wan ea am.

Q: How did it taste when you ate it?

A: As I was eating am, I no fit tell lie that he no sweet but it just be like something wey no get pepper or salt.

Q: Didn't you add pepper while cooking?

A: No, I use pepper but as he dey taste for my mouth, it be like eno get pepper or salt or oil. As I chop am, I vomit am.

"I don't think Salihu is not normal. The truth is that he is a wicked man who is now unlucky to be caught," Ochonu told *Tempo*. "I'm sure he has been killing for long and he has been enjoying human flesh. This one may not be his first attempt."

Regarding allegations that the head and limbs had been sold on the black market, the Police Commissioner contradicted his earlier statements and dismissed the issue, declaring that all of the remains had been taken into custody by his department.

"His case is peculiar but not very complex," Ochonu said. "Unlike what was reported sometime ago about one Clifford Orji, also a cannibal in Lagos, Salihu has not been found to be connected to anyone. Salihu is possibly new in the act but as soon as we are through with a mental test on him, we will charge him to court."

A year later, Salihu Ojo still has not been tried, and there have been no further investigations into the Police Commissioner's initial statements to Reuters, confirming cult involvement and claiming his troops were hot on the trail of those who had purchased the missing parts. So due to a lack of evidence, this one goes down as just another lone nut who eats people when his head gets turned around.

SPARE PARTS

Spare parts are showing up all over South Africa. Human body parts are highly prized on the black market, with genitalia, eyes, breasts, and brains being the most valuable, and the less potent parts often being casually discarded.

Ghoulish gangs are often used to assassinate a person and bring in the prized parts, but trying to freelance it without knowing the go-to guy is risky. In 1990, when Johannes Mohlale Monareng killed a six-year-old girl and tried to sell her head on the open market, he was arrested, tried, convicted, and committed to a mental institution—only to be released four years later, no doubt much improved.

In June of 1999, children attending the Isaacson School in Soweto were shocked to find the head of one of their schoolmates, 11-year-old Tshepo Molemohi, glaring down on them from the roof of the school.

The child had been abducted the day before by two burly 18-year-old thugs, and taken to two aged witchdoctors, who ceremonially restrained him, then stripped and slaughtered him. After the removal of the head, the genitalia, and some of the organs, the head was taken back to the school and placed on the roof.

Investigation of this shocking display led to the young accomplices, who confessed and implicated the witchdoctors. A search of their quarters turned up the victim's shoes, and all four were charged with murder.

"Witchdoctors use body parts to prepare different medicines, depending on what the client wants," said Gordon Chavinduka, president of the Zimbabwean Traditional Healers Association and former vice chancellor of the University of Zimbabwe, explaining that usually the motive is money. "Mostly it is for self-enrichment and business improvement."

Throughout South Africa, magical workings are spoken of in all languages by their Zulu names. Thus a traditional healer is a *sangoma* or *inyanga*, a fetish such as a skull is a *tokoloshe*, and the magical substance ingested by the client is *muti*.

There are more than a quarter million traditional healers in South Africa. Most use herbal ingredients for their *muti*, though special occasions might call for spicing it up with a monkey hand or a chicken foot. But there are less scrupulous *sangomas* who provide the *muti* that packs the most power, and there are well-heeled and highly-placed customers who pay very well indeed.

Throughout South Africa, *muti* is thought of as a form of insurance. New construction requires consecration by a *sangoma*; taxis pay a high *muti* fee to protect their territory and business; sports and politics are rife with the use of *muti* to gain an edge over the competition; thieves use *muti* to give them invisibility and the ability to dodge bullets; courtrooms are often cleared because a *tokoloshe* has been found and the case has been compromised.

"If the business is not doing well, get a boy or a girl's head—someone who has a future—and your business will have a future too," Chavinduka explained.

More than 300 people have been murdered for their body parts in the past decade in South Africa. And at the Institute for Human Rights and Criminal Justice in South Africa, Dr. Anthony Minnar fears that the situation is only bound to get worse.

"We have children going missing every week from our townships," he says. "The assumption is that those missing children are being put into prostitution and also that they are being used for *muti* murder."

To make a brain *muti* according to traditional practices, the corpse's head is chopped off and the top of the skull removed. The brain is removed and sun-dried. Later it is ground with fresh herbs and eaten from the skull.

"If a witchdoctor is going to go out at night to practice witchcraft, they eat human flesh, drink the soup and smear their bodies with some medicine," Chavinduka said. "The connection is that they will be brave, feared and even invisible at night."

"A girl's vagina brings productivity to the business," Chavinduka said. "The connection is that women are productive because they produce children. Testicles are used for enhancing sexual strength and performance."

Johannesburg *muti* shop owner Kessavan Naidoo, an herbalist for 30 years and close observer of traditional healing methods, explains that human hands are considered an effective anti-stroke remedy. Strokes are seen as the result of a spell being cast by the hands of a *sangoma*; thus a human hand may be burnt, reduced to a paste and rubbed onto the wrist of the stroke victim.

According to Naidoo, hearts are used to treat heart disease, while eyes are believed to counteract the "Evil Eye" of an enemy.

On October 8, 1998, the *Weekly Mail and Guardian* in Johannesburg published a list of magical results that may be obtained by using *muti* with the following ingredients:

+ Blood gives vitality.

+ The heart is used for bravery.

+ Hands and heads beckon customers to a new business. Hands or parts of a hand also symbolize possession, success or illegal appropriation.

+ Eyes symbolize vision and foresight.

+ Genitals ensure virility.

+ Brains are for academic success.

+ A skull can be built into the foundations of a new building to ensure good business.

+ A brew containing human parts may be buried to ensure a good harvest.

+ Lips make one a good orator.

+ Human fat strengthens *muti*.

There is nothing merciful about a *muti* murder. The more the victim screams and struggles while the organs are being removed, the more potent the *muti*, so extraction of the desired parts is preferably accomplished before slaughter, and free rein is given to the brutal instincts of the captors to commit the most gratuitous atrocities.

Jeffery Mkhonto was one of the lucky ones who lived to tell the tale of an encounter with *muti* rustlers. The South African native was 12 years old when they came to his village looking for live body parts to harvest. A neighbor called him over for some food, but when he got in the door they ganged up on him and cut off his genitals with a butcher knife. "They took me home and left me in front of my father's house. As they left I heard them say they are going to sell my parts so that they can get money."

Few have described the horror of *muti* like Elizabeth Matsuku. In 1996, in the village of Suurman in northwestern South Africa, the 46-year-old woman had a visit from a distant cousin who came from a nearby village. She welcomed Albert Baloyi to her home with her customary hospitality, and he settled in comfortably until one night when he came home smelling of drink.

"I was tired as I had been helping my neighbor prepare for a wedding," she told *The Independent*. "Albert called me and said he was looking for human body parts. He said a traditional healer had offered him ten thousand Rand if he could bring her a tongue, a buttocks and a left breast."

Elizabeth thought her cousin was just kidding. "But when he said he was going out to look for those things, I realized he was serious. He said there were many people who drank liquor and walked in the streets late at night. He would find one of them and cut off their body parts. I told him not to do it. I told him people would accuse our family of practicing witchcraft."

Her cousin seemed to understand and the family all turned in for the night. The visitor slept on the floor of the lounge, while Elizabeth shared her bedroom with her grandson, Jabu.

"Late that night, someone pulled me from my bed. He hit me with fists and open hands. It was Albert. He said he was looking for *my* tongue and breast, not someone else's. He said to me: 'You thought I was joking when I told you that I want body parts. Tonight you are going to die.'"

Elizabeth was dragged from her bed and her hands were belted behind her back. "He threw me on the floor and told me to pray because I was going to die that night. I prayed to God and my ancestors so they could accept me when I died. When I had finished praying, he also knelt and prayed. He asked God to help him in what he was doing. He said he was poor and needed the money the *sangoma* had shown him that day. He said he was unemployed and he had never seen so much money in his life. He said if it wasn't for the money, he wouldn't kill me—but he had to because he had never seen a R200 note before. I wanted to scream to attract the attention of Jabu, who was still sleeping. But each time I tried to scream he put the knife to my throat. He undressed me and raped me."

After he raped her, he intended to cut out her tongue, and she was ordered to open her mouth. "I refused. He tried to force my mouth open, but I fought, even with my hands tied behind my back. He cut me on the chin with the knife, but still I would not open my mouth. When he realized I was not prepared to let him get my tongue, he went for my breast. I tried to scream but then he put the knife on my throat again. I pleaded with him to kill me before cutting me to pieces, but he refused. He said the *sangoma* had told him to cut me up while I was still alive because that would make the *muti* strong. He refused to kill me."

He cut off her left breast and a large piece of flesh from her buttocks. "He then covered me with a blanket and left."

Convicted of the brutal assault and serving a 20-year prison sentence, Baloyi never mentioned the *sangoma's* name in court. "I think the *sangoma* threatened to cast a spell on him if he ever talked," said Elizabeth. "Up to this day, we don't know who that person is."

Much less the *sangoma's* well-heeled clientèle who were the ultimate consumers of Elizabeth Matsuku's breast and buttocks.

In April of 2001, the BBC aired a documentary called *Nobody's Child*, relating the story of Naledzani Mabuda, who was a *sangoma* in the Thohoyandou area in South Africa. In the mid-nineties, his youngest wife, 18-year-old Helen Madide, had dutifully borne him an infant son.

"He began to tell me stories," Helen told the BBC. "His ancestors said that he must kill me and the child so that he can be rich. He showed me the path and forced me to go along that path. He was pushing me and demanding me to go whether I like it or not. He said he was going to kill the baby first while I see the baby, then secondly he will kill me."

Helen tried to run away, but the wily *sangoma* caught her by the neck and forced her to restrain their son's legs while he cut his throat. "When the child was dead, he started to cut all those pieces, the hands, the legs and even the sex organs."

Mabuda was sentenced to life in prison, and although Helen Madide was acquitted of all charges, according to the BBC, she will never be free of the guilt she suffers for participating in her own son's ritual sacrifice.

But *sangomas* have no immunity to their own evil. Jim Kgokong Shego was the most successful *sangoma* in the Mountainview area of the South African province of Mpumalanga. He was seeing 40 clients a day, and it was said that his *muti* could cure AIDS—until June 7, 2000, when four less successful *sangomas* conspired to make *muti* of the *muti* man.

First they rousted Shego's apprentice, John Msiza, and forced him at gunpoint to take them to Shego's house. When Shego greeted his colleagues at the door, they shot him in the leg and hauled him out into the open veldt.

"Madonsela took out a knife and he ordered us to pin Shego's legs wide open." According to Msiza, who testified on May 23, 2003 against the four defendants at their murder trial, two of the men held his legs and two more pinned down his shoulders. "Madonsela took the knife and cut out the man's testicles. He then cut around his navel and took it out. He also cut around his anus and took that tissue out."

While the *muti* man's ruined flesh was placed in a plastic bag for later use, a rock was tied around his waist. Still crying and pleading for his life, Shego was thrown down a mine shaft to drown in the dank water.

Traditional *sangomas* hasten to condemn *muti* based on human remains. Fanyane Matsaba, the president of Lwandlelubumbene Health and Herbalist Association in the Eastern Transvaal, says that *sangomas* are born with a healing gift and that the herbs they use as medicine are revealed to them by their ancestors in dreams. This knowledge can also be imparted in training. The use of human remains indicates the sorcerers "are not in direct link with the ancestral spirits."

Claude Makhubela concurs, denigrating sorcerers who use human remains as witches. "True *sangomas* and *inyangas* would never use human organs for *muti* because the ancestral spirits who work through them would remove the power of healing," said the traditional healer from Soweto.

"Spirits work through the living, not the dead."

Lacking the power to heal, he concluded, "They are just there to exploit people with a desperate need."

In September of 2001, a boy's torso was found in the Thames River in downtown London, England. Though police were unable to identify the victim, they suspected it was, in fact, a *muti* murder, and turned the investigation over to the Occult Crime Unit.

In April of 2002, Scotland Yard investigators traveled to Johannesburg to confer with a wizened *sangoma* of highest repute about the case. Credo Mutwa was horrified at the photographs the detectives showed him, as reported by the *Guardian*.

"They sacrificed an innocent child who had not yet reached puberty," said the *sangoma*. "They would have drank his blood and used it to wash themselves. The finger joints would have been used as charms and his bones would have been ground into a paste to give them strength."

Mutwa said the child had not been killed by a South African for *muti*, because the genitalia had been left intact. Nor was it a satanic ritual, he felt sure. The way the child had been dismembered indicated that the killer most likely came from Nigeria, as it appeared to be an *obeah* ritual, involving sacrifice to a Nigerian sea goddess.

On July 9, 2002, a 31-year-old Nigerian woman was arrested in Glasgow, and questioned in connection with the boy, who had been dubbed "Adam" by police. Joyce Osagiede was not charged, but she did cooperate, and was soon released and deported back to Nigeria.

In September of 2002, police announced that forensic analysis had revealed that shortly before death Adam had ingested a potion of human bone fragments, clay, quartz and gold.

In January of 2003, further testing suggested that the victim had been alive upon arrival in London and had been slain very shortly thereafter. Pollen found in his system was traced to a rural area just north of Lagos, and in March, Scotland Yard investigators spent several weeks in Nigeria pinpointing the boy's origins and identity.

On July 2, 2003, Joyce Osagiede's 37-year-old ex-husband was arrested in Dublin. Sam Onogigovie was wanted in Germany, where he had been convicted of human trafficking, and was questioned by Scotland Yard regarding the ritual murder of the boy they believed to be the suspect's own son.

"It is a breakthrough at this point in time," Detective Andy Baker told Reuters. "We intend to interview the suspect at the earliest opportunity following the search in conjunction with our Irish colleagues."

MORGUE MURDERS

The same superstitious beliefs about the magical powers of human remains are driving bustling businesses around the world that show no signs of becoming relics of a benighted past. In cultures as diverse as Cambodia, Venezuela, Nigeria and South Africa, the odd documented case signifies much more than a singular circumstance of isolated insanity; rather, such crimes are dependent upon the existence of a whole criminal subculture involving victims, clients, and perpetrators, promoted by the exploitation of indigenous superstitions via primitive conjurer's tricks ranging from the use of psychoactive drugs, hypnosis and old-fashioned sleight-of-hand, to threats, intimidation, outright bribery and corruption of the local power structure, with significant infiltration of law enforcement and the trades that involve the handling of the dead. The mandatory blood oath of silence keeps the low-level functionaries bound to the organization for life; occasionally they may be sacrificed to draw the heat off the vested interests.

Tjaart Schutte, for example, was a sergeant with the police department in Krugersdorp, South Africa, while also being ideally positioned as an employee at the Hillbrow State Mortuary in Johannesburg. A private detective first became suspicious of Sgt. Schutte when he was seen following an apprentice *sangoma* during a *muti* investigation.

That private detective testified against Schutte in May of 1995, when the 33-year-old mortuary attendant stood trial for corruption, mutilation, and contravention of the Human Tissues Act, after cutting out a human heart and three gallstones, and selling them to be used for *muti*. On July 21, 1995, Schutte was sentenced to three years of "correctional supervision," and the matter was settled without any of the clientèle being brought to justice.

In Sanaa, Yemen, an Iraqi student disappeared in December of 1999, and her bereft mother appealed to authorities. The mother's vociferous appeals finally resulted in the May 2000 arrest of a 48-year-old Sudanese anatomy instructor and morgue worker at Sanaa University named Mohammed Adam Omar. Upon arrest, at first he "tried to commit suicide by slicing open his wrists with glass from his spectacles," but under interrogation, he confessed to a 20-year killing spree spanning Lebanon, Kuwait, Nigeria, Yemen, Jordan, and Sudan, claiming 51 victims.

Authorities required him to focus on the 16 he had killed in Yemen, and Omar obliged by describing his M.O. Half of his victims were university students; he would take them to the morgue and knock them out by blunt force blows to the head. Then he would skin them, cut off their hands and feet, keep their bones, and dissolve the spare parts in chemicals. Substantiating his tales, he led investigators to nine skeletons, six headless corpses, and two skulls.

"I regret what I did and executing me will purify me from my sins," Omar told police. "Sometimes I used to hate what I did, but when I saw women, especially beautiful ones, something happened inside me that I could not resist at all." He had started out slaughtering and skinning rabbits as a child, but since the age of 22, women had been his prey of choice.

In court, Omar recanted the multiple confessions and admitted to murdering only two women; a Yemeni student and the Iraqi student whose mother had sought justice for the death of her daughter. He related "charging a fee for high grades" and when the Iraqi student refused to turn over the $2,500 bribe he demanded, Omar lured her into the morgue and killed her in his usual manner.

Police suspected that Omar had been involved in the smuggling of body parts abroad, and many believed that he had been the scapegoat in a sex-and-murder scandal, possibly involving dozens of murders and powerful figures. The medical school morgue was said to have been used to dispose of the bodies of young women who had died in exclusive brothels in Sanaa. "The general belief among the public is there are partners and motivations for committing these crimes," said *The Yemen Times*, "and those partners may amazingly be among the highest classes of the society."

Yemeni parliament formed a commission to investigate the killings, "insisting on the need to conclude quickly the police enquiry to explain the circumstances of the crimes," but nothing ever came of it.

On November 20, 2002, Omar was convicted of two murder charges and sentenced to death. On August 22, 2001, Omar was executed by firing squad in front of a crowd of 30,000 people. Before he was shot to death, he was forced to kneel, and his face was pushed down into the dirt while he received 80 lashes with a knotted leather whip. This was for drinking liquor, under the repressive Muslim code of Sharia a serious offence that had to be formally rectified before the execution could proceed.

EYEBALL STEW

A man-eating troll under a bridge in San Cristobal, Venezuela, hit the wire the first week February of 1999, with a string of lurid crimes that were echoed across the globe in Nigeria that same week with uncanny synchronicity.

Upon his arrest, Dorangel Vargas became an instant international celebrity upon confessing to having eaten about ten men over the past two years. He then went on to offer culinary tips. "I rejected overweight men because they had too much cholesterol, and I spared the elderly because their flesh is contaminated and very tough."

While police refused to discuss the case, they gave the press open access to the confessed cannibal, who clearly appeared to be enjoying all the attention, including the obligatory Hannibal Lecter jokes.

"Sure, I eat people," the lanky, bearded man told reporters. "Anyone can eat human flesh, but you have to wash and garnish it well to avoid diseases."

There had never been any crimes this sensational in this remote part of Venezuela, near the border of Colombia. So the shack under the bridge where the "Hannibal Cannibal of the Andes" cooked up his eyeball stews immediately became a tourist attraction, with camera crews tracking down the bones and entrails nearby, and the pans he used to prepare eyeball soup and tongue stew.

"I only eat the parts with muscles, particularly thighs and calves, which are my favorite," Vargas said, then embellishing his story in the next breath. "I make a very tasty stew with the tongue and I use the eyes to make a nutritious and healthy soup."

But Vargas has the discriminating palate of an epicure. He prefers the male to the female, and he doesn't bother with the hands and feet. And "although I've been on the point of trying them on various occasions," he does have his limits. He balks at eating testicles.

But where did he get the bodies? This seems less certain. Press reports have claimed that he found his victims among the homeless, but Vargas said he was "given" the bodies by various people, including the police.

Preliminary reports that Vargas has a history of psychiatric admissions, as well as a criminal history on similar charges have yet to be confirmed, and it's too soon to say for sure what went on under that Venezuelan bridge.

Then there's the talk that Vargas may be the designated fall guy for a ring of traffickers in human organs.

As recently as January of 2002, a ring of body-snatchers were arrested in Callao, Peru, and investigators believe they had been selling human remains for research and ritual use for 20 years without being discovered. Police caught Carlos Alberto Chávarry, the administrator of the Baquijano y Carrillo cemetery, red-handed with a collection of human bones and forged death certificates, cremation permits, and disinterment permits. "With these forged certificates you could murder someone, certify them dead and then cremate them yourself," Prosecutor Mirtha Ramos told *Ajá*.

One month later, a judge in Wellington, New Zealand was shocked that a trio of grave-robbers had used the skull of an infant as an ashtray, and part of its jaw as a necklace. The baby had been buried in a crypt in 1924. The coffin had been removed from the crypt and a hole had been cut in it; the baby's skull and a jawbone had been removed through the hole. The skull was in use as an ashtray until recovered by police, and the baby's left jawbone was attached to a leather tie and used as a necklace. Found guilty of interfering with human remains and burglary were Denis McCarrison, 21, Harlen Wright, 19, and Lachlan Holland, 18.

BRAZILIAN BONES

On June 23, 1999, police arrested a spare parts dealer in the remote state of Mato Grosso, Brazil. After they found 16 skulls and other bones buried beneath his home, Jose Augusto dos Santos, 40, was taken into custody on suspicion of robbing graves and making human sacrifices. He was suspected of the ritual sacrifice of a small child and a man, said police.

"He says he bought all these bones from a worker at the cemetery," said homicide investigator Marcio Peironi. "But we have reason to believe he may also have committed human sacrifice. This man had pictures of Lucifer, Satan, all over the house."

Known as a *pai-de-santo* or head priest of the popular *candomblé* religion, Augusto dos Santos told authorities that his *terreiro*, or house of worship, was used in ceremonies of dancing and drumming in which West African gods possess the minds and bodies of the devotees.

However, while *candomblé* involves no human sacrifice, sources have told authorities that in addition to his role in *candomblé* ceremonies, dos Santos was paid by middle- and upper-class followers of the darker religion of *quimbanda*, where the *pai-de-santo* summons evil spirits to win favors from them.

"We have done the big job, discovering these remains," Peironi said. "Now we have to send them for DNA tests, hopefully identify them and notify the families."

With all of the occult practitioners plying their trade in the streets of Rio de Janeiro, the murder count in the city is normally quite high, although most of the poor street urchins are unremarkably eliminated by extremist vigilantes. There are also more sinister kinds of Brazilian vampires working the same streets.

Marcelo Costa de Andrade, for example, found 14 victims among the rootless youth in nine months starting in April of 1991. He would attract them to dark and deserted places, rape and strangle them, before defiling their corpses and drinking their blood "to become as beautiful as them."

In December of 1991, Costa met two brothers, ages eight and ten, in a bus terminal and invited them to come to church with him, offering them money to help him light some candles. As they passed through a dark area on the way to the church, Costa pounced on the younger brother, Ivan de Abreau, raped and strangled him to death while his horrified brother Altair stood by, rooted to the spot with fear.

Then the vampire turned to the boy, hugged him and told him that he loved him, and wanted him to stay with him. Altair had no choice but to spend the night with him there in the bushes. The next morning he managed to escape his tormentor and hitch a ride home. At first the terrified child refused to discuss what had become of his brother, but eventually the truth came out, and Costa was arrested. After two months in custody, he confessed to 13 other murders, and led police to their remains. He was sent to a mental institution, but escaped in 1997, and was on his way to the Holy Land when captured a month later. He reflected:

> I preferred young boys because they are better looking and have soft skin. And the priest said that children automatically go to heaven if they die before they're thirteen. So I know I did them a favor by sending them to heaven.

Despite the atrocities committed by real Brazilian vampires, the fascination with vampire lore has gone mainstream in São Paulo, with April 13, 2002 being declared Vampire Day. "Our intention is to pay homage to a good vampire," City Councilman Jose Laurindo de Oliveira told the *Jornal da Tarde*, of "Lizvamp," poster girl for a campaign seeking donations to the local blood bank. Promoters' hopes were to ride the vampire mania coinciding with the debut of the hot new Brazilian TV soap opera, *Kiss of the Vampire*.

COLOMBIAN BLOOD RING

Over a six-month period in 1963, there were ten adolescent boys found dead in Cali, Colombia, their bodies drained of blood and dumped in vacant lots. The cause of death was found to be deliberate exsanguination, and the police suggested that these might be victims of an elusive black-market "blood ring" that was selling blood for as much as $25 per quart.

A pair of 12-year-old twin boys went missing for four days in December of 1963, and when they were finally found, they were in badly weakened condition. The surviving victims described a house where they and other boys were held against their will and injected with drugs to make them sleep. But the house was never found, the murders went unsolved, and apparently the black market in blood has continued unabated.

In 2002, the Colombian National Department of Administrative Security identified 250 separate active satanic cults. Nearly 50 different groups of blood-sucking vampires have been identified in Bogotá alone, and experts fear they are on the increase.

Gathering at night, dressed in black and feasting from silver flasks of blood laced with brandy, these vampires often satisfy their ritualistic requirements for sanguinary refreshment by bribing staffers at transfusion centers to sell them bagged human blood. Or they might purchase a bag of animal blood from an abattoir, like any mortal. When their usual sources dry up, they cut themselves and drink their own blood.

Until recently they were shy types who kept their ghoulish habits mostly to themselves. But police say that over the past year, the urban vampires of Bogotá have grown bold and hungry, accosting passers-by at gunpoint, forcing them to bare their neck or their wrist to be sliced so the vampires can drink their blood as it flows fresh from the wound.

Interpol official Juan Prieto told newspaper *El Espectador* that he was worried that vampires could be responsible for several unsolved murders in Bogotá, "but we have a problem proving it."

A police spokesperson said these crimes are notoriously difficult to prosecute because witnesses are afraid to come forward. And Colombia's freedom of religion laws mean that people can't be stopped and searched just because they happen to be wearing corpsepaint and black capes, hailing Satan, and quaffing bloody cocktails.

As one of the authors of *Worlds at Night*, anthropologist Miguel Álvarez-Correa spent over three years interviewing almost a 100 Colombian urban vampires. He relates their belief that like Nosferatu, they have extraordinary powers of seduction. They believe that being vampires gives them superhuman strength, second sight, and even invisibility. Nevertheless, when the nighttime wanes, they still manage to pass as normal enough to go to school or work at a day job.

For Álvarez-Correa, the vampiric craving for blood is a symptom of a psychological disorder that is being seen in youth who are searching for identity. He believes that satanism and *vampirismo* are born of same existential restlessness, and arise from the same low-to-average socioeconomic circumstances, which are becoming increasingly devoid of cultural values and significance.

Along with the hematophagia, or consumption of blood from humans and animals, Álvarez-Correa found poor school performance, addictions to drugs, sexual promiscuity, rebellious conduct, obscene and profane language, and a certain pleasure in hatred and violence.

BITE MY NECK!

Even the peaceful little nation of Wales is not exempt from a visitation of vampires. On November 24, 2001, Mabel Leyshon, a dainty, hearing-impaired 90-year-old widow, was watching television in the living room of her semi-detached bungalow in Llanfair, a rustic little village in the northern region of Anglesey, when a 17-year-old vampire threw a slab through the sliding glass door to the patio, then crept up on the elderly woman from behind and went at her with a six-inch knife.

The vampire stabbed his helpless victim 22 times, then carried out "a bizarre and macabre ritual," in which her heart was ripped out and her blood was drained and drunk. The still-beating heart was wrapped in newspaper and placed in a saucepan on top of a silver platter. Two fireplace pokers were placed at her feet, arranged in an inverted cross, and candles were burned.

Mabel, who was under five feet tall, had been "a determined, lively lady with a sharp mind," and was "justifiably proud of coping on her own," a police spokesperson told the press. Now this charming lady had been reduced to a form of inanimate evidence in an unspeakably grisly murder trial.

Mathew Hardman was taken into custody a month after a BBC Crimewatch reconstruction of the crime was aired. His quarters were searched, and among the evidence to be used against him in court was a rather suggestive selection of reading material, including a copy of *Running with the Demon*. Special note was made of an issue of *Bizarre* magazine, opened to the feature "Cooking with Claux," in which the Vampire of Paris expounded upon the culinary aspects of the preparation of human flesh for dining. Investigators also searched Hardman's browser history, where there were logged recent visits to the Vampire/Donor Alliance and the Vampire Rights Movement.

When questioned by police, he denied any involvement in the crime. He claimed he had not shown up for work that night because he "forgot." He said he had spent Saturday night with a friend, but the friend denied it. When asked about vampires, Hardman deadpanned: "I don't know anything about the occult."

Sure enough, he said, he had visited the vampire websites, but he had done it "just to have a look." Vampires were actually nothing more than a "subtle interest." But he did admit to somewhat more of an interest in immortality, and was willing to concede that inasmuch as vampirism would provide a route to immortality, he would be "somewhat interested."

But most damaging would be the blood evidence, backed by DNA testing, placing the defendant in the victim's home, as well as the victim's blood on the knife seized from his home. Against this hard evidence, his feeble attempts to distance himself from his vampire crime would pale.

When the Welsh vampire went on trial for murder in Mold Crown Court on July 16, 2002, prosecutor Roger Thomas presented a picture in his opening statement of a defendant who was fascinated by vampires.

"He may now deny it, or seek to play it down, but we submit in November, 2001, he was fascinated by, and believed in, vampires," Thomas said.

"He believed they existed, believed they drank human blood, and believed most importantly that they could achieve immortality—and he wanted to be immortal. What may have started out as a bizarre interest became an obsession, and led ultimately to murder."

The prosecutor stressed that far from being a sudden, uncontrollable outburst of violence, this vicious murder had been planned and prepared well in advance.

"By 24 November, 2001, the defendant had learned quite a lot about vampires, certainly enough to satisfy his two main questions—how do I become a vampire and how do I become immortal?"

"He had decided what he had to do—a sacrifice, the murder of another human being was necessary to achieve his ends. With his parents away, he committed what, we submit, was a deliberate murder to satisfy his own grotesque and selfish ends."

Thomas insisted that Hardman was not mentally unstable, but instead was fully responsible for his actions: "These are not the views of a mentally unstable defendant—he is perfectly sane and there is no medical issue whatsoever for you to consider."

The prosecutor apologized to the jury for the shocking nature of the testimony, then drew down on the choice detail: "At some stage, the saucepan had been filled with blood, as there was a tide mark around the rim." And... there was a lip mark on the edge of the pan. "In other words," Thomas said, "the blood had been poured from the saucepan to the edge so it could be drunk."

And the chilling charge: "The person who murdered Mrs. Leyshon, removed her heart and drank her blood is this defendant."

Thomas told the jury that the youth had been arrested on September 23, two months to the day before the killing, after he forced a 16-year-old German exchange student to bite his neck, because he believed she was a vampire and he wanted to become one too.

In a preview of witness testimony, the prosecutor described how Hardman had become friends with the German girl, who lived in a nearby group home with other exchange students. He apparently had long talks with her about vampires. The girl said she told him that according to legend, if he wanted to become a vampire, he would have to be bitten by a vampire and drink blood.

Hardman asked her if he could become a vampire if he had been bitten but didn't drink blood. Then he posited: "If I killed somebody, maybe an old person, as it wouldn't matter too much—kill him after I got bitten, am I a vampire then?"

The girl recalled, Hardman had previously told her that he thought Llanfair was "a perfect place for vampires," because so many of the residents were elderly, and "if they died, no one would be suspicious."

He showed the girl his neck, ordering her: "Bite me!" Nervously, the girl changed the subject, but the troubled teen threw himself on her and forced her back on her bed, pressing his neck against her mouth.

Concluding his opening statement, the prosecutor related that when interviewed about the incident, Hardman had told police he had felt crazed and was holding back anger "as if it had been bottled up for centuries."

The next day brought the testimony of two witnesses who described that strange and frightening incident in their own words.

The first witness was the German exchange student, who had returned to the UK from Germany to testify. She admitted having an interest in vampires—and described how she'd had to fight Hardman off after refusing to bite him.

Hardman had said it would be "great" and "cool" to be a vampire. He told her, "I have been waiting for this moment all my life," as he tried to get her to bite him. She was overwhelmed at the situation. "It was too much," she said.

"I was really afraid of him because of the look in his eyes. I was really scared," she told the court. "I felt responsible because I told him so many things about vampires before, and he got it messed up in his head."

"It was really sick the way he advertised his neck. He said: 'Here's my neck, and this side is even tastier.'"

Next, a 21-year-old Chinese male exchange student described the night he heard a commotion coming from the German exchange student's room, and he came out of his room to see what was happening:

"The landlady went upstairs and opened the girl's bedroom door and saw the defendant. The landlady shouted my name and I went to the girl's bedroom. I saw the defendant; he appeared to be crazy and shouting. He said he recognizes that the girl is one of the vampires and he knows she is hungry and he asks her to bite his neck. The girl looked scared. I tried to stop him and I slapped him on the face once. He kept on asking the girl to bite him."

According to the student's testimony, he and the landlady managed to drag Hardman out of the girl's bedroom and into a downstairs dining room. But Hardman, who believed that the landlady was also a vampire, continued to rant and rave.

"He was not scared of anyone. I tried to slap him again but it didn't really work. Then he punched himself on his nose and he bled. He told the landlady and the girl to smell his blood. He wiped his face and wiped his nose and then raised his palm."

The Chinese student had also been named by the defendant as providing his alleged alibi. Hardman had told police he had been at his home on the night of the killing. But the student testified he had been at work that night, not at home, and he had not seen the defendant.

The next day, testimony was heard at Chester Crown Court, as the arresting officer described the behavior of the defendant upon the occasion of the biting. Sergeant Peter Nicholson, who was based at Llanfair, stated that he had reported to the house at around 1:30 in the morning on Sunday, September 23, 2001.

"Inside the house I saw a male youth sitting on a settee. I later discovered this was the defendant," testified the officer. "I attempted to speak to him to try to get him to leave peacefully. He didn't make any sort of coherent response. All he could say was, 'Bite my neck!'"

The defense elected to put the defendant on the stand, and for his own part, he denied killing Mabel Leyshon, claiming he had never set foot in her home and that the DNA evidence placing him there, and placing the victim's blood on his knife, must have been contaminated at the lab.

As for the biting episode, Hardman blamed cannabis ingestion, and the court heard that he had experienced something that felt like "a rush of adrenaline exploding all at once" inside him. He said he did not want to release it through violence, not wishing to harm anyone. "It was just something inside me, my genes started going crazy," he said. "I could not stop myself going crazy."

The defense put on several witnesses who painted a mundane picture of a fairly forgettable fellow. "He was a quiet lad, who kept to himself," said a former pupil.

A special-needs tutor, who had helped the defendant with dyslexia, described him as "a well-behaved boy with a good sense of humor," a pleasant, cooperative young man who was eager to learn. He would ask questions, she said, but his writing and spelling were affected by his condition. His interests appeared to be unremarkable; he enjoyed computer games, television, pop music, art, drinking and getting high with friends.

Testimony revealed that Hardman was born and raised in Amlwch, on the north coast of Anglesey. His parents had separated in 1998 when he was 13 years old, and his mother, Julia, had moved to Llanfair, taking him. That same year, his father died, which upset the boy badly.

He attended David Huws School in Anglesey, leaving at the age of 16 to study art and design at Menai College. He had completed one term, and when he was arrested, like Issei Sagawa, he was an art student. He was also holding down a part-time job working in the kitchen at a local hotel, while living in Llanfair with his mother and her partner, who was a former fireman.

The most significant detail of his past history to emerge was that for three years starting at the age of 13, he serviced a paper route, and one of his customers, who lived just a few houses down, was Mabel Leyshon. The unstated implication was that whether or not he would admit it, his predatory sensorium had been at work long before the predator fully emerged. He had been scanning his environment for vulnerability, and perhaps subliminally, focusing his attention on Mrs. Leyshon, who was advanced in age and hearing-impaired, standing under five feet tall, and living alone near his own lair.

As the 14-day trial drew to a close, the jury took almost four hours to return a unanimous verdict of guilty. The vampire wept in the dock, while his mother shrieked in the gallery. Mr. Justice Richards banged the gavel and ordered Mathew Hardman to be detained at Her Majesty's pleasure—a life sentence—and ruled that he must serve a minimum of 12 years for the murder of Mabel Leyshon.

"You have been convicted by the jury on the strength of the most compelling evidence," said the judge. "The horrific nature of this murder was plain to all. It was a vicious and sustained attack on a vulnerable old lady in her own home, aggravated by the mutilation of her body after she had been killed. It was planned and carefully calculated.

"Why you should have acted in this way is difficult to comprehend, but I am drawn to the conclusion that vampirism had indeed become a near obsession with you, that you really did believe that this myth may be true, that you did think that you would achieve immortality by the drinking of another person's blood and you found this an irresistible attraction.

"You had hoped for immortality. All you achieved was to brutally end another person's life and the bringing of a life sentence upon yourself."

After the trial, Detective Superintendent Alan Jones, who led the murder investigation, spoke in a press conference on the courthouse lawn. "The evidence against Hardman was carefully gathered as a result of the inquiries into Hardman himself, a detailed forensic examination of both the murder scene and his home address, and finally by in-depth examination by the Forensic Science Service of the items seized," he said. "Through 16 hours of interview, he at no time offered any sympathy, any concern about Mabel Leyshon and what happened to her."

DON'T KNOCK IT

Dean Wride was becoming a vampire. He had already drunk the blood of two humans from syringes to hasten the transition, but he wouldn't become a full-fledged vampire until he drank the blood of the third one. He needed a victim who was prepared to give more than just blood.

His wife wasn't as enthusiastic as he would have liked about their S&M sessions, and then there was Melanie. Sometimes Melanie would invade his very soul and have her way with him. And Melanie was so jealous of his wife she wanted to kill her. The wife was so depressed about the entire situation, she wanted to jump off a bridge just to end it all.

And thus it happened that the 32-year-old man helped his 55-year-old wife Esther commit suicide in the summer of 1996 in Winnipeg, Canada. It was as simple as that.

That's what Wride told the police when he turned himself in three days later. But a closer inspection revealed a more demented scenario. Whether he was in proper persona as the vampire or whether he was possessed by the evil succubus Melanie, he had forced his wife to swallow a non-lethal overdose of sedatives. But she wasn't dying. He waited awhile, smoked a cigarette, watched a porn video, went shopping, smoked another cigarette. He slit her wrists. Still hanging in there. So finally he just went on and stabbed her to death.

At his murder trial in April of 1998, Wride grinned and chuckled as Dr. Stanley Yaren, director of forensic services at the Health Sciences Center in Winnipeg, described how he had poured chemicals on the body to preserve it and cut out one of the eyes because he didn't like the way it kept looking at him. "His plan was to somehow mummify the corpse in order to keep it in the apartment," said Yaren.

Yaren described how Wride had giggled as he related eating parts of his wife's corpse. When the psychiatrist suggested that this would disgust normal people, the vampire quipped, "They shouldn't knock it if they haven't tried it."

"This is not a mentally healthy individual," conceded the doctor. "I don't think that what's wrong with Mr. Wride can be fixed." Ever since a brain aneurysm at age 13 had damaged the frontal lobe of his brain, he had experienced partial paralysis, epilepsy and hallucinations.

Notwithstanding his damaged brain, "He knew his own actions were wrong," said Dr. Yaren. "That was clear to me. He as much as told me so."

"Cannibalism is beyond the pale," says prominent forensic psychologist Park Dietz. "It's the last frontier of being a bad boy."

Regardless of how deranged or demented a criminal defendant may be, in Canada as in the United States and England, all that matters under the law is whether or not he is capable of appreciating the nature and consequences of his actions, and of distinguishing right from wrong. Thus, another demonstrably damaged creature was convicted of second-degree murder and sentenced to life in prison.

GIRLFRIEND CASSEROLE

David Harker was becoming a cannibal. At 6'5", this 24-year-old skateboarding skinhead cut a striking figure, sporting menacing tattoos on his scalp reading "Subhuman" and "Disorder," and entertaining his peers with a line of fashionably gruesome patter.

For years, he had been stoking his fantasies about becoming a "notorious serial killer," describing his favorite films as *Henry: A Portrait of a Serial Killer*, and *A Clockwork Orange*, which are both still banned in Britain. His favorite book was a true-crime potboiler on the cannibal serial killer Andrei Chikatilo.

The unemployed resident of Darlington, a town in northeast England near Newcastle, was also into witchcraft and proudly displayed his satanic accessories on a silver chain about his neck. A 14-year-old girl described a picture of himself he had drawn for her, with devils' horns, brandishing a staff in the shape of a huge penis.

"My main ambition in life is to kill someone," he would proclaim, then typically discourse at length on how he wanted to hang bodies from hooks in a deserted warehouse and mutilate them, or as Jenny Jordan, 16, recalled, "remove the intestines of girls and bathe in them." David Shaw told investigators how the avowed devil-worshipper had leered at a passerby of the female persuasion, musing, "She'd look good... pinned to my wall."

But even though he eagerly boasted to at least 25 people of turning his lover into a yummy casserole of sautéed thigh with macaroni and cheese, none of them took his outrageous claims seriously enough to report them to police.

When 32-year-old Julie Paterson, a mother of four with chronic poly-substance abuse problems, disappeared in April of 1998, nobody really thought that much about it. Long-term boyfriend Alan Taylor told police he had not worried about Julie because she often went off for days on end.

She had been missing more than a month before her partial remains were finally found in a garbage bag by a police dog on May 16. Medical experts told police that the limbs and head had been chopped off the torso "with confident strokes." Although police searched sewers, a garbage depot and other sites, they failed to recover her legs, arms and head.

Shortly after Julie disappeared, Harker began boasting of the murder in the most graphic terms. He told Stephen Crane, "I took some black tights and I've strangled her." Crane didn't believe him.

Neither did another friend, when he told him, "I've killed a woman. I've chopped up her body," and went on to boast of where he had dumped the body—naming the exact spot where Julie's remains were to be found a month later.

Rebecca Hoyland, the mother of Harker's four-year-old son, had grown accustomed to his eccentric behavior and his lurid chat, having watched her ex-lover do things like carve the words "Fuck You" on his chest with a broken beer bottle, and talk about how he would love to "stretch her limbs and gouge out her eyes."

"I strangled Julie to death in the flat," Harker told Rebecca. She blew him off. "I cut up the body and dumped it." She laughed.

"Smell my hand. What does it smell of?" he demanded of Chris Bradley. "A farm," was his pal's best guess. "No, try a rotten corpse," chuckled the ghoul. "I've been chopping up a rotten corpse."

It was only after Julie's remains were found and her photo appeared in the local news that witnesses finally alerted police to Harker's incredible boasting.

When confronted by police, Harker initially denied that he had killed anyone, but a search of his apartment turned up Julie's bloodstained tights, and when confronted with the forensics, he told a team of psychiatrists the whole story.

He had met Julie when she was out drinking with Alan Taylor on Valentine's Day. Soon they were seeing each other behind Taylor's back. On that fatal day in April they were drinking cider in a park for a while before going back to his apartment together.

Harker said he had no intention of killing Julie. He related having sex consensually with her, when "I got bored and strangled her with her tights." Apparently the murder perked up his interest, so he had sex with her corpse.

Then dismembering all that fresh meat with a knife and a hacksaw must have worked up his appetite, because he fried up a couple of chunks from one of her thighs and mixed them with pasta and cheese and feasted upon her mortal remains before passing out for the night, with the rest of her mutilated corpse tossed casually in the corner of his room.

The next day he put his girlfriend's head, legs, arms and torso in plastic trash bags, dumped the torso a mile from his apartment and put the head and limbs out for the trash collectors.

When doctors asked his impression of Hannibal Lecter in the film *Silence of the Lambs* he schooled them, "People like me don't come from films—them films come from people like me."

He told them that he had befriended a demon named Quasak, and had been hearing the voices of demons in his head since the age of 18, adding, "They told me to do it."

During an interview with one doctor, Harker claimed that he had previously murdered three homeless prostitutes, using a plastic bag to suffocate them. While he has described in considerable detail the killing of two tramps, investigators have been unable to substantiate his claims and have dismissed them as fantasies.

The psychiatrists placed him in the top four per cent of the most disturbed psychopaths, and concluded he was "an extremely dangerous individual who had shown no remorse."

Dr. David Green advised, "Harker obtains pleasure from killing and may kill in the future for pleasure."

Even his own attorney, Aidan Marron, had to admit as much to the court at Harker's trial. "He is a grossly disturbed individual. He is an intense and very dangerous psychopath," he observed, going on to conclude, "It seems inevitable that a life sentence must be imposed in a case such as this."

On February 10, 1999, Harker admitted to manslaughter on the grounds of diminished responsibility. His Honor Mr. Justice Bennett addressed the defendant from the Bench. "You have shown no remorse and I am satisfied that given the slightest opportunity you would kill again. You are an evil and extremely dangerous person," he pronounced, and sentenced him to life in prison, with a recommendation that at least 14 years be served before being considered for parole.

A subdued Harker muttered, "Thank you," and was escorted from the court by three burly guards.

He was taken to Durham Prison and locked up on the maximum security wing, just a cell away from a serial-killing cannibal twice his age, 46-year-old Robert Mawdsley, who had killed four times—the last three times behind bars. In 1978 he beheaded William Roberts, 43, with a shiv before eating his brain.

Doing lunch with two notorious cannibals would be enough to give even the most hardened cons the willies. "Harker is boasting about the killing to people in prison," said one prison insider. "He told people he kept his victim's head on the sideboard."

"He shows no remorse," observed a guard. "He even told officers how he cut strips of flesh from his victim's legs and fried them."

Julie Paterson's former husband, Freddy Newman, wrote to Harker in prison, begging him to tell where the rest of her remains were, so she could be properly laid to rest. The vicious fiend refused to cooperate and wrote back: "I have no inhibitions, remorse or regret and care not one bit if your wife has a full-body burial or not."

YOU GOT ME

Tristian Lovelock had been mates with Richard Markham for eight years, and was with him the night he was last seen, as the two of them were tossing back a few at a friend's house in Basingstoke, Hampshire. Both men were unmarried fathers; Markham of one, and Lovelock of two. They shared years of an easygoing friendship.

Richard Markham lived alone in a one-bedroom house, within walking distance from the drinking party. The already-intoxicated pair left their friend's house at 8 p.m. on Thursday night, May 30, 2002, and walked to Markham's house, where they proceeded to drink some more.

Markham was the son of a former Queen's Guard. The 27-year-old furniture importer was born in York, and at a burly six-foot-one, he had played ice hockey as a junior member of the Basingstoke Bisons. He was a clean-shaven guy, with green eyes and short dark-brown hair who liked to watch martial arts videos, had one pierced ear, and sported a tattoo around his navel declaring him "Made in England." He had been arrested twice, for criminal mischief and drunk driving.

"Everyone knew Richard as a druggie and a psycho," one of their friends, a window cleaner named Wayne Scaife, told reporters. "He was quiet but there was a weirdness about him. He was really into Samurai swords and had his own collection. Tristian was always arguing with Richard but that was the friendship they had."

Tristian Lovelock, a 25-year-old unemployed carpenter, was a troubled man who had done a prison term in 1998, and was living at home with his parents and a sister. He was a long-term drug user, described by a family friend as having a violent temper. On April 15, he had posted a quixotic message to a Friends Reunited website: "A carnival of words magical & mystical a circle of friends mad & hysterical, watching a mad man dazed and bewildered shouting demands from the top of a temple! I Tristian Robert Lovelock now announce I am clinically insane."

On Friday afternoon, May 30, a retired gentleman was walking his dog in a Basingstoke park, when the dog dived into a hedgerow, barking excitedly. "I went with him to see what he had found," said Victor Mansi. It was Tristian's head.

"At first I thought it was some sort of animal but when I looked closer I saw an ear. It was a terrible sight. I could hardly believe what I was seeing. There was a blood-stained rag lying next to it. It looked as if the head had been tossed into the hedge and somehow the rag had come off."

Police were summoned, and as they gathered at the scene, a young couple were dismayed to discover a human arm in their flowerbed. Police followed gouts of gore along the sidewalk to the little terraced house on St. Nicholas Court, where Richard Markham resided.

Upon forcing entry into the house, police discovered the resident was nowhere to be found, but he had left more surprises. Tristian's torso was tossed ignominiously on the floor of the front room, and in the kitchen was his other arm, freshly baked inside the still-warm oven. In a truly macabre touch, a place setting had been laid on the table with a plate bearing hamburger buns and tomato sauce.

It was two more days before police found Lovelock's missing legs, which had been hidden in underbrush at the park.

The post-mortem examination showed that the cause of death was several heavy blows to the head from a blunt object. The remains were chopped into pieces post mortem. The way the body was treated suggested it was a desperate and foolish attempt to dispose of the body, rather than a ritual dismemberment killing.

Meanwhile, Markham had caught a cab to Heathrow at 3 a.m. Friday morning, and at 5:30 a.m., booked a flight on British Airways to JFK. During the six-hour wait before departure, he calmly and quietly relaxed at the terminal, calling a few friends on his cellphone.

Airport surveillance cameras caught the casually dressed homicidal maniac smiling benignly as he clutched his boarding pass, and proceeded in an orderly fashion through the queue, finally arriving in New York City at 2:33 p.m.

Hampshire detectives forwarded a warrant for Markham's arrest to Interpol in Washington, but Interpol must have uncommonly slow modems, for New York police claimed they didn't have the paperwork they needed to apprehend the killer for four days.

Adding to the dismay of New York's shell-shocked populace, Robert Giannelli, Deputy Chief of the NYPD detective bureau, announced: "This is someone who is obviously in a distorted mental state and is possibly now walking the streets of New York. If you see this person, do not approach him. Call police immediately to report his whereabouts."

The world press went wild with the news of this utterly gratuitous butchery and the transatlantic fugitive killer on the loose in The City. At first, armed with a paucity of information, the New York police and press billed the crime as a gay slaying, and warning leaflets were distributed at gay clubs in The City.

As days went by, the word trickled in from England that this was probably not the case, but the hysteria didn't entirely abate until finally on Wednesday, June 5, a couple of female British tourists did what New York's finest backed by the FBI and Interpol couldn't seem to do: they dropped the dime on the young man wearing a blue-and-white checked summery shirt and khakis, lounging on a bench at 67th Street and Park Drive in Central Park, reading the *New York Post* and the *Daily News*, both of which had his face on the front.

The ladies summoned two patrol officers, who radioed their supervisor. When he arrived, he approached the suspect. Markham initially made a move like he might run, but then turned and said, "You got me."

NYPD Officer Francisco Alvarez asked his name, and "he just said, 'Richard Markham,' at which point he lifted his shirt and showed me a tattoo that said, 'Made in England,'" said Alvarez in a press briefing. "When he lifted his shirt, I thought, 'Oh God!' I didn't know what he was going to do." He added, "It feels really good to have gotten this guy off the street."

The nonchalant fugitive came along quietly, offering his wrists for the handcuffs. He spoke freely with police and volunteered that he had been registered under his own name at the St. James Hotel on West 45th Street since he had arrived in town. Upon arrest, he had $80 in his pocket, along with ticket stubs to *SpiderMan* and the Museum of Natural History. He told police that like any other first-time visitor to Gotham City, he had toured the Empire State Building and Ground Zero. He had also enjoyed the hospitality at a choice selection of East Side Irish pubs.

After settling into his new accommodations, the debriefing continued. Officials described Markham as calm and collected. He readily cooperated and confessed to beating his mate to death with a hammer and then using a saw and a Samurai sword to slice up his corpse.

"Tristian was a bully, so I smashed him over the head with a hammer," he told detectives at the Central Park Precinct. "Then I had to get rid of the body."

A police source told *The Times* in London: "He claims the victim would get drunk and beat him up, so this time he decided to turn the tables."

Markham also hotly denied that he was homosexual or that Lovelock was his lover. "I'm not gay," he told police. "Tristian was my mate."

At a five-minute preliminary hearing the next day, Markham waived extradition, and while being led out of the Central Park precinct by federal agents, all at once the press shouted a barrage of questions at him.

"New York is great, man!" he yelled. "I went to the Metropolitan Museum of Art—Egyptian exhibit!"

When asked why he killed Lovelock, he tossed off: "I didn't do it."

Then when asked if he and Lovelock were lovers, he yelled: "Fuck off! No!"

DANK VOICES

They call it *dank* in Kansas City. Known elsewhere as *illy*, *fry*, *sherm*, *wack*, and *water*, it smells like gasoline and tastes like rubbing alcohol. First spotted in Trenton, New Jersey, in the early Seventies, it now permeates the underbelly of America, where a cheap way to alter reality is always much in demand. If a joint doesn't twist your head, for 20 bucks you can buy one dipped in embalming fluid. And if you smoke it, it will eat your brains out.

"What they're getting is often PCP, but the idea of embalming fluid appeals to people's morbid curiosity about death," Dr. Julie Holland of

New York University School of Medicine told ABC News. "There's a certain Gothic appeal to it."

Users smoke it hoping to attain a comfortably numb, floating sensation. Short-term effects also include paranoia and delusions, dissociation and toxic psychosis, coma, renal failure, and respiratory arrest. PCP alone causes hallucinations, seizures, aggressive behavior and violence.

When 21-year-old Marc Sappington smoked dank, he hallucinated menacing voices ordering him to find victims and kill them, "eat flesh and drink blood," threatening that if he refused, he himself would be killed.

A cheerful, quiet youth who had never known his father, Sappington lived on Troup Avenue in Kansas City, Kansas with his mother. She struggled to raise her only son in a neighborhood rife with crime, and took him to church regularly, where he sang in the choir and learned to quote scripture. He'd had a few brushes with the law, but there were no crimes against persons.

His first murder was a rather casual affair. Armando Gaitan, at 16, was what their elders call a *GIT*, or Gangsta In Training. He lived by the code of the street, and Sappington thought he was cool. On March 16, 2001, Gaitan obtained an assault rifle and he and Sappington decided to use it to rob an automobile detailing shop on State Avenue. At the shop, the two young toughs approached David Marshak, 25, demanding cash and jewelry, with Sappington brandishing the weapon. Marshack immediately gave them all he had, and that should have been the end of it. But for reasons no one can explain, Sappington shot the cooperative robbery victim dead.

Gaitan fled to Texas, where he was arrested, but refused to name his partner in crime. Sappington was home free, and once again, that should have been the end of his criminal career. But now that he was a real killer, his voices began to clamor for blood.

"What about him?" he would ask the disembodied entities as he wandered the streets. "What about her?"

But it was three weeks before the voices picked a victim. Terry Green, 25, had been a friend of Sappington's for years, and when he knocked on his front door on April 7, 2001, the voices commanded Sappington to lure his friend down into the basement and attack him with a hunting knife he had hidden there.

The sudden violence splashed blood on the walls, the floor, even the ceiling. Once the body had been rendered lifeless, the voices commanded Sappington to drink the blood pooling on the floor. Afterward, their orders were to get rid of the body.

The inexperienced killer loaded the body into his mother's car and drove across the river to the Missouri side of the city. He found a nightclub he had visited with Green, and offloaded his body into the back seat of a car in its parking lot.

Three days later, using the same victim-selection technique of wandering around asking his voices for guidance, he chose another homeboy, 22-year-old Michael Weaver. He approached Weaver as he sat on the front stoop of his home late at night, and suggested they go for a ride in Weaver's car. Three blocks from home, Sappington attacked his friend with a knife and stabbed him to death, dutifully quaffing the red fluid that drenched the car as it flowed from the wounds. With this, his third murder, Marc Sappington would defy the stereotype by becoming a youthful black serial killer. But he was not one to rest on his laurels.

On the way home early that morning, he spotted a 16-year-old boy named Alton Brown, better known as "Freddie," who looked up to him and liked to tag along on his adventures. The voices told him to "do it," so he invited the boy over to his house, and took him straight down to the basement. This time he used a shotgun, and when it was over he took his time, not only lapping up the fluid flowing from the wounds, but severing the victim's arms and legs and sawing the torso in half at the waist, carving off a portion of bite-sized pieces, and taking them upstairs to cook and eat.

When Sappington's mother came home, her son was nowhere to be found, but she followed a trail of blood down the basement stairs, and when she caught sight of the gruesome scene, she immediately called police.

Taken into custody three days later without a struggle, he refused to talk. Lt. Vince Davenport, commander of the police homicide unit, tried every technique he knew but was getting nowhere. Davenport decided to call it a night, and was reaching for his coat, when Sappington spoke. Uncertain of what he had heard, Davenport asked the boy to repeat it.

"Vampirism," he simply said. "Cannibalism."

And then he gave a full, detailed and emotional confession.

Charged with four first-degree murders and bound over on $2 million bail, Sappington was sent for a series of psychiatric evaluations, and in January of 2003 his trial was postponed indefinitely, as he was declared not competent to stand trial.

BLOOD FRENZY

When a killer says he has become someone else, or that some malignant spirit has taken him over, he may not be just looking for an excuse to shift blame. He may be frankly describing a form of dissociation in which a criminal alter takes over the more benign host personality. Or he may be describing an uncommonly persuasive hallucination.

One such case that recently occurred not far from Washington, DC, in Leesburg, Virginia, bore a certain thematic resemblance to the double murder Rod Ferrell committed in Florida.

The quartet of disaffected teenagers in Virginia included 18-year-old Kyle Hulbert, a gawky kid who was on three different psychoactive medications to treat him for delusions, confusion and hallucinations. He carried diagnoses of bipolar disorder, grandiose psychosis, schizophrenia and dissociative identity disorder, or multiple personalities, and had been in and out of foster homes and psychiatric facilities since he was seven years old.

His father, Matt Hulbert, later told police that Kyle thought of himself as a "ninja warrior," and was obsessed with role-playing games and vampire lore. Friends said Kyle often carried a dagger and talked about drinking blood.

The unstable teenager had what he called "problems with irritability" when he didn't take his medications, but believed that "violence was not really an issue because he would usually just seclude himself."

A young friend of Kyle's told the *Loudon Times-Mirror* that he had met the hapless teen when Kyle lived with a foster family in nearby Woodbridge. The friend, who prefers to remain nameless, said that Kyle had been a student at a Prince William County PACE school for at-risk students. However, when he threatened a school bus driver, he was taken out of the program and sent to a mental hospital in Richmond.

After being moved to a different facility in Staunton, in early September he was released "because he was fine," as he told his neighbor. Then Kyle turned 18, and was legally emancipated. The hapless teen "didn't have no place to go," so his young friend took him in. "I tried to do what I could for him in the time he was here," he said. "I had no problems with him."

A social worker helped Kyle get Social Security payments in September and October. "This would have helped him get his own place, get his medications," the friend said. In mid-October, he moved in with another friend in Maryland, and without coverage from Medicaid, he went off his meds again.

Kyle's unnamed friend was disappointed with the response from local social services. Though county agencies might have provided help for the clearly troubled youth, "they washed their hands of him," he said. "They said he was on his own."

Kyle had met Clara Jane Schwartz in October at a Renaissance Festival. She was his "closest, most dear friend," his "sister in spirit." The youngest of three children of Robert Schwartz, Clara carried diagnoses of schizophrenia and depression, but was not being treated. Soon after meeting the girl who liked to be called "CJ," Kyle became convinced that her father was trying to kill her.

The widower Schwartz, 57, was executive director of the Center for Innovative Technology, an acclaimed biophysicist who had done extensive work in genetics in major corporate and university settings. His other children deny being mistreated, and there is no substantiation for these claims.

On Thanksgiving weekend of 2001, Kyle picked up CJ at her house, and she pulled a pork chop out of her bag and handed it to him, telling him ominously that her dad had "cooked it separately" for her. That was more than enough for Kyle, who was actively hallucinating conversations with demons.

On December 8, when they picked up Kyle, Michael Pfohl, the eldest of the group at 21, was driving, and his girlfriend, 19-year-old Katie Inglis, was along for the ride. In a confession penned for the police, Katie describes how a typical suburban weekend of shopping at the mall came to comprise a renowned scientist, down on his knees pleading for his life with a deranged swordsman, "What did I ever do to you?"

From the Confession of Katie Inglis:

We got up at noon on Saturday when Megan called again to confirm that we were going to meet her at Bennigan's in Springfield Mall and do some Christmas shopping. We stayed with her and Heather while they shopped. They bought some gifts for us and Megan bought stuff for Heather for her birthday.

We left them at 5:15 p.m. and drove out to C.J.'s and Kyle with us because he said he had a job to do. Kyle's definition of job is assassination and he refused to tell us who. Kyle got out of the car with his sword strapped to his waist wearing Michael's trench coat. He walked up the road and disappeared. We lost sight of him because it was about 6:30 p.m., dark, and rainy. I saw a flash of his sword just before he disappeared and knew he was doing a job seriously.

Mike backed up into a large empty and very muddy spot to turn around and head out when Kyle came back. We got stuck and tried to get out any way possible and couldn't. Kyle got back around 7:00/7:10 and looked shaken up. He was still on his feet. He saw our predicament and we asked him to go up to the Schwartz residence to ask Mr. Schwartz if he could help us, not knowing where Kyle had gone and who he had killed.

He told us very seriously that nobody was home twice and I did the math. I knew he had done something to Mr. Schwartz and he tossed his sword in the car. He climbed behind the car to try and push to get us out. It didn't work. He kept on pushing, still wearing the trench coat. He finally got fed up with it getting in the way. He pushed it in the car and I saw a reddish tint smear on it. That confirmed that there had been blood drawn, but I couldn't be sure that Mr. Schwartz was dead. I hoped he wasn't, but in the back of my mind I knew he was.

We got home at about three in the morning and discussed our alibi with each other on the way there. It took us about an hour to get home. We discussed what we were going to tell the police and that was that we had gotten stuck going up to Clara's house trying to get some notebooks for her and we sent Kyle up to see if it was okay to go up there and get some stuff and that we had also gotten confused and thought we had taken a wrong turn and tried to turn around but again we got stuck and Kyle went up to the house in the same trip to ask if Mr. Schwartz could help us get out and there was no one home.

[The next day] Clara called and told us to be careful because the police had our name and address and that her dad had been found that morning by them and they came knocking on her dorm room door.

She sounded like she had been crying or was about to. She told me briefly that she was sorta sad and didn't know what she was going to do and told me that she was going to stay with her grandparents for awhile in Maryland.

Clara had told us that her father had hit her on several occasions and tried to kill her more than once. She told me that he had tried to poison her at least 11 times not just kill her but she had been considered to have serious mental illnesses, such as schizophrenia and manic depression by more than one psychiatrist.

And Kyle trusted her wholeheartedly in everything she said, but Kyle has a thirteen year psych ward history and isn't all there. He's been diagnosed with most of the mental illnesses in the book including schizophrenia and multiple personality disorder.

I am sorry that all of this happened and I hope that Mike and I can go on living our lives, along with Clara and her family. I know what was done was wrong and so does Mike. I know that telling on Kyle, as bad as that may sound, was the right thing to do. I just hope that Kyle can be brought in unharmed and proven guilty and do his time and suffer the punishment decreed on him even though he is my friend.

I am willing to testify in court that Kyle did commit murder and that if proven guilty suggest that he be sent to a mental facility for the criminally insane because he is truly ill mentally and has committed a murder that may be caused by that mental illness.

I am sorry Kyle. It was the right thing to do.

12/11/01

For his part, Michael Pfohl revealed himself to be utterly out of touch with his own guilt. After being ordered to write apologies, he grudgingly complied, minimizing his responsibility, reaching the apogee of banality with his comment that he "made a big oopsie," and finally inserting a remark intended to covertly tip off his criminal accomplices of his real loyalties.

From what the investigating officer/interrogator tells me, I have a lot of apologies to write. I have been asked to write them.

I suppose I should begin by apologizing to the investigating officers. I put you guys through a lot of trouble. I've given Kyle a lot of rides to places. I probably should have turned him down this time. You've lost a lot of sleep because I couldn't say no to a friend.

The Schwartz family shows up next on my list. I made a big oopsy here... I got your dad killed. I'm sorry for your suffering. Clara, I'm sorry to you especially... you've suffered enough.

Kate. She's important. She means the world to me. I'm sorry to traumatize you like this. You, too, have been through a lot of trauma. I'm so so so so sorry for bringing you with me.

Kyle. You are the one who will suffer most from this. There is no worse horror than prison. I am sorry for giving you the wrong ride to the wrong place, and letting you do this. I am doubly sorry for so utterly betraying you. I should not have admitted even an inkling of guilt on your part. You are my brother, and I did a piss-poor job of protecting you.

Robert Schwartz. I am sorry for the painful, violent nature of your death. Please tell me, by some sign, that you are well. And please don't blame Kyle. He did what he thought was right. Perhaps he was right. Perhaps you can tell me that. Or that he was wrong. I'd like to know one or the other, though.

Myself. I don't know if I should apologize to me. I knew what I was getting myself into, even if only vaguely. I'm fully responsible for that. But I'm sorry to me for letting this happen to me. And for breaking my honor and sacred trust by betraying Kyle. And for betraying myself by apologizing. If I wasn't dead before, I am now.

That's all I can think of. I drove Kyle to Clara's house (well... I didn't KNOW it would be Clara's house...) to assassinate someone.... I must come to terms with that now. I don't now how. But Life finds a way.

Michael Pfohl

Fortunately, Kyle Hulbert provided an articulate, though delusional, account of how he struggled with a cast of demonic characters urging him on. He went on to render a blow-by-blow description of the slaying, and related with a certain awe his own sense of transformation in the frenzy triggered by the taste of his victim's blood.

I, Kyle Hulbert, being of sound mind.

I am writing this so those who read it will know my side of the story as to what happened on Saturday, Dec. 8, 2001 in reference to the death of Robert Schwartz.

It began when I met Clara Schwartz at a Renaissance Festival. We got close very quickly and I consider her my closest, most dear friend and as a sister as well. Soon after meeting her (in October by the way) I learned that she had been suffering from mental and emotional abuse from her father, Robert Schwartz, since her mother died. I got concerned once I learned of the death threats her father had given her. I convinced her to write a list of significant times that her father had abused her as well as any death threats she had received. I have been angry about the fact that anyone would treat someone as such. He had poisoned her on several occasions with various chemicals. I fail to see the logic behind anyone, let alone a father to his daughter, could be so cruel as to put someone through that. I have always told Clara that I would protect her.

I have met Robert Schwartz a total of three times. All three times he seemed extremely hostile toward me. I first thought about killing him when the visions got out of control. I could no longer sleep without seeing him doing something to Clara. I would close my eyes and see him poisoning a lemon or a pork chop as he did the last time I was at his house before I killed him. I know he poisoned the pork chop because when I went to Clara's to pick her up to take her back to JMU, she handed me a piece of cooked pork chop and said "taste this and tell me what you think, Dad cooked it." I took a small bite and immediately spat it out. I could tell it had been tampered with both by taste and by smell. Clara informed me that her dad had "cooked it separately."

After that incident, I had a really hard time dealing with the visions. I would walk from my room and somehow end up in Clara's. I would watch as her Dad comes in and begins to yell at her, to tell her she is worthless, that she is nothing. he would leave and Clara would cry. I think that is what did it ... seeing Clara cry. I could not bear the sight of that.

But Sabba, Ordog, Sarin and Nicodemus would argue with me whenever I told myself that it would be easy. They said to just kill him would be a violation of my desideratum. I could not kill him without just cause. If I was not defending myself or someone else I loved, I could not kill.

Then I found out that Clara was going to the Virgin Islands for Christmas vacation. I also found out both from her words and what I could glean from her mind that Robert was planning on making sure she did not come back. That was all I could take. I asked Ordog and the rest and they told me that doing such now was in no way a violation of my desideratum.

I asked Mike to take me to Mt. Gilead. He complied. We were halfway up the driveway and I told him to stop the car and let me out. He did so and I told him to wait, that I would be back in a bit.

I walked up to the house. After knocking on the door, Robert answered. I asked if Clara was there. He said that she was not and that she was at JMU.

I asked if he had her number so I could reach her. He invited me in and I used the bathroom and followed him in to the dining room to the computer desk. He started writing and a conversation ensued as thus:

(me) "So how have you and Clara been getting along?"

(Rob) (Stops writing, back still to me, turns his head slightly) "What business is it of yours"

(me) "Because I care about her."

(Rob) (turns around to face me with a slight grin) "And?"

(me) "I know your plans you will not get away with it."

(Rob) turns his back on me.

(me) (step closer to him on his left side just behind him) "I won't let you hurt her."

At this point, Robert backhanded me. He made contact just above my left eye. (I believe he had a ring of some sort as I got a slight cut on my eyebrow.) At this point, a struggle ensued.

I will say this before I go farther. Had he denied it, had he not struck me, had he not grin in such a way that haunts my mind even now, had I not seen his confession in his eyes, I would have left and let him live. But none of those things happened. He struck me and we struggled. When he hit me, my body turned and I pulled my sword.

I slashed at him and struck him in the back of the neck. I do not believe I broke the skin as he just seemed to shake his head and continue. At some point, he ended up behind me with one hand on my neck in an attempt to force me to the floor, the other tightened around the blade of my sword. I pulled the sword through his hand.

Somewhere in the back of my mind, someone laughed at a fool who would grab an attacker's blade. As I pulled the sword away and through his hands, I turned it so that the point was toward me and drove it backwards just above my right hip into him.

I do not know exactly where it made contact, but his grip loosened and I pushed away. At this point we were circling each other. I was, even at this point, willing to let him live. I told him to back off and let me pass, and I would be gone. He grinned at me again and that grin echoes itself in my mind's eye to this very moment as I write. He advanced on me and we ended up grappling again at some point.

I got his blood in my mouth, possibly when I drove my elbow into his face in an attempt to get him away from me. However it happened, the blood drove me into a frenzy and I became incoherent. When I returned to the state of mindfulness and sanity, I was withdrawing my sword from his back. I had apparently stabbed him several times after he had fallen face down on the ground.

I rinsed the blade off in the sink, and turned off all the lights save the one in the living room. Nicodemus, wise Nicodemus advised me to make haste from the house as his soul had departed. I returned to my brother all the while listening to Ordog, Sarin, Sabba, Nicodemus and Michelle attempt to soothe me. Their words had a comforting effect and I suppose it did calm me down to an extent.

I do pity Robert for he was a living creature after all... but only so much. He deserved to die. Maybe not in the way I delivered it, but somehow nonetheless. I still hear his voice and see his smile when I told him that I knew... "And?" I do not believe I will ever forget that. But Clara is now safe. Robert will never harm her again... Whatever happens to us, we will survive.

"Damon"

"I can guarantee that Kyle doesn't know where the fantasy world ends and reality begins," said his father Matt Hulbert. "Kyle thinks this is all a game, but there is no reset button."

According to Loudoun County court records, Mike Pfohl and Katie Inglis admitted "they were involved in the planning, execution, escape and cover-up of what was described as a planned assassination of the victim."

Police searched their homes and seized numerous swords and knives, "as well as black cloaks and clothing related to the pagan religion Wicca," and handwritten and word-processed documents "that contain language of killing and human sacrifice in a Wiccan fashion." The warrant goes on to describe Wicca as "a cult which involves pagan rituals and sacrifices."

Pagan witchcraft does not cause murder. As with vampire lore, it is intended to be practiced nonviolently. It must be stressed that in the case of the prominent DNA researcher who was hacked to death in his home, it was chiefly because a mental patient was struggling with delusions and hallucinations. To add to the fatal mix, the youth had been influenced and manipulated by the victim's disturbed daughter. The other two companions are culpable due to their knowingly inciting and enabling the slaughter. Despite the listing on the search warrant, there is nothing about any of this behavior that is legitimately endorsed by Wicca.

The murder itself was not performed in a ritualistic fashion, nor did the behavior before or after the murder reveal concerns of an occult nature. Even though some of those involved apparently possessed a few occult books, it does *not* follow that these four dysfunctional youngsters were capable of the discipline and concentration required to conduct actual rituals. And even if they did gather together with the intention of having their own rituals from time to time, there is no evidence that anything of that nature was involved in this murder.

The same goes for the vampire role-playing. The crime was not committed in a role-playing context, and despite the significance of the blood frenzy, the blood-drinking itself was just happenstance. The murder was already committed by the time Kyle "crossed over" into a blood-drunken stupor beyond his conscious recall. He did not feast meticulously, in the style of the urban vampire.

The witchcraft and vampire role-playing games were no more the causes of this brutal slaying than the somber style of the killer's trenchcoat. Yet they were contributing factors to the social fabric that predisposes toward violent crime. These young people were drifting aimlessly, looking for some lore to endorse frank deviance and morbid fantasy, which in the absence of common sense and moral restraint, can unfortunately lead to the destruction of more than just the life of the murder victim.

Although Clara Jane "CJ" Schwartz was at her dormitory at James Madison University in Harrisonburg at the time of the killing, not in the car with Kyle, Katie and Mike, still "she knew the murder was going to happen up front," Sheriff Steve Simpson said. Documents seized in police detectives' searches revealed Schwartz "discussed with at least one of the suspects the planning and subsequent murder of her father Robert Schwartz."

Documents seized include emails from the account "gothicvamp@ yahoo.com" and another account under the name "Apocalyptic Chaos" that CJ had used to post a message to a web-based bulletin board, listing her home page as "www.hell.com."

The scientist's daughter and the other three "Gothic vamps from hell" were all held equally responsible under the law, and charged with first-degree murder and conspiracy to commit a felony.

BIZARRE AND EVIL THINGS

On February 4, 1999, Sean Sellers became the first American since 1927 to be executed for a crime committed when he was 16, bringing to ten the total number of juvenile offenders put to death by the American criminal justice system since 1990.

Born in 1969 to a 16-year-old mother who divorced his alcoholic father four years later to marry a truck driver, throughout his young life the boy was dropped off with one relative or another while his mother traveled with his stepfather. By the time he was 16, he had been moved over 30 times. Though intelligent and sensitive, he became withdrawn, emotionally disturbed and detached from reality.

After being convicted of three murders in 1986, Sellers settled down to a life of soul-searching and religious conversion on Death Row. He urged others to forego their sinful ways, renounce Satan and accept Christ. Attractive and articulate, he gained supporters.

In 1992, his supporters funded a full battery of psychological tests, which resulted in a diagnosis of multiple personality disorder. Doctors testified that they had interviewed Sellers while in three alternate identity states: "Danny" was sweet, soft-spoken, immature and left-handed; "Ninja" disliked handcuffs; and "The Controller" boasted an impressive vocabulary and expressed frustration because he was not allowed out more.

Psychiatrist Richard Flournoy wrote in his affidavit that one of them "must have been in executive control of Sellers' person or body, and that this alter personality neither understood nor cared about the nature of his acts, nor that the acts were either right or wrong."

Sellers himself resisted the diagnosis. "As is consistent with many of the MPD patients I have treated, Sellers did not like my indication to him that he suffered from MPD," he testified.

"Ironically, persons who attempt... to fake MPD generally will readily accept an assessment that they are MPD; persons who are MPD almost always deny the fact even when presented with overwhelming evidence that they suffer from this disorder."

"Even if it's a different me, it's still me, isn't it?" mused Sellers philosophically. "And if it's some other me who does something horrible and evil, isn't it an evil part of myself that did it? I want to take responsibility for it. I don't want to rationalize it away, and that's usually what it sounds like whenever I try to explain it."

An appeal was filed based on this new evidence, and the Tenth Circuit Appeals Court wrote in 1998: "Although troubled by the extent of uncontroverted clinical evidence proving Petitioner suffers from Multiple Personality Disorder... and that the offences were committed by an 'alter' personality, we are constrained to hold Petitioner has failed to establish grounds for federal *habeas corpus* relief."

The following narrative, in his own words, is a composite of three different web-published autobiographical articles written on Death Row by Sean Sellers.

I tossed my cigarette onto the pavement and sighed. From out of my pocket I took a small vial of blood. Tilling it back and forth, I watched the bubbles snap leaving specks on the glass until I turned it over washing it crimson again. I removed the cap and touched my tongue to the top, tasting it. Then I poured it into my mouth and let the warmth of it cover my teeth. Swallowing it I thought, "And people think vampires only live in the movies."

I was not a cruel person. I didn't commit murder because I enjoyed causing pain. I had pets all my life, and I wanted to be a veterinarian. I never was a bully, or provoked fights, or picked on people weaker than I was. In fact I got into a few fights standing up for people who were being picked on. When we're kids we just feel things. When we're adults we look back on our childhood and we figure out some of what we were feeling and why. There was a *LOT* of anger in me as a kid. I didn't know that, but it was there.

Mom had me at 16, and when she was 21, I was 5. I don't remember much before 5, but at 5 she left me with her father, my "Papa" (PAW-PAW) Jim Blackwell, his wife Geneva—"grandma" to me—and Papa's parents— Great grandpa and Great grandma to me. And she left. She met Lee—Dad to me—and she was gone. I only saw her when she managed to make it in every few weeks. And every time she and Dad left, I smiled, waved goodbye, and went to the bathroom, closed the door, and cried. Every time. And I never once let anyone see me do it.

Over the next few years, Mom and Dad kept picking me up and moving me here and there. We never lived in one house more than a few months, or in one town more than a year, so I had several different schools, and never made any lasting friendships. That built up a lot of resentment.

Then there were things like Mom's temper. She always spanked me with a belt, but she also just hit me. Slapped me in the face, "mashed my mouth"—a flat palm, straight-on blow to the lips that mashed my lips into my teeth. She did that when I got "mouthy" and it made my lips swell. It always shut me up though. She hit me in the head with wooden mixing spoons, butcher knife handles, hair brushes, whatever she had in her hand. Usually it was because I said something wrong, or if she was cutting my hair and I was fidgeting, *SMACK!* "Be still dammit!" I never knew what would get me smacked, so I learned to be very careful around Mom. I walked on eggshells and avoided her when I could. I tried to live in my room as much as possible. I hated her as much as I loved her.

Beneath the few books I carried home with my football equipment was a notebook filled with Dungeons & Dragons material. I did four things. I played football, practiced Ninjutsu, collected comic books, and played D&D. I was a Dungeon Master and I also played a character. Nobody understood the game as well as I. I read, I studied the manuals. I created new and more intense Dungeon modules. All of my spare time in school was taken up in my study of D&D.

We moved to Colorado and I continued to study with what had become my hobbies. After a year, football had been left behind and I joined the Civil Air Patrol (CAP). I attended special training schools became a NEAT (National Emergency Assistance Training) qualified Ranger graduating with art outstanding cadet merit. A few months later, I was the squadron cadet commander.

We moved again. Returning to Oklahoma, I was reunited with old friends, but l had changed. I left a short-haired football player who wore Wranglers. I returned with long hair, wearing my NEAT Ranger beret, a Levi jacket and 501s, carrying a double-edged boot knife tucked in my pants at the small of my back, and Nike high tops. When I left, I had been in a few fights and shown I could fight. Now, I carried an air of being downright dangerous. I was cool.

Dad had killed people in Vietnam. Being able to do so and not be bothered by it was a sign of strength to him. I wanted to be like my Dad, and as crazy as this sounds, a part of that was to have the strength to kill someone, and not be bothered by it. I didn't want to kill anyone, I just wanted to have that strength. I wanted to be like Dad, and be able to shrug and say, "It's not hard to kill someone," like I'd heard him say, and knew with conviction he's done it.

Time heals wounds, and in time, I met a new girl. This one, knowing I was interested in witchcraft, introduced me to a witch named Glasheeon. By Glasheeon's instructions, I stripped naked and laid down. "Satan! I call you forth to serve you," I prayed aloud and recited Glasheeon's incantation. I felt the room grow cold and experienced the unmistakable presence of utter evil enter. My blood pressure went up. The veins on my arms were bulged. I got an erection and began to feel a lifting sensation.

Then something touched me. My eyes flew open but saw only spots, as they had been closed so tightly. Again I felt something touch me, and I shut my eyes terrified and thrilled, It felt like ice-cold claws began to rake my body caressingly, and I shook in an erotic pleasure as they explored every inch of my body. I heard an audible voice speak three words in a whisper, "I love you." I continued to pray, telling Satan I accepted and would serve him.

One by one the invisible clawed hands touching me disappeared, and my blood pressure fell. I was alone. I sat up exhausted, hooked, unbelieving. I hadn't been on drugs. I'd never smoked a joint. It had been incredible, and I knew it was real. I made a pact to Satan. In my own blood. I wrote, "I renounce God, I renounce Christ. I will serve only Satan. To my friends love, to my enemies death... hail Satan."

We began performing rituals, but something seemed to be wrong. There was a barrier put up between us and the power we needed to invoke. We brought forth demons, but we wanted more. It was time to prove our allegiance to Satan. We began breaking the Ten Commandments. Only one remained, "Thou shall not murder."

I began doing solitary rituals, invoking demons and asking them to enter my body as a sanctuary. During a ritual, in sacrificing my own blood to Satan, I received my Satanic name: *Ezurate*. Scars began to appear on my body, on my arms and chest where l continually gave blood to my master. I had begun to drink blood... I took blood from my friends and myself, storing it in vials I had taken from a clinic. To keep my parents from questioning the scars, I used needles most of the time.

I'd been carted all around the state and Colorado all my life, slapped, smacked, hit, and had whatever I wanted ignored. I was mad and the idea of controlling my life to get what I wanted was like candy to me. Plus I looked at the way everyone around me lived and the stuff I read in *The Satanic Bible* in principle was lived out in lifestyle by Mom and Dad and everyone else I knew. No one was a real Christian. We didn't go to church. We didn't talk about God. Mom and Dad cussed like the truck drivers they had been for so many years, Mom bought me a box of condoms when I was 13 and Dad told me to use them, we'd stolen stuff out of the trucks Dad drove, I'd seen Mom lie to people's faces to get a deal or sell something, my aunt and uncle, and mom and dad smoked pot, and bought speed, so what was the point of pretending to serve God when we lived like Satanists? Satanism taught me that I should make my own rules to live by in life, and that's just what everyone I'd grown up around did, so I got very involved in Satanism. I truly thought it was an honest way to live, and the rituals of it would enable me to control my life. Even then I didn't want to kill anyone. That desire didn't start until later.

As I began to do all those Satanic rituals, I found myself having some strange problems. As a kid I'd heard voices in my head. I'd tell my friends, "You know that voice inside your head that argues with you and tells you things?"

They'd say, "No."

I'd be like, "Never mind, then." I just figured I wasn't explaining it right.

Those voices were just a part of the way I thought, and I never gave them any consideration. But as I did all these rituals those voices changed. They started sounding different—and being a Satanist, I decided they were demons and it was no big deal. Demons were the beings that would *DO* the things I wanted done. They were the keys to the power Satanism promised me, so I wasn't afraid of them. Other things began to happen too, though. I began to have "blackout" periods where I couldn't remember what I'd been doing. I also felt so empty inside. Cold. All that anger which had turned into contempt was now becoming a cold hatred toward Mom specifically, and by proxy toward Dad.

My head started really going crazy on me. I was inviting demons into my body, and I was hearing all these voices in my head. I thought they were the demons. They were telling me stuff like, "Shoot the class, kill everyone in the class." They were giving me answers to tests, things like that.

I thought it was really cool at first. Then I got to where I was losing touch with my emotions. I hadn't felt anything for so long. I couldn't cry anymore. I just felt empty inside. It wasn't so much hateful or angry as empty.

Richard Howard, my best friend, and I had begun to talk about bizarre and evil things together. I honestly don't know when it started or why. We were both involved in Satanism, and Richard talked about raping and killing an old girlfriend of his, torturing her, of stealing the cash from the money bag his boss took to the bank at night, and killing her. I fell right along with him. I enjoyed talking about this evil as much as he did. We planned robberies and rapes and violence, *NEVER ONCE* with any intention of doing them. We'd just say, "Wouldn't it be a kick to do this!" And we'd laugh about it.

Somehow, one night, during one of those kinds of conversations, right after we'd done a Satanic ritual in the yard beside his house, we decided to kill Robert Paul Bower. I wish I could tell you how it came up, but I can't. I honestly don't remember anything after that ritual except a haze and images of me and Richard talking. Richard got the guns. His grandfather's .357 revolver that was loaded with five shells that looked like hollow points to me, and a .22 rifle of his brother's.

I had said I wanted to know what it felt like to kill someone. I'd said that many times, but that was not the reason we were going to kill Mr. Bower. He worked the midnight shift at a very remote Circle K store and one night, because Richard stopped in and talked to him a lot on the way home from seeing Tracy, Richard thought Robert would sell him beer. When we got to the store, Mr. Bower refused, and that had made Richard mad. That had qualified him as someone we'd like to kill, and we'd talked about him in those conversations about killing. That night we just somehow decided to really do it, and it would be an offering to Satan to prove ourselves.

We went to the store and Richard talked to Mr. Bower for probably an hour. We bought fountain drinks, questioned him about not having a camera in the store. Wasn't that dangerous? Someone might kill and rob him. Robert wasn't concerned. There was only 50 dollars in the cash register at any one time, the rest was in the safe, and no one was going to kill him for that. Richard and I gave each other amused glances. A few customers came and went. Finally as Robert came out of the store to look at Richard's clutch pedal, since we'd just put a new clutch in his car and Robert's also needed one, Richard looked at me and said, "Let's do it."

I took the revolver and followed them back in, but I froze before I got inside. I went around the side of the store. I couldn't do it. Just couldn't. Then this voice spoke inside my head and said I was weak, I was a coward, and something blinked inside my mind. That's the only way I can describe it. One second I was shaking and saying I couldn't do this and then *BLINK!* I was cold, determined, heartless, and evil. I walked back around straight and tall, opened the door and stepped in. Richard saw me and held up something in the aisle where he stood. "How much is this?" he asked.

Robert Bower was taking a sip of coffee. He peered over the brim of the cup, swallowed, said something and set the cup under the counter. As he stood up, I raised the gun over the counter, aimed it at his head, and just as he looked at me, fired. He flinched and it missed. He ran and I fired again, but he slipped and fell and I missed again. I heard him cry out, though.

He grabbed a green windbreaker which he wore when stocking the walk-in refrigerators and held it up in both hands, hiding behind it as he ran bent over back and forth behind the counter. Richard came up to the counter and he ran from him and almost into me. I saw his eyes over that jacket, filled with panic, and I heard Richard say, *"DO IT!"*

I fired, and Robert Paul Bower flew backward landing hard on his side. Blood splattered everywhere. He didn't move. When I turned around, Richard was leaning over the counter trying to figure out how to open the cash register. I said, "Go," but he didn't move. I took a few steps and said, "Go!" and he sprang out the door. We got in the car and left.

In the car, we laughed as the evil delight of our action gripped us. We were not human. We were completely possessed by our demonic servants. We were stripped of all love, mercy and kindness, and were consumed with hate, anger, and eroticism. We were Satanists.

After that, I had killed someone. Sometimes I wanted to tell Dad so he'd be proud of my strength. He'd see me as strong, not weak. And sometimes I didn't even remember doing it. I didn't live under a constant awareness that I'd killed someone. Most of the time I didn't even know what I'd done. It was that blinking in my mind. The person who couldn't do it didn't know he did, then *BLINK!* And the person who did do it, remembered. That's the best I can explain that. When I was that person, that murderer, I felt superior. I looked down on people with the secret knowledge that I had killed and was capable of killing them too. When I was not that person I was just a confused teenager, going to school, working, learning to drive, still full of anger, and counting the days when I'd be 18 so I could move *OUT* of that house.

Things turned very, very stressful at home. I decided to kill my mother. I bought some rat poison and put it in her coffee, but it didn't work, even when I served her 3 cups of it. But after that, *BLINK!* And everything was different. We argued, but I just wanted to leave, I didn't want to kill her. Then *BLINK!* And I'd be planning her death.

One night that blink happened and when I came home from work I was the cold murderer who had killed Robert Bower. I went to their room before they went to bed and took Dad's .44 revolver from the drawer beside the bed. I put it in my room and waited for them to go to bed. Dad talked to me about rebuilding the engine of my pickup together. When they were in bed I went to my room, did a ritual, dressed only in my black underwear, and then crept quietly into their room. There was nothing but cold hatred in me. There was some sense of, "Sean needs to be free and this will free him. This is the only way." That was not a conscious thought, just a sensation. It's like that was the motivation behind it. I wasn't committing murder, I was removing an obstacle from my way. I was knocking down a door to a prison cage. All I felt, however, was coldness.

I put the gun close to Dad's head and fired, then immediately fired again at Mom's head. Her head raised up, neck craning backward, and I fired again. Then I laid the gun down in the hallway and went back to the room. I felt relieved. I felt like a great weight had been taken off my shoulders. I went to take a shower and the blinking started again. There was a lot of blinking. So much so that nothing is clear. I ended up at Richard's house, and we planned what to do for the police. But it wasn't all an act. There would be a blink and I'd cry real tears in real grief. Then another blink and I was calm and cold and putting on a show.

I've lived for twelve years now with the memories, knowledge, and grief of those three murders. This doesn't matter, but after years of work the blinking is gone and I remember everything both parts of me did. The stuff I don't remember is when—I think—there was too much blinking, like a light switch going on and off. Flick flick flick flick *ON*. Flick flick flick flick *OFF*. I remember the *ON* and *OFF* parts, but not the flick flick parts. What I remember horrifies me.

THE DEVIL MADE THEM DO IT

The belief that a supernatural entity is to blame for a bloody misadventure is as old as crime itself. "The Devil made me do it" is nothing more than a worn cliché. Yet we continue to hear of the voices of demons and devils when inquiring into the motivations behind the most egregious criminal behavior.

In 1988, Michelle Moore, a 21-year-old convenience store clerk in Las Vegas, Nevada, was shot in the face with a .45-caliber handgun and killed instantly. Edward Bennett was 19 years old when a jury sentenced him to die for the murder. Writings used to show the murder was "ritualistic and satanic" included the following passage:

> I need to kill somebody or tear someone apart. I got to satisfy my need, cure this thirst for blood. So as I make the sacrifice by doing it just for you and kill this child, for it is a first born, I'm giving you my soul, Satan. Where is my reward? My thirst for blood is now calm, but it shall rise again. My power is so strong I need to cause some death. For Lucifer's inside of me, and I don't want to let him out. I look in the mirror, I see him in my eyes. I feel his heart beating in my chest, and I know it is not mine. For I feel so privileged for I'm with number one. I'm so fucking powerful and my reigning has just begun as I kill and kill again. I feel my rewards come on. My power's growing even greater. I'm so fucking strong for I am the devil's right-hand man. I carry out his every chore. I make this sacrifice in his name, Lucifer the Great, blood splattered on my face from the kill I've just done.

In another case with occult overtones, in 1990, 15-year-old Stephanie Dubay was stabbed to death in Warren, Michigan, by a couple of professed satanists, Jaime Rodriguez and Augustin Pena, who boasted that she had been slain in preparation for a satanic feast on August 1.

Both victim and killers wore satanic tattoos; the victim's breasts were marked with a 666 and a cross with a line through it. Rodriguez sported a large pentagram encircling a goat's head on his chest, along with a 666 emblazoned over his right breast.

The victim's organs were removed with surgical precision, and her head was skinned and placed in Pena's fridge, only to be taken out to be shown off to a pair of teenaged girls. The right hand, the tongue, and the spleen were also preserved for special purposes. Rodriguez prepared the victim's right index finger to wear as a "charm" around his neck.

At trial in July of 1991, as Rodriguez was convicted and sentenced to life he showed no remorse, and his claim that he had been automatically and unconditionally forgiven for his act of human sacrifice suggests he might be *non compos mentis.*

On April 21, 1999, Darrel Wayne Harris and Robert Menendez engaged in a ritual in Ft. Lauderdale, Florida, in which the teens cut their hands, mingled their blood, and chanted lines from *The Satanic Bible.* Harris drew a pentagram in the dirt, and told Menendez to look down at it. As Menendez looked down, Harris stabbed him six times in the throat and back.

"Somewhere along the line the culprit just started to hack him with the knife," Detective Arturo Carbo told the *Sun-Sentinel.* "The victim told us that the stabbing was not part of the ritual and he firmly believed he was going to die. Harris and Menendez were part of a network of 30 to 40 local young people who are involved in satanic activities."

Menendez told police that he and Harris had known each other for more than a year, and that they hung out at local public libraries to use computers to access satanic websites and send email to other satanists.

Harris was charged as an adult with attempted first-degree murder on May 27, 1999. In this case, although the attack occurred during a satanic ritual, it was not endorsed by the text recited or the symbolism invoked. However, the ritualism provided the context under which the borderline was approached and then crossed into frank criminality. It is inevitable that the conclusion be reached that were it not for the ambiance, with its implicit endorsement of deviance and its appeal to the blood senses, there would have been no criminal assault; if these two unstable young people were not indulging in blood rituals, it is more likely they could have continued to socialize without one going into a spasm of violence and trying to cut the other to pieces.

Three young satanists were convicted of a ritual murder on August 11, 1999, in Helsinki, Finland. 24-year-old Jarno Sebastian Elg was sentenced to life for instigating two others to participate in a ritual that included torturing a 23-year-old victim, strangling him to death, and ingesting certain of his body parts. For their participation, Terhi Johanna Tervashonka, 17, and Mika Kristian Riska, 21, received prison sentences of two years and six months and two years and eight months, respectively. Ruling that the three youths "were strongly influenced by satanism," the District Court in southern Finland declared most of the details of the case secret.

Asperger's Syndrome is a rare form of autism which can involve a fascination with death as well as an inability to relate to the sensitivities of others. Although it is not considered insanity, in December of 2000, it was used in a British courtroom to explain the actions of 21-year-old Simon Gibson, the "ringleader" of a trio of grave-robbers who broke into a centuries-old crypt, stealing bones to be fashioned into ceremonial accoutrements. They were caught after a photo turned in for processing was reported. It showed a juvenile gang member mugging for the camera, posing Hamlet-style with a human skull. Bristol Judge Simon Darwall-Smith called actions "offensive to the public and disrespectful of the deceased," and sentenced the ghoulish Gibson to 18 months in prison, with his sidekicks getting lighter sentences.

UNDER THE INFLUENCE

The American Academy of Pediatrics has published a study supporting their policy statement: "Extensive research evidence indicates that media violence can contribute to aggressive behavior, desensitization to violence, nightmares, and fear of being harmed."

American children between 2 and 18 years of age spend an average of 6 hours and 32 minutes each day using media (television, commercial or self-recorded video, movies, video games, print, radio, recorded music, computer, and the internet). This is more time than they spend on any other activity, with the exception of sleeping. When simultaneous use of multiple media is accounted for, that exposure increases to 8 hours a day. A large proportion of this media exposure includes acts of violence that are witnessed or "virtually perpetrated" (in the form of video games) by young people. It has been estimated that by age 18, the average young person will have viewed 200,000 acts of violence on television alone.

Unfortunately, most entertainment violence is used for immediate visceral thrills without portraying any human cost. Sophisticated special effects, with increasingly graphic depictions of mayhem, make virtual violence more believable and appealing. Studies show that the more realistically violence is portrayed, the greater the likelihood that it will be tolerated and learned. Titillating violence in sexual contexts and comic violence are particularly dangerous, because they associate positive feelings with hurting others.

It's not unusual for people to identify with characters in movies and TV, and incorporate them into their dreams, memories and fantasies. While millions of people manage to enjoy the entertainment while keeping it all in perspective, there are those whose sense of reality is so fragile, that when shown the suspension of the laws of nature and society, with suggestions of evil forces and alternate realities, their paranoia and their fears can be heightened; they may abandon their attempts to orient towards reality, and plunge headlong and oblivious into the world of fantasy.

Most experts agree that there is no such thing as a work of art that has the power to compel someone to commit a crime, and anyone who blames their crimes on a movie is only looking for an excuse to escape responsibility for their lawlessness. And yet each contributing factor is worth noting when it comes to understanding the roots of crime.

"When somebody commits a violent crime, you can't point to just one cause," Joanne Cantor told the *Washington Post* in May of 2003. "I think these things can have really devastating effects on really vulnerable people," said Cantor, who has studied television and movie violence. "If people are saying they were influenced by that movie, then that movie was probably on their mind when they were planning these things."

In March of 1987, Tim Erickson and two other Minnesota teenagers, claiming to be inspired by the movie *The Lost Boys*, formed a "vampire cult," murdered a 30-year old drifter, and drank his blood. Erickson was sentenced to life in prison.

Another horror flick, *Warlock*, was viewed at least ten times by a 14-year-old boy in LaRonge, Saskatchewan, before he developed the delusion that as a vampire, he would be able to fly if he drank boiled fat from a virgin child.

This delusion prompted Sandy Charles to lure seven-year-old Johnathan Thimpsen into a bush on July 8, 1995 on the pretext of finding a lost toy. Once there, he stabbed the child to death, using a knife from his mother's kitchen. He then flayed strips of flesh and fat from the boy and took them home, where he cooked them on the stove to render the fat into a liquid. When he drank the viscous fluid, he was disappointed, like Manuela Ruda, to find he still could not fly.

Because of the grisly nature of his crime, the teen was tried as an adult, convicted of first-degree murder, and sentenced to life in prison.

A BUCK FOR YOUR BLOOD

In February of 1998, a man from Scott, Wisconsin was taken into custody, accused of sucking the blood out of a teenage girl's arms.

Other teens reported that Phillip K. Buck, 39, held underage drinking parties at his home where they slashed themselves and licked or sucked their wounds. He had been arrested a month earlier after neighbors complained of the ritual abuse of juveniles taking place in his home.

At such a party on December 27, 1997, Buck reportedly told a 16-year-old girl that he had a wooden stake and was going to kill himself. Then he handed the girl a razor blade and suggested she cut herself, telling her that "it would make you feel better."

The girl made several "criss-cross" cuts on the inside of each of her forearms. Buck then placed his mouth on one of the profusely bleeding wounds and sucked the girl's blood for about 15 minutes.

Another witness reported seeing Buck use a razor to cut his arms in front of intoxicated teens before giving the razor to them, and recalled Buck warning that there was an informant among them and that if he ever found out who it was he would "crush their throat."

Sinister items taken from Buck's home when the Sheriff's Department executed the search warrant included cloth restraints, a whipping device, a razor blade, a penknife, and a book about vampires.

Police denied any connection between this vampiric activity and a group of vampires in nearby Wisconsin Rapids known as "hissers" because of the sound they made when confronted. In a bizarre razor attack in October, one hisser had ostentatiously licked the victim's blood off the razor.

But the Buck case does bear a certain thematic similarity to a 1993 case in Toronto, Canada, where 25-year-old Donald Kuntz was convicted of assault for slicing open the arm of a 21-year-old woman he had met in a bar. The woman had agreed to let him drink her blood, but when Kuntz opened the wound, the woman panicked, wept and headed for the emergency room, bleeding copiously, in pain and distress. After she left, Kuntz dropped to the floor and licked up the spilled blood before fleeing.

In July of 2001, a couple of teenagers in Hartford, Connecticut, engaged in a "love ritual" involving mutual cutting and sharing of blood. David Coakley used a razor to carve "Forever Yours" into his 16-year-old girlfriend's back and posted the photos of the mutilation on his website.

One of the girl's shocked girlfriends told a parent, who reported it to police. The girl was treated at Connecticut Children's Medical Centre in Hartford and released. Coakley was taken to jail, where he re-opened the love-wounds in his arms and used his own blood to festoon his cell wall with romantic hearts and flowers entwined with his lover's name.

A BITE OUT OF CRIME

On March 10, 1999, the *New Orleans Times-Picayune* reported a relatively minor crime that gives a distinct taste of the crude reality beyond the mythic image of the vampire that has become such a friendly, familiar media virus.

On Sunday afternoon, Duncan Murray and Betty Latino were playing pool with the other regulars at Rumors Lounge in Lacombe. William Brewer was passing through from Alabama, he said, but the stranger fit right in with the regulars.

"He seemed like a nice, friendly man. He hung around here much of Sunday talking to everyone and playing pool," said Pepsi Briggs, the bartender. "He had a few drinks but he was not falling down drunk and his speech was not slurred. He was polite and neat and well dressed."

Briggs said she shut down the bar at 10:15 p.m. "This Brewer man was still at the bar and there were two other customers who needed to get home. I offered to give those two a lift and when Brewer said he was staying at the Star Motel, Betty and Duncan offered to give him a ride. If they had not done that, I would have taken him to the motel myself," she said.

When the car pulled up to the motel, without any warning whatsoever, Brewer became enraged and screamed that they had taken him to the wrong motel. Reaching over the driver's seat, he severely gouged at Murray's eyes. Murray got out of the car and tried to flee, but Brewer was on him at once. Like a ravenous Fiji warrior, he bit off one of Duncan's ears and swallowed it whole, along with a portion of his other ear.

Brewer, 30, was charged with second-degree battery and aggravated assault, and held on $1 million bond.

Murray, 60, was hospitalized in fair condition; he has subsequently lost the vision of one eye and may lose the other one as well.

"It is just awful," said Bern Trosclair, a friend of both Murray and Latino.

"He is a nice man and a hard-working man. It just makes you sick."

"Duncan and Brewer had played pool all evening and everyone had been getting along fine; no problems; no one drunk, none of that. I just can't believe it," said Pepsi Briggs. And so it goes in New Orleans.

In Chester, Ohio, Jonathan Ferris went to jail on June 26, 2001, for 45 days because he attacked his own grandfather, biting away at his neck and ear, yelling that he was a vampire, according to the *News-Herald*. When hauled before Chardon Municipal Court Judge Craig Albert, the 24-year-old vampire offered two mitigating factors: first, that on the day of the attack he had been drinking; and second, that he suffers from manic depression. Family members added that he had also been diagnosed with schizophrenia, a double-barreled diagnosis that would be hard for any drunk vampire to endure without biting the nearest living creature.

A month later in Pittsburgh, Pennsylvania, a high school band director was suspended from his duties on July 31, after sinking his teeth into the arms and ears of several of his students. James Wilson was suspended while the allegations were investigated, but he was supported by a rally of past and present pupils. In his defense, they told the *Pittsburgh Tribune-Review* that the popular teacher, who had guided the Albert Gallatin School marching band to several awards, simply enjoyed "horsing around" with youngsters. Sometimes that rambunctious spirit would apparently just well up and before you knew it, jolly old Mr. Wilson would be taking another chunk out of a kid!

A wild serial biter was cornered in the lobby of Pike's Waterfront Lodge in Fairbanks, Alaska where he was snarling, threatening to eat people and trying to bite them. Alaska State Troopers summoned to the scene arrived at 4:30 a.m., February 5, 2002 to find a highly intoxicated 24-year-old man named Kelly Loudon.

Once handcuffed and placed in the back of a squad car, the miscreant boasted loudly that he "eats fresh meat and feeds the rest to his dogs," which posed no particular problem. But when he commenced hissing and spitting, a pillowcase was borrowed from the hotel to place over his head. On the way to the Fairbanks Correctional Center, he wiggled out of the pillowcase and smashed his head against the window, injuring his forehead, so the Troopers transported him to the Fairbanks Memorial Hospital emergency room. There, the raver threatened the hospital security guards and made chomping noises at them, verbally abused the nurses and doctors, and tried to escape several times while being examined.

On the way back from the ER to the lockup, Loudon kept at it until he kicked out the windows of the squad car, causing nearly $400 worth of damage. Charged with disorderly conduct and third-degree criminal mischief, the serial biter undoubtedly settled down after he sobered up, and returned to his usual good spirits, cheerfully eating his fresh meat and feeding the rest to his dogs.

It was two weeks later on February 18 in New York City, when police were called by a man who heard "bloodcurdling screams" from his neighbor's apartment, where Felix Rondon and Jessica Mencia lived with their four-year-old daughter.

Police broke down the door to the locked bedroom to encounter a shocking sight: Jessica was still screaming and Felix was on top of her, biting and tearing her face with his teeth.

As they pulled him off, Felix's face and mouth were covered in blood. Jessica was bleeding heavily from her face, and there were bite marks on her arms as well. Police said that one of Jessica's earlobes was nearly torn off, and chunks of flesh were missing from her ears and around her eyes. They believe significant portions of her face were actually eaten by her boyfriend. Felix Rondon was charged with assault and harassment, and put under psychiatric observation.

SPECIAL RECIPES

Since 1985, the serial killer had been terrorizing Southern California, murdering at least two dozen women. He seemed to be taunting law enforcement by leaving corpses displayed like haunted sculptures. He had dressed some of his victims in men's clothes, surgically removed the right breasts of some, and excised the navels of others. He inserted a lightbulb in one victim's vagina, and left another one with her head buried in the ground like an ostrich.

Then on September 13th, 1991, Catherine McDonald was found stabbed in the chest and genitalia, and posed provocatively in a spread-eagled position. And in signature fashion, the right breast had been removed, with the killer apparently taking the human trophy with him.

The next day the sheriff's homicide task force took a break from the investigation to enjoy the annual picnic for Riverside County employees. As usual, county employee Bill Suff was in charge of the annual chili cook-off competition. And as usual, his "special" chili won first prize.

Though ultimately convicted of 12 murders and connected to at least as many more, Suff has maintained his innocence, and has slyly sidestepped the obvious conclusion that the secret ingredient that made his chili so "special" had once been known as Catherine.

After he settled in to life on Death Row, Suff went on to play the gay raconteur with the usual claque of serial killer groupies, littering the internet with murderabilia for sale. Screenwriter and attorney Brian Lane collaborated with Suff to release a grotesque book featuring his blood-curdling recipes.

Cannibalism may simply be a primitive attempt to dispose of the proof of the crime, according to Dr. Park Dietz, a national expert on criminal psychosis who testified at the Jeffrey Dahmer trial. There is no reason to think such corpse disposal methods are inspired by occult motives, but they do provide an *ad hoc* ritual that functions at a primitive level to purge a very intimate rage that might be seen as akin to the passion of the vampire sucking the life from a victim.

Feeding human remains to others serves to deeply victimize those one resents, while allowing one to "quietly enjoy knowing you got them," Dietz told the *Great Falls Tribune*. "As practical jokes go, it's on the extreme end."

BOYFRIEND STEW

In October of 1994, the *Rocky Mountain News* reported that Carolyn Gloria Blanton of Alamosa County had been charged with murder in the shooting death and dismemberment of her boyfriend, Peter Michael Green.

Judge Jean Paul Jones admitted 40 items into evidence, including a .25-caliber pistol, as well as a cooking pot and bowl that a sheriff's deputy testified had contained bite-size chunks of human flesh.

Green's torso was found in a closet at his home, and his legs were found in a nearby dumpster. "The flesh and the meat were off the legs," Sheriff's Capt. Les Sharff testified. "They had been totally cut away from the bones themselves, from the ankle up."

In another case of feminine gastronomic rage, in October of 2001, a guilty plea to murder was filed by a jilted Australian woman who skinned her lover then cooked and dished up his flesh before his family. "Served him right!"

Katherine Knight, who worked as a butcher at a slaughterhouse in Sydney, had conscientiously explained her murder plan in a home video she made for her teenage children. Then she went to John Price's house, where she found her lover of six years unconscious—most likely from a drug overdose.

The 44-year-old mother of four slaughtered him like a pig, cut off his head and certain other body parts, and boiled them in a big pot with vegetables. According to *The Mirror*, she left his skin hanging in the hall, and carefully arranged three dishes of boyfriend stew in the kitchen, with the names of his three children next to them.

The scene was so grossly disturbing that a year later, case-hardened investigating officers told the court they were still in mandatory therapy.

The victim's daughter, Rosemary Price, was relieved that the guilty plea would keep any further upsetting details out of the courtroom. "It would have haunted the jury for the rest of their lives like it haunts us," she said.

"Apparently Dad wanted out of the relationship. He had applied for an aggravated violence order against her because he was frightened of what she might do. For her to do what she did to him makes it really hard to bear. Dad was a great bloke."

A restaurateur in Jackson, Michigan, tried a similar culinary approach to a marital dissolution.

One of the officers investigating the disappearance of Pat Artz in July of 2000 came to the family restaurant and found a box containing a skull and cooked flesh. "I recognized burnt flesh on the counter," related the disgusted officer.

Kevin Artz claimed he couldn't remember a thing, probably due to an emergency operation to relieve a blood clot on his brain, several weeks before the killing. He told police he had no idea what he was doing. All he could remember was that after 12 years of marriage, he looked at his wife and saw the Devil staring back at him.

Artz was seen carrying his wife's head around in a box, though employees at the restaurant insisted that he was devoted to her. Said dishwasher Alex Lazaroff, "He loved Pat."

IT TASTES PRETTY GOOD

Down through the years, the Bowery in New York City has been home to more than a few eccentrics. But even among that world-class crowd of colorful characters, Daniel Rakowitz managed to stand out. It wasn't just the cockerel that was always perched on his long-haired shoulder. The small-time dope peddler claimed a special dispensation had given him the revelation that the Dark Lord had changed His Number from 666 to 966, and he exhorted all and sundry to join the Church of 966.

"I'm the new Lord, and I will take leadership of the satanic cultists to make sure they do everything that has to be done to destroy all those people who do disagree with my church," Rakowitz ranted in a later interview. "And I'm going to be the youngest person elected to the U.S. presidency."

Born in Rockport, Texas in 1960, Rakowitz had been given psychiatric care quite early, and psychotropic medication even as a pre-teen. He came to New York sometime around 1985 and quickly established his reputation.

Monica Beerle was a Swiss dancing student who took pity on the goofy guy, and let him move into her apartment at 700 East 9th Street. But she respectfully declined to join the Church of 966, and after a few weeks she asked him to clear out. On August 19, 1989, just 16 days after he had moved in with Monica, Rakowitz murdered her, and over the next few weeks, he dissected her remains in her own kitchen.

He boiled her head and made soup out of her brains, serving the nutritious meal to several of the rootless ramblers in Tompkins Square Park, telling them, "It tastes pretty good."

Rakowitz was having such a fine time he celebrated his enjoyment by scrawling on the door of Monika's apartment: "Is it soup yet?" and "Prey!"

He put her skull and bones in a bucket, which he carried around for awhile before he finally deposited it in a locker at the Port Authority bus station. Then he started bragging about what he had done on the street. Not surprisingly, he was soon taken into custody, and so were the skull and bones.

Once in jail, he demanded to be addressed only as "The New Messiah." The police humored him, and soon had a full confession.

Stubbornly representing himself, he petitioned the judge to empanel a jury of marijuana smokers so he could "get a fair trial."

"I just want everybody in New York City and the world to be happy and have a smile on their faces," the demented messiah explained. "If everybody smoked marijuana, there would be no violence in the world."

On February 22, 1991, Rakowitz was found not guilty by reason of insanity, and remanded to a state hospital for the criminally insane.

His status has been reviewed periodically since then. Each time Rakowitz has contended that he does not require hospitalization. However, the Special Projects Bureau has argued that based on the evidence, he remains dangerous. To date, each presiding judge has ruled that Rakowitz continues to suffer from a dangerous mental disorder.

In 1995, he exercised his statutory right to have a civil jury review his case. Based on evidence provided by the Special Projects Bureau, however, that jury unanimously confirmed that he had a dangerous mental disorder. It is unlikely that Rakowitz will be released in the foreseeable future.

In 1992, Randy Charles Easterday, 27, was charged as a participant in the crime, and evidence in that case pointed towards Rakowitz and Easterday belonging to a cult operating out of the Church of the Realized Fantasy. Police sources claimed the two men butchered the dancer "in a ritual sacrifice and a satanic offering."

Nathan Smith was the manager of The Sunshine Hotel, and in an interview with *The New York Historical Society* he reminisced:

My most famous tenant was the cannibal Daniel Rakowitz. Very nice guy. A little weird. He lived right there. One day I knocked on his door and I saw he had a cage with twenty-seven gerbils. I said "Rack Baby"— that's what I called him—I said "Rack Baby, this is not gonna work. Me and you are good friends, buddy, but you're going to have to leave." Next thing I know he's serving a girl in a stew to the homeless in Tompkins Square Park. But he was a down dude, a very nice guy. Listen, they can be murderers or whatever, they're all right with me. We've always had "different" people here. Different people go with the territory.

 Daniel Rakowitz

 Gary Heidnick

Gary Heidnik was another crackpot with a pseudo-occult approach to the depraved exploitation of women. This one involved the forced consumption of the human substance of fellow victims. While running his own homegrown church, he kept a harem of sex slaves chained to water pipes in the basement of his Philadelphia home. One of his slaves starved to death, and he murdered another one with electricity. Then Heidnik chopped up pieces of their flesh, mixed it with dog food, and fed the unholy goulash to his other captives. He went to the electric chair for his crimes in 1999.

I'VE GOT A PROBLEM

On July 13, 1970, a couple of longhaired hippies were speeding down the wrong side of a dirt road near Lucia, California, in a 1969 yellow Opel Kadett when they crashed into a pickup truck. The truck was slightly damaged but the Opel was totaled.

The bearded hippies stepped out of the car and approached the truck. The tall powerful one with shoulder-length blonde hair wore a leather vest and bellbottoms. The shorter one with curly dark hair wore cowboy boots and an Army field jacket.

The driver of the truck was a Detroit businessman on vacation. He offered to give the scruffy pair a ride to the nearest phone so they could report the accident. The hippies just shrugged and got into his truck. They finally came to a service station in Lucia that had a payphone. But while the truck driver was on the phone summoning the police, the two men jumped from the truck and dashed for the woods.

Patrolman Randy Newton was out cruising the Pacific Coast Highway when he got the call over his radio, and he figured the two fugitives could not have gone far. He came upon the suspects two miles from Lucia, trying to hitch a ride. Newton arrested them and radioed for backup. When his fellow patrolmen arrived, the suspects were cuffed and their rights were read. They readily admitted having been involved in the accident.

Though neither man carried identification, the 22-year-old tall blond man identified himself as Stanley Dean Baker and his road-dog as 20-year-old Harry Allen Stroup. Though Stroup exercised his right to remain silent, Baker was eager to talk.

The prisoners were patted down, and in Baker's pockets police found a copy of *The Satanic Bible* and a couple of small bones. Officer Newton studied them curiously and asked what they were. Baker told him, "They ain't chicken bones. They're human fingers." There was a stunned, disbelieving silence. Then he shocked them all with one of the most memorable one-liners in the world of crime: "I've got a problem. I'm a cannibal."

Peter Schlosser had gone camping in Yellowstone Park, and Baker told police that on July 10, he had murdered the 22-year-old camper. After shooting the victim and stabbing him 27 times with a 5-inch knife, he had cut out his heart and eaten it, chopped up the corpse, and disposed of it in the river, pocketing the fingers as macabre mementos. He went on to claim that he had felt the urge to eat human flesh and to refer to himself as "Jesus" ever since receiving electric shock treatment at the age of 17.

While exonerating his road-dog Harry Stroup from any involvement in the Montana murder, Baker voluntarily incriminated himself in further crimes, claiming he had been recruited when he was in college in Wyoming into the "Four P Movement," called by cult-watcher Maury Terry an "offshoot, fringe-type" organization spawned by the Process Church, which in turn is thought by many to be derived from a certain vast, affluent, highly litigious quasi-scientific mind-control cult.

After swearing allegiance to the "Grand Chingon" of the Four P Movement, Baker told police, he had been involved in human sacrifices in the Santa Ana Mountains.

Fingerprints linked him to another homicide in San Francisco, for which he was not prosecuted, due to being denied a speedy trial. At trial, Baker boasted of his magical power to change the weather, and confessed he was partly responsible for the demise of Jimi Hendrix.

Sentenced to life in prison, he was confined to a Montana prison, where he kept busy recruiting for his jailhouse coven. Corrections officers noted that the full moon would find Baker crouched in his cell, howling like a wolf. He also developed into a security risk, with weapons being confiscated from him 11 times.

Baker was transferred to a supermax prison in Illinois, where he continued to proselytize for his idiosyncratic occult belief system among the population. Although he proudly called himself a satanist, the compliment was not returned. In 1976, he tried to join Anton LaVey's Church of Satan, but was disappointed to have his application rejected.

Harry Stroup served his sentence and was released in 1979. Baker was paroled in 1985. He asked for his whereabouts to remain confidential, but a TV journalist tracked him down outside Minneapolis and got an interview in 1991. He described himself as "a good man," denying any connection to the San Francisco murder, and blaming the Montana murder on "that outfit in California."

SACRAMENTO DRACULA

In Sacramento, California, on January 23, 1978, a 22-year-old pregnant woman was found slashed to death, eviscerated and mutilated, with evidence left at the scene of her blood being collected and drunk by the slayer. Three days later, less than a mile away, a quadruple murder occurred, with a similar mutilation of the adult female victim and evidence of blood drinking.

After Richard Trenton Chase was identified as the "Dracula Killer" he was also connected with a drive-by shooting that killed a man a month earlier, and two near-miss shootings of the man's neighbors. A serial fetish burglar and abductor of numerous animals, Chase had most recently been arrested four months earlier on an Indian reservation carrying firearms and a bucket of animal blood.

This 28-year-old white male of average intelligence and known history of sexual impotence and substance abuse was arrested in 1965 for marijuana possession, in 1972 for drunk driving, and in 1973 for carrying a gun without a license and resisting arrest. In 1976, he entered a nursing home after injecting rabbit's blood into his veins. Nursing home staff started calling him Dracula after he repeatedly bit the heads off birds.

After antipsychotic drugs demonstrated some relief from his symptoms of mental illness, he was released from the nursing home, but upon release he remained unable to support himself. He was speaking of UFOs and Nazis that were out to get him because he had been born Jewish and had a Star of David on his forehead, and he believed that these Nazi-commandeered UFOs had telepathically ordered him to kill.

Chase reportedly believed he suffered from "soap-dish poisoning" and his own blood was being turned to powder, which justified his compulsion to replace his disappearing blood with whatever blood he could ingest orally. Starting with the blood of birds and rabbits, he progressed to dogs, cats

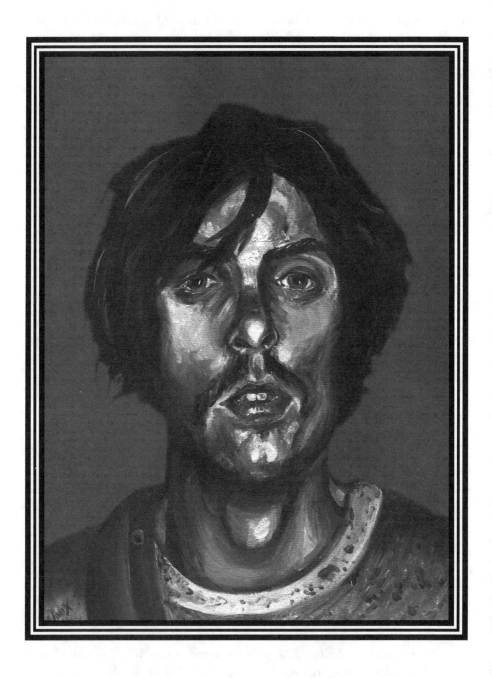

 Richard Trenton Chase

and cattle, then finally sought relief by drinking the blood of humans he claimed were slain for that purpose.

His insanity plea rejected, Chase was sentenced to the electric chair in 1978. After saving up the antidepressants prescribed to alleviate his symptoms, this demented creature was found dead from an overdose the morning after Christmas, 1980, in his Death Row cell at San Quentin.

The first person I killed was sort of an accident... The second time, the people had made a lot of money and I was jealous. I was being watched, and I shot this lady—got some blood out of it. I went to another house, walked in, a whole family was there. I shot the whole family. Somebody saw me there. I saw this girl. She had called the police and they had been unable to locate me. Curt Silva's girlfriend—he was killed in a motorcycle accident, as a couple of my friend were, and I had this idea that he was killed through the syndicate, that he was in the Mafia, selling drugs. His girlfriend remembered about Curt—I was trying to get information. She said she was married to someone else and wouldn't talk to me. The whole syndicate was making money by having my mom poison me.

I NEED BLOOD

In 1996 Arvind Balu, a student at the University of California at Berkeley, won a free vacation to Lake County in the Clearlake area in a radio contest, so he took Brendan Loftus, a fellow student, with him to celebrate a long Fourth of July holiday weekend. It was there that they allegedly met a 14-year-old girl, who waited a year to tell police that Loftus had raped her while Balu had cut her and licked her blood in their room at the Konocti Harbor Inn.

Upon conviction, Balu was sent to Atascadero State Hospital for evaluation, and Loftus went to prison for a five-year term. In July of 2000, Loftus was freed when his conviction was reversed on appeal, while Balu's case remained on appeal.

It was a warm summer night in August of 2000 when Joshua Roise picked up a hitchhiker about ten miles north of Santa Cruz. He was headed toward San Francisco, and his rider asked to be dropped off at the corner of Haight and Stanyan.

"He was calm during the ride but he changed when I went to drop him off," Roise wrote in a police statement. "He thanked me for the ride and attempted to hug me. He then bit my neck and proceeded to clamp down.

"I asked him repeatedly to stop, but he only clamped down harder and restrained my arms so I couldn't get away. He continued biting and sucking on my jugular vein for about two minutes."

Roise flagged down a patrol officer, who apprehended the man after a brief pursuit through Golden Gate Park.

"I need blood," blurted Eric David Knight immediately upon being taken into custody, and went on to explain that he suffered from a disease that left him unable to eat food. "I need the cure," the self-professed vampire told police, and reiterated, "I need blood."

Roise was treated for a bite wound at UC San Francisco Medical Center and released. The 39-year-old homeless man, who had a record of assault and battery, was found guilty a month later of misdemeanor battery, false imprisonment and resisting arrest. Sentencing was deferred pending the results of a psychiatric evaluation.

"The judge also ordered the adult probation department to suggest a sentence appropriate to his condition," said Fred Gardner of the San Francisco District Attorney's Office. "Knight will not be going back on the street, but it is clear to me that California needs a whole new layer of custodial facilities for people who are nuts in this way."

SAN FRANCISCO SAMURAI

On October 16, 1998, two men sleeping in the streets of the Nob Hill district of San Francisco had their throats cut several hours apart, but fortunately the wounds were not fatal; both men recovered. Two weeks later, 48-year-old Shirley Dillahunty, who was sleeping in a doorway in the Mission Hill district, was less fortunate. When her throat was slashed, this crime would be declared a murder.

Evidence tying each crime scene together included a cryptic symbol scrawled on the pavement in the blood of the victim. It was later deciphered as the Chinese symbol for Death.

People on the streets were horrified, but gained little support from the community at large. Because of the perceived worthlessness of their lives, these serial assaults were of little interest to the advertisers supporting the local media, and thus to the editors and producers who decide what is "news."

San Francisco has a long-standing history of frequent arrests and sweeps of homeless encampments. Though the city claims 1,800 emergency shelter beds, thousands more are sleeping outside, where they're isolated and vulnerable. The two years leading up to the serial slashings had seen 34 homicides of the homeless.

Homeless advocates accused the police of allowing a mad slasher to run amok in their midst, and otherwise chronically failing to protect and defend them, with Coalition on Homelessness spokesperson Paul Boden telling the San Francisco Chronicle, "If a rash of tourists were stabbed over several days, there'd be a major response," a notion which Police Chief Fred Lau promptly rectified by pointing out that it was "absolutely untrue."

Then in Chinatown on November 10, a 48-year-old unidentified homeless man whose throat was slashed as he slept on a park bench fought off his attacker, and the staggering, blood-soaked victim managed to contact the police.

In what Captain John Goldberg called "pretty good police work by the guys on the street," officers Alane Baca and Gregory Huie snagged a 21-year-old half-Asian diagnosed schizophrenic two blocks away with a bloody knife in his pocket and a Chinese symbol tattooed on his chest.

Deputy Chief Richard Holder said that Joshua Rudiger had "admitted some guilt to the four incidents," but he expressed some reservations as to the credibility of some of the statements he had made.

Claiming to be a 2,000-year-old vampire with "special psychic powers" who had lived all over the world, Rudiger told police he had sucked the blood of all of his victims after he had cut their throats.

Rudiger said that as a samurai in another life, he had burned down the holiest temple in Japan, killing worshipers, and so now he was to be punished by God by being forced to drink human blood to maintain his vitality in this life.

However, none of his surviving victims complained of even so much as an attempt at blood-sucking, so such statements might have been just another symptom of the mental illness that had been plaguing him for years.

"We'll never know if he really drank the victims' blood," said Lt. David Robinson, "but we're sure he's the guy who slashed their throats."

As to where Rudiger might have picked up such an idea, "His roommate says he had been watching vampire films," remarked a neighbor, "so he may have got it from that."

The self-proclaimed vampire had been charged with stabbing a homeless man in the neck in February of 1997, but ironically the victim went to jail for drugs and was stabbed to death by another inmate before a case could be put together.

Then on August 3 of that same year, Rudiger attacked another man with a bow and arrow. This time he was charged with attempted murder, but the defendant was found incompetent to stand trial and sent to Atascadero State Hospital. But by the time he was declared fit, victim Myron Scholes had moved to the East Coast and was less than enthusiastic about coming back to testify.

Thus it was that in May of 1998, Joshua Rudiger was given three years' probation for assault with a deadly weapon with great bodily injury, and turned loose. Although one condition of his probation was "intense psychiatric supervision by the adult probation department," that wasn't enough to keep him from becoming a vampire.

"You can't put someone in jail just because you think they're dangerous," said prosecuting attorney John Shanley. "You need evidence. To win a trial, you have to have witnesses." When the witness left in the bow-and-arrow case, "we had no choice but to accept the plea agreement. Our only other option was to dismiss the case and release him with nothing."

"We didn't take this situation to the level we should have to ensure his compliance" with the probation agreement, conceded Armando Cervantes, chief probation officer for the San Francisco Adult Probation Department, while admitting that Rudiger had not reported for any psychiatric supervision whatsoever.

Looking back at his record, it becomes clear that this is not a case of film and fiction corrupting an otherwise stable and healthy youth. The social conditions that created this vampire were nothing short of grotesque. He had long been rummaging through the dark corners of his cultural heritage for imagery exotic enough to correspond to his own grossly degrading experience, as his primitive impulses spontaneously formed deep within his damaged psyche, taking shape as they rose to consciousness, finally crossing over from fantasy to the Theater of the Real.

The fatherless son of a homeless drug-addicted prostitute, Joshua Rudiger had been discarded and abandoned, and was found weeping and terrified at the age of seven months amidst his own filth in a bathtub, unattended for two or three days.

Over the next two years, he passed through four foster homes. By the age of four, he carried a diagnosis of psychosis with mental retardation, and had an IQ that never tested higher than 81. As a preschooler, he would bang his head, bite his tongue and force himself to vomit. He later told doctors that it was about that time that he began living his double life.

Rudiger lived in a succession of foster homes until his attempted suicide at age 15. He had tried to kill himself with a samurai sword, and went in for his first psychiatric admission, passing through six psychiatric hospitals in eight months, and winding up at Napa State Hospital, where his evaluation stated, "Mr. Rudiger exhibits low frustration tolerance along with the delusional belief that he is a samurai whose duty it is to 'kill all bad people.'"

"I'm a samurai. I was samurai before I was born, even in another life," the young patient had told the doctor. "I'm like a tiger. I'm OK if you leave me alone, but if you bother me, I strike."

When he left at age 18, Rudiger was in worse shape than when he went in. He would sneak out of his room at night to lick the chests of other patients. "I'm going to be a vampire and suck their blood out," he told one therapist.

Relocated to an adolescent treatment center in San Jose, he walked away after three months, and was found wandering the streets carrying a dead fish, saying he hoped to use a lighter to cook "ninja sushi" on his way to Japantown in San Francisco.

Joshua Rudiger entered a plea of not guilty to ten felonies, and on December 10, 1999, a jury found him guilty as charged of second-degree murder and all related charges. Despite his lifelong psychiatric diagnoses, as in so many other cases, his insanity plea was rejected. There would be no therapy. 20 years to life.

BIG LURCH

It was broad daylight, around noon on the tenth of April, 2002, in the City of Lost Angels. And there was Big Lurch, all six-foot-eight of him bucknaked, loping down South Figueroa gazing up at the sky, ranking wack on the dust of paranoid angels, otherwise known as PCP; his mumbling mouth slathered with blood, raw gore streaking down his bare chest and loins.

Police were summoned, and took the appalling apparition into custody. Just as they were placing him in the squad car, Alisa Allen ran up to the officers screaming hysterically. She had just come from the apartment where the raver resided with her friend, known as Pocahontas, whom Alisa had just found dead on the floor. "She was cut up really, really bad," she said in court at the preliminary hearing on May 30.

Alisa identified the killer as Antron Singleton, an aspiring rapper who had come out from Texas for the past few months to lay down tracks for his debut album. Man or beast, Big Lurch might have been on his way to stardom. He had, after all, rapped with such artists as Mac Dre, RBL Posse, C-Bo, and Mystikal, another rising rapper who three months later would commit several felonies in Baton Rouge and wind up in prison himself.

Big Lurch was one-third of the Cosmic Slop Shop, and was slated to appear on C-Bo's next album. But this was no Hollywood publicity stunt, and the blood streaming from his mouth was not for theatrical effect; it was the blood of a young mother. The 21-year-old victim, Tynisha Ysais, had two babies, aspired to be a model, and was known for her gentle ways, her generous smile, and her wide, dreamy eyes.

When Los Angeles Detective Raymond Jankowski found her body on the floor of the apartment, there were teeth marks on her face, and a broken knife blade embedded three inches in her left shoulder.

"Her chest was open, exposing internal organs," Jankowski testified at the preliminary hearing, and went on to describe how pieces of her right lung, which had been pulled out of the chest cavity, had apparently been chewed and eaten.

And worst of all, a medical examination found human flesh and blood in the rangy rapper's stomach.

"That is so gross," the victim's mother muttered under her breath during the gruesome testimony. "The police told me not to believe the rumors, but they were true."

"I can't believe it," rap producer Scarface told AllHipHop.com. "I've known him for awhile. His people were in touch with me about doing some material three or four months ago. For some reason, I decided not to work with him. He had a nice voice and he could rhyme. No one would have expected this."

Big Lurch was held without bail and ordered to stand trial on one count of murder with special circumstance of infliction of torture, and one count of aggravated mayhem. He entered a plea of not guilty on June 13, 2002, and finally appeared in *Billboard*.

The victim's mother made a run for the deep pockets in April of 2003 by filing a wrongful death suit enjoining not only the rapper, but also the ex-con music producer Suge Knight and his corporate entities, Death Row Records, Tha Row Records, and Stress Free, whom Carolyn Stinson charged with turning her talented young daughter's suitor into a true vampire, by providing him with drugs "to encourage him to act out in an extreme violent manner so as to make him more marketable as a 'gangsta rap' artist."

"Part of what makes a gangsta rap artist marketable is the fact that the artist is a current ongoing participant in violent gang activities," stated the lawsuit. "Singleton met this criteria and was even more marketable because his songs were as violent as his lifestyle and included rape, murder and ended with him eating his victim's body organs."

"I don't know this guy," Knight told Reuters the next day. "Nobody from our company knows this guy. I never even heard the guy rap." The music mogul's demurral was found credible, as the plaintiff promptly withdrew Knight along with Death Row Records and Tha Row Records from the suit, leaving only corporate fledgling Stress Free liable to pay damages for providing money, drugs, an apartment and a bodyguard for Big Lurch, thus encouraging him to become a true vampire at the expense of the mother who loved a young California girl fondly known as Pocahontas.

ROCKET SCIENTIST, VAMPIRE RAPIST

In the summer of 1985, a 19-year-old woman hitchhiking through Florida was picked up by a vampire who took her to his home, handcuffed, raped and tortured her throughout an 18-hour ordeal in which he drained her of over half her blood and drank it. Naked and handcuffed, she escaped through the bathroom window, and was picked up by a passing motorist and taken to a hospital to be revived.

Police arrested 38-year-old John Crutchley, an aerospace engineer working for The Harris Corporation in nearby Melbourne.

"This is a guy who had to pass a CIA background check, working for

Harris like he did," said Matt Wilson, an actor who interviewed Harris employees who had worked alongside Crutchley, as he researched making a low-budget film about the case in May of 2003.

"But everything I've read about him, the people I've talked to, everything indicates he had this kind of goofy persona around the office," Wilson told *USA Today*.

By all accounts, Crutchley would chat up female co-workers, find out about their interests, then research them to develop conversational gambits he would use to ingratiate himself. Male colleagues became aware of his ruse and advised the women not to feed him any personal information.

"You ask him how he's doing, and he says 'Peachy.' That's it. Everything was 'peachy.' And he had this walk," Wilson said, "Like this," demonstrating a loping, bouncy stride. "He drew attention to himself."

Although Crutchley had also been a suspect in at least two dozen murders in Florida, West Virginia and two other states, he was never charged. Sources close to the case suggest that prosecutors elected not to accept a plea bargain agreement proffered by Crutchley's defenders, for him to admit to other crimes in return for a reduced sentence. Instead, the State pressed for a life sentence, but Crutchley was actually sentenced to 25 years.

The prison rules in effect at that time gave Crutchley 3,000 days off his sentence, and after 11 years, he had accumulated 2,250 days off for good behavior. At the age of 49, the vampire rapist had served his time and was ready to return to society.

As his release date drew near in the summer of 1996, Florida Department of Corrections officials had trouble finding a place for him. The people of Melbourne did not want him back, nor did they in his mother's home in West Virginia. Finally, he was scheduled for release to a halfway house in Orlando, but the anxiety of being freed apparently motivated him to smoke a joint, and when mandatory urine testing turned out positive, the "three strikes" sentencing guidelines were used to sentence him to life.

On March 30 of 2002, he was found in his cell with a plastic bag wrapped around his head, an apparent suicide.

Crutchley is an example of a highly intelligent, sexually sadistic vampire who might very well have been a full-fledged serial killer, but due to the vagaries of the legal system, whatever could have been learned by his confessions will forever remain a mystery.

MACABRE MÉNAGE À TROIS

On the golden coast of the Sunshine State, on November 21, 1993 another vampire struck a 19-year-old woman, and this time the victim was to lose more than just her blood.

Chubby teen Tiya Whetsel had a crush on Greg Mason, a broodingly handsome 24-year-old former mental patient. After partying with him one afternoon, she couldn't shake the enchantment of his hypnotic gaze. The lovestruck girl couldn't wait to see this dangerously fascinating man again.

Mason had given her his number, and she prompted a friend to give him a call. Upon hearing of Tiya's desire to see him again, he had agreed to pick her up later on that evening. But when Tiya stepped into his truck, she came face-to-face with Mason's satanic sweetheart, a 19-year-old witch named Angela Perez. *The National Enquirer* just up the road would call it a classic love triangle. But this affair was much more sinister than that.

The macabre *ménage à trois* ended badly, with the infatuated ingenue throttled, beaten with a baseball bat, and stabbed about the head and neck with a nine-inch blade; the brutalized body hidden in the glades outside Boynton Beach; and the bloody knife stashed in Angela's trailer.

Angela was accustomed to keeping dreadful secrets, but her troubled partner was not. He broke down and confessed to his father, who alerted police.

Angela knew what it meant to take an oath of silence; her bedroom was virtually a satanic shrine, with black-draped walls, pentagrams and baphomets proudly positioned.

Bright and lively, with snapping black eyes and a thick shock of glossy black hair, Angela enjoyed a fairly normal youth until her high school graduation at age 16, when she carved a bloody pentagram into her palm and took to dressing in colors of the night.

Stephan Giarritta was a member of Angela's coven. He described to state's investigators one of the times they had sacrificed a cat. The bloodthirsty high priestess reached into the viscera of the writhing animal and ripped out its liver with relish—biting into it while it was still throbbing hot and sucking the life-blood as a ritual sacrifice.

But the jury would hear none of that. "We knew, of course, she had done things with cats—and had eaten their livers," admitted prosecutor Bunnie Lenhardt. "But you can't convict someone because of certain beliefs."

And since you can't convict them, you must not allow the jury to hear about the matter at all, lest their primitive emotions be inflamed unjustly against the defendant.

After confessing, Greg Mason entered a guilty plea and was sentenced to 19 years in prison.

Angela Perez went to trial. The jurors saw a meek, pitiful young lady weeping openly on the stand as she testified that it was all Greg Mason's fault, that she had only helped out because he forced her to, and that she was afraid if she didn't, her fearsome accomplice would kill her too.

Without recourse to the known facts about her character, the jury accepted her pitiful testimony at face value, and instead of finding her guilty of murder, found her guilty only of manslaughter.

After the trial, once jurors learned the gory details of this vampire's background, two of them appeared at the sentencing hearing, protesting that their verdict would have been different, had they been able to more accurately assess the extent of the defendant's bloodthirst.

Taking into consideration the objections of the jurors, the judge did what he could within statutory guidelines, and maxed her out at ten years. On May Day of 1998, her time off for good behavior put this homicidal vampire back on the streets again. But like the vampire rapist, John Crutchley, she was not ready to be free. Not quite yet.

Angela Perez violated parole by failing to see a psychiatrist, and in July of 1999, she went back behind bars until March 13, 2000, when she was released. Her court files reveal that this sworn satanic priestess has apparently been rehabilitated from her wicked ways. Last seen living at home with Mom and Dad, she was driving a nice car, while working a part-time job and attending school full-time, ranking as an honor student in graphic arts at Palm Beach Community College.

HIDDEN FIRE

Among the most despicable true vampires are those who sexually abuse children, kill them and then suck their substance and gnaw upon their tender flesh. Arthur Shawcross and Nathaniel Bar-Jonah are a couple of American serial killers who were arrested, convicted, and served time for violent crimes against children. After release, their cases show another striking similarity. With forced relocation into a new community, they both went on to offend again in the worst way. In both cases, they admitted to eating the flesh of their victims. There are no occult overtones to this type of crime. These killers are functioning at a primitive oral level. As the most cowardly of sexual predators, they prey upon children chiefly because of their vulnerability.

Arthur Shawcross was two months premature at birth on June 6, 1945. His 18-year-old mother Betty and his 21-year-old father Arthur Senior married when she turned up pregnant, and settled in Watertown, New York, where they raised a family of four. By the time Artie turned 13, he was living in a close-knit village that became known as Shawcross Corners, just outside Watertown, with his extended family living nearby.

Throughout his entire life, many of the intimate details of his personal history have been provided by Shawcross himself, and often seem incredible. One explanation for such stories is confabulation. He attempts to present a plausible explanation for his actions, but the cause may well be a fully inexplicable organic malfunction. So he may not actually be lying, but just totally out of touch with his own mental processes and trying to bridge that gap with something he thinks makes sense.

There is no evidence to support the allegations Shawcross has put on the record about being sodomized by his diminutive mother and forced to provide oral sex not only for his sister Jeannie, but for a female cousin and sometimes an aunt as well. He also claimed that as a child, he had sex with a sheep, a cow, a horse, and even a chicken, which was killed in the course of the assault.

Notwithstanding the reliability of his accounts, early sexual deviance would not be inconsistent with his known record of sexualized violence. Certainly, his sexuality maintained a primarily oral focus throughout his life, and even if his early sexuality was somewhat less colorful, still, these stories came out while Shawcross was preparing a legal defense based on his mental state. It would not be illogical for him to be "playing crazy" to some extent under the circumstances. In any case, even if the personal history he relates never actually happened, still the content of his fantasy life is significant, inasmuch as it sheds light on his motivations.

His younger siblings deny the allegations of abuse. However, the extended family tends to agree on the fact that Arthur Senior was verbally humiliated by his wife Betty, especially after it came to light that he had married a woman in Australia and fathered a child before marrying Betty. So there was a rather unpleasant atmosphere in the home. All sources agree that young Artie spent most of his time away from the house, and his parents complained early on that they were unable to control him.

Interviews with neighbors and relatives reveal that the eldest son of the Shawcross family had always been a bully. He tortured animals, snapping the necks of rabbits, drowning kittens, tying cats together, shooting darts at frogs, and releasing bats inside parked cars, hiding and watching as the drivers returned and panicked.

He was a chronic bed-wetter into his teens, and he enjoyed setting fires; his was a classic case of the "homicidal triad" of fire-starting, bed-wetting, and animal abuse as a precursor of adult violence. He held conversations with imaginary friends, spoke in strange voices, and gained the nickname "Oddie."

At nine, he complained of a debilitating leg pain, but doctors could find nothing wrong. A year later he sank in four feet of lake water at a family outing, and when rescued, claimed he was paralyzed. Six days of hospitalization and testing failed to reveal anything abnormal, though he was finally assigned a diagnosis of encephalomyelitis, or inflammation of the myelin sheath of the brain. Throughout the rest of his life he would often feign illness, chest pain, and even unconsciousness. Most often, no medical cause for his maladies could be detected.

As life went on, multiple traumas were sustained. At 12 he was struck in the head with a discus and spent four days in the hospital with a skull fracture. In his youth he was also to be knocked unconscious for a half-hour by a sledgehammer, electrocuted by a faulty switch, hospitalized after falling on his head from a 40-foot ladder, and hit by a truck.

Extensive investigations have revealed that Shawcross has frontal-lobe brain damage, as well as a rare blood disorder named pyroluria and the controversial XYY chromosome. Each of these conditions is known to contribute to sudden, unreasoning paroxysms of violence.

As he matured into his early teens, he became fixated on oral sex, and like Andrei Chikatilo, suffered the humiliation of impotence. At 14, he claims he was raped by a man who held him by the throat and sodomized him. Since that alleged assault, Shawcross claims he linked the achievement of a sexual climax with the infliction of pain.

He did poorly in school and was held back repeatedly until, like his parents and grandparents, he dropped out of high school short of graduation. Crimes of petty vandalism and theft escalated until in 1963, when at age 18, he broke into a Sears store and was caught at the scene by police. As a juvenile, he was sentenced to 18 months probation.

The next year he met a girl named Sarah Chatterton at a store where they both worked, and they soon married at a Baptist Church and enjoyed a honeymoon in Canada. They moved into a trailer owned by her family, and he began to drift from one menial job to another. A few weeks later he revealed that his marriage had still not been consummated, telling a cousin in his customary crude way, "I ain't got her yet." Eventually he did manage to perform, for a son was born a year later.

Shortly afterwards, he committed a hot-headed assault on a 13-year-old boy who had hit his car with a snowball, and spent three days in jail before being sentenced to six months probation. A court-ordered psychiatric workup noted Shawcross was an "emotionally unstable personality" and said he reacted "with excitability and ineffectiveness when confronted by minor stress."

His young wife chose to terminate their marriage at that point, and after their separation in August of 1966, he began dating Linda Neary. He was drafted in April of 1967, and in 1968, he made her his second wife while on leave. Two weeks later, he was shipped out to Vietnam to serve as an Army supply clerk in Pleiku. He claims he was trained as a predator and became an animal, attacking and ravishing not only enemy soldiers, but even Asian prostitutes as young as 11. He spoke of first tasting human flesh in Vietnam, and the war stories he told psychiatrists were horrific:

Yeah, I go out there and came across a woman—a girl. She was putting an AK-47 on the side of a coop and I shot her, tied and gagged her, took her up where I had a clear view of the area and tied her to a tree... I didn't have nothing to eat that day, and I took a big chunk off the hip of the girl... I took off all the skin and took a piece of green bamboo and I ran it up inside the bone and I roasted it on the fire... After it cooked down, it was almost like eating charcoal-broiled pork, the consistency of a dry roast beef... I was just in the mood, that's all. After I was eating it—it didn't taste that bad—I took the body and carried it down through the jungle area where I knew there was a big anthill and laid it beside the anthill, went back to the tree, and was sitting there sharpening the machete and eating that meat. The other girl had the sweat running off of her. I untied her hands and tied her on the ground and raped her... and I cut her throat, took her head up there where the house was and put that head on a stick right in front of the house.

It has not been possible to substantiate his accounts of war atrocities, and investigation of his military records revealed that he was assigned to a quiet post and never came near any such action. Be that as it may, he was a changed man when he returned home in 1969.

"I was home three days before I was asked if I was going to see Linda," Shawcross recalls in Jack Olsen's *Misbegotten Son*. "I said Linda who, I had forgotten that I was married."

The Army sent him to Fort Sill, Oklahoma and Linda went with him, but he became progressively more disturbed and assaulted her. He visited an Army psychiatrist who recommended therapy and hospitalization, but his wife didn't feel comfortable agreeing to it, and his parents refused to sign the papers, protesting that there was nothing wrong with their son.

He was honorably discharged from the Army in the spring of 1969, and the couple returned to upstate New York, settling in Clayton, near her parents.

Shawcross continued to deteriorate, and for the first time, started drinking. He went into a rage when he applied for a job and received no veterans' preference. For months he wouldn't do anything but go fishing, and refused to look for a job. In April Linda was four months pregnant when he got drunk and beat her so brutally she was left unconscious, and miscarried. After her family returned from the hospital, Shawcross was found on the floor with his wrists slit in two places. Police asked Linda if she wanted him arrested, but she demurred, and simply had her father deliver the message that she wanted out of the marriage. Two weeks later when she was released from the hospital, he refused to leave the house and had to be forcibly evicted by Linda's father.

Shawcross moved to a nearby village and went on a crime spree, burglarizing a gas station and burning down a barn and a milk plant, telling police upon arrest that he was upset about losing his wife. Arson had been a recurring theme in his criminal history since childhood. He had spoken of finding sexual excitement in fires, a trait also found in Ottis Toole, another neurologically-damaged serial killer who claimed to have been sexually abused by a parent and forced to give oral sex to a sister.

Shawcross was convicted of two counts of arson, and in 1970, sentenced to five years in prison. At Attica, he claims he was raped by three black convicts, and that he raped each of them later in return. Other sources say he was simply shoved into a door and knocked unconscious; that there was never any rape on either side. The truth of the matter may lie somewhere in between. In 1971 there was a prison riot, and Shawcross saved the life of a prison guard, so he was given early release.

Since Linda had divorced him while he was locked up, the brand-new ex-con was once again in the market for a mate. In January of 1972 he started dating a friend of his sister's, Penny Nichol Sherbino, who had two children. He had known her since junior high school, and the instant family soon moved in together. Shawcross made Penny his third wife in April, and got a handyman job at the Watertown Public Works Department.

He "walked cross-lots" or rode his bike all over town, and spent a lot of time fishing along the Black River. Before long he met ten-year-old Jack Blake, and they sometimes went fishing together. On July 4, 1972, little Jack went out to play and never came back. His fishing buddy became a suspect but was never arrested due to lack of evidence.

Three months later, eight-year-old Karen Ann Hill was found dead under a bridge, where she had been raped, strangled, and mutilated. When police learned Shawcross had been eating an ice cream cone at the bridge that day, they picked him up for questioning.

Upon tenacious interrogation he finally cooperated, and under the terms of a negotiated plea, he admitted to killing Karen Ann Hill as well as Jack Blake. Though at first his account of the murder was ludicrously self-serving, eventually the truth emerged: he had taken the little boy into the woods, stripped him naked, strangled him and beat him in the head. Shawcross showed police where he dumped the body, but the skeletal remains were too deteriorated to confirm his claims. He told psychiatrists that he had also removed the child's heart and genitals and eaten them, and returned to have sex with the rotting corpse. Again, we will never know if Shawcross was just "playing crazy" when he confessed to these gratuitously ghoulish details, but it takes a seriously depraved personality to think it's a good idea to confess to the necroerotic cannibalization of a child—*especially* if they didn't really do it.

Shawcross was on his way to prison again, this time on a 25-year bid as a convicted child molester, considered behind bars everywhere to be the lowest of the low. His confessions to eating parts of a little girl and a little boy didn't help with his prison popularity. He incurred numerous disciplinary reports and ran into a great deal of conflict with other prisoners. But he managed to "improve himself," and by 1985, he had completed his high school education and taken courses in locksmithing and horticulture through Penn State University, eventually working his way up to "model inmate" status.

During his incarceration he was examined by psychiatric professionals who sketched a contradictory but provocative picture. Dr. Albert Dresser examined him first, and wrote that he did not consider Shawcross a "psychological risk," because he saw no evidence of delusions, hallucinations or sensory deceptions.

Upon the administration of the Bender Motor Gestalt test and the Wechsler Adult Intelligence test, Dr. J.R. McWilliams stated he had found no evidence of neurological impairment. He noted that Shawcross was deeply depressed and "relied heavily upon fantasy as a source of satisfaction." He opined that Shawcross seemed to be "a normal individual who knows he has done wrong and would like to help himself get back on the right track for his eventual return to society." Inexplicably, on the medical chart submitted into evidence, the words "normal person" were crossed out and the words "psychopathic killer" were written above them in pencil.

Dr. Michael Boccia observed that Shawcross had not come to terms with the reality of his crimes and continued to blame others for his problems. He stated that in his opinion, when Shawcross requested the first examination, he had not done it to deal with his mental problems; he had merely done it to impress the parole board.

Finally, Dr. Y.A. Haveliwala wrote that although Shawcross had adapted readily to prison routine, he had a schizoid personality, was antisocial and had a distinct personality disorder. "This man does not show a good degree of evidence of successfully resolving or working out his psychosexual conflicts."

A parole report stated that Shawcross "exhibited a belligerent reaction representing a foreboding potential for a possible re-enactment of his tragic behavior." The report criticized him for his disdain for the Sex Offender Program, and for displaying his "fury" during a parole interview. Thomas Connolly, a parole officer, wrote in 1981: "This writer is strongly opposed to parole release at this time... obviously he is quite dangerous and capable of horrible crimes."

Despite his negative evaluations, in March of 1987, Shawcross was declared "fit to re-enter society" and given early release. Another prescient parole officer, Robert T. Kent, wrote: "At the risk of being melodramatic, the writer considers this man to be possibly the most dangerous individual to be released to this community for many years."

The citizens of Watertown made it clear that this known sexual predator was unwelcome in their community, so he was sent to Binghamton, where he moved in with Rose Marie Walley, who had been a prison pen-pal for 12 years. Although she was still married to an older man, they had been separated for years. She was smitten with the convicted killer, and considered herself fortunate to have him at home with her at last. Binghamton's residents were no happier with him than Watertown's. They protested and insisted that Shawcross be moved.

He and Rose next moved to Delhi, but were asked to leave there too almost immediately. They fled to Fleishmanns, but within days were recognized, and an angry, torch-bearing mob led by the town's mayor assembled before his house, demanding that he leave town.

Finally the loathed vampire and his common-law wife were relocated by the Parole Board to Rochester, New York; this time, in hopes of avoiding another roust, it was a year before the local police were notified of the record of the murderer in their midst. Out of 1,300 parolees in the town of 250,000, 80 of them were killers. But despite this heavy case-load, the local parole officers managed to keep a relatively tight rein on Shawcross as he was eased into the community.

Shawcross got a job packing salads at night. So now he had a job, an apartment, and a faithful woman. Life should have been good—except for the time bomb ticking away in his own mind. It would have to be something. In this case it was a trivial matter that triggered his descent into a primitive state of uncontrollable *lustmord*. It was Christmas of 1987 when he asked his mother to come to Rochester to meet Rose, and she declined the invitation. Then he learned that the family had returned the gift he had sent them. This upset him more than it would the average person. He ranted and raved and rode for miles on his bike.

About that time, he met Clara Neal and started a long-term relationship with her, telling Rose that he was only being nice to Clara so he could borrow her car. He brought Clara to meet Rose, and often went out with the two of them. Remarkably for a man who was essentially sexually dysfunctional, he always managed to keep a woman at home, and still be on the lookout for someone to fool around with on the side. Even when he had two loyal women competing for his attention, he was still looking for someone else to slake his increasingly violent sexual hungers.

"After a while I found out what was going on in my mom's car and bedroom," Linda Neal told Jack Olsen. "He bit my mother. Not love bites—*hard*! I saw the marks on her breasts and upper arms and inner thighs. I saw him pinch her so hard she almost cried, and I saw him bite, too. From the first times she ever went out with him, she carried black-and-blue marks, bite marks, pinch marks."

The first to go was Dotsie Blackburn, a prostitute last seen strolling on Lake Avenue. The story Shawcross told of what happened to Dotsie has all of the features he has recited obsessively in case after case, so they are probably a mix of fact and fantasy.

At any rate, the story starts when he is just driving by in Clara's car, and Dotsie flags him down and asks if he wants a date. He tells her he wants to have mutual oral sex, and she gets in. She agrees and he pays her. She directs him to park his car in a dark spot behind a warehouse. He gets into position to enjoy the sex, and she bites him, drawing blood. In rage and pain, he reflexively bites her vagina while squeezing her throat. When she passes out, he lets her go and tries to stanch his own bleeding. He ties her up and drives her out of town to one of his favorite fishing spots along the Salmon River. When he threatens to rape her, she taunts him and calls him names. He strangles her to death to keep her quiet. Then he spends a couple of hours in the car with her before carrying the body down to the river and tossing it in.

It was the end of March before Dotsie's frozen body was found washed up in a culvert. The ice had preserved the remains well enough that upon close examination, the gnawed-upon portions of the vagina were observed.

Shawcross was under stress because he had been fired when his boss learned about his criminal record. He had become a regular, using the *nom d'amour* of "Joe" or "Mitch," trolling the Lake Avenue strip in Clara's car.

On July 8, 1989, he picked up Anna Steffen and drove to the river near Driving Park Bridge, where they had sex outside in the woods. The way Shawcross described it, several children were heard approaching, and he panicked out of fear of being found naked by children, and thus violating his probation. He urged the woman to be quiet but she kept talking, and he strangled her in the process of silencing her. The children passed them by without noticing them. Later he told police he "couldn't be bothered" to dispose of her body, and just threw it in the river and let it drift downstream, where it rapidly decomposed in the warmer weather, and was not found until October 21.

Perhaps sensing the dangers inherent in losing control, Shawcross forced himself to settle down and resist the temptation to prey on the populace. He got another job packing salads at night, he split his time between Rose and Clara, he went fishing and bike-riding, and he managed to go another whole year before he killed again.

It was around the end of July when he found himself fishing with 58-year-old Dorothy Keller. He had been paying the homeless woman to clean the apartment he shared with Rose, and had carried on an affair with her for the past two months. He was cuddling with her under a crude shelter when they argued. According to Shawcross, Keller threatened to tell Rose and Clara about their affair, so he beat her over the head with a log and she died instantly. He stuffed her body under a fallen tree, and returned several months later to interfere with the remains and to remove the skull, tossing it in the river.

In August, he finally made Rose an honest woman. They were married in front of the courthouse and exchanged rings. Although they had sent out a quantity of invitations, it was a rather forlorn affair. Nobody showed up except the boyfriend of one of Rose's daughters, and nobody sent any gifts.

On September 29, Shawcross picked up Patty Ives, another Lake Avenue prostitute. She offered him sex for $25, and they went to a construction site to lie down on the ground. Shawcross claims he caught her trying to snatch his wallet, so he knocked her down, raped her anally, and strangled her to death. He spent some time with her body, then stuffed the body under some construction materials and went home. It was a month before her desicated remains were found.

June Stotts was a young developmentally-disabled girl who often visited Rose at their home. Shawcross was out cruising around in Clara's car one warm November day when he saw June sitting by the river, so he stopped and asked her to go for a ride with him. They went to a beach area where they fed the birds and strolled around until they found a secluded spot, where they proceeded to enjoy consensual sex. All went well, according to Shawcross, until he made a harmless little joke about her not being a virgin. She started screaming, so he had to put his hand over her mouth to silence her. He silenced her to death, then gutted her with a knife, excising portions of her vagina and other organs, and either ate them, as he claimed, or effectively disposed of them, for they were never found. He covered the body with a blanket and threw some brush over it and left it there by the water.

It was November 5 when he picked up Maria Welch from Lake Avenue and took her to the banks of the Genesee River for oral sex. Once again, Artie's story starts with haggling over price, escalates with an attempted wallet theft, and climaxes with strangling to death. He dumped her body in some underbrush alongside the road.

The next murder was only five days later. This time he claimed he choked Frances Brown to death with his penis while she was giving him oral sex, and then continued to use her orally after her death. After he finished with the body he dumped it down an embankment, where trash covered it superficially.

On November 14, the *Rochester Times-Union* picked up the story of the eight murders—calling for the apprehension of "The Genesee River Killer" or "The Rochester Strangler." Shawcross was well aware of the media coverage. He often chatted with police officers at a donut shop about the progress they were making on the case. Nobody suspected "the fisherman."

In any case, a profiler looking at a string of prostitute slayings would not have suspected an ex-con with a record of killing children. And while Shawcross was indeed perpetrating a series of murders of prostitutes, he was also breaking the pattern with atypical murders. So the killing continued.

At the end of November, Shawcross was having a late dinner at a restaurant when Elizabeth Gibson got in his car to keep warm. After he found her there, the usual oral sex led to an attempted wallet grab, which led to strangling. This time the victim fought so hard she broke the gearshift on Clara's car. Fearing that the police might be on his tail, he drove out of the area to dispose of this body.

Two weeks later he picked up Darlene Trippi from Lake Avenue and drove her to a remote spot where they had sex, but the hapless prostitute made fun of Artie when he couldn't sustain an erection. She called him a little boy, so he had to choke her to shut her up. Her body was dumped in a wooded area.

A week before Christmas, even though the police were indeed out in force, right under their noses the serial predator picked up June Cicero, and drove her out by the Salmon River. Then when Shawcross revealed his inability to sustain an erection, the unfortunate prostitute mocked him. They enacted the whole familiar failed-sex scenario before he strangled her to death. He dumped her off the bridge, then came back two days later with a handsaw and cut the frozen vagina from the corpse. Shawcross later claimed that he ate it.

Finally, a young black prostitute named Felicia Stephens disappeared the day after Christmas. Shawcross first said he had no memory of this murder, but later he related a tale in which she stuck her head in the window of his car and he rolled the window up, catching her in it, then grabbed her and pulled her into the car and killed her instantly, without having sex. At any rate, he had no trouble remembering what became of his only black victim: he dumped her body in the same spot he used for Dotsie Blackburn and Jean Cicero.

Jean Cicero was probably his prettiest victim, and on January 3, 1990, Shawcross decided to visit her corpse. He drove Clara's car out to the bridge over the Salmon River and stopped to eat a salad he had brought from work.

The helicopter above that had been patrolling the Salmon River saw him parked there, just as they saw the outline of the body under the ice.

As soon as he noticed the copter, he got back in his car and drove to the nursing home where Rose worked. Police followed him there and took him in for questioning. Finally after 12 straight hours of interrogation, in which he identified photos of victims and confessed to their slaying, Arthur Shawcross was charged with ten murders.

At trial he pleaded not guilty by reason of insanity, and several prominent psychiatric experts testified, including Dr. Park Dietz for the prosecution and Dr. Dorothy Otnow Lewis for the defense.

Dr. Lewis testified that Arthur Shawcross had been "hideously traumatized" in his childhood, and cited post-traumatic stress disorder as a contributing factor to his behavior. She suspected neurological damage, noting hallmarks of temporal lobe seizures in the auras, amnesias, and somnolence surrounding the episodes of violence.

Regrettably, Dr. Lewis was unable to persuade the defense team to order the necessary testing to provide support for her suspicions in time for trial. Later on, a quantitative electroencephalogram did reveal spiking in the temporal and frontal lobes, confirming her suspicions. As Dr. Lewis later summed up her conclusions in personal correspondence, "I do believe that the combination of early extreme sexual abuse coupled with brain injury and seizures created in Shawcross a recipe for violence."

Though Dr. Robert Kraus did not testify, he spent 15 months on the case and prepared a report stating that Shawcross was "an emotionally unstable, learning disabled, genetically impaired, biochemically disordered, neurologically damaged individual, psychologically alienated from significant others during his entire life, venting his frustration and rage, mixed with fear and defiance, in a lifetime of ever more violent and destructive aggression, which ultimately turned to overpowering murderous fury." Kraus stipulated that the man was not normal, but neither was he insane, dissociated, or post-traumatic. Rather, he found Shawcross to be "extremely dangerous, impulsive, unpredictable, emotionally unstable, and subject to overpowering outbursts of murderous rage and temper in those situations he perceives as personally threatening, demeaning and humiliating."

It was Dr. Kraus who uncovered the pyroluria diagnosis, in which the blood is overloaded with kryptopyrroles, or "hidden fiery oils." Shawcross' blood contained ten times the high-normal level. Like porphyria, the so-called "vampire disease," pyroluria is a genetic disorder in the metabolism of blood. Dr. Kraus explains:

The presence of elevated kryptopyrroles in humans is described as similar to another medical condition called porphyria, a well known but also uncommon disorder associated with psychiatric disturbance (emotional instability, long histories of vague nervousness and in some cases severe psychosis which looks like a schizophrenic disorder).

The clinical correlates of abnormally elevated kryptopyrroles in humans are partial disorientation, abnormal EEG's, general "nervousness," depression, episodes of dizziness, chest and abdominal pains, progressive loss of ambition, poor school performance and decreased sexual potencies, all of which are found in the history of Arthur Shawcross.

Abnormal levels of kryptopyrroles also correlate with marked irritability, rages, terrible problems with stress control, diminished ability to control stress, inability to control anger once provoked, mood swings, poor memory, a preference for night time, violence and antisocial behavior...

Mr. Shawcross could never live very long in the unstructured setting of community life, and I believe he feels more secure in a prison setting. I also believe he knew he was completely out of control as the homicides increased and, without conscious awareness, desired to be apprehended and returned to prison. I do not believe his presence at the Salmon Creek Bridge was "accidental."

Arthur Shawcross was not "born bad," but the influences which shaped his life and behaviors were beyond his awareness and control. He was born with an unusual combination of predispositions to violence...

The recommendation I am attempting to make is that early recognition of future dangerousness by itself is obviously not a sufficient safeguard. But early recognition combined with a careful diagnostic evaluation of all risk factors for future dangerous behaviors and a realistic plan of corrective action/intervention offers, in my view, the best opportunity for protecting both the individuals at risk and the community.

Despite the best efforts of the defense in mitigating the liability of the unrepentant, if disordered, serial killer, it only took six-and-a-half hours for the jury to return a verdict of guilty to all charges, and to sentence him to 250 years in prison.

Rose Shawcross died of natural causes in the spring of 1977, and it was only a matter of time before her wayward husband married his longtime mistress, Clara Neal. They tied the knot on July 10, 1997, in a simple ceremony at Sullivan Correctional Institute in Fallsburg, New York. "It was nice and all," the blushing bride told the press. "It took ten years to make the grade," smiled the ever-loyal Clara, "but I finally made it."

Artwork and personal items from Shawcross have become a flashpoint in the movement toward enforcing and extending the unconstitutional Son of Sam laws, originally aimed at prohibiting felons from profiting from crime. Although prison art shows have been held for years, much has been made of the situation because of the Shawcross name. The first round of headlines appeared in September of 1999, when protests were made about Shawcross murderabilia being advertised for sale on eBay. Officials said that he had been mailing drawings and oil paintings to killer art dealers. In return, they would send him gifts like clothes and shoes instead of cash. Doing particularly well on the market at the time were his repetitive drawings of Marilyn Monroe and Dale Earnhardt.

Such artifacts had been traded in less publicized venues for years, but all of the publicity generated by the protests caught the attention of the prisons officials, who declared that Shawcross had not violated the state's Son of Sam law because he was not accused of benefiting from the actual crimes that led to his arrest. Nevertheless they found a way to punish him to satisfy the highly vocal critics. Shawcross was given two years in solitary confinement and he lost his art privileges for five years. On appeal, the solitary time was reduced to nine months.

Then in April of 2001, New York Governor George Pataki ordered that all violent criminals be banned from showing and selling their art at an annual exhibition by inmates organized by New York Department of Corrections. The order was prompted by the inclusion of ten paintings and sketches by the infamous killer. His paintings of Princess Diana, a unicorn with a Pegasus, and butterflies were selling for up to $500, of which the prisoner would keep half, with the remainder donated to the Crime Victims Board, the plaintiffs in the original Son of Sam litigation.

 Arthur Shawcross

LITTLE BOY PIE

For some, the question, "Does evil exist?" is philosophical. But for those who have confronted or been victimized by predatory pedophiles, there is no question at all. We are what we do.

    +Andrew Vachss

It's an innocent town of 56,000 nestled deep in the heartland, the wheatfields of Montana, the kind of place where a little boy has every expectation of being able to walk a couple of blocks to school without being eaten by a monstrous troll.

"A friend said this stuff doesn't happen in Great Falls," said Laura Detrick, who lived across the street from ten-year-old Zachary Ramsey, who was last seen walking his usual route to Whittier Elementary School at about 7:45 a.m. on February 6, 1996. "Well, I guess maybe it does," Ms. Detrick concluded bleakly. "Nobody is exempt."

"Zachary Ramsay was a special little boy with a spark in his eye and a great smile," said Diane Long, Whittier Elementary Principal. "Zach was a perky kid, a talented artist and a good citizen. He obviously had great potential and a very involved, caring mother."

One witness spotted a light-colored sedan as it nearly struck a young boy crossing the street on foot; another saw a hulking middle-aged white man in the alley where Zach was last seen the day he vanished; others reported seeing a frightened, crying boy running away from an angry man.

At about 11 a.m., Rachel Howard, Zach's mother, received a call from school officials. She knew there was no reason for her son to run away; he was not having any problems, and in fact was due to receive an award for his artwork that very day. She began to frantically search the neighborhood, and an hour later, called the police.

Detective Bill Bellusci headed up the investigation at the beginning. At the time, sex offenders were not required to register with police where they lived, nor were they evaluated to determine their risk for re-offending. But upon request, the state gave police a list of a dozen sex offenders living in Zach's neighborhood.

When he saw the name Nathaniel Bar-Jonah, he recalled a chilling interview with him, as Bar-Jonah protested his innocence in the sexual assault of an eight-year-old boy right before Christmas in 1993, assuring Bellusci that if he had fondled the boy, he would have also killed him.

"Bar-Jonah stood out in my mind because I'd worked with him before," Bellusci told the *Great Falls Tribune*. "I knew he had been violent before and I knew he was still active."

When Bar-Jonah arrived in Great Falls in 1991, the local probation office had been alerted by their counterparts in Massachusetts to Bar-Jonah's past criminal violence against young boys. "The day Zach turned up missing I went over to Nate's place," Bellusci said. "He wasn't there. The house was dark."

Meanwhile, police and FBI agents were following tips from across the country. When police finally got back to Bar-Jonah, he lawyered up, referring them to his attorney, and there the matter rested. "I don't know if we dropped it or we overlooked something," Police Chief Bob Jones said years later. "We were going to get back to it, and we didn't."

Bar-Jonah and Zachary had both attended the Mount Olive Christian Fellowship Church. Bar-Jonah had also been involved in the Christian youth group, Royal Rangers, through Central Assembly of God, and Zachary had attended the Royal Rangers in nearby Fairfield. Bar-Jonah also might have had contact with Zachary through the Whittier Elementary In-School Scouts program.

In a choice of vehicle oddly echoing the Shawcross case, Bar-Jonah was driving his mother's off-white 1987 Toyota Corolla around the time of the crime. This would be a vehicle consistent with the witness' description of the close encounter with the little boy.

Bellusci took a photo of Bar-Jonah around Whittier to see if any of the teachers or children had seen him recently, and asked Zach's mom if she knew him. He asked County Attorney Brant Light to get a search warrant to enter Bar-Jonah's home, but the request was never brought to a judge. "We just had nothing to tie it to him," Bellusci said. "There were a lot of other sex offenders living around there at the time."

One of the most tantalizing leads came in within the first few months. A known sex offender was driving a semi across the Canadian border, when he mentioned Zachary to a border patrol officer, who took him into custody and contacted local authorities. The FBI searched his semi, plucking at the carpet fibers for clues. Under questioning, the trucker actually confessed to kidnapping Zachary. It took another month of police work to prove that he was lying. At the time of the abduction, his truck had actually been broken down in Missoula.

"If you don't clear something like this in 48 hours, you get all these calls," Sgt. John Cameron said. "There were thousands of rumors and thousands of bogus tips." After the story aired on *America's Most Wanted*, FBI agents chased leads across the country, going to New York, Canada and even to Italy, where Zachary was reportedly spotted.

"Every time we got any kind of lead we followed it as far as we could," said FBI special agent James Wilson. "Although there were lulls, there was no lulls when you had something to go on. We followed (tips) across the country. Even in other countries, someone would spot a kid who looked like Zachary Ramsay. Each one of those we were able to verify that they were not Zachary Ramsay."

As the momentum of the investigation expired, in the absence of viable leads, the child's bereaved mother was treated as a suspect by default. "It's not unusual that we'd look at the parents first," Chief Jones said. "The FBI more or less instructed Detective Bellusci to look at the parents."

Franz Ramsay was Zachary's father. Since he had been stationed in Colorado Springs, Colorado, he was ruled out as a suspect. But Rachel Howard's polygraph tests were inconclusive. And her demeanor was suspiciously stoic.

"We couldn't eliminate her," Bellusci said. "People react differently to tragedy. Her reaction was to stay strong." Then shortly after Zach disappeared, Rachel Howard's boyfriend shot himself in the chest. Investigators tried to connect this tragedy to the little boy. Perhaps the boyfriend had known something and tried to kill himself under the weight of his guilt. But no evidence to support this theory could be found.

On the first anniversary of Zach's murder, FBI and police staked out his mother's home, hoping to no avail to catch her visiting his grave. "The family was put through every investigative resource we had and we weren't able to link Rachel Howard to anything," said Detective Tim Theisen.

In the fall of 1997, Bar-Jonah's roommate contacted police. Notes show that Sherri Deitrich called Detective Bellusci, and arranged a meeting. But in her interview, she was hysterical and frightened from a fight with Bar-Jonah. In what must have seemed a colossal waste of time to the weary but dutiful officers, she jumped from topic to topic, rambling on at length about her truck, and giving police nothing whatsoever to go on. Her statements, and her potential as a valuable witness, were to be buried until police found her in Idaho in 2001.

The frightened woman had become suspicious of Bar-Jonah and years later, she told police that when she cleaned the apartment, she found boy's clothing in a plastic bag in Bar-Jonah's closet. It was a blue jacket with green sleeves, jeans, briefs, socks and a pair of black tennis shoes covered with dirt. Zachary had been wearing a blue denim jacket with green sleeves over a blue football jersey with his name on the back in gold letters, stone-washed blue jeans and black high-top tennis shoes. Sherri Deitrich had quite a tale to tell, but it would have to wait.

Bellusci was transferred to another division in 2000, and the cold case of the disappearance of Zachary Ramsey was taken over by Sergeant John Cameron and Detective Tim Theisen, who admitted that all roads led to

Bar-Jonah; nothing had been turned up to eliminate him as Zachary's abductor, and in fact over the years more evidence had piled up against him. "There's no excuse," Cameron said. "He was a suspect by day two. They knocked on his door, and they didn't go back."

Nathaniel Benjamin Levi Bar-Jonah's given name was David Paul Brown. He had been raised a Catholic, in a family who had always struggled just to stay afloat. For the first nine years of his life, they lived in subsidized housing, only moving to a nicer home in Bonnette Acres on the Connecticut border of Massachusetts as he hit pre-puberty.

With a brother and sister nine and eight years older, David spent many years as virtually an only child. He had few friends and rarely dated.

"He was a little different from the rest of us," recalled Gene Stark, one of his classmates. His few male friends also were loners. A camera club member, he contributed photos to the school yearbook. He also helped with fund-raising efforts for shop, one of his favorite classes. He worked in the Bartlett High School cafeteria and in the print shop.

Neighbors found it curious that young David seemed to avoid friendships with kids his own age, and preferred the company of younger children. Though he would join in the occasional street game, the odd chubby boy with mismatched eyes was neither graceful nor athletic, and in fact injured his right leg in a sledding accident, an accident which left him with a disability that later surfaced as a strange concatenation of leg pain with an uncontrollable, dissociated episode of violence.

Though life in Bonnette Acres was a step up from the projects, he found it hate-filled and racist. "Blacks didn't last long in that neighborhood," Bar-Jonah reminisced in a letter to the *Great Falls Tribune*. "We were threatened for having a black Bible student living with us."

His father, Phil Brown, was a mechanic who retired early because of heart problems, and spent nearly seven years at home before his death in 1974. By all accounts, he was a harsh disciplinarian. His mother, Tyra Brown, was a stabilizing force in the boy's life. Friends said he never wanted to shame her, but described their relationship in terms of love-hate.

"He didn't realize all that his mother had done for him," said Sherri Deitrich. "He felt he wasn't given the support from his parents when something happened to him as a child." Years later in a psychiatric evaluation, he recalled choking a young girl while his mother screamed at him to stop. He was only six years old at the time.

No charges were filed in 1973, when 14-year-old David Brown was caught in a Massachusetts cemetery, lying in wait for two young boys he had attempted to lure there. For days, he had been scrawling menacing messages in chalk on the sidewalk outside the home of Alan and Kevin Dupont, then aged nine and ten.

Next a letter came to them in the mail, with words cut out of magazines telling the boys to come to the cemetery and get $20: "DON'T TELL ANYONE!" Of course, the boys told their mother, Dolly LeBlanc, who promptly called police. They found David Brown lurking in the cemetery. However, Ms. LeBlanc declined to press charges. Whether she was merely hoping to minimize the deleterious impact on her children, or whether the juvenile pedophile had managed to ingratiate himself or intimidate her, will never be known for sure. He was later to demonstrate a marked predilection for witness-tampering.

In 1975, the budding vampire graduated from a vo-tech high school, then spent a few months studying journalism and the ministry in Pennsylvania and South Carolina, before returning home to mother.

That same year, 17-year-old David Brown was driving his mother's car one winter day in Webster, Massachusetts, when he flashed a badge on an eight-year-old boy walking to school, and ordered Richard O'Connor into the car for a trip to the police station. But the fake cop drove right past the police station; he drove all the way out to Webster Lake, where he forced the child to strip, and wrapped a seat belt around his neck, repeatedly choking and releasing the child, while he wept and begged for his life. Finally he released little Richard, who was hospitalized because the blood vessels in his neck had ruptured. Brown admitted his guilt and was sentenced to one year probation.

Two years later, Brown was working at a fast-food restaurant for a living when according to Massachusetts police records, on a September evening, dressed like a state trooper and once again flashing a badge, he accosted Billy Benoit and Al Enrickias, ages 13 and 14, outside a Shrewsbury movie theater, and ordered them into his mother's car. Threatening the boys with a knife, he handcuffed them and drove them to a rural spot outside Charlton, where he had set up a tent.

"I took the larger boy into the woods," he confessed to police. "I started to strangle him, I guess mainly because he could identify me, and I wanted to kill him." Enrickias played possum, and when the predator moved on to his friend, he saw his chance and ran for his life.

When police caught up with Brown, he had the younger boy in the trunk of his mother's car. Billy's face was swollen and discolored from strangulation.

Brown pleaded guilty to two counts of kidnapping and attempted murder. A psychiatrist pronounced him "dangerously disturbed," and he drew 18-to-20 in the state prison system. He spent less than two years in prison before being transferred to Massachusetts Treatment Center for the Sexually

Dangerous in Bridgewater, where he spent the next 11 years.

At some point during his stay at Bridgewater, he left behind his white-bread identity as David Paul Brown, assuming Nathaniel Benjamin Levi Bar-Jonah as the most pretensiously Jewish-sounding name he could think of. He wanted people to think he was Jewish, because he wanted to experience being discriminated against and persecuted.

His psychiatric evaluations revolved around dire themes. "Mr. Brown's sexual fantasies outline methods of torture extending to dissection and cannibalism," wrote one of his therapists in 1980. "He expresses a curiosity about the taste of human flesh."

As the years passed, psychologists continued to regard him as a menace. Dr. Robert Levy warned in 1983 that without long-term help, he was almost certain to commit other sexual offenses. Seven years later in 1990 another psychologist, Dr. Leonard Bard, reported that the inmate had made only minimal progress. Citing "a profound lack of feelings of effectiveness and control," Bard noted that the inmate had "a rich fantasy life distinguished by themes of revenge and rage."

Contradicting the negative evaluations in his jacket were several psychologists who testified that Bar-Jonah had improved markedly. Dr. Eric Sweitzer stated that he was a changed person from the man who had kidnapped the two boys years earlier. He described him as "a far more thoughtful, insightful, controlled and wiser 33-year-old," and declared that he was no longer sexually dangerous. Dr. Richard Ober testified that the inmate had exhibited "increased self-esteem and social relationships," and he, too, declared Bar-Jonah to be no longer sexually dangerous.

Bar-Jonah's lawyer, Richard Boulanger, argued that his client had "resolved the underlying psychological conflicts, which resulted in the commission of crimes... Rather than being an impulsive individual, he is a controlled, thoughtful person. I find that the petitioner does not require the secure setting of the treatment center."

Despite the two evaluations from state psychiatrists urging Judge Walter E. Steele *not* to release Bar-Jonah, the judge released him anyway, finding that even though Bar-Jonah had been deemed sexually dangerous, he had never even been charged with a sexual offense; he had pled guilty to assault and kidnapping. At that time, Massachusetts law decreed that any time spent in the sex-offender facility was considered part of jail time. Once a prisoner's sentence was served, he had the right to ask to be released from the sex-offender facility as well.

Barely six weeks after Bar-Jonah's release, Nancy Surprise stopped off at the post office in Oxford, Massachusetts, leaving her seven-year-old son briefly alone in the car. Upon her return, to her horror, the young matron found a 280-pound sex offender sitting on top of her little boy, practically crushing him. She ordered Bar-Jonah out of her car, and as the disturbed predator withdrew, she dragged her son away and ran for help. By the time the police arrived, they were both crying hysterically.

Bar-Jonah was arrested on assault charges, and freed without bail. Several days later, the Surprise family reported seeing him hanging out near their house, and prosecutors asked to have him returned to jail. The judge refused.

The next day, Judge Sarkis Teshoian made the decision to send the recidivist sex-beast somewhere far, far away from the good people of Massachusetts. Without being informed of the defendant's troubling history, the judge accepted a guilty plea to several charges, including intent to commit a felony, and approved a plan packing Bar-Jonah off to the wilds of Montana, on two years' probation. When pressured by reporters from the Associated Press years later, the judge responded defensively that the deal was "an appropriate sentence based on the information available at the time."

In response to written questions from the Associated Press, Worcester County District Attorney John Conte, whose office handled the Massachusetts cases against Bar-Jonah, responded that prosecution of the assault on the Surprise boy "would have been difficult, if not impossible" because the mother refused to let her son to testify, and because both she and her son failed to identify Bar-Jonah within hours of the incident.

"If Mrs. Surprise had been willing to permit her son to testify, I expect that the case would have gone to trial," Conte said. But given the facts of the case, "we saw no cause to object to Mr. Bar-Jonah's transfer."

The formal terms of the plea bargain specified that Bar-Jonah would receive an open-ended sentence to the state prison in Concord, which in turn would be suspended with the requirement that he undergo immediate psychiatric treatment. He would be placed on two years probation, but the probationary fee would be waived, on the condition that he leave the Commonwealth of Massachusetts and move to Montana.

"He was dumped on us," said Montana prosecutor Brant Light bluntly. "And we are deeply offended by that." Light called Bar-Jonah's criminal history a "clear red flag" that he was too dangerous to be released.

"I think clearly the prosecutor and police were aware of his past and wanted to get rid of him," Light said in a telephone interview with the *Washington Post*. "When his mother said she'd take him, they said, 'Good-bye, see ya!'"

Bar-Jonah's older brother, Bob Brown, already lived in Great Falls, and their mother, Tyra Brown, was planning to move here. In fact, according to the attorney for the Surprise family, Tyra Brown was "the instigator behind the deal." John Towns remembers the police chief telling him, "We have a bad apple here. Attempted murder and sexual abuse in Shrewsbury."

Even though Bar-Jonah had been charged with breaking and entering and assault, and even though he had a record of preying on young boys, the state of Massachusetts "never laid a glove on him" after he was picked up. "The question is, why not?" asked Towns.

According to Brant Light, the reason is obvious: Massachusetts simply wanted to get rid of their troublemaker. "They just said, 'Get out of our jurisdiction.'"

"That's where the system really fell apart," Light said. "A guy who just gets out of a mental institution for assaulting boys, and then he assaults another, and you decide 'Let's give him probation and make him move to Montana'?"

"On their own initiative, they could have energetically prosecuted that man, filed a motion to have him committed for evaluation," John Towns told the *Great Falls Tribune*. The case against him "should have had a prosecutorial life of its own and it did not. We're not talking about some little sneak thief's case falling through the cracks," he added. "He should not have walked away from it. But he did."

On Oct. 2, 1991 Bar-Jonah reported to probation officer Mike Redpath, in Great Falls, Montana. Redpath had no idea who he was. "He just showed up," Redpath told the *Great Falls Tribune*. "They sent him out here but didn't tell us. We didn't know anything about him."

Weeks later, he received a "pretty thin file" that revealed only that Bar-Jonah was on two years probation for the assault on the Surprise child, but other than that, he later described it as "very inadequate." Redpath called Bar-Jonah back in to discuss his file.

"He divulged to me that he was in Bridgewater and all the other things," Redpath said. "I was taken aback by that, because it was not included in the packet of information." Montana authorities wrote to Massachusetts for more history and psychiatric records on their uninvited guest. However, the Massachusetts probation office told the Associated Press it had no record of sending any additional information on Bar-Jonah to Montana.

Montana Corrections squared off against Massachusetts Probation: "Montana officials were unaware of what occurred in the Massachusetts courts," the Montana Corrections Department said in a statement, "and did not have a complete record to evaluate Bar-Jonah."

"If there were any problems, and the state of Montana felt that they didn't have adequate information," countered Coria Holland, spokeswoman for the Massachusetts Commissioner of Probation, "they shouldn't have accepted the case."

The state of Montana duly kept Bar-Jonah on probation for 21 months, until August 19, 1993. But he never received the counseling that Judge Teshoian had ordered under the terms of his probation.

It was almost Christmas, four months after his probation expired, when he was arrested for sexually assaulting an eight-year-old boy. While he was in jail, he met Keith "Doc" Bauman, who had been arrested on charges of sexual assault and unlawful transactions with minors. Years later, a search of Bar-Jonah's home produced a letter from Bauman thanking him for the delicious "deer burgers" he had brought him.

Tyra Brown bailed her aging son out of jail, and hired a lawyer. The child's mother decided she did not want to let her son testify, so charges were dropped.

When he first moved to Great Falls, Bar-Jonah had moved in with Bob and Jill Brown, his brother and sister-in-law, then later he moved in with his mother. After that he lived alone or with a roommate. All told, during his eight-year tenure in Great Falls, he lived in four different homes. He had dreamed of opening a general store, but fell back on working at fast-food restaurants, as he had done before his arrest in Massachusetts.

He shoveled shrimp at Skipper's Seafood, offered fries with your order at Hardee's, and passed out cookies to your kids at Fuddruckers. "He was strange," said Dan Binstock, Fuddruckers owner. "He was pretty isolated and didn't say much. He made other employees nervous because he would sit and stare at them for long periods of time."

Bar-Jonah was dating a woman he met while working at Hardee's, Pamela Clark, and before long he asked her to marry him. "He was 40 and had never been married," observed Sherri Deitrich, who would later be his roommate. "He desperately wanted a normal lifestyle. He wanted to get married and have kids."

In Bar-Jonah's apartment were thousands of photographs of young boys. Some were innocent reprints from magazines; others were apparently snapped at local playgrounds. He was a regular customer of the Great Falls elementary school and middle school yearbooks, buying one for every year he lived there.

He worked odd jobs around the neighborhood, shoveling walks and mowing lawns. Sometimes he would barricade himself in his bedroom for hours, or stroll aimlessly along the Missouri River alone. He prided himself on his Christianity and his cooking, and he collected "Star Wars" memorabilia.

He also collected dolls, comic books, trains and stuffed animals. He especially cherished his teddy bear collection, perhaps because his mother sometimes called him her Teddy. His garage was described by one neighbor as a child's paradise, filled to the brim with toys to light the eyes of the children he would attract when he had a garage sale or hawked his wares at the local flea markets.

Years later, Pamela Clark would reveal the sinister side of these garage sales and flea markets: under the table, this pedophile was selling pictures, magazines and games depicting torture and murder.

He joined his family in attending church at the Central Assembly of God. He had asked Pastor Alan Warneke if he could be a leader of the church's youth group, the Royal Rangers. When an alert police officer quietly advised the pastor about Bar-Jonah's past crimes against children, Warneke made a nearly-complicitous decision to allow his sinful parishioner to participate in the youth group, though he decreed that he could not be a leader, nor should he be left alone with youths.

"We had heard of his past and based on that we did not give him a position with any of our children's ministries," Warneke said. "To the degree that I knew Nate, he was always a pleasant guy to be around. He was always generous and always willing to share what little he had."

Bar-Jonah was able to meet many people his own age at church, at work, and at the flea markets, but he spent most of his free time with their kids. "Children liked him and he liked younger children," Sherri Deitrich told a reporter. "He said if he ever got married and had children, he would raise them until they turned into teen-agers, and then he would make them legally adults because they are such pains."

Sharon Freeman shared a back yard with Bar-Jonah, and her ten-year-old son played football and chess with him. Freeman and her son went out with him several times—for Bible studies, Christian concerts and other wholesome family occasions. "I thought he was a nice man," she said. "I thought he was really friendly."

Julie Watkins met Bar-Jonah at church. She and her eight-year-old son would have cookies with him, and Bar-Jonah would drive her son to Sunday school. "He's kind of a strange-looking person," she reflected later. "He just didn't fit in. He didn't show a lot of emotion. He didn't smile or get angry, he was just always somewhere in the middle. It seemed a little odd."

Despite the misgivings she later expressed about the man's oddness, occasionally Ms. Watkins would even leave her little boy in the care of this "strange-looking" convicted pedophile.

It was after such an occasion in 1994 that Watkins brought her son to the police with charges that while the parents were in Helena for a Christmas party, Bar-Jonah had fondled the boy. He was arrested, and prosecutors pressed charges, hoping for a plea bargain. Bar-Jonah contacted friends of the little boy and urged them to testify that the child was a liar. This resulted in additional charges of witness-tampering.

A psychiatric evaluation by the Massachusetts State Hospital reports that on November 11, 1994, Bar-Jonah complained of a severe pain in his leg, which he claimed stemmed from his childhood injury. "When the pain gets too bad," the report clinically stated, "he sort of steps aside and watches himself behave violently."

Then on February 6 of 1996, little Zachary Ramsey disappeared while walking to school.

Police analysts later observed that during that period of time, a number of factors had conspired to raise Bar-Jonah's stress level, making an episode of violence more likely to occur:

+ A family member recently had died.

+ Pamela Clark had left him to move in with her ex-boyfriend.

+ His car was towed for vehicle violations.

+ He was awaiting disposition of charges from 1994.

+ His protective mother had been out of town for three weeks, and her stabilizing influence was needed.

+ Employment records at the Hardee's reveal that Bar-Jonah hadn't shown up for work February 4, 5 or 6.

Instead of going to work, Bar-Jonah had rented a car, and put 510 miles on it in a couple of days without leaving town. Although he was in debt at the time, and had the use of his mother's car, he spent $175 on the rental. The car was returned at 3:30 PM on February 5. Police believe Bar-Jonah stalked Zachary in the rental car, planning ahead to use his mother's car for the actual abduction.

Medical records at the Doctors Convenience Center across the street from his duplex reveal that Bar-Jonah came in at 2:20 p.m. the day Zachary vanished, complaining of a recurrence of the pain in his leg, as well as a dislocated left index finger. Police sources later observed that this type of finger injury often occurs to a police officer when handcuffing a struggling suspect.

On February 7, Bar-Jonah took several taxi rides and the checks written to pay for them were altered. The dates were erased and new dates were written in to indicate he took the taxis on February 6. These checks were the only ones he kept.

Police took these manipulations of vehicular data as evidence that Bar-Jonah was making a ham-handed attempt to deconstruct the eyewitness testimony placing him in the pale car that was seen nearly hitting the little boy on February 6.

One of the taxi trips he took the day after Zach vanished was to the dry cleaners, where he left his police jacket to be cleaned and to have its zipper repaired. The bloodstain on the sleeve, however, couldn't be removed, though after dry-cleaning it was no longer useful for DNA matching.

Before February 1996, Bar-Jonah had frequently purchased food. But his check registry abruptly showed a marked departure from that consistent pattern. For the month of February, the only check he wrote for food was one for a Subway sandwich. What could he have been eating?

Unfortunately, these suspicious circumstances, along with Detective Bellusci's chilling memory of his conversations with Bar-Jonah on the 1993 molestation case, were not noted at that time, and further revelations about what happened to Zachary would only be made after more crimes were perpetrated and prosecuted.

Untouched in the midst of the far-ranging investigation into the abduction of Zachary Ramsey, Bar-Jonah was free to pursue his special interests. In the fall of 1996 after nearly three years, no plea bargain had been reached on the molestation of the Watkins boy, so after speedy trial motions were granted, all charges were dropped.

Debby Cotes met Bar-Jonah when she and her ten-year-old son lost their home in a fire in 1996, and she recalls that on Christmas, he brought them spaghetti, stew meat, chili, and a pie—all with meat that tasted a little strange. He boasted to her that he had slaughtered, butchered and wrapped the meat himself.

That first Christmas without her son, Rachel Howard saw that there were some small toys and a set of brushes and paints awaiting Zachary under the tree. All to no avail, for no trace of her little boy would ever be seen again.

In August of 1997, Bar-Jonah rented a booth at the American Antique Mall, the better to display his teddy bears and trains, his dolls and comic books.

That same month, the free-spirited Sherri Deitrich was muscling a truck through Montana on her way from Colorado, when she ran out of gas and money at the same time in Great Falls. She went to the American Antique Mall to liquidate some of her belongings, and met Bar-Jonah there. He invited her to dinner at his house, and offered her a place to stay. His mother had been living with him in the duplex, he explained. She had just moved into her own place across town, and he could use the company.

At first, Deitrich recalls, Bar-Jonah was the perfect host, cooking her dinner, loaning her his car, always quite the gentleman. But when his mother left town to return to Massachusetts that fall, he underwent a drastic change.

"Within the first week he started becoming angry," Deitrich said. "He didn't have his security net there to keep him in control. Within a very short period, I saw a definite change."

Bar-Jonah even told Deitrich he might become violent. "He was concerned about putting himself in the position where he would hurt other people," she said.

Bar-Jonah often talked to Deitrich about Zachary, always referring to him as if he were dead, rather than missing, saying he had played games with him and waved to him from his window. He admitted he saw the boy at the end of the alley and waved to him on the day Zach went missing.

Bar-Jonah also knew accurate information about the boy's family, including the fact that Rachel Howard's boyfriend had moved out two days before that fatal day.

Bar-Jonah told Deitrich that a policeman who was a friend of his friend, Doc Bauman, had been spending time with Zachary and had probably abducted him. Bauman has related that he has no such friend. Bar-Jonah told Deitrich that children were taught to trust policemen and that Zach must have been kidnapped by a police officer.

Sherri listened to her roommate's discursive ruminations and put up with his obvious eccentricity, but when Bar-Jonah commenced throwing things at her, she finally decided to go to the police. Unfortunately, she was too upset to make a coherent complaint. Finally, Bar-Jonah evicted her, claiming he had two video cameras that had caught her going into his bedroom. She left town immediately. "There was an anger that started bubbling up inside him," she said. "I was given a couple of weeks to see that anger."

In the fall of 1997, dressed as a police officer, Bar-Jonah approached the home of a Great Falls family and knocked on the door. When the young woman answered the door, he asked to take her five-year-old son to the police station. The alarmed mother refused, and slammed the door in his face. The timid predator went away, and the mother called police immediately. Charges of impersonating an officer were filed, and he was awaiting trial when he was caught doing it again.

In the summer of 1998, Bar-Jonah's home was graced with a new roommate: a 19-year-old boy named Casey Sullivan. And throughout that summer, there were three Native American boys who would come downstairs to visit Nathaniel Bar-Jonah almost daily: a 15-year-old boy, his six-year-old brother, and their nine-year-old cousin. His apartment was always open to them, and was well-stocked with potato chips, hot dogs and the apparatus required to keep three boys there, munching away happily while being groomed by the pedophile. He wore only his underwear in the apartment, and was always snapping photos of them while they slept on his couch, lay in his bed, wrestled in his living room, and played outside in the yard. He took them to the State Fair, the ice cream shop, and the movies they wanted to see. He bought them lunch at Hardee's and McDonald's and the Pickle Barrel.

At first it was fun, but eventually their friendship soured when Bar-Jonah predictably began to perpetrate. As the story came out later in courtroom testimony, one day Bar-Jonah handcuffed the eldest boy to a pole hidden under stairs outside his apartment and left him there. Another time, he sat on him wearing only boxer shorts.

One night, the boys were staying over in his apartment when the eldest was locked in Bar-Jonah's bedroom with him. "He told me to take my pants off," the boy later told the court. "I was scared." The boy, who is mildly retarded, wept as he related what had happened to him after he took his clothes off. "He touched my butt and... in the front." Then, according to testimony, Bar-Jonah stripped and told the boy to touch his genitals. Suddenly, the boy's nine-year-old cousin knocked on the door, and Bar-Jonah unlocked it.

The cousin said Bar-Jonah made him remove his clothes and then choked him. "He touched me on my penis and on my butt and he also tried to touch me again," said the nine-year-old. "I moved his hand and went upstairs."

On another occasion, Bar-Jonah turned to a page from the Book of Gacy and asked the nine-year-old boy if he wanted to play the "rope game." Standing behind the boy, Bar-Jonah placed the rope around his neck.

"It was like a pulley, and he would just start pulling it," the boy later testified. "I started choking and I went up... I was scared, I thought I might die."

Then Bar-Jonah eased back on the rope and the boy slipped the noose, and ran crying to his father. His father went downstairs and pounded on Bar-Jonah's door, but when nobody responded, unaccountably he left and never went back.

The six-year-old also reported in his limited and hesitant manner that Bar-Jonah had touched him in front and in back, in a way he did not like. And his brother confirmed his story, saying he had watched.

The boys were ashamed and afraid to come forward to report these criminal sexual assaults to police, so charges were not filed until July of 2000. At that time it became a little more clear why they had remained silent, as once again Bar-Jonah would be charged with witness-tampering.

On December 15, 1999, an off-duty Great Falls police officer spotted Bar-Jonah decked out in full police regalia, lurking around Lincoln Elementary School, armed with pepper spray, a fake badge, a toy pistol, and a real stun gun. A quick check of his record showed that he was awaiting trial on charges of impersonating a police officer in 1997. He was taken into custody immediately and charged with impersonating an officer and carrying a concealed weapon.

A search of his apartment yielded 28 boxes of evidence, much of which linked him to the 1996 disappearance of Zachary Ramsey, as well as the more recent molestation of the three Native American boys. As these concurrent investigations gained momentum, charges on the 1997 and 1999 officer-impersonation cases were eventually dropped, over legal "strategic concerns," according to prosecutor Brant Light.

Among the evidentiary items seized by police in the search of Bar-Jonah's home were a book on autoerotic asphyxia, several books on ropes and knots, and two three-ring binders filled with roughly 14,000 pictures. Most of them were snapshots Bar-Jonah had taken. Others were magazine clippings. The pictures were taped onto fluorescent paper and inserted into plastic sleeves, like those used to hold sports cards. Most of the photos were of young boys, but a few celebrities appeared, including the outrageous cross-dresser, Dennis Rodman.

Prominently featured in the photo albums were the three Native American boys Bar-Jonah had assaulted in 1998, and the photos sparked the investigation that brought the offenses to light.

In July of 2000, the incarcerated defendant was charged with multiple felonies involving the sexual assaults on the three boys, along with a separate charge of kidnapping involving the eldest, stemming from the time he locked the boy in his bedroom.

Casey Sullivan had come forward to support the nine-year-old's story, and turned state's witness against Bar-Jonah. He had witnessed the "rope game." Bar-Jonah had tied the boy's hands with a yellow nylon rope, Sullivan told police; and he had heard the boy choking from another room.

On December 20, 2000, a year after police arrested him and searched his home, charges were filed against Bar-Jonah in the abduction and murder of Zachary Ramsey; he was arraigned January 11, 2001, and entered a not-guilty plea on January 15.

The charges rocked Montana, to say the least. In the 46-page affidavit were the most horrifying allegations, with evidence supporting charges that Bar-Jonah had kidnapped little Zach, killed him, and eaten those of his remains he hadn't fed to others.

Among the papers seized under the search warrant was a list of 22 names. There were no spaces between the words on the list, and according to Pamela Clark, that is exactly how Bar-Jonah always wrote when he was angry—a peculiar trait that hints at a possible neurological defect. Zachary Ramsey's name was on that list, as were most of Bar-Jonah's known victims.

And then there were his journals, where he gleefully penned such memorable comments as: "Lunch is served on the patio with roasted child." This arresting detail caught the eye of investigators, as Doc Bauman had told them that Bar-Jonah had suggested they eat the special "deer burgers" he brought them *out on the patio.* And these odd-tasting "deer burgers" had come from a man who had never owned a real gun or a hunting license in his life.

Most of the sensitive portions of Bar-Jonah's journal were encrypted, and had to be decoded by the FBI. Others were just coyly phrased, like "barbecue bee sum young guy." In the encrypted portions, he wrote about cooking little boy pie, little boy stew, and "Christmas dinner for two." Investigators believe the latter notation pertained to the dinner he had shared with Debby Cotes and her ten-year-old son. So this, then, is what happened to the little boy last seen running from the angry man in 1996.

While the Zachary Ramsey case was breaking wide open, there was a new development in the case of the assaults on the three boys. On February 8, 2001, Brant Light announced that Bar-Jonah had written a letter threatening his former roommate and asking him to lie for him regarding his eyewitness of the "rope game." Bar-Jonah chided the youngster that he had lied for him before, and charged he "owed him one." Then Bar-Jonah dramatically suggested that if anything happened to him, his blood would be on Sullivan's hands. Two counts of witness tampering were added to his charges for this letter, and for another letter he had sent Sullivan the previous September that only came to light after the witness came forward upon the second offense.

An affidavit filed with the tampering charges stated that Bar-Jonah had written letters to the boys. In one, he asked the youngest boy to draw a picture of himself and send it to him, so Bar-Jonah could hang it on his cell wall. Regrettably, no tampering charges could be filed in that instance, because the boys had yet to be named as victims.

Bar-Jonah's brother also talked to the boys and their parents, saying that the police and social services might talk to them about Bar-Jonah and warning them that the police might make them say something that wasn't true.

February 11, 2002 the trial commenced in Butte, Montana, on the charges involving the three boys, and the constant perp faced a jury for the first time in his life. Midway through the trial, as the heartbreaking testimony unfolded, in histrionics worthy of Arthur Shawcross, he complained of chest pains and had to be whisked to the emergency room. Not surprisingly, no cardiac pathology was found, he was returned to court, and the trial ground on inexorably toward the verdict.

After only six hours of deliberations, Nathaniel Bar-Jonah was found guilty of fondling the eldest boy and locking him in his bedroom, and guilty of perpetrating the "rope game" on the nine-year-old boy. The jury deadlocked on a second charge of sexual assault, and returned a not-guilty verdict on the charge of fondling the youngest boy. Facing his fate alone, without family or friends in his corner, Bar-Jonah sat with his hands in his lap, impassively listening to the verdict.

Bar-Jonah's trial on the Ramsay murder was set for October 8, 2002. While prosecutor Brant Light put together the State's case, Rachel Howard desperately clung to the belief that her son was still alive, and seized upon a video of a boy resembling Zachary as "proof," closing her ears to reports from investigators that the boy had been ruled out.

One week before trial, with a half-million dollars invested in preparation, prosecutors were putting in 12-hour-days, when suddenly the case fell apart. Rachel Howard delivered a letter to their office, stating that she was still upset at being considered a suspect in 1996, and setting limitations on her testimony.

Later that night she and her lawyer were seen dining out with Bar-Jonah's defense attorneys and investigators. Though this was neither illegal nor improper, still, it was unheard of. "Usually, victims don't want anything to do with defense attorneys," Light told the *Great Falls Tribune*.

The next day, Howard came to Light's office and accused Investigators Detective Tim Theisen and Sergeant John Cameron of trying to silence her and force her to lie.

"She indicated that she didn't believe he did it and she was told to keep her mouth shut, and if she didn't, she would be charged with a crime," Light said. "That was really upsetting."

"This was out of the blue," said Theisen.

Cameron said he understood Howard's dilemma, and sympathized with her. "If you're a mother and you don't have a body, it's a lot easier to believe he's alive than the grim reality."

But as for her charges, "It's ridiculous. It's false. We did nothing but treat her with respect."

"These guys did a hell of a job," said Chief Bob Jones, clarifying that their interviews had all been taped, and clearly demonstrated that no witness had been influenced, much less pressured to lie.

Light's strategy called for Howard's testimony as to what Zach was wearing when last seen. To establish the facts, he wanted her to simply state that she had not seen or heard from her son in six years. "It's sad testimony, but it's testimony we needed," he said.

However, Rachel Howard insisted that she would not cooperate, and intended instead to testify only that she was sure her son was alive.

With his star witness taking this position, on October 1, 2002, Brant Light asked District Judge Kenneth Neill to dismiss the case without prejudice, leaving the door open for charges to be filed if new evidence were to come forward, or release from prison should appear imminent.

DEVIANT OR INSANE?

Gerard John Schaefer was an uncommonly nasty serial killer who was murdered in prison in 1995, after having his necrophilic ravings revealed in court at his murder trial, and as in the case of Nathaniel Bar-Jonah, used to convict him. What might have been missed by the casual reader of this paradoxically self-revelatory tome, *Killer Fiction*, was that Schaefer was a college graduate, a creative writing student under Southern Gothic author Harry Crews, and as such, perverted and diabolical monster though he most assuredly was, he still managed to display a winsome way with words on topics so *outré* they are seldom addressed at all. Here he muses on being called *ghoulish* in newspaper coverage of his crimes:

> When I was accused of being a ghoul, I had to look the word up to get a clear meaning of *ghoulism*—which is defined in law as either robbing corpses or feeding on corpses. I wanted to clarify the distinction between a ghoul and a cannibal.
>
> I might mention that Ted Bundy took a pretty good bite out of that girl at the Chi Omega house. Bundy bit off the girl's nipple and ripped a hunk out of her buttocks... Rip a hunk out of her ass and she's going to bleed plenty. Did Ted relish the taste of blood?
>
> Was he a cannibal or a ghoul? Out in Washington they found this corpse with fresh lipstick and recently painted fingernails, but she'd been dead for several weeks. She was rotten and decomposing. Ted admitted to doing her up on a regular basis. What he was doing, having sex with rotting corpses, is incomprehensible.

 Gerard John Schaefer

Disingenuous as ever, Schaefer goes on to parse the distinctions among those who consume human flesh, providing cameo glimpses of a couple of classic cannibal killers:

It's a well documented historical fact that a number of world leaders in African nations have practiced cannibalism: Jomo Kenyatta, Idi Amin, and Jean Bokassa are three names that readily come to mind. While I've seen printed references to their cannibalism, I've never seen one called a *ghoul*, so perhaps there is a distinction. The "savage cannibal" of Africa or Amazonia feasts on human flesh as a matter of choice, not of necessity. The major difference is in how the local social structure perceives the custom.

Albert Fish, an American gent who enjoyed eating little girls, was tried and executed for murder — not cannibalism. Interestingly enough, it is not in violation of law to eat human flesh in New York or Florida. Mr. Fish had a taste for human flesh and went out and picked up children as if he were selecting vegetables at a greengrocer's stand. He slaughtered them, dressed them into select cuts and cooked them up in accordance with his favorite recipes. Nothing too fancy… a basic cutlet sautéed with onions. I'd expect the Africans would serve up a spicy repast. Bokassa favored a young girl, prepubescent if available.

Fish was caught dicing up little Grace Budd, also a prepubescent girl, so it does seem that the preference is not necessarily cultural. Maybe the older ones are tough. Pullets and hens are both chicken, but I'd prefer a pullet… more tender and juicy than a stewing hen. Apparently cannibals see things in a similar light.

Human flesh was Fish's meal of choice, and the motive for the murders he committed was called cannibalism. In New York, such an act is regarded as deviant but not insane, and is socially unacceptable.

Compare the Ed Gein case. Gein murdered women and ate them. He also dug up fresh female corpses and ate them. Dressed them out like deer into appropriate chops and steaks and roasts, and put them into the meat locker. Gein was regarded as insane and after he was caught, spent the rest of his life in an insane asylum in Wisconsin.

These two cases are very similar, yet in one state the murderer/cannibal was executed, and in the other he was hospitalized as insane. Both cases involve fellows who simply enjoyed a dish commonly unavailable in our society.

In all, Albert Fish molested and killed 15 children. He was executed in Sing Sing in 1936, but not before saying what a thrill he anticipated in dying by electrocution. He sent his victim's mother a letter relating in rapt detail how he despoiled the child with the most depraved indifference to her suffering, although, he consoled the distraught woman, "She died a virgin."

 Albert Fish

Ed Gein

FEAR OF VAMPIRES

While most of the people who commit crimes stemming from a fascination with vampirism enjoy playing the role of the vampire, another type of crime proceeds from a superstitious fear of vampires, the "vampire hunter" role taken to the point of striking out at other individuals, perceived to either be vampires, or less clearly, to embody the nameless, shapeless menacing Other. Some take comfort in rituals. Others enmeshed in the machinations of supernatural evil find more violent ways to enact the dramatic potential of blood.

In January of 2002, Ion Ionescu told Romanian police he had killed a 73-year-old woman because it appeared she turned into a vampire.

According to *The Evenimentul Zilei* newspaper, the 36-year-old man from Herendesti had been hired to watch the woman during the night after she suffered a stroke. He struck her in panic, he said, when she woke from a coma and "went after him."

On May 28, 2002, Romania's Romnet press agency reported that a Transylvanian man had plunged a silver dagger into his own mother's heart, because he feared she had become a vampire. Nicolæ Mihut's mother, Anghelina, had died, but before her funeral, Nicolæ spied a cat jumping over her coffin—a sure sign of a corpse being transformed into a vampire, according to Romanian folklore.

The apprehensive Nicolæ inspected the corpse and found that his mother's lips and cheeks were tinged red. He summoned the village priest, who advised taking the ancient precautions.

"We know from our ancestors that when a soul doesn't leave the body of a dead person, somebody has to stab that person with a silver knife in the chest or the stomach," he told reporters, adding, "When the knife pierced her heart we all heard a very long sigh and the body became rigid and very pale, unlike before. It was terrifying but we had to do it. We were told that if we didn't release her soul, she would have come back to haunt us or even to kill us."

Fear of invasion by a dark supernatural spirit is not limited to Transylvania. In August of 2001, an Ecuadorian man told the daily paper *Extra* that his wife Digna was bearing Satan's child. Vicente Suárez first realized who he was dealing with when his wife underwent a sonogram, and the seven-month-old fetus "looked nothing like a human baby."

Suárez claimed that Digna suffered from fits during which she gained superhuman strength and shouted in a deep, otherworldly voice: "Let me out, let me out!"

"When the Devil is in possession of her body, she spits at anyone who approaches," her husband said. "She kicks out and she drinks urine as if it were water."

The neighbors said that the woman would go into a trance and praise the Devil. While entranced, she would behave as if she could not bear the presence of children or of religious images.

Digna's family and friends said she had always been a shy, home-loving girl, but that Satan must have taken control of her body during a Ouija board session. When last heard, they were hoping to raise money to pay for a medical examination, although an exorcism would be a last resort.

Exorcism is not always an option, though, when superstition meets ignorance under the influence of a persuasive myth. And even with a wealth of folk wisdom to draw on, these strange creatures can be hard to recognize, especially when they are still changing shape. In August of 2001, a Malaysian witch doctor told *The Straits Times* that he had trapped a shape-shifting vampire in a jar. Hairul Hambali appeared on television to talk about his find.

The spiritual healer described how he caught the vampire near a cotton tree in Selangor. He said it took about an hour to catch the elusive phantasm, whose body appeared to be covered with cotton. This vampire was described as about the size of two tennis balls, resembling a big wad of cotton with a small face.

Hambali reassured viewers that the pest would eventually be thrown into the sea to keep it from harassing people. And so another *ad hoc* ritual was contrived to banish the ill-tempered spirit once and for all.

According to *La Cuarta*, a 28-year-old man in Copiulemu, Chile, didn't want to exorcise the Devil; instead, he had met up with The Evil One in a nearby cemetery, and agreed to a pact to bring him wealth and fame. In return for these promises, he killed his own mother. Upon arrest he boasted of plans to kill his sister as well, to claim the further benefits the Devil had promised, beyond the supposedly already attained wealth and fame: not only making him handsome, but increasing the size of his manly apparatus. In a sepulchral voice, the man assured investigators that he could kill them with one piercing glance from his "Evil Eye," and that he could dissolve their bodies by spraying them with his saliva. He was bound over for psychological testing—one more case of superstition and delusion causing mortal mayhem.

But it's not just third-world people who believe in such phenomena. According to a 2001 Gallup survey, 41 percent of Americans believe humans can be possessed by the Devil, while an equal percentage refuse to believe it, leaving the rest to ride the fence.

"There are no clear clinical guidelines to distinguish between 'normal' religious beliefs and 'pathological' religious delusions," Dr. Joseph Pierre, a psychiatrist at UCLA's medical school, told the *Atlanta Journal-Constitution*.

"The church holds that people are subject to demonic influences," said Mark Jordan, a Roman Catholic professor of religion at Emory University.

But what if the most fearsome and powerful vampires have shifted shape so as to appear to be ladies and gentlemen of wealth and taste? Author David Icke has appeared on Channel Four telling Great Britain that her elite public figures are descended from monstrous, shape-shifting, reptilian vampires.

"Many will laugh and that is their entitlement, but this is not sensationalism," claimed a senior Channel Four source. "Icke has his theory and he is sticking to it. In many ways what he has to say is revelatory. He expects to be dismissed but he wants to be heard."

On October 8, 1998, *The Sun* tabloid announced that Britain's Prince Charles and Queen Elizabeth II were direct descendants of the original Count Dracula, Vlad Tepes. Quoting *Roots of the Rich and Famous* by Robert Davenport, *The Sun* revealed that the Dracula bloodline entered the British royal family through the consort of George V, Queen Mary, whose Austrian ancestors were traced directly to Dracula's Romanian bloodline.

According to *Der Spiegel*, Russian president Vladimir Putin has what it takes to join British royalty and the rest of the global power elite in the pursuit of power by means of vampirism.

"His two green eyes are like two hungry, lurking predators, like weapons," wrote Irene Pietsch in her April 2001 book, *Fragile Friendships*, after spending a week with the Putins at a Russian government guesthouse in Archangelskoye.

"Unfortunately, my husband is a vampire," Lyudmila Putin confided ruefully to her friend Irene. "But he is just the right man for me—he doesn't drink and he doesn't beat me."

POTENT FANTASIES

Jerry Burden of Portsmouth, England, was a mild-mannered, middle-aged man who could do no wrong, until he lost several members of his family, and subsequently began suffering the horror of impotence.

His attorneys blamed these sad circumstances for the fact that in the spring of 2000, Burden took to donning a Dracula mask and lurking in a graveyard. Detectives described the mask, which was later discarded, as "terrifying."

Worse yet, he sexually assaulted six women and girls, the youngest being 11 years old. The women all described their attacker as weak and slim, wearing black gloves and a hideous mask with blood-dripping fangs.

Judge Keith Cutler handed down a life sentence, saying he believed the crimes were sexually motivated, and that the planning that had been involved showed that Burden had been trying to live out some kind of fantasy. "It may be that you were unable to live up to the potency of your own fantasies, but I consider that you might keep on trying."

Judge Cutler told the would-be vampire he would serve at least eight years hard time, and would be placed on the sex offenders register.

"In some ways you are every woman and every girl's nightmare, causing women to fear ever walking alone in public places in case they should be attacked in such a frightening and brutal way."

On April 2, 1996, Jon C. Bush, a 26-year-old heating and air-conditioning mechanic, was indicted in Virginia Beach, Virginia, on 26 felony charges involving sex with minors. The tall, dark man had built up a "family" of about 30 youngsters who followed him in a role-playing game called *Vampire: The Eternal Struggle*. He would troll the local malls adorned in full vampire attire: snap-on fangs, white face, black lips and nails, swirling his black cape, with several similarly decked-out teenage boys in tow.

This display was intended to attract girls into their circle. Once drawn into the vampire fantasy, he would offer to "initiate" the underage girls, giving them three options: they could allow him to bite their neck and drink their blood; they could perform oral sex on him; or they could submit to sexual intercourse. Nine girls, ages 13 to 16, were used sexually in this way, thus resulting in one count of rape, 11 counts of carnal knowledge, six of indecent liberties, and eight of crimes against nature, as well as nine misdemeanor counts for contributing to the delinquency of minors.

Although this charade seems to be a case of cynically using a pretext simply to get sex, police spokesman Mike Carey said, "He really thinks he's a vampire. What we have here is a young man who got so immersed in a game that he took it to the next level. He was living it."

Lead investigator Detective Donald Rimer said that Bush told police he believed powerful forces were arrayed against him, and that he could only increase his personal power by recruiting new players into the game. Rimer considers this case an example of the hazards of fantasy role-playing games.

"I see an innate problem with any role-playing game that suggests violent behavior, suicide and death," he told the *Richmond Times-Dispatch*. "These games are different than most games. You don't see kids getting arrested for multiple embezzlements after playing Monopoly."

DEVIL'S TOWN

In Texas, on February 13, 1999, 21-year-old Pablo Lucio Vasquez was sentenced to die for the slaying of David Cardenas, a 12-year-old boy who was found scalped and dismembered in Donna, Texas, just across the Rio Grande from the infamous Matamoros.

Vasquez confessed that the previous April 17, he had stunned the victim by striking him with a pipe, slit his throat, hoisted the still-living child onto his shoulder, and drank the fresh blood flowing from his mortal wound.

Vasquez told his cousin he did it because the Devil told him to kill the child and drink his blood as a human sacrifice. While Vasquez had not made any statements to authorities about his beliefs, one of his gang members described him to police as a satanist.

Vasquez' 15-year-old cousin was also charged with murder, and six others, including two of Vasquez' uncles, were accused of helping to destroy evidence to cover up the crime.

The obvious occult connections were downplayed, as usual, but the Donna Police Department identified 23 gangs in the area, including three who were self-identified as satanic. Local gang members openly flashed the sign of the Devil, and many buildings in town were tagged with inverted pentagrams and 666 graffiti.

Most of the department's information on occult gangs came from gang members themselves. "They won't come right out and let you know," said Detective David Fuentes, the department's resident gang expert, who had been studying occult crime during his five years on the force. "Most of them are very discreet. It's very unusual when one will tell you his affiliation." But when the known elements of the crime fit, the conclusions are obvious.

Police Chief Miguel Carreon said members of occult gangs had moved to the Rio Grande Valley, and had organized local gangs and taught them to perform rituals. "Donna is the first to open their eyes to a problem we have," he said. "It's all over the Valley."

"We're not happy kids," an 18-year-old Donna gang leader known only as "Hector" told Carreon. "Nobody loves us."

Hector, who calls Donna "D-town" for "Devil's Town," had been a gangbanger since he was 13. He believed "the Devil has power," and got a kick out of the notoriety. "We're famous. We like that," he said. "When we do something bad, it's really bad."

Gang members who practice occult rituals are like other kids attracted to gangs in that they are looking to be "in with the in-crowd." Poverty is the most significant factor that breeds this sort of peer-group oriented activity. These youth predominantly come from single-family homes where their parent is chronically overworked or otherwise unavailable. Membership in a gang gives them the attention they crave; it makes them feel wanted and gives them a frame of reference that enables them to further a more far-reaching purpose, by swearing blood oaths of secrecy that lock them into moving drugs, weapons, fake identification documents, and other valuable commodities.

Fuentes believes that gangs who call on the Devil are seeking protection for illegal activities. "Most of them are praying 'take care of us while we're dealing our drugs.'"

"Satanic involvement relieves people of the responsibility of their own thoughts and actions," says Michael Cuneo, the author of *American Exorcism*. "Overwhelmingly what people are suffering from is some neurological, psychological or psychiatric disorder, or, in many cases, they've taken their cues from the popular entertainment industry."

Susan Robbins, associate dean for academic affairs and an associate professor at the University of Houston Graduate School of Social Work, wrote an article on satanic cults for the *Encyclopedia of Social Work*. She is one of the plausible and persuasive experts who continue to maintain that despite cases like this, there is no evidence whatsoever of organized satanic activity involving kidnapping, ritual abuse, murder or mutilation of children and animals.

Robbins attributes these crimes to self-proclaimed satanists who form their ideas of satanic worship from songs, television, movies, games, books and the internet, and then come up with a set of rituals. "The link between the crimes that they commit and ceremonial satanic worship, however, is quite tenuous."

The official position she articulates as well as Ken Lanning himself is that people who would commit such crimes are disturbed, and would commit them whether or not they were sanctioned by a satanic group.

As the supervisory special agent at the FBI Academy in Quantico, Virginia, likes to say, "People love this idea of 'The Devil made me do it.' This is not only not new, this is the oldest theory of crime that there is."

"I don't see it so much as a cause for crime as a justification of crime. I see individuals who go out and kill and rape," Lanning told the *Atlanta Journal* in 1988. "The satanism is a symptom of their problem, not the cause of the problem."

And again Robbins echoes Ken Lanning in pointing out that organized groups such as Anton LaVey's Church of Satan and Michael Aquino's Temple of Set are open churches that are not linked to any criminal activity.

"There are lots of published accounts of people saying they were victims and they witnessed murders, which may very well be true," Cynthia Kisser, executive director of the Cult Awareness Network, told the *Atlanta Journal*. "But as far as I know you're not going to be able to substantiate it."

"You have a dead body, malice, a murder," says Donald Sparry, a police instructor in Georgia who lectures on occult crime at law enforcement seminars. "Why complicate it with all these allegations about rituals?"

And so even though quite often occult involvement in a crime is strongly suspected, and may even be well-documented, the allegations are not presented in court because if it can be shown that sensational evidence serves to unnecessarily inflame the sensibilities of a jury, an otherwise solid conviction may be thrown out on appeal. Prosecutors are increasingly cautious about placing these allegations on the record, because even if the evidence of occult motivation is not inflammatory, they are all too well aware that it may simply be disbelieved, since ritual crime falls so far outside the ambit of the everyday lives of jurors. This is the very same dynamic that allows criminal organizations to operate under the radar.

SNUFF

In a Nebraska pedophile ring involving the ritual consumption of human flesh, the cover-up extended to the highest levels of state and local government. Perpetrators were protected against investigation by law enforcement or prosecution by the State, because key individuals in both organizations were compromised. A great deal of money was embezzled, drugs were smuggled, and there was evidence connecting all of it to the Iran-Contra scandal.

Even law enforcement at a federal level was involved in intimidating witnesses who insisted upon naming names and places where they and other minor children had been prostituted, drugged, transported, and photographed while being forced to participate in depraved rituals. The names the kids named were well-known, and the places the perps held were high. One of the two witnesses convicted of "perjury" won a million-dollar judgment after doing time; the other is still serving a sentence. None of the perps were convicted of these alleged crimes, although several of them did fall on other counts.

The kind of occult organization that came to light in Nebraska is very different from the situation with Tex-Mex gangbangers seeking power over their rivals via satanic sacrifice. When it comes to the "devil making them do it," the devil in this case is the power named by the occult practitioners who compel children to commit these bloody acts for them as live-action pornography. In the Nebraska case, the assaults were videotaped, and the victims re-traumatized by forcing them to watch the tapes in the presence of other powerful perverts, all blood-bound to keep their dreadful secrets at any price.

Paul Bonacci gave a videotaped sworn statement to investigator Gary Caradori on May 14, 1990, and less than two months later, while pressing this investigation even further, Caradori died when his single-engine aircraft mysteriously blew up in midair and crashed. This frightful situation was investigated by State Senator John W. DeCamp, who released his report in a self-published book called *The Franklin Cover-Up*.

According to Caradori's report on Bonacci, he was brought into the pedo ring in 1979 at the age of 12, and unsuccessfully tried to get away from them many times, even attempting suicide. By his own account, in 1984, at the age of 17, Paul Bonacci was taken on an airplane to Sacramento, along with a boy about 12 or 13 called Nicholas.

From his sworn statement:

We were picked up by a white limo and taken to a hotel. I don't remember the name of it. We meaning Nicholas and I were driven to an area that had big trees, it took about an hour to get there. There was a cage with a boy in it who was not wearing anything. Nicholas and I were given these Tarzan things to put around us and stuff.

They told me to f--- the boy and stuff. At first I said no and they held a gun to my balls and said do it or else lose them or something like that. I began doing it to the boy and stuff. And Nicholas had anal sex and stuff with him. We were told to f--- him and stuff and beat on him. I didn't try to hurt him. We were told to put our d---s in his mouth and stuff and sit on the boys penis and stuff and they filmed it. We did this stuff to the boy for about 30 minutes or an hour when a man came in and kicked us and stuff in the balls and picked us up and threw us. He grabbed the boy and started f---ing him and stuff. The man was about 10 inches long and the boy screamed and stuff and the man was forcing his d--- into the boy all the way. The boy was bleeding from his rectum and the men tossed him and me and stuff and put the boy right next to me and grabbed a gun and blew the boys head off.

The boys blood was all over me and I started yelling and crying. The men grabbed Nicholas and I and forced us to lie down. They put the boy on top of Nicholas who was crying and they were putting Nicholas hands on the boys ass. They put the boy on top of me and did the same thing. Then they forced me to f--- the dead boy up his ass and also Nicholas, they put a gun to our heads to make us do it. His blood was all over us. They made us kiss the boys lips and to eat him out. Then they made me do something I don't want to even write so I won't.

After that the men grabbed Nicholas and drug him off screaming, they put me up against a tree and put a gun to my head, but fired into the air. I heard another shot from somewhere. I then saw the man who killed the boy drag him like a toy. Everything including when the men put the boy in a trunk was filmed. They took me with them and we went up in a plane. I saw the bag the boy was in. We went over a very thick brush area with a clearing in it. Over the clearing they dropped the boy. One said the men with the hoods would take care of the body for them.

I didn't see Nicholas until that night at the hotel... we took a shower together and then were told to put on the Tarzan things. After we were cleaned up and dressed in these things we were told to put on shorts, socks and a shirt and shoes, and driven to a house where the men were at with some others. They had the film and they played it. As the men watched, they passed Nicholas and I around as if we were toys and sexually abused us.

They made Nicholas and I screw each other and one of the men put the dead boy's penis in mine and Nicholas' mouth. I didn't want to write this because the man forced me to bite the boys' penis and balls off. It was gross and I saw the film where it happened and started freaking out remembering what they made us do afterwards to the boy. They showed us doing everything to the boy. I was there for about five days attending parties but only recall cutting my wrist, which is why I stayed two days in a hospital under a name I can't recall. Some guy paid for me.

The question, then, is: who are the true vampires—the boys who bit the balls off, or the men who forced them to do it so they could watch?

THE DEVIL'S CHILD

Ottis Toole, in the words of his crime partner and lover Henry Lee Lucas, was "one of the worstest killers in the world." Alone and with Lucas, this killer drag queen restlessly roved all over America—robbing, raping, burning, killing, drinking blood and cannibalizing, attacking the nation more like an epidemic plague than a mere human being. Estimated casualties range from 50 to 500 victims. He confessed to numerous murders, and many cases are considered closed, even though due to the economics of prosecuting murder cases, especially those involving the death penalty, formal charges were only brought in a handful of cases.

Murder was a way of life for Toole and Lucas. There were no boundaries, no consistent motivations, and there were a half-dozen concurrent patterns, creating the overall impression of no pattern at all.

The crimes described in a confidential interstate law enforcement report, which have been solved to the satisfaction of the respective investigating officers, probably show the widest variety of types of murders in criminal history. Together and separately, Ottis and Henry killed the old and the young; men, women, and children; whites, blacks, Native Americans, Mexicans and Orientals; straight and gay. There were stabbings, shootings, stranglings, drownings and burnings; robberies and sexual assaults; sadistic mutilations and tortures; ritual killings and drive-by thrill-kills.

While the crimes seemed to be almost "desperately random," the recurring theme was overkill. It was not enough to simply extinguish the life of the victim. Over and over Toole's victims were subjected to multiple assaults, and their lifeless bodies raped or mutilated. With this kind of organic rage, it is as if the fury is so great that murder alone is not enough to satisfy the blind impulse to destruction.

"What do psychiatrists say about you, Ottis?"

"They can't figure theyself out, 'less figure me out. They got to figure theyself out 'fore they can figure me out."

Ottis Toole may have been naive, and he may have employed the provincial speech of the underclass, but in his own poignant way, he succinctly summed up the crux of the dilemma he embodied. This blood-drinking, cannibalistic devil-worshipper embodied one of our most extreme forms of social pathology, and it is in the process of understanding such unfathomable creatures that we are compelled to discover disturbing truths about ourselves, the world we have created, and its inevitable strange fruit. Before we can even begin to understand Ottis Toole, it will be necessary for us to examine ourselves, and to face the unpleasant evidence of the shredding of our social fabric by the prevalence of impersonal violence. Extreme cases like these serve as evolutionary drivers, insofar as the challenge of coming to terms with them forces us to evolve into a higher consciousness of ourselves.

But our search to understand the roots of violence is hampered by a criminal justice system that apparently interprets such inquiries as posing a direct threat to their mandate to render punishment and exact revenge. While investigations have been conducted for years into the connection between brain dysfunction and criminal misbehavior, attempts to conduct research into the brains of these incarcerated human disasters have been systematically suppressed.

Time after time, motions by public defenders for diagnostic testing have been rejected by the courts. And such was indeed the case with four death-penalty murders in the Florida panhandle that Lucas and Toole faced in 1991. Dr. Joel Norris wrote a recommendation for the defense, stating that adequate diagnostic testing necessary to demonstrate the extent of Toole's deficits would run about $250,000.

Faced with the option of giving the deadly duo a trial that would hold up on appeal, they accepted guilty pleas and sent them both back to prison with another four murder convictions. Lucas did have some diagnostic tests done in Texas, which revealed significant abnormalities, but Toole went to his grave without ever having a thorough work-up done.

This is characteristic of one way our social system has failed to respond adequately to the challenge of our Tooles and Lucases, and they epitomize all of our social failures—those who have fallen into the underclass in any way— whether they be incarcerated, unemployed, impecunious, abused, neglected, insane, physically or mentally infirm or defective, or perhaps involved in prostitution, drugs, gambling or petty crime—or merely of a less than desirable age, weight, nationality, sexual orientation, or complexion.

Insofar as the difficulties experienced by these elements of our population are not addressed, to that extent we put our entire body politic at risk. This underclass makes up the majority not only of criminals, but of victims. The dynamics that contribute to the unchecked proliferation of mindless murder will continue to fulminate, until the damage extends beyond the strata of throw-aways and write-offs, and crosses over to take a savage bite out of the lives of the happy, shiny people who expect to be protected and defended from such chaos.

This grim social dynamic has been piercingly articulated from inside the belly of the beast by none other than Charles Manson, as quoted by Nikolas Schreck in the *Manson Files*:

> There is a price and you will pay. You may not see it, but the beast you created will devour you. That is to say, your social subconsciousness. There is a subconsciousness that lurks below your awareness. The social subconscious beginning to make its move is called anarchy.
>
> Things happen every day the newspapers don't print and the TV's don't show. You're only told a small part of what's going on and that part is only to control your mind, to get you to stay in line, to avoid panic and to create a social thought to keep down total chaos of the masses. The lie is becoming so big that no one can believe it. This is what isolates people, for soon no one will know what to believe.
>
> The last battle of Armageddon will be when the social consciousness reaches a high fear level, as fear has always and will always induce madness.

During three three-hour sessions with this author and the late Dr. Joel Norris in 1991, Ottis Toole described a life story that to most people simply does not seem possible. Scuttling through the sludge in the bottom of the social swamp, forever on the prowl for prey, Toole and Lucas exemplified the true vampires whose personal habits and crimes are too loathsome to inspire romantic fancies of a criminal elite.

With over a hundred murder cases to his name, Toole summarized his life: "It was living a nightmare. It won't never be over with. It don't make no difference what I do or say, it won't *never* be over with."

Interviewing any maximum security inmate is intimidating. It's not so much the inmate as the prison environment itself. Every prison is different, but there's always that distinct and unforgettable institutional ambiance: the musty disinfectant smells, the loud harsh sounds, the hot hungry eyes of the inmates frankly appraising any evidence of femaleness, the coldness of the immense, burly guards, the invasiveness of the no-nonsense matrons as they conduct a body search, the irrational fear of being thrown out or worse—confined... and the sick feeling of finality as those big steel gates slam behind you with a haunting *crash-BANG!*

After a seven-month correspondence with Ottis Toole, I finally met him in July of 1991 under the highest security conditions afforded by the State of Florida. The East Unit of Appalachee Correctional Institution was completely locked down: all prisoners were confined to their cells the entire day

 Charles Manson

of our interview. While I was undergoing security processing, six double-armed guards brought Toole from his solitary cell to the tiny interrogation room, cuffed and chained hand and foot. When I commented to the guards on the extent of the security precautions, one of them chuckled, "If I let *this* 'un get away, I could forget I ever even *wanted* a job in the state of Florida!"

As I was escorted through the prison to the interrogation room by a cadre of various uniforms, I was so tense I could barely speak. I had heard so much about Toole's sudden fits of irrational violence, and as eager as I was to finally meet him face-to-face, I had the feeling anything might happen, anything at all. I maintained my composure, but frankly, I was scared.

So they opened the double-locked door, and suddenly there he was, looking at me—this savage killer drag queen that was said to eat the flesh and drink the blood of his victims in ghoulish devil-worshipping rituals. As I approached him, he rose to greet me with a tight, anxious smile. Ottis Toole was not some kind of brilliant, clever Hannibal the Cannibal. To say he lacked charm is an understatement, but while his manners were most often crude and offensive, rising to greet a lady was one of those few little social graces he did manage to acquire at his mother's knee.

As I squeezed through the door into the cramped little room while he was rising to his feet, I found myself standing less than six inches away from a human being as unpredictable as a rattlesnake—I was right in his face. I stopped there to greet him, intending to shake his hand. But his hands were both cuffed to his waist, and as he started to reach toward my extended hand, the gesture was caught up in his restraints, and in that cramped space, chance brought his face bare inches from mine.

In first moment, I stood there looking deep into his eyes—braced for wildness, cruelty, hatred—and I was surprised by what I saw way back there, far beyond the flat coldness projected by his hooded eyes. Behind that cold menace, I caught a glimpse of a tormented child, crazed with pain, and cringing with fear of more pain. He wore a tentative smile, yet it was fear that filled his eyes. I was stunned to realize that deep inside, this brutal killer was even more frightened than I was.

As I saw the fear in his eyes, I placed both hands lightly on his shoulders and quickly brushed his cheek with mine, in an impulsive gesture of reassurance. "It's OK," I was telling him without words. "I won't hurt you." I wished there were some way the damage to his soul could be undone. But of course, therein lies the tragedy of the whole situation. There would be no rehabilitation for him, no return to a normal, healthy state—for since birth Ottis Toole had truly been the Devil's Child.

His head was so full of devils, he told me, that if a priest were to run all those devils out with "that thing they called an exorcism," there would be nothing left of him at all; he'd go "stark, raving insane." I believed him.

Born in the shadow of the Gator Bowl, Ottis Toole was a real live gator—a bottom-feeder almost more reptilian than human, scuttling through the swamps of society, ceaselessly scanning for helpless prey. But how did he get that way? This was what I had come to find out.

He was not a pretty sight, I'm afraid. Tall and gaunt, with poor tone and rough, pallid skin, he looked as if he might have AIDS. When he died on September 15, 1996, however, the cause of death was listed as liver failure, and prison authorities stated that an AIDS diagnosis was not listed anywhere in his medical records.

Though he did not appear robust when I met him in 1991, when he was arrested, he had been a strapping six-foot-two with large hands and a lank, muscular 200-pound physique. His mannerisms veered from tough macho to delicate femme. He must have been a real sight when he donned his makeup, his long blonde wig, and the flashy, full-length ballgowns he used to wear when he performed his one-man drag shows for his neighbors, lip-synching "Sugar Shack" and "It's Raining Men."

Though he had a wicked laugh, and every other word was an obscenity, he was usually passive and soft-spoken, and guards called him a model prisoner. Inmates called him Grandma, because in prison society, he played the femme, and the jockers highly prized the feel of his toothless mouth. He rarely wore his dentures except for the rare court appearance or interview.

He was unaccustomed to talking around his dentures, and on top of that, he had a speech impediment. Quite often, he was unable to articulate a word, and if asked more than once to repeat it, he became frustrated and irritated. His accent and idioms were pure gator, to the extent that his speech was often unintelligible to those who did not emerge from the swamps. Apparently, I was able to interpret his efforts better than most, as he told me gratefully, "Ain't nobody understands me the way you do."

I quickly learned that his concerns were two—coffee and cigarettes—and any interview had to begin by satisfying those basic needs before the conversation could proceed. Once he had his fuel on board, I found him relatively cooperative, but inaccessible. His literacy was at about third-grade level; he could not grasp abstract concepts; and while he might not actively resist questioning, his ability to respond was severely limited. While he could write simple letters, and we did share correspondence, he was unable to put his thoughts in writing, and all of the significant statements I obtained from him were through interviews—either with me personally or with reporters conducting interviews that I produced from behind the scenes.

When asked how many he had killed—or when, or where, or how—most often he would just say he didn't know. When asked why, he would just shrug or respond vaguely. "I don't know why I did do it, to tell the truth. I'd have a pistol in my hand, and that's just what I done at the time."

The closest Toole came to verbalizing to *why* it happened was in one image that summed up the years he spent roaming the country with Lucas: "It was like playing Bonnie and Clyde. It was just a murder rampage."

Once, after a particularly barren interchange, he leaned forward. "Listen," he said with a pained squint, "Some people keep track of stuff. I don't keep track of *nothin'*. Most times, I don't even know if it's *day or night*."

Psychiatrists variously diagnosed Toole as schizophrenic and psychopathic. With an IQ testing on the borderline of being developmentally disabled under the law, he was functionally illiterate; he dropped out of his special-education classes in the eighth grade.

In a court-ordered psychological report, Dr. Wallace Kennedy concluded in 1985:

He is a creature of impulse that seems incapable of premeditation. He has always acted instantly on impulse without the slightest sense of right or wrong at the time. Life itself, to him, is so unmeaning, and the distinction between living and dead people so blurred, that killing to him is no more than swatting an annoying fly is to normal people. A severely disturbed individual who is competent and sane in spite of his bizarre history, Ottis Toole seems incapable of premeditation or self-control. He trivialized the distinction between living and dead, believing himself to be dead. Retarded and illiterate, he has been out of control since early childhood. A severely drug-dependent individual, he is unsafe under any conditions outside of a secure prison, and perhaps unsafe there. He is neurologically damaged, definitely in the frontal area, and the psychological evaluation indicates other neurological deficits. He is a classic case of severely diminished capacity to control his impulses.

A psychiatrist who analyzed Toole in 1983 described him as a man with "a bizarre sexuality and impulse disorder, pyromania." Dr. Ernest Miller reported: "He states that he occasionally sees little 'devils' and wonders if this is because he lives with the devil and has all the 'devil things' in his mind." He also stated: "At times he fancies he hears voices saying he should kill himself and go to rest. These occur when he is asleep and sometimes when he is awake. He regards the origin of these voices as from his mind or from the devil."

Dr. Eduardo Sanchez reported that Toole "stated that at times he feels like the devil is telling him to set fires and 'do bad things.' The patient went on to state that he thinks he is the devil himself." Dr. Sanchez felt that Toole was "quite capable of acting out at a psychotic level with complete lack of reasoning and inability to foresee the consequences of his actions and the magnitude of it."

His memories were fragmentary, remote, and recovered only with a marked effort. When asked a question about his past, he would often lapse into a far-off, dreamlike state which might be quite extended before he would respond. Law enforcement found this behavior particularly unnerving, when all they wanted was the facts; yet it was fascinating to observe, as you could practically *hear* the gears of his brain grinding away.

As Toole explained it to me, "Whatever I talk about, I always go back and try to remember and sympathize. And it's just like I'm living it, you know, like I'm doing it, when I'm talking about it. Like it's really happening to me all over again." It was as if he would leave his inert body there with you in the interrogation room and time-travel back to the remote event, go through it again, and then find his way back to the room. Only then could he respond to your question. His eyes would come into focus and then he would speak.

One of Toole's defense attorneys once said facetiously, "The best way I can describe Ottis Toole is that he represents the lower end of the gene pool." While his dismissive comment was not intended to be taken literally, it was actually very descriptive of Toole's legacy.

Prenatal factors including poverty, alcoholism, and nutrition that was marginal at best, combined to give him little opportunity to maximize his genetic heritage, which was not overly predisposed toward success in the first place.

By the age of four, Toole had been run over by a car and sustained a broken leg, and by the age of eight, he had fallen through a hole in his front porch, impaling his forehead on a nail that went three inches into his skull, damaging the frontal and limbic portions of his brain and resulting in *grand mal* epileptic seizures for the rest of his life.

His tendency to black out resulted in confusion about what he had done. When questioned about the details of his crimes, he explained, "Well, some of them I don't even remember doing until it's been done, until the next day somebody says you done this, you done that, I don't really remember, you know. Cause I'm an epileptic, too, you see."

To some extent, his memory loss could be attributed to brain damage, but his mind was further impaired by years of consumption of commercial and bootleg liquor, along with a stunning array of street drugs, starting at his mother's knee, with her "nerve pills."

"It gave me a foul mind," is the way he put it. "With my mind fouled up so much, how was I going to know where I was at, my own self? I didn't pay that much attention to where we was going, because if we had some pot to smoke I was smoking pot, and if we had some pills to pop, I was popping pills, and if we had beer to drink, we was drinking beer."

During the years he spent roaming the country with Lucas, he claimed that between the two of them, they regularly downed a case of beer a day, often topping it off with a fifth of liquor, and the cult leaders ensured that they had unlimited access to drugs including acid, coke, heroin and his drug of choice, speed. "Oh shoot," Toole said, "I would take it all. Whatever I could get my hands on, is what I would take. Something to get me real high, you know."

The abuse of alcohol and drugs not only impaired his memory, it undermined whatever tattered remnants of moral training he might have had. "Dope makes you wild. It really brings out the hate in you more, because you don't care who you would have to rob to get it. You'd probably rob your own mama to take her pocketbook." He would even go so far as to blame his string of murders on drugs. "If I was in my right mind at the time, it wouldn't have never happened. I was on dope, strung out, just wild and crazy, you know?"

In prison, he was consistently medicated with Thorazine and Dilantin, given a regular balanced diet, and punished when he was caught with street drugs or jailhouse brew. Though the rigid control of his environment provided some ballast for his fragile equilibrium, it was not sufficient to restore him to a soundness he had never known in the first place.

He had difficulty telling the truth. "If I tell the truth, I'll get in trouble," he explained, sensibly. "If I don't tell the truth, I won't get in no trouble. So I'll just keep on telling lies." Like Lucas, he had given numerous false confessions. "I figured what's the difference between one murder and another, if you killed one or if you killed a thousand. I was playing a dangerous game."

It's hard to imagine this living death. "I'm already dead," he said plaintively. "I'm already down in my grave. The sides just ain't caved in on me yet.." In this undead state, he tried to kill himself by hanging, cutting, and overdosing many times. "I lost count. I'd say about a dozen times."

He told me of a psychiatrist who had asked him if he thought he was crazy. "I told him yeah, and the doctor said, I believe you are too." Nevertheless, he had been declared competent to stand trial, and the M'Naghton guidelines for legal insanity did seem to apply, in that he did appear to know the difference between right and wrong and to understand the nature of his acts. Still—it is hard to avoid the use of an old-fashioned unscientific term like "crazy" once you have beheld the evil joy radiating from this fiend's face as he is relating his vicious crimes and depraved pleasures.

His mother Sarah Cooper Harley, whom he idolized, was a hardshell Baptist who chanted Bible verses to cure his ills, and dosed him with barbiturates to calm his nerves. He remembers his alcoholic father sexually abusing him from the age of six, and when the man left to go live with his own mother as man and wife, a stepfather came along who picked up where his real dad left off—but this time, the child was passed around to his stepdad's friends as well. All along, his mother turned a blind eye to the abuse, denying to herself and her son that her husbands would ever do such a thing.

Ottis was the youngest of a brood of nine, and his roughneck brothers beat up on their sissy kid brother regularly. One of them, Howell, shot at him numerous times, once wounding him in the head.

His older sisters, Drusilla and Vonetta, dressed him as a girl and made him wait on them like their own private little Cinderella. "I started to think I was a girl after a while. Sometimes I feel like I'm about half and half, I do." He said that he enjoyed dressing like a girl so much that "when someone would take my wig off, I'd snatch it back and put it right back on."

Drusilla was the first one to teach him about sex with females. She had begun consorting with grown men when she was 12, and she compelled her little brother to service her sexually. When I asked him about this, he denied any sexual contact with his sisters, but upon being reminded that juvenile authorities had removed Drusilla from the home for it, he changed his story without batting an eye: "Oh yeah, Mama did catch us once."

He always considered himself homosexual. "Well, I was raped when I was a little kid. A real little kid about six years old. I told my mother about it, and she said he wouldn't do nothing like that, you know." Although he was twice married briefly, and behaviorally could be considered bisexual, he denied enjoying sex with women. "Tried 'em. Didn't like 'em."

Since early childhood, he obtained sexual satisfaction from setting fires, which culminated in his conviction in 1983 of murder by arson. "I been doing fires since I was a little kid. See, the little fires don't excite me, you know. Only big fires excite me," he told Steve Dunleavy on A Current Affair.

"Just like if an ugly woman don't look good to you, you don't get excited. You have to get a pretty woman to get excited. It's like the same way with fires, you know. The bigger the fires, the more I get excited."

A little-known aspect of the neuropsychology of arson involves the observation that damage to the limbic brain can result in a stimulation to the central nervous system being felt in the genitals, thus forging a connection that creates a sexual sensation that essentially arises from brain damage.

Taunted in school for being dirty and slow-learning, and for playing with fire, stuttering and wetting his pants, Little Ottis often played truant to visit his father's mother Cornelia. He loved this tall, striking woman in her long, dark skirts and high-heeled boots, and yet he feared her, for she was a spell-casting, grave-robbing witch from the Okefenokee Swamp, a member of an hereditary death cult whose blood-drinking rituals had been passed down through the family for generations.

"If you believe in God, you believe in the Devil," Toole recited. "If you believe in the Devil, you believe in God."

Toole told us that his earliest memories were of midnight trips to graveyards, where Cornelia commanded him to rob graves for her, while the voices of the dead cried out to him of their anguish and dismay, and the menacing "devil-trees" waved their black branches at him, and leered down at the frightened child "like they were looking for something to eat."

He trembled as he recalled falling through one rotten casket right into the flesh of a decomposing corpse. Screaming hysterically as he clambered out, the child was shoved back down into the grave and forced to pull the bones from the rotting flesh. Cornelia needed those bones for her witchcraft, she told him, and he was the one the Devil had chosen to help her do her sinister work. He was born, his grandma told him, to be the *Devil's Own Child*.

Ottis described a typical scene from his home life. Cornelia would go to bed with the chickens, but get up again late at night and take the old black dresser drawer that had served as his cradle, turn it upside-down, and arrange her makeshift black altar with the magical implements: the glass filled with blood, the black candle, the knife, the bones, and the wooden hands Cornelia called the *Hands of Death*.

The child would awaken to hear the chants she mumbled and smell the herbs she burned. "What you saying, Grandma?" he would ask. "Hush!" she would tell the curious little boy, "You don't need to know! You know too much already!" And as she made up her bags of herbs, feathers, roots and bones, the drowsy child would drift back to sleep, with the Devil's chants weaving through his dreams, becoming as much a part of him as his own mother's prayers to Jesus.

Ottis believed his grandmother didn't want him to learn enough to outdo her as a sorcerer, but she always had plenty of work for her young apprentice. She'd get him to grab a chicken and wring its neck and catch the blood in a bowl. She would have him taste the blood and tell her whether it was still warm enough to drink, or had clotted and grown too cold to gag down.

She peddled her magical charms and spells to superstitious folk on both sides of the color line, and Toole speculated that she must have been doing all right for an old lady, because she always had blood-rare steak for dinner—except when she ate raw liver.

Cornelia had brought her roots work from her birthplace on the edge of the Okefenokee Swamp, where the skull and crossbones had been posted as a warning to the hapless wayfarer of the evil conjurers that had been practicing their black arts deep in its miasmal mists for as long as memory served.

Toole said that he thought that devil-worshipping was a kind of game, but when he was forced to go down into the graves and pull at those putrid bones, he began to really feel its evil power. By the latter phase of his life, he was disappointed in that power. "At first I thought it was something special, but it didn't do me no good, it just dug me deeper into the hole I was in."

After his father had moved back to live with Cornelia as man and wife, Little Ottis kept a pet cat at Cornelia's house, and when she bore a litter of kittens, his father told the child to get rid of them. When he resisted, his father punished him by tying the kittens together by their tails and suspending them from a clothesline. He forced his son to stand underneath the kittens as they tore at each other and their bloody guts drenched him. "Brat, you stand there," he sneered. "You let that blood fall all over you!"

He would never forget how he looked over towards his grandmother, only to see her standing in the doorway, laughing at him as his weeping mingled with the howls of his dying pets.

I used to hear voices...

Right now I could go to my mother's grave and lay down on the dirt and hear and feel the dirt vibrating... and I can hear her moving around down there... and I know she was hearing me when I was talking to her... laying down and talking to her... and I could feel the dirt vibrating... I used to go out there all the time...

And I used to go with my grandmother into graveyards... we used to dig up all kinds of bones... get all kinds of herbs... and she used to take the bones and do devil worship... she would put spells on you with the bones... she would make voodoo dolls... take a chicken and wring the chicken's neck... I had to do what she said... she told me I belonged to the devil...

she'd say you do what I tell you to do... you can't quit... you ain't never going to quit... you do what I say... I said, well maybe she's akin to the Hands of Death, you know... but she was a real witch... she wore long dresses... long hair... she covered her face... she went through graveyards... and barns... putting spells... burning altars... she had skulls in her house... she showed me how to take a drawer and turn it upside down and build an altar out of it... and take hands and a knife and a cup, and put it all up there... it was real interesting... there was no slowing up...

When I was real little, my dad put me under the clothesline and he tied these two cats tails together... I was under the clothesline and these cats just scratched each other's guts out... blood was running over the top of me... I was yelling... I was real young... and he was akin to the Devil... and they used to make meat with a dog...

I was real little... he made me have sex with him... my real dad and my step father too... so I just kept going... couldn't stop...

I used to dress up like a girl when I was real little... so it got wilder and wilder over the years... couldn't stop... worse and worse... it just kept coming... wide open... I didn't know what to do... stop or quit or what, so I kept going... doing what my grandma told me to do...

I just kept going... sometimes she'd get a fresh body... and cut the head off and all... and then she'd take the head in her hands and hold it until the skin dried and sometimes she'd take the skin and put it up against her skin... I don't know why she was doing that... she'd cut the skin open and put it over her skin... I don't know why... she said it made her skin stay young... I don't know why she did it... I just did what she said...

Sometimes she would pee in a big jar and pour it all over me and tell me it was a way to keep the Devil in me... so that's what I did when I was a little kid... right or wrong... I couldn't figure it out...

The late Dr. Joel Norris was widely recognized for his book *Serial Killers: the Growing Menace,* and other case studies of serial killers including Henry Lee Lucas. His background as an art therapist was less well known. Looking like a furry troll who had been separated at birth from Jerry Garcia, he explained the principles he applied to his admittedly offbeat analysis of the criminal mind via artwork.

"It is easy enough to lie with words," Norris would say, "but the hands don't lie. It is impossible to fabricate in a drawing." Eyeing me out from under his grizzled thatch, he showed me how drawings can be used as X-rays of the unconscious mind. Even the primitive scrawls of the most limited intellect reveal something about his character and perception. Most revealing is observing the artist at his work.

During a series of interviews, Ottis Toole was asked to "draw a person," which is the first phase of a psychological profile involving drawing a person, a house, and a tree, each of which is symbolic of the self.

Though Toole's wrists were cuffed and shackled to waist chains, he was cooperative. Standing at a table with his body awkwardly twisted to one side and his range of motion severely restricted, he quickly sketched out the head of what appeared to be an immature young male. Then he stopped.

Norris later observed that the tendency throughout all of Toole's drawings to depict only disembodied heads could be an indicator of a lack of connection between his mind and body.

The age of the figure, said Norris, was an indication of the intellectual or emotional age of the subject. Since Toole's IQ testing revealed the intellectual development of a ten-year-old child, the pre-adolescent figure he drew would be consistent with the age at which his own development had apparently halted.

Toole was finding it enormously difficult to draw a complete human figure, or to identify what body parts were missing when asked. When Dr. Norris prompted him to go on by asking, "Can you draw the *whole* person?" Toole started at the neck and hesitantly drew the simple outline of the trunk, arms and legs, without any hands and feet. He was making small talk as he tried to concentrate on the task, but he seemed to grow increasingly nervous.

At one point he stopped and said, "I don't think I'm going to be able to draw it," but he persisted, using jerky, tentative strokes to affix primitive, claw-like hands at the ends of the arms.

Observing his evident strain, Norris asked, "How do you feel when you're having trouble drawing a whole person? Afraid you'll make a mistake?"

"Yeah, that's what it is."

"What if you do?"

"I'll just mess up the picture."

"What's the worst thing that can happen?"

"It won't look right."

"Would somebody fuss at you or spank you?"

"This teacher used to spank my hands with a ruler when I messed up."

Again he stopped, apparently satisfied with the figure.

"There's one thing missing still," pointed out Norris, without saying what it was. He was hoping Toole would notice that there were no feet. Norris interpreted the lack of feet as evidence of a mind that is not psychologically "grounded," or firmly related to the mundane, physical world.

Toole's response to this prompting, however, was not to draw feet on the figure. Immediately he directed his pen back up toward the upper portion of the figure. First he stopped at the throat, making a small line. Then his attention was drawn to the face, where he added details—first lines from the nose to the mouth, then more detail on the eyes.

Encouraging him, I commented, "You put some detail on the face—that's good!" He responded to my interest by adding a small horizontal line to the cheek. It didn't seem to correspond to any recognizable anatomical feature.

"Oh, what's that?" I asked.

"Oh, just something," Toole responded, and again stopped drawing.

"Now is there anything missing there?" prompted Norris once again.

Inspecting his picture at length, finally the puzzled convict noticed. "Oh, his feet!" Then he gave the legs of his man a pair of feet. However, Norris later observed that the feet Toole had drawn would never be able to actually support a man the size of the character he had drawn.

After the drawing of the full figure was completed, Toole sat down, lit up a cigarette, and asked, "Now what's that all about? What does that drawing mean?"

Norris answered, "Well, shrink that I am, it does makes me think of some stuff. Tell me some more about that teacher."

"She knew I could do things right, so she used to slap my hands."

I asked, "Then did that make you do better or worse?"

"Sometimes I'd do better, and sometimes I wouldn't do nothing at all."

Norris asked, "How did it make you feel?"

"It made me feel like reaching up and slapping her. It burned my hands, you know, it hurt. Then I had a man teacher, and he really worked on me."

Norris said, "One of the things I saw in the drawings that you sent to Sondra, was there was always a little boy that looked scared. And as you were drawing this man here today, I got the feeling that somewhere way back in your mind, you were really scared. Does that make sense?"

"I am scared of people to a certain extent. I'm the kind of person that don't get deep involved with people, you know. Ever' time I get deep involved, I know they'll be gone, and I'll be by myself again. I always get left behind, ever' time. Makes no difference who it is, everybody I get close to, I always get th'owed back again, th'owed back to the wolves. That's the way I thought this trip was going to work out today."

Norris responded, "Well, I know you don't know anything about me, but you're welcome to ask me any questions you want."

"I know you're a doctor. You gone send me a picture too?"

Norris smiled and answered, "Yeah, I'll send you a picture. See, Ottis, the kind of doctor I am, I don't believe people should be put to death for crimes. I've known a lot of people—Charles Manson, your friend Henry, and he's about as difficult as anybody I've ever met in my life, difficult to get along with, I mean. And even Henry, I don't believe he could help what he was doing. I don't believe anybody that's healthy and has had a good life would do this. Am I right?"

Ottis swallowed and said softly, "Yeah."

"And I don't say that I will always be your close friend, because I don't have time to be friends with everybody I know."

"Oh, you know what I mean, just by talking to 'em for a while, you know."

"But getting you through the trial, I would make a commitment to get you through the trial."

"Yeah?"

"There's something in your drawings and in interviews I've seen that people have done with you, there's a kindness about you, and you're like a hurt puppy, or a hurt child. And if that could be translated to the jury, I don't think they'd give you the death penalty."

Ottis slumped in his seat. "I've got four trials to get through."

"My impression of what you just said was, 'Yeah, but I'm just going to give up, it's just too much.' Is that what you just felt?"

"Yeah. I started the other day to say, well, I'll just go on and take the death penalty and be done with it."

"You mean cop a plea and not go to trial?"

"I said shoot, just cop a plea, you can't get death on a trial, once you cop a plea."

The most productive application of the principles of art therapy involves the therapist interactively discussing the drawing with the artist. Most of the drawings Toole sent me in 1991 showed people with unusually large ears, some almost as big as the heads. Before discussing these drawings with Toole, Norris had speculated that the large ears might mean that sounds seemed unusually loud to Toole, or that there had been a great deal of yelling in his family. However, the truth turned out to be much more significant.

When I asked Ottis why the people in his drawings had such big ears, at first he laughed. Then he said, "That's because when you get mad at one of 'em you can grab a-holt of their ears and pull 'em back."

"Big enough to use as handles, huh?" I bantered back, echoing his brittle laughter.

"Yeah," he cackled. "Handles." Another percussive laugh. We had to wait a while before he settled down.

Asked who had pulled his ears, he answered, "Mama used to pull my ears."

"What about the girls? Did they pull your ears?"

"Yeah. They did. Drusilla did."

Intuitively, Norris went for it: "What about your stepdaddy?"

Toole hesitated and lowered his hooded eyes, then in a soft voice said, "Yeah."

"And your daddy?"

Almost inaudibly, "Mm-hm."

"What did they do with your ears?"

At this point he withdrew completely into a troubled silence. He sighed, rested his forehead on his hand, and shifted uncomfortably in his seat. Finally he whispered, "I don't want to talk about it," and asked for another cigarette.

We went on to discuss several more drawings, but he remained subdued, still lost in memories of his own pain and degradation.

He had explained, "Whatever I talk about, I live it all over again in my mind. It's just like I'm doing it when I'm talking about it, like it's really happening to me." The tears in his eyes and the trembling in his chin left no doubt that he was once again experiencing the disturbed emotions of the little boy whose his ears were big enough to use as handles.

After Toole regained his composure somewhat, Norris probed the matter a little further, asking what his father had done to him.

"Oh, little bit of everything," he sighed, but he couldn't say exactly what.

Norris asked why he found it easy to relate the details of the crimes he had committed, but close to impossible to discuss his own abuse.

"Well," he shrugged, "some things just hurt too much."

Asked if he had been thinking about what had been done to him as a child, as he crushed the skull of a homosexual who was giving him oral sex and then stabbed him 106 times, he said, "I get all that kind of stuff in my mind and I just keep on going. I can't stop."

"Do you think that in a way you were killing your daddy or your stepdaddy when you did that crime?"

"I just kept killing 'em over and over."

 Otis Toole

On July 6, 1988, Henry Lee Lucas was interviewed in Texas by Florida Department of Law Enforcement Special Agent Joe Mitchell regarding the four homicides committed in the panhandle of Florida. In this interview he told Mitchell that he and Toole had discussed that if they ever got caught, they would confess to crimes they had not committed, and then recant their confessions, saying they hadn't done anything after all, in a deliberate attempt to muddy the waters. Their strategy succeeded all too well, leaving a trail of disbelief behind all of the murders they actually did commit.

An article by Marlene Sokol published in *Florida Times Union* on Oct. 22, 1983, reported Toole's first confession to killing Adam Walsh. The TV special about the case had just aired on October 10, and it was shortly after seeing it on TV in jail that he confessed to Duval County detective J.W. "Buddy" Terry.

"We had established quite a rapport over the months," said Terry. "He knows I won't lie to him, and he's generally been pretty honest with me. I guess he just needed someone to talk to."

Terry described Toole as quiet, soft-spoken and polite. "If you didn't know Toole was a murderer, you'd probably like him. He is honest in interviews, but sometimes he likes to play little games with us. Like he'll look at the wall and pretend he doesn't remember something, then say things like, 'If I was going to do something like that...' and then he'll come right back and tell us the whole story."

Police took him down to Hollywood, Florida, and then returned him to the Duval County Jail.

"We feel quite confident that Toole is the individual who killed Adam Walsh," Leroy Hessler, Assistant Hollywood Police Chief stated for the record. "I heard some of the details. It made Charles Manson sound like Tom Sawyer or Huckleberry Finn. Very gruesome. Of all the homicides he talked about, this is the only one that really bothered him. He can discuss other homicides and it doesn't bother him. He was remorseful about hurting this young boy. He broke down and cried when he talked about killing Adam."

John Walsh said, "I cannot comment on this individual, but I am relieved that he is off the streets. My heart will be broken for the rest of my life. I will always miss Adam."

In 1988, Toole described to reporter Bruce Ritchie how he had killed and cannibalized Adam Walsh:

The way it happened to Adam Walsh reminds me of my childhood too. It's really a filthy killing. It ain't no killing is clean. His head was chopped off and th'owed in a canal. Otherwise he was molested and chopped up, and I left some parts all through the canal, and I took some of the parts back to Jacksonville, and I barbecued it just like ribs and ate it, ate his ribs, you know. I deal in cannibalism too, I do. I mostly chopped him all up in little pieces.

I can't really deal with people too much, 'cause I don't know how to approach being around people. So I have to stay locked down. I can't approach the population or anybody else, because I might go haywire again, and just start chopping up somebody... I been doing all this since I was a child, I didn't just start doing it yesterday or the day before.

How this one happened was... [Adam] started whining a little bit, wanting to get out, you know. I hit him real hard on the chest and knocked the breath out of him. Then I got further down the road and I chopped his head off. Soon's I hit him in the chest, I put a blade up to his throat and cut him inside his neck, so I reckon that went on and drownded him inside his lungs, you know, that blood got inside of him. And then I put him face down and I took out my machete and chopped his head off. And I used a butcher knife on him too.... After I cut his head off, I drunk some of that blood.

Even though Toole remained the prime suspect in the Walsh murder, police never charged him, and many believe his lurid confessions to be a product of his vivid imagination, fueled by the desire to compete for headlines with Lucas. Even so, many of the details of other crimes he confessed to have been corroborated by witness statements and forensic evidence, and there is no doubt that, regardless of the actual count, he was every bit the dangerous homicidal maniac he claimed to be. Even though some of the stories he and Lucas have told might involve some degree of confabulation, still, it takes a certain type of person to seek status and acceptance by making such despicable boasts... it takes a *true vampire*—a thoroughly depraved, bloodthirsty serial killer.

Like every other serial killer I have dealt with personally, Toole exhibited extreme mood swings, inexplicable changes in demeanor, and indignant disavowal of his previous contradictory statements and actions. "I'm happy one minute, and sad one minute, then I forget all about it the next minute." Sometimes he might realize that he has changed and dismiss it casually; other times he wouldn't even realize that he was contradicting himself, and when confronted with the discrepancy, he might calmly admit that he'd been lying, or he might angrily deny it.

I have come to suspect that this combination of denial and instability is an essential component of the personality of many serial killers, inasmuch as the violence is sealed off from the more acceptable behavior, providing a mask of sanity that will allow him to interact at some level of society in daily life, while conducting his criminal career unapprehended for long enough to rack up the numbers that earn the *serial* rank.

When a killer is more overtly disturbed, he is more likely to come to the attention of law enforcement, and be apprehended rather quickly after the first offense. A serial killer might be articulate and attractive, like Ted Bundy, or he might be your subnormal gator like Toole and Lucas, but whatever level of society he occupies, he must be able to split off that part of his personality that commits crimes.

Whether this trait is actually a symptom of a dissociative disorder, or merely an artifact of legalistic denial combined with typical psychopathic blame-shifting, it is disconcerting at the very least, and can play havoc with the most carefully-laid plans.

In one interview, I asked Toole whether he ever got confused over whether he had done something or not, and he responded with a typical *non sequitur*: "That's just like that case in Colorado, I still say that's my case." He repeatedly insisted that the case, a double murder at a massage parlor, was his. I asked him if he wanted to tell me about it. He nodded. "Uh-huh."

I asked him three times, reminding him that we were on tape, if he was *sure* he wanted to talk about it, and after thrice repeating that he was sure, he added, "After *he* gets done here," with a nod towards Dr. Norris. I told him I would make the necessary arrangements.

It took phone calls, letters, affidavits and time, and meanwhile, Ottis was going through quite a few changes. For a while he was furious at me for "turning state's evidence" against him and "trying to get him electrocuted." He raved about wanting to stuff my head in a toilet. It reminded me of a statement he had made about the love of his life, Henry Lee Lucas: "My love turned to hate. That's what kind of love I got."

I continued to write to him throughout his vacillations, explaining the situation over and over and reminding him that I was merely following through on what he had told me he wanted to do. He wasn't being charged with murder, and I would not testify against him. I assured him that if he didn't want to talk about it any more, he could always *JUST SAY NO* and forget about the whole thing.

I'll never know what he understood from my letters, or why he abruptly changed his mind, but eventually he recovered his sunny demeanor, and seemed to grasp that I was not about to betray him. At any rate, he went back to writing that he loved me, and demented old queen that he was, even asking me to marry him. At least for a while...

I will write to you long as you keep me in stamps. I love you Sondia.

Ottis Toole

Nine months later, in April of 1992 we found ourselves in court, where Toole had been transported by Lear jet at a cost to the People of Colorado of a half-million dollars. Another man, Park Estep, had been convicted of the crime, had served his sentence, and had recently been released. He had been attending the Air Force Academy when convicted of the double murder, and at this point he just wanted his record cleared. If Toole would tell the court he had done it, Estep's conviction would be reversed and the records would reflect his innocence.

Ottis Toole had given detailed confessions to the two slayings in 1988, to the legendary homicide detective Lou Smit, and the entire series of videotapes was played back as Toole sat there in court watching himself describing every detail of the crimes, even drawing an accurate layout of the massage parlor and diagram of its location on the street. As he told the story to Smit in 1988, he had stabbed one woman and shot the other, raping one and setting the other one on fire.

The tape was periodically paused while Estep's lawyer Richard Tegtmeier questioned Toole on the details step-by-step. Toole denied everything, pouting like a child, petulantly taunting Estep, Tegtmeier, Smit, the prosecutor, the public, even spitting filth at Her Honor. "Y'all can take that confession and shove it up your ass whichever way it fits!"

The confession on the tape showed Toole stating that before he left the scene of the crime, he had taken some petty cash from a jar in the kitchen.

Tegtmeier stopped the tape and turned to Toole. "So you took some money from a jar on the kitchen counter..."

"I did *NOT*, stupid!" snapped Toole, "The jar was on top of the *refrigerator*!" He smirked, pleased with his slap at the attorney, but lacking the insight to realize that he had incriminated himself.

The State of Colorado promised him that he would not be prosecuted for this crime; they just wanted to know whether there was sufficient reason

 Henry Lee Lucas

to give Park Estep a new trial. But Toole adamantly refused to cooperate.

Several times, when he acted up, he would grin and mug at me like I was in on the joke. He claimed the 1988 confession was just a game he was playing to embarrass the police, and said the details he had furnished were just lucky guesses. "I ain't killed *nobody* in the State of Colorado!"

For three days, Toole sat on the witness stand in waist-chains, shackled hand and foot, watching himself chain-smoke his way through his explicit confession. By the third day, he was more fractious than ever. He leaped to his feet and shook his fists, rattling his chains and hurling obscenities in all directions. Her Honor sat perfectly still and made no response at all.

After one outburst, Tegtmeier asked him how he felt. "I feel like I'm about to go *off*," he leered, panning the courtroom to gauge the reaction of Lou Smit, myself, and the rest of his rapt audience. "Y'all won't let me smoke a *damn* thing, that's why I'm not going to cooperate!" He had not been allowed to have a cigarette since he left Florida. Colorado was a non-smoking state, and no exceptions were to be made.

Even though the Court had brought me out there directly pursuant to his statement that he wanted to tell me about the case, they would not allow Toole to talk to me. So the crimes he had insisted he wanted to tell me about were stubbornly denied, as a mischievous Ottis Toole once again had his fun with law enforcement, gloating and gaping, basking in his moment of glory.

Her Honor found no reason to reverse Park Estep's conviction on the massage parlor murders, and so Ottis Toole was flown back to Florida State Prison to continue serving his time back home in the swamps of Florida, a state where a guy could still enjoy a smoke.

> Ottis Toole was a big old 220-pound queer with nothing good-looking about him at all, and Henry Lucas was a one-eyed dirty thing that never took a bath, so they kind of went together, because too many people wouldn't have either one of them.
> + James Redwine

Love was only part of the tangled emotions Ottis Toole and Henry Lee Lucas had for each other. Ultimately, in their twisted world, just as murder was not enough, neither was love. Police descriptions paint Lucas and Toole like bookends—sometimes as twins, sometimes as opposites.

Profound confusion about sexual identity exists in some serial killers, with many displaying endocrine dysfunction. Like a revolving yin/yang, these two men would trade roles—both physically and psychologically.

When arrested, Toole was a large, robust man—6'1" and 200 lbs. His services as a roofer were in demand, because he could take buckets of tar in both hands and walk straight up a ladder. Yet, this burly Neanderthal loved to dress up in drag and solicit sex with men.

Even though Henry Lee Lucas often spoke as if he were the macho one of the pair, he was also known to refer to himself as Toole's wife. Lucas denied any homosexuality in himself; yet his appearance was always more soft-spoken, more passive—more feminine, if you will—than that of his rangy partner. Toole described their lives together as "just like Bonnie and Clyde," and said they would take turns with which one would play Bonnie. They'd also, he confided, play games with their crimes, trying to outdo each other.

There are conflicting stories about when Toole met Lucas, and the version repeated most often was that it was in 1974, when Lucas was working at a Pennsylvania mushroom farm. Regardless of the questionable details of their prior association, sources agree that it was in 1976 that Toole ran into Lucas at the Mission near Springfield, and took him home to begin the ultimate phase of their conjoined murder spree.

Betty Redwine, the woman Ottis Toole called "Mama Betty," who had been the landlady and employer of both Toole and Lucas, sat out on the porch on a summer's day in 1991, rocked and talked about two of the most prolific serial killers in modern history:

> Ottis just brought him in here one day and said, "Betty, I want you to meet my friend. His name is Lucas and he's gone be around the place and help me work around here."
>
> And Lucas looked like he was staying pretty drunk and Ottis looked like he was staying about half-drunk or pilled up or something, and he got where he was falling down on the work and wasn't helping me, and all they wanted to do was get in that old car and go to ridin' and ridin', half-drunk and doped up, and they come in there in the dining room and want some money off'n me and I said, "Listen, I'm gone tell y'all right now, you ain't gone get a dime outta me, 'less you get outta here and go to work or help me do this work around here. I'm not givin' you nothin'!"
>
> But I didn't worry about them none, because I always had a pistol pretty handy too, you know. And Ottis and Lucas are not gone come in here and jump on me, because Ottis knew how I was and he knew I wouldn't back down from 'em, and if they jumped on me, I would've just shot 'em, that's all. I put my foot down pretty much, and Ottis knew that what I said WENT. It HAD to go. And he looked up to me, you know.

Ottis was a mama's boy. He was a queer, and she knew he was a queer, and she was the sole person between him and his brothers, you know. And it was always my mama done this, and my mama done that, and then after she died, I was his mama then. You see them letters he wrote me, he'd say, "Mama Betty, Mama Betty, Mama Betty." And "I love you, Mama Betty." That's how he always ended the letters.

He always relied on his mother for everything and she told him everything to do, and he listened. That was his love and the only thing in his life that he really loved. I never heard anything about his father.

But his mother, she give him a bed to sleep on and she give him something good to eat and a roof over his head and kept ever'thing warm, and they always had somebody living there with 'em, she had her grandchildren and all of them out there.

I remember when he would go all the way out to his mother's grave and he told me when he got out there, the grave would tremble. He went out there quite often. He said he'd sit on the head of the grave and it would just tremble. He'd come back wore out and tired, with the sweat just pouring off of him. Look like he'd run all the way home from the cemetery.

I don't think that any man Ottis ever had really cared anything about him. So when he got Lucas, he got him a companion. And Lucas got a home to stay in. He was on the street, didn't have no place to live, and Ottis come and took him out of the mission and carried him home with him, and Ottis was expecting something, you know, expecting to have a love affair with him. He ain't gone drag a man out there and give him free rent and do this and do that for him unless he, you know... but Henry just more or less wanted a place to live.

I always looked at Lucas as the man and Ottis as the woman. He always said Lucas was the only man he ever loved. And Ottis was jealous over Lucas. Just like Ottis told me, he said Lucas was not a queer. He said, "I'm the one pushed it," he said, "because I wanted sex with Lucas." He said, "I'm the one that forced Lucas to have sex with me."

Ottis had Jesus Christ's picture on his wall in there for a long time. Then one day he come in with the Devil's picture. And he said, "Well, I'll put one on each side of the room, and I'll look at the Devil and then I'll look at Jesus Christ."

Ottis said him and Lucas went to California and that's where they got into this group. When they went in there, the rite was that they would kill somebody and they would have to drink the human blood, and they had some kind of insignia that they'd put on your skin showing that you would belong to the group.

I understood that they did put something on Lucas, but I never have seen it. But when they got to Ottis, they looked into his eyes and they said,

"You're the very Devil himself, we don't need to put no mark on you."

He told me they had one in Florida. He said they would notify him when one was going to happen. He said, don't you know when I'd disappear once in a while... and I didn't know when that would be, because the only time he could disappear would be at night. He'd get off at about 8 o'clock and he would go do whatever he'd want to. He was in and out all the time.

But he said these guys wore hoods and they had the meetings way out in the woods. He said he would go to it whenever it was being held. But they wore hoods, you know, and he said you never knew who was under them hoods. He said they didn't want nobody to know who they was.

And he said once you got in that thing, there was no pulling out of it, and if you tried to get out of it, that was your death warrant, because they'd come out and kill you. He said that's the reason they wore them hoods, because if they took a notion to kill somebody, if they thought somebody was out running their mouth about it, they would come out and kill 'em.

He said they sacrificed human beings and drank human blood. But he never told me about that when he was living here. He didn't tell me that until he was in the county jail. He was in there about three or four months and he'd call me nearly ever' day.

One morning I came in here in the office, and Ottis was sitting at the office desk, and he smiled, and he said, "I want you to meet my two friends." And when I looked at them guys, and they looked at me, and they hung their heads down like they were shamed. And he said, "I'll tell you sons of bitches right now," he said, "Y'all shamed of me? Get your asses up and get 'em out! Right now!" That's what Ottis told 'em.

Cause when I come in, both of 'em was sittin' on that couch right there, and both of 'em hung their heads down. I don't know if they knew me or saw me before, or didn't want me to catch up with 'em being with a queer or what, but they were ashamed of him and he knew it. "Both you sons of bitches get out of here! Shamed of me? You get out of here and don't come back!"

Ottis calls himself a woman. When he's out at work, he don't talk about that stuff too much, he just does his work, he don't have time for all that gay talk. But otherwise, he's like a woman. He wants to get in there and fix up things and make them look pretty—kind of feminine, you know. And he would put a wig and a dress on and go down there on Main Street looking like a woman.

There was an old attic I had in that house at 217 First Street and he asked me if he could have it and I told him, you want to stay up in the attic, it's all right with me. It was a big place. And he put two or three couches in there and two or three beds in there, and the next thing I know, he's chargin' 'em so much a night to stay up 'ere in that place.

Then it come to me about his shows up there. These guys will get to talking, you know, and know pretty much ever'thing that goes on around here. Said Ottis would get flowers and plants and hang 'em from the rafters up there in the ceilings. The attic had some little windows on the sides and he had some curtains rigged up there. It wasn't nothing fancy or nothing like that, but he did have it fixed up right nice. And he would have these men up there and put on a show—dress up like a woman and fix all this food and beer and stuff.

And I told him I was going to have to put a stop to that, because he was running me some competition, renting out the bed and serving the food and putting on a show. That was when I fired him and he went to live over there in that shack on Market Street. But no sooner did he move than he come begging me to take him back and sayin' he wouldn't do nothin' like that no more, he'd work for free and he'd do anything I want, if I'd just take him back.

The reason Ottis wanted to stay here is we got 50 to 75 men in these houses, and he's always in and out cleaning up, and he sees all these men. It's just like at the penitentiary. He gets in that penitentiary, he probably likes it. Because he's queer, he's a female, and he's got all them men.

> If you still want to come do the interview its open to you. But I already turned down Geraldo But you are welcome to come.
>
> Sincerly Henry Lee Lucas

Ottis Toole's eldest sister, Drusilla, grew into an unstable woman who spent some time in a mental hospital. Later, she bounced from man to man, giving birth along the way to three ill-fated children—Sarah Pierce, Frieda (Becky) Powell, and Frank Powell.

Sarah Pierce, Drusilla's eldest, came closest to repeating her mother's pattern—indulging in drugs, alcohol and promiscuity, often having sex with men her Uncle Ottis would bring home, while he would watch. She was considered a nymphomaniac, and like Uncle Ottis, she had gone to jail for arson.

The situation in the Powell household was so chaotic that Sarah Harley, Ottis and Drusilla's mother, took the initiative to turn little Becky and Frank over to the custody of Uncle Ottis and his constant companion Henry, who took them along on their odysseys.

Henry had already become enamored with nine-year-old Becky, and by the time they went on the road together, their relationship had become sexual. Henry claims that he thought of her mostly as a daughter, but that he occasionally indulged Becky's desire for sex.

When they returned the children to their mother in Jacksonville, it was not too long before Becky was raped by her stepfather, and Drusilla committed suicide because of it. Sarah had already left home by that time, and Becky and Frank were institutionalized.

Henry Lee Lucas missed his child bride, and drove to the state home and broke her out. He took Becky with him back to Jacksonville, where Toole's wife Novella informed him, in her typically abrasive fashion, that the juvenile authorities were already looking for Becky and were sure to take her back when they found her. So Henry took Becky and left town in the dead of night, leaving Toole behind.

Little Becky and Frank had been used as bait by Toole and Lucas to attract victims to their death. As innocent children, they were abused and traumatized by these men who were supposedly acting as their guardians. When Lucas took Becky with him, Toole took leave of his senses, worrying and wondering why they had left him behind in Jacksonville.

Toole set out for Texas to find Lucas, but before he could catch up with him, Lucas had killed Becky in a fit of pique. According to Toole, it was the murder of his niece that finally turned his love for Lucas to hate.

Becky's brother Frank was committed to a mental hospital, allegedly driven hopelessly insane by the horrors he had been forced to participate in and observe.

While Lucas' statements about Becky's murder angered Toole, he claimed that what offended him most was Lucas' accusations that Toole had sexually molested Becky himself. Though the most unbelievably out-rageous behavior may be tolerated, even the most bloodthirsty serial killers apparently have their limits—at least in their own minds. While indignant that Lucas would even so much as say such a thing about him, Toole readily compartmentalized recall of the documented incest with his sister Drusilla, and conveniently expunged the years of his complicity in the consensual relations between Henry and Becky, while they were trav-eling together.

In 1985, a book by Max Call was published called *Hand of Death*, which was allegedly written with the cooperation of Henry Lee Lucas and at the behest of Clementine Schroeder, the lay minister who had become Lucas' close personal friend. In this book, Call described how Lucas was recruited into a cult of devil-worshipping criminals by a Florida man he refers to by the pseudonym of "Don Meteric."

Call also claimed that Ottis Toole had been in the cult for years before Lucas was initiated, in a ritual that required him to kill a man and eat portions of the victim's body. This book consistently portrays Henry as the reluctant participant in hundreds of abductions and murders, with Toole the enthusiastic instigator. While Lucas was very vocal about the details of his alleged cult activities, throughout the years Toole remained comparatively silent, lending an air of mystery to his role.

In the latter part of 1983, after Henry experienced a religious conversion in the Williamsburg County Jail in Texas, he began to talk openly about the cult. "I want the Hand of Death to be exposed. I've told people about the camp in the Everglades but they never include it in any of their stories. I've told the police but they don't seem interested. The FBI and the Texas Rangers believe me, yet I'm not seeing any action," Lucas was quoted by Call.

Ottis Toole's family background in a generational form of "devil-worship" that involved the ritual use of human remains and the drinking of blood has been well-documented. Years later, he volunteered information about his lifelong cult involvement in debriefings with law enforcement and attorneys as well as interviews with journalists. He named the real "Don Meteric" as a man who had known his grandmother and provided cars for Henry to drive on their journeys, as well as plenty of drugs and booze to use along the way.

He identified the location of the Process Church headquarters in New Orleans, and accurately described their occult philosophies. He mentioned the cult name "Dagon Abraxas," which is not the sort of name you hear on every street corner, as being in charge of a ranch south of the border where they took guns and minor children. He explained how their Florida employers and/or associates would sign them in and out of work to provide alibis, when they were really off doing jobs for what he called "the cult."

It's true that authorities have been less than impressed with these stories of a devil-worshipping death cult. Since investigating officers have been unable to find any tangible evidence of such a criminal conspiracy, they remain skeptical of its existence. Why, then, would these stories be circulated? Ken Lanning, Supervisory Special Agent at the National Center for the Analysis of Violent Crime at the FBI Academy, explains why many criminals rely on a negative spiritual belief system to justify their lawlessness:

Some psychotic people are preoccupied with religious delusions and hear the voice of God or Satan telling them to do things of a religious nature. Offenders who feel little, if any, guilt over their crimes may need little justification for their antisocial behavior. As human beings, however, they may have fears, concerns and anxiety over getting away with their criminal acts. It is difficult to pray to God for success in doing things that are against His commandments. A negative spiritual belief system may fulfill their human need for assistance from and belief in a greater power or to deal with their superstitions.

Lanning further cautions against confusing cause and effect, even when there is evidence of occult activity on the part of an offender.

It is easy to blame involvement in satanism and the occult for behaviors that have complex motivations. Blaming satanism for a... murder is like blaming a criminal's offenses on his tattoos: both are often signs of the same rebelliousness and lack of self-esteem that contribute to the commission of crimes.

Al Washington, who represented Toole in the Sonenberg arson-murder that put him on Death Row, said, "I don't believe Ottis Toole or Henry Lucas are competent to function in a criminal organization, or to follow a sophisticated philosophy or belief system. They might have been exposed to something of this sort at some time but I don't think that explains their crimes."

Ottis tells me of a snake emerging from the mouth of a woman's severed head in the Cave of Skulls, and later I uncover substantiation that the Hand of Death is a snake cult that deals in lycanthropy... Ottis says he ate people because he enjoyed it. He ate the meat of women sacrificed during cult rituals. Eating meat sacrificed to idols is routinely Baalist, and isn't the Hand of Death simply Neo-Baalist or even Neo-Molochean?

The bottom line is satanism. Real satanists are super secret, which should come as no surprise. Who is going to do an exposé of a group that can summon lycanthropic powers? Voodoo, *Santeria, obeah*... all these are real and powerful dark forces, and virgin sacrifice is nothing new either. And I don't doubt it still goes on at Snake Island and Rancho Diablo.

+ Serial killer Gerard John Schaefer

THEY FELT LIKE VAMPIRES

"Serial killers are psychological monsters who have taken the place of werewolves and vampires," says author Harold Schechter, a professor at Queens College.

"They are the cream of the crop and only the most crafty stay on the streets for decades because they are careful and invisible," says criminologist Jack Levin. It's only when they begin to slip that we find out about them.

"I just don't believe people are born evil," says professor of psychiatry Dorothy Otnow Lewis. "To my mind, that is mindless. Forensic psychiatrists tend to buy into the notion of evil. I felt that that's no explanation. The deed itself is bizarre, grotesque. But it's not evil. To my mind, evil bespeaks conscious control over something. Serial murderers are not in that category. They are driven by forces beyond their control."

But Andrew Vachss doesn't agree: "The truth is as simple as it is terrifying: Sickness is a condition. Evil is a behavior. Evil is always a matter of choice. Evil is not thought; it is conduct. And that conduct is always volitional. And just as evil is always a choice, sickness is always the absence of choice. Sickness happens. Evil is inflicted."

To decide whether a serial killer like Jeffrey Dahmer is actually evil, or just sadly sick, consider above all his behavior. When he was arrested, among the items found in his apartment were a fresh torso ripped open in the kitchen sink; two 50-gallon garbage cans full of rotting torsos; a bucket of hands; skulls on shelves and in fridge, next to a lobster pot with a stewed penis in it; a pickled penis in a jar, and a fresh one in the sink.

Something stronger than my conscious will made it happen. I think some higher power got good and fed-up with my activity and decided to put an end to it. I don't really think there were any coincidences. The way it ended and whether the close calls were warnings to me or what, I don't know. If they were, I sure didn't heed them... If I hadn't been caught or lost my job, I'd still be doing it, I'm quite sure of that.

I've always wondered, from the time that I committed that first horrid mistake, sin, with Hicks, whether this was sort of predestined and there was no way I could have changed it. I wonder just how much predestination controls a person's life and just how much control they have over themselves...

 Jeffrey Dahmer

Am I just an extremely evil person or is it some kind of satanic influence, or what? I have no idea. I have no idea at all. Do you? Is it possible to be influenced by spirit beings? I know that sounds like an easy way to cop out and say that I couldn't help myself, but from all that the Bible says, there are forces that have a direct or indirect influence on people's behavior. The Bible calls him Satan. I suppose it's possible because it sure seems like some of the thoughts aren't my own, they just come blasting into my head... These thoughts are very powerful, very destructive, and they do not leave. They're not the kind of thoughts that you can just shake your head and they're gone. They do not leave.

I should have gone to college and gone into real estate and got myself an aquarium, that's what I should have done.

Jeffrey Dahmer was beaten to death with a piece of weight-lifting equipment on November 28, 1994. Convicted of the murder was psychotic killer Christopher Scarver, who claimed to be Jesus Christ because not only was his mother's name Mary, but he was a carpenter.

Dahmer's brain was preserved in formaldehyde upon the request of his mother, who intended for it to be studied. His father sued his mother for overriding their son's wish to be cremated. On December 12, 1995, the judge ruled in Lionel Dahmer's favor, and the brain was destroyed.

Six months later in the same court, Circuit Judge Daniel George compelled the City of Milwaukee to turn over Jeffrey Dahmer's personal belongings to an attorney representing the families of his victims. Robert Steurer intended to auction them off to settle claims filed against the City by the victims' families.

Finally a Milwaukee civic group pledged $407,225 to buy the Dahmer estate and burn it, rather than see the macabre murderabilia put on the auction block, and so on June 28, 1996 his belongings were destroyed. Yet his depraved legacy lives on in the Slayer song named *213*, after Dahmer's apartment number.

Serial killer Ted Bundy told police the night of his last arrest, "Sometimes I felt like a vampire." Although the multi-state serial slayer and escape artist was more interested in necrophilia than the drinking of blood, still he was a biter, and the vampiric element of psychic predation apparently resonated with his psychosexually-motivated murder mentality.

These are excerpts from an interview Ted Bundy gave Dorothy Otnow Lewis the day before his execution; the full transcript appears in *Defending the Devil*, by Polly Nelson:

I think that there's more, an integration there, an interrelationship, which when the malignant portion of my personality or consciousness, call it what you will—the entity—is more or less directing the mood and the action, I'm still on another level of consciousness of this, I'm not totally unconscious of, or unaware of it.

There are times I've, the rage and the madness was just so strong, I was just so... I'd be screeching, screeching, cursing, you know. That's when I was, deep down inside I was watching this, I said, You're absolutely mad. This is just madness. Oh, yes.

Initially, of course, I was nauseated and horrified, just frightened, more than I can say. I couldn't sleep for days the first two times this happened. I just couldn't sleep. I just was appalled by what had happened. Now as the years passed and the incidents happened, I reached the point where I just suffocated. I would always feel that sense of despair and horror kind of combined, but it wouldn't really last for more than a few hours. And then I'd go home and go to bed or whatever and just go back to being myself.

That whole kind of consciousness was just totally dominant. I mean, the need, the thought, the feeling, the excitement of harming, of getting some sort of sexual gratification at harming someone, was absolutely paramount. Driving me. I mean, that was coming from some source within me, and yet it was not me.

But you see, this is what I'd never done before. I'd never bitten anyone before, and this is an indication, you know, how... I don't know... supercharged or whatever, bestial, even, I was at that time.

There was another serial killer who said, when he heard that Ted Bundy had felt like a vampire, "Myself? I-oooh... Grrrr-snap! My transfiguration leaned more towards a werewolf. The sun would go down and the gentle voices of the night drew me out. I couldn't resist their urgings."

Later, in his cell on Death Row, he wrote of a dream in which he observed, "I could fly, because I was a vampire." What began as an actual dream became the basis of fiction, as he turned his favorite rape fantasy into an illustrated short story called *Vampire's Dream*. One year after he wrote this fantasy, into the cell next to the dreamer moved a confessed double murderer and leader of a teenage vampire cult, who at the age of 17, arrived to become the youngest man on Florida's Death Row.

While crimes of dreams and dramatic fiction tend to be heavily symbolic, the murders committed by the true vampire who moved in next door to the dreamer paradoxically had no vampiric components whatsoever. In his case, although his fascination with the trappings of the occult

 Ted Bundy

seemed to stem from the same generalized disaffection, when it actually came to murder, he was far less organized and more primitive.

The dysfunctional lifestyle that predisposes toward crime proceeds from an inclination toward all transgressive behavior. In other words, they were vampires and they killed, but although much of their behavior did proceed from their vampire role-playing games, the crimes they committed did not. Rather, both the role-playing and the murders proceeded from the same malaise, a sense of alienation so profound that they have utterly disassociated from their own common humanity.

In this case, as well as the other remarkably similar Kentucky vampire cult case, crimes were committed for motives no more occult than the theft of sports utility vehicles from the innocent victims they slaughtered, the better to make it to New Orleans in proper vampire style.

VAMPIRE MOM AND HER FERAL SPAWN

Born into a broken home in rural southwestern Kentucky, Roderick Justin Ferrell grew up immersed in role-playing games and deviant behavior. Sondra Gibson had divorced his father and worked sporadically as a waitress, dancer and hooker. Sometimes she would keep the boy with her in the small, quiet, predominantly Baptist college town of Murray, Kentucky, perhaps best known as the home of the National Boy Scout Museum. Sometimes Sondra would leave young Rod with her parents in Eustis, Florida, while she pursued other interests. In either case, the boy more or less ran wild.

By the time he reached 16, Vampire Mom and her feral spawn were both involved in a community of about 30 role-playing Kentucky vampires. It started out with playing *Vampire: the Masquerade*, the White Wolf game.

"There didn't seem to be anything wrong with it," Gibson told Reuters. "I played it with him. It's hard enough to find something you can do with your kids today, and the game was fun. It was something, anyway." Gibson said the game had remained a fantasy. "It was a thrill, sure. But it was still role playing. People pretended to do stuff, but didn't really do it."

Vampire Mom's indulgence in inappropriate socializing with minors of the opposite sex eventually landed her a felony conviction for writing a sexually explicit letter to a 14-year-old boy, inviting him to join her in a vampiric ceremony involving close personal contact with her distinctly undead genitalia.

Rod Ferrell was repeatedly suspended from school, and in September of 1995, was finally expelled. When police asked him why, he smirked, "For being a little asshole." His lifestyle degenerated into sleeping all day and staying out all night with his vampire friends, who gathered at a ruined building littered with empty liquor bottles and the detritus of drug use, and messages like "Please deposit dead bodies here" scrawled on the walls.

In October, Ferrell was among a group of teens accused of breaking into an animal shelter, beating 40 dogs, and mutilating two puppies. "They had stomped one of them to death and one of them, they pulled the legs off," said Sheriff Stan Scott of Calloway County, Kentucky, about 180 miles southwest of Louisville. Ferrell later confessed to the crimes, and told psychiatrists he had been torturing and mutilating animals since the age of nine, boasting of beating cats to death, and laughing, "I did much worse to the dogs."

One of the Murray vampires who had engaged in role-playing games with Ferrell since the fourth grade said that Ferrell "had become possessed with opening the Gates to Hell, which meant he would have to kill a large number of people in order to consume their souls." John Goodman told reporters Ferrell claimed that by doing this, he believed that he would obtain "super powers."

Besides drinking blood in a search for eternal life, there was also morbid self-mutilation. "I cut it to watch the blood roll down," Ferrell later admitted. "Sometimes I cut to hope I can die."

A connection to early abuse emerged as Ferrell explained his self-mutilation. "A lot of shit happened to me whenever I was little and it triggers off in my memory sometimes and I freak out."

Charity "Che" Keesee, Ferrell's 17-year-old girlfriend who was pregnant with his child, mutilated herself as well. "The same thing with Che... I had cut myself because I override my pain, cause like Che, she was raped by her stepfather when she was 12, and that's what triggers off in her mind."

On Friday, November 22, 1996, Ferrell abruptly informed Che that she was coming along on a trip with him and his best friend, Scott Anderson.

"I told her either she agreed or I'd hogtie her," said Ferrell. "I told Che beforehand that I was going to take her with me and just take like a half-ass road trip, because I was sick of Murray, because all the cops were bugging me there for something I didn't do." Che's best friend Dana Cooper, 19, came along voluntarily, out of concern for her pregnant friend. Ferrell describes the chaotic process that set the four Kentucky vampire teens on the road to murder:

> So I was going over to Dana's house to see her, and Scott pulled up because that night he was taking his little brothers to the skating rink and whenever he got there we all decided just to pick up and leave, cause we'd planned on that a week before we got caught, and before we had charges brought up against us for making explosives, and there was like seven warrants out for us; after that was cleared that was when we decided to pick up and leave, so we had Charity and Dana go tell his brothers that we had been beaten and kidnapped, so they wouldn't think about looking for us. They, we told them that the car was totaled because we took the Buick. Right after we told them that, it was around 11:00. We headed straight, ah, for 20 West, or 20 East, to reach 75 going southbound. Basically the rest of that was driving to Florida.

Their ultimate destination was New Orleans, but first they headed for Eustis, Florida, a small town about 35 miles from Disney World, to pick up another aspiring vampire. While living with his maternal grandparents the year before, Ferrell had met a girl who had been planning to run away to New Orleans with him over the previous seven months.

Heather "Zoey" Wendorf, 15, wore purple hair and a dog chain around her neck. Though her granddaddy had been Billy Graham's lawyer, Heather had told friends she had been a demon in past lives and boasted of invoking spirits during blood rituals.

"She was a real nice girl, but deep down you could tell she had some heavy problems," said Joe Barrett, 15, a friend of Heather's in Eustis. "When she started hanging around a different crowd last year, she went from being real nice to being quiet. She started dying her hair—purple mostly—and wearing all-black clothes." Some said she swore she was a vampire.

Heather confided her deepest, darkest secrets to Ferrell, considered him to be a "father figure" and looked forward to the day he would return to Florida for her and they could live together "like a family."

The Murray vampires arrived in Eustis, Florida, on Monday. "Whenever we got here we just chilled out for a couple of days," said Ferrell in his detailed statements to police, "and on Tuesday we, ah, got pulled over by a state cop for a flat tire and they checked our plates and they checked our identities and all that and we got nervous so we decided we were leaving that night, still going along with the same plan, just pick up the girls and leaving."

Heather Wendorf's best friend Jeanine Leclair, who was another one of Ferrell's former girlfriends, had been planning to come along, but when the summons came, "she like tried crawling out of a window and then decided that it was too hard. Told us to come back for her later."

That afternoon, Ferrell took Wendorf to a cemetery, where they conducted a blood drinking ritual to "cross her over" as a fellow vampire. Ferrell explained the ritual: "You cut yourself, let them drink it, it runs through their veins for a few moments and then your blood becomes tainted and you drink from them and become the untainted. You go around feeding on humans."

"The person that gets crossed over is like subject to whatever the sire wants," Wendorf later said in a deposition. "Like the sire is boss basically. They have authority over you."

Ferrell and Wendorf differed in the accounts they gave later about the conversation in the graveyard, with Ferrell maintaining Heather told him she wanted her parents killed, and Wendorf claiming the opposite. Heather's story is that she only learned her parents had been slain afterwards, as the five vampires fled the scene of the crime.

Jennifer Wendorf told investigators that "within the past 30 days, Heather Wendorf has asked me if I had ever planned to kill our parents" and that her sister had gone on to state that if she needed anyone killed, "next time Rod's down, he can do it."

Police apprehended the runaway teens driving the stolen Buick in Eustis shortly before the murders. "They ran our I.D.'s and shit and couldn't find anything so they let us go."

Rod Ferrell had never met the victims, and later commented that, "I went to the wrong house first. Didn't kill anybody though, cause I looked in and saw there was little kids and that's my rule, I don't kill anything that's little. Now adults, that's perfectly fine, 16 and up." And so he and Scott proceeded to a house that better suited their slaughterous intentions.

Heather's father Richard Wendorf, 49, and his wife Naoma Queen, 53, were found by Wendorf's 17-year-old daughter, Jennifer, bludgeoned to death in their home with a "V" sign surrounded by five circular marks burned into Wendorf's body.

Ferrell explained that their interest was chiefly in the Explorer. Besides the vehicle, a credit card and some small change, the only items Ferrell admitted to taking were Heather's father's knife and her mother's pearls which were around her teddy bear's neck. Heather had already taken all the money, he said.

The four Murray vampires joined by Heather Wendorf were headed for the elegant city that haunted their vampire dreams. After switching the tags, they ditched the Buick, and took off in the Explorer, stopping only for gas—after they learned the hard way to keep an eye on the gas gauge.

Scott had not been driving the Explorer for long when they ran out of gas. "A state trooper came up and said he thought we were broken down."

Police had their third chance at the fugitives at a rest stop. "One of those state cops were talking to a security guard and I was letting the state cop bum cigarettes off me," said Ferrell.

"I think we got stopped at least three times on like the highway itself by state cops and they just came in—they asked us if everything was okay, everything is fine, where we were headed, then let us go."

And so they "took off like a bat out of hell going as fast as the Explorer would go, straight to New Orleans."

"Got to New Orleans about a day, exactly a day later," recalled Ferrell. They found New Orleans all right, but they never did find their mythic city of intrigue. "I went there at night. That's when we arrived, right as the sun was setting, and we parked the Explorer on Second Street, and that's when we started walking around. Got pulled over by the New Orleans police... it's not common to see white people walking through the complex. They let us go."

As the disenchanted teens toured the crack side of New Orleans, they were less than charmed with what they saw. "That's when Che freaked out, because she's never been to a big city, and she's never seen black people carry around AK-47's in their back yards," Ferrell told police. "I still have a lot of friends in New Orleans and that was where I was going to live. And if Che didn't freak out that's where I would have been right now. What can I say, it's a bitch about living in the big cities, you learn to be good friends with the cops and crime lords."

The dissatisfied desperados left the city and took the back roads, looking for "a nice forest area." Ferrell said, "I was just going to fucking ditch the fucking Explorer in some lake and start going through the fucking woods, killing deers or whatever I could find for meat... We went into a secluded forest area to rest so that way no policeman could see us. My idea of course, they cut down camouflage and shit to cover up the Explorer. Worked quite nicely."

After resting up, they headed for Baton Rouge. Ferrell told police they were "flat broke, had no food and the only thing I could do, cause I didn't want to kill anymore, was to look for an empty house, and I found one... made sure they were gone for Thanksgiving or something. I broke the door down..."

"Then we did food, weaponry detail, and money detail. Any kind of money we found, any kind of food that was actually eatable and could last for awhile, and any kind of weaponry that would upgrade us, we picked up. I was on weaponry detail. I had them on food and money. They found a jar full of money which equaled about $20.00. That got us our gas. They found plenty of food in the refrigerator and cupboard. Searched the house looking for the weapons that we found. I found a 12 gauge, box of bullets, which weren't 12 gauge bullets which didn't help, ah, one compound bow, a shitload of arrows, and I think that's all the weapons we found there."

They were finally taken into custody on Thanksgiving night in a motel room in Baton Rouge, Louisiana, after Che called her mother in South Dakota, and her mother told her to charge the room to her credit card.

"Believe it or not, they fell for it," said Sheriff Scott.

"Her mother was asking way too many fucking questions," said Ferrell. "I knew she was going to turn us in. I told Che to hang up right then and get the fuck out, don't tell her where the fuck we were, because I knew she was going to turn us in. Against my wishes she did, while I was ditching the shit, and within the next half hour the police pulled up at the Howard Johnson's Inn, and that's whenever I just walked straight to the cop car and put my hands behind my back and said, 'Okay, let's go.'"

Upon being taken into custody by Baton Rouge police, Rod Ferrell gave detailed confessions, which were videotaped and played in February of 1998 at Ferrell's murder trial. This author sat behind the sobered-up, cleaned-up, scrawny, sullen youth with short light brown hair at the defendant's table, watching his tanked-up, Mohawked doppelganger casually describe exactly how he had callously bludgeoned his friend's parents to death.

 Rod Ferrell

Went into her house, her mother was taking a shower, her father was asleep on the couch, so I took the liberty of rummaging through the house and getting something to drink, because I was thirsty. Scott was following right behind me like a little lost puppy and then before her mother got out of the shower, I went to her dad and smacked the fuck out of him until he finally quit breathing so yes, I'm admitting to murder... Actually it took him about 20 fucking minutes to stop, I swear, I thought he was immortal or something...

[I hit him with] a crowbar. I was going to use a machete or chainsaw but that was too messy, just nasty... it only got a little blood spot on me—surprisingly—but anyway, so after that I basically picked his body up, screwed him around and looked for his wallet and stuff and that's where we found his Discover card...

And about two minutes after that I flipped him back over, he was, the mother came out of the shower with a nice hot cup of coffee that she spilled all over me, cause she was asking me what did I want, cause she thought I was just robbing them... she just basically looked straight at me and said, what do you want? By that time, you know, it was pretty obvious, I had blood on me and a crowbar in my hand. I was fixing to say, yeah, I want to have coffee with you, son of a bitching smartass, but anyway then that's when she lunged at me, cause I was actually going to let her live, but after she lunged at me I just took the bottom of the crowbar, and kept stabbing it through her skull and whenever she fell down I just continually beat her until I saw her brains falling on the floor, cause that pissed me off... She clawed me, clawed me, spilled fucking scalding hot coffee on me, pissed me off... So I made sure she was dead.

Rummaged through the house looking for car keys, money, whatever. Thought about waiting for Zoey's sister but decided, nah, why bother. Let her come home, have a mental breakdown, call the police, which I was correct, she did. Anyway, went through the parents bedroom, found the keys to the Explorer... casually walked outside afterwards, unlocked the door, peeled out of the driveway.

Although a vampire initiation ritual had been held in a cemetery immediately before the murders, there were no signs of blood-drinking, and Ferrell himself denied any ritual significance. Basically, it was just a brutal double murder committed utterly without any remorse or any other form of mitigation. A police affidavit described the motive for these murders as nothing more than part of a plot to steal a sport utility vehicle for a trip to New Orleans.

In this case, as in the other Kentucky teen vampire cult case, the connection between the violence and the vampire ideology is less causal than tangential. The Byzantine twists and turns of logic of a troubled mind with an inability to distinguish between reality and fantasy can encompass even brute violence, especially when the barriers that normally emerge out of the socializing process have been absent, or the child's own barriers have been violated. A background of early abuse would predispose one to break-through violence upon virtually any slim pretext.

"There was a rush, actually," he admitted. "To feel that fact that I was taking a life. Because that's just like the old philosophy about if you can take a life, you become a god for a split second, and it actually kind of felt that way for a minute."

But as he considered the absurdity of such a proposition, his delusion-ary beliefs crumbled before the actuality of his incarceration. "But if I was a god, I wouldn't exactly be here, would I?"

His memory was skewed by an inability to appreciate the reality of the suffering of the victims of his grandiose delusions. "His face was just, it looked like a rubber mask. It didn't even look real. And her head, her brains were just like oozing out of her skull."

He described his absorption in role-playing games as a continuation of a lifetime of exposure to macabre occult activity, characterizing his own family history in phantasmagorical terms.

> I've fucking seen murders like all my life, every since I was five... cause my grandfather for one, he's never been caught either... He's part of an organization called the Black Mask. Whenever I was five they chose me as the Guardian of the Black Mask and the Guardian has to become one with everybody. In other words, they raped me. And they have to sacri-fice a human to the Guardian so they sacrificed someone right in front of me... I've been hanging around gangs and cults and all that shit all my life, so I've seen like sacrifices and drug buys... otherwise I don't care. I'm used to seeing people's brains fly out the back of their head, so it's really nothing to me... Killing is a way of life, animals do it, and that's the way humans are, just the worst predators of all actually... We did it like one after another, we always took time in between each kill so we wouldn't get caught as easy. Well, the hell of a thing is some of the law enforcement is part of that cult...

After rambling on at some length in this manner, in a portion of his statement that was redacted when presented to the jury, he concluded flatly, "I like to watch people die."

Sergeant Odom responded evenly, "Well, Rod, I'm not going to sugar-coat this thing, buddy, 'cause you know what you've done."

"It's pretty simple, I'm fucked... Is it actually possible for somebody my age to get like a death penalty?"

"It depends, ah, I don't know what the laws are in Florida, ah, when you are 16 years old in this state you can be tried as an adult and you're subject to adult penalties."

"'Cause what I was thinking, what I would have done if I was an adult would equal the death penalty."

"Sure."

"So I was kind of hoping, you know, I was like, please go ahead, ha!"

"Well..."

"I've tried suicide, it hasn't worked, so maybe they can kill me."

"To be straight up with ya, yeah, it's probably going to entail the death penalty. But I mean you know that's, if you appeal it, then it's seven or eight years down the line if you are convicted."

"Like if I just did what I did now, like just fucking admit everything, why don't they just fucking kill me?"

"Well, they can't do that. We're bound by higher laws than the people that kill people, you know."

Rod laughed. "I'm sorry, this is just like a big fucking joke. My life seems like a dream. My childhood was taken away at five, I don't know whether I'm asleep or dreaming anymore so whatever, for all I know I could wake up in five minutes."

"Rod, I can assure you, it's not a dream."

Later on, in his second recorded session, he uttered a plea to the justice system in general. "Suicide has never worked for me, so that's why I was kind of hoping at this rate now I could maybe be tried as an adult and get electrocuted or something... Just give me the fucking death penalty. I mean, I'll just walk straight up, you don't even have to chain me like you do most of them. I will put the chair on myself. That's why I thought about actually resisting, in hopes that these Baton Rouge police would actually shoot me in the heart or head or something. Something that would actually give a fatal wound."

Baton Rouge Police Corporal Don Kelly noted that other than the self-inflicted cuts on their arms, the teens had not "exhibited any vampirish behaviors." Though allowing that some of them did wear black clothing, "they're not in black capes and fangs."

"They just look like screwed-up kids," Kelly told reporters. "There's no shortage of those."

Upon learning of the boy's arrest, Ferrell's grandfather Harold Gibson broke into tears and gasped, "What if they come after me?" He told a reporter,

"They're saying Rod is a monster. A monster! He's not a monster, he's not."

Calloway County prosecutor David Harrington described Dana Cooper as "a follower, someone who wanted to be liked. Probably easily manipulated." A woman who graduated from high school with her said she craved attention. "But this vampire stuff? There was nothing that suggested that. She was just strange."

Martha Anderson drove all night from Kentucky to attend a juvenile court hearing in Louisiana for her son Scott. "He fell under the spell of something," she told reporters. "I don't know what it is."

David Keesee said his daughter Charity had never been in trouble before. "She basically ran away from home," he said, "but I don't think she knew what she was getting into."

"The animal shelter thing was the first visible sign that it had gone beyond game-playing," said Harrington. "I think you had a group of kids that just wanted to be a part of something, wanted to belong to a group. And it went too far. Hopefully, it's over."

On November 14, 1997, while awaiting her son's murder trial, Vampire Mom Sondra Gibson, 35, was sentenced to five years probation for writing to a 14-year-old boy: "I longed to be near you... to become a Vampire, a part of the family immortal and truly yours forever. You will then come for me and cross me over and I will be your bride for eternity and you my sire." Originally charged with solicitation to commit rape, she instead pleaded guilty to a felony charge of unlawful transaction with a minor. A stipulation of the plea was that although Gibson was guilty of the crime, she was mentally ill when it was committed.

In February of 1998, Rod Ferrell entered a guilty plea to two counts of first-degree murder, and at the death penalty hearing, this author spent over three hours in private conversation with Sondra Gibson (who announced on the stand that she was changing her name from Sondra to Star).

A diminutive woman with kohl-smudged ice-blue eyes, dressed in black with lipstick and nails to match, and clutching a well-thumbed Anne Rice novel, she testified that she had taken Rod to church as a child. Her parents, tongue-speaking Pentecostals of the "Oneness" persuasion, tried to persuade this writer to attend church with them.

The allegations Ferrell made about satanic ritual abuse implicating his grandfather have not been verified by law enforcement. However, Rod's aunt testified in Rod's defense that she had been molested by her father at least three times, and that she refused to allow her children to be near the old man to that day.

Harold Gibson stoically endured the incriminating testimony from members of his own family and blankly denied to this writer that he had ever molested the boy. Whether or not the crimes the defendant related ever actually occurred, suggestions of generational incest permeated this case.

Several witnesses described how Rod and his mother were commonly seen walking hand-in-hand, carrying on "more like girlfriend and boyfriend" than mother and son. Testifying for the defense, Vampire Mom described how she caught her son cutting a girl and drinking her blood. She was mad, she said, and told him to stop it. However, she conceded that she did endorse the open display of black drapes, pentagrams and candles in his room, as well as his use of *The Necronomicon*.

Sondra Gibson also admitted to her own prostitution and drug use, and described one of her long-term consorts as "a satanist" who dressed in drag and died of AIDS.

Though she did plead guilty to writing the sexually explicit letter to a 14-year-old boy named Josh Murphy, she testified that her seductive letter was just a ploy aimed at the boy's brother, Stephen Murphy, also known as "Jayden—Prince of the Vampires," and she proudly announced on the stand that she was now "in love with Jayden."

She identified a Valentine she had just sent Jayden and testified that he was now an adult (just barely, apparently). "I made sure of that before I sent it!" Privately, she confided that she had been on the outs with the vampire clan but was "back with them again"—a development which apparently took place during the trial.

She gave this writer a statement for release during a commentary on Prime Time Justice to the effect that she had raised her son in a creative environment and that in her opinion, this trial was a modern-day witch-hunt.

Her comment that some of the vampires "were a little too weird for me" may be compared to her son's confessions, where he describes how Scott had wanted to throw the bodies in the swimming pool, but Rod nixed the idea because that was "just too sick."

Video footage of Ferrell's arrest shows him flipping off the press, distorting his features by smearing his face against a glass window, and sticking out his tongue, wiggling it like a snake—an endearing gesture he repeated in court for the benefit of the jury, who quite naturally sent him directly to Death Row.

Scott Anderson, charged with being a principal accessory to murder, also faced the death penalty, but on March 30, 1998, he agreed to plead guilty in exchange for two life sentences.

Charity Keesee and Dana Cooper, both charged with being principal accessories to murder, refused to accept a plea that would send them to prison for 40 years.

In appreciation of Heather Wendorf's role as State's witness against her vampire sire, all charges against her were dropped, and she announced plans to go into seclusion while she tried to rebuild her life with the help of a court-appointed guardian.

"She was near hysterical crying," her attorney James Hope said. "It doesn't change the fact that she has been orphaned by the murders. But it certainly gives her some reprieve in the immediate sense."

On March 10, 1998, it was announced that Heather Wendorf had accepted $1,000 from Aphrodite Jones for her exclusive story. Because of Wendorf's cooperation with the State, her profits from accounts of these crimes, and those of her co-author Aphrodite Jones, were not subject to a lien under Florida's unconstitutional Son-of-Sam law, while presumably profits from Rod Ferrell's account of the same crime would be.

Wendorf had received more lucrative offers from movie and television producers, attorney Lou Tally told reporters, but had rejected them because she didn't want to make money off her parents' deaths. "Aphrodite already planned to write a book. We were concerned if we stonewalled her and didn't have anything to do with it, the one enduring piece of work out of this story would be without her," Tally said.

"She didn't need to sell her story. We're just appalled," said Gloria Wendorf, an outraged aunt. "This indicates to us exactly what Heather Wendorf is."

On May 14, 1998, Florida officials announced that they would no longer supervise Sondra Gibson's five-year probation sentence. She had wanted to move to Florida from Kentucky permanently so she could visit her son at Florida State Prison, but four of her neighbors told Department of Corrections investigators that they didn't want this convicted sex offender in their community, and started a petition drive which drew 44 names and 15 letters.

"I strongly object to allowing this person, with her background and connection and cults... in this area," read a typical letter. "I have grandchildren and great-grandchildren."

"The danger to her could become great if the local community or citizens were to realize that she was living in their neighborhood," observed Umatilla Police Chief Doug Foster, hinting that perhaps it would be best for everyone if *all* of the vampires among us would just move on.

"There is a certain anxiety in the vampire subculture that events like this will get hung on them," said J. Gordon Melton, who runs the Institute for the Study of American Religion in Santa Barbara, California. His sentiments were echoed throughout the internet, as those of the undead persuasion scrambled to distance themselves from the gross butchery.

"Vampires are another way of life for those whose lives need excitement," wrote "Child" on Glen Roberts' Full Disclosure website. "Rod Ferrell should be tried as an individual, not a vampire. The media is making a bad name for those who are interested in the Dark Side."

"First of all, what kind of pathetic idiots torture puppies and bash their parents to death?" wrote Marjean Stewart, 35, of Denton, Texas, on alt.vampyres, "This doesn't follow any tenet of vampiric belief."

March 2, 1998

Dearest Sondra,

Greetings. Let me begin these writings by first introducing myself properly, I am ROD FERRELL. I am seventeen years of age and of course, as you well know, the youngest man on Death Row. I have heard much about you... You appear to be a most interesting individual. It would seem that you have the ability to grasp the complexity of the unbinded mind. In short, I would like to befriend you if I may. Perhaps we may find that we have much in common, perhaps not?

I don't know if you would be interested or not, but I would like to share some of my art with you. At the present I am in the process of creating what I have titled "Lost Enigma." It basically has no purpose as of yet, but I assure you when and while I make it I'll keep you updated on it if you like. You must forgive me, my mind is in a state of roaming. I have so many thoughts and ideas and yet just when they gather they scatter just as quickly. Thus is the reason that "Lost Enigma" has no real plot as of yet.

Do you know what the most beautiful word in the universe is? It is ONE! To reach the essence of One is to find true sanctification. Sometimes I lose myself in meaningless ponderings, but they give safe haven from the harshness of reality, so...

Forgive the shortness of this letter, but my mind is blank. If you have any questions then by all means—please ask. I shall go now.

Eternally

Rod J Ferrell

SPAWN OF SATAN

In April of 1997, a sinister sextet of teenage vampires stole guns, ammunition and $500 cash, and fled their east Kentucky homes, crammed into a Chevrolet Citation driven by the eldest of them, 20-year-old Joseph Risner. Like the quixotic quintet from southwest Kentucky, they were heading towards the vampire's dream of New Orleans when murder intervened. It wasn't planned, they said, and it had nothing to do with being vampires. It just sort of happened.

At a rest stop on Interstate 81 near Baileyton, in northeast Tennessee, the children of darkness met a young family on their way home from a Jehovah's Witness conference that had taken as its theme Isaiah 54:13: "All your children shall be taught by the Lord, and great shall be the peace of your children."

There had been precious little peace, however, for these children. They all came from extremely unstable homes; all but two had documented sexual abuse.

"Apparently they felt like they had nothing to hold onto and nothing but hate for the world," said Brandon Reynolds, a 22-year-old friend who met with the group right before the slayings. "The fact that everything they see, if they don't think it's bad news then they think it's bullshit. The fact that they ain't never seen nobody do nothing that they felt they would have faith in... They just felt like they had one long death to live out."

"They had no faith in the world, and I mean, once somebody reaches that point, what can you say to them?"

The Spirit-filled young couple at the rest stop apparently thought they had something to say to the kids sporting pierced ears, noses, lips and eyebrows, black-dyed hair and razor-cut arms. Vidar and Delfina Lillelid approached the six youngsters to engage them in a conversation of a religious nature.

Risner and the youngest vampire, a tall, skinny 14-year-old with spiked hair named Jason Bryant, walked back to the car to change shirts while 17-year-old Karen Howell and the gang's 18-year-old ringleader Natasha Cornett chatted with the Lillelids and played with their two children.

Though Cornett had proclaimed herself the "Daughter of Satan," six-year-old Tabitha Lillelid didn't see her that way. She smiled on the troubled teen and handed her a Hershey's kiss.

What a cute little girl, thought Cornett. She'd like to take both of these pretty little children with them on the road, and like, raise them. How cool it would be to go out in a blaze of glory. And then afterwards just ride off into the sunset with the kids in a van—you know, like Mickey and Mallory in *Natural Born Killers*.

These musings were cut short as Bryant and Risner returned, and suddenly Risner drew a 9mm pistol from under his shirt and pointed it at Vidar. "I'm sorry to have to do this, but we need your van," he said and directed the family to come with him. "We're going to walk to the van, and you're going to take us for a little ride."

Risner ordered Vidar to drive and took the passenger seat next to him. Bryant sat in a captain's chair behind him with a .25-caliber pistol drawn on Delfina and Tabitha, who sat in the back next to the toddler in his safety seat. Cornett and Howell sat on the floor behind the van's front seats.

Tabitha started crying and Delfina was singing and praying, as much to calm herself as her children.

"Shut up," ordered Bryant, and she tried to, but she couldn't.

In front, Vidar Lillelid talked on and on about God as he drove, while Risner brandished the 9mm pistol.

"Please let us go," begged Delfina, "We wouldn't recognize you."

Vidar agreed. "You kids all look alike nowadays."

"Well, you better remember your religion," snarled Risner, "because Christians are not supposed to lie."

When Delfina kept pleading, praying and singing, Bryant again snapped, "Shut up!"

"Calm down," Vidar urged his wife.

"Nobody's gonna hurt you," whispered Cornett to the woman, "I promise." But the spawn of Satan lied.

Vampire clan members Edward Dean Mullins, 19, and Crystal Sturgill, 17, were following in the Citation, and when they caught up with the van on a dead-end dirt road, Risner stopped and ordered everyone out.

As the terrified family clung together at the side of the road, Tabitha was crying uncontrollably and Vidar put his hand over her mouth to quiet her.

Bryant asked Risner what to do with the Lillelids.

"I don't know, man. What do you think?"

"I think we should kill them."

"Don't!" cried Cornett at once.

Risner said "I can't do this," and put the 9mm pistol in the floor of the van.

Karen Howell later testified that Bryant ignored Cornett's pleas to spare the family as Vidar Lillelid took out his wallet, offered it along with the van, and asked, "Just please don't hurt us."

Cornett asked Vidar to give the children to her "so they won't be hurt."

"No," replied the anguished father. "If we die then the kids will be hurt anyway."

So they shot them all. Later the vampires gave conflicting stories about how it happened, with some saying the first shot hit Delfina in the side, and others saying Vidar took it first in the eye. The judge strongly suspected it was young Bryant who fired the first shots, then emptied the .25-caliber pistol into them as they wept and begged, though others implicated Risner, and Risner implicated Mullins.

By most accounts, Bryant headed back to the van for the second gun, when Karen Howell looked back and saw Tabitha. "She was standing over her mother. I yelled, 'No!' And he went right up to her—oh, God," she wept, "he went right to her and shot her, shot them all over again. He came back laughing."

Meanwhile Risner was trying to turn the van around. All six vampires piled into the van. Risner jerked the steering wheel to the right and deliberately ran over the couple as he drove their van away.

Bryant laughed at the sight of Tabitha lying with her arms out reaching out towards her father. He predicted that within a couple of hours the shooting wouldn't bother them.

When the family was found in a ditch, the children were clinging to life and their parents' lifeless bodies. Altogether, the four victims had taken 17 bullets. Vidar had six bullet wounds; Delfina had eight. Shot through the head, the unconscious Tabitha clung to life until the next day. Only two-year-old Peter, shot in the back and through one eye, survived.

All six vampires were arrested two days after the murders in Arizona, trying to enter Mexico in the Lillelids' van.

At a pretrial hearing, detention officer Shawn Ferrell of Cochise County, Arizona, told the court that as he was booking Mullins, "he asked,

'What's going to happen to me? I said, 'I don't know,' and then he asked, 'What usually happens to people after they've done what I did?'"

Ferrell's incident report also quotes Mullins as saying, "Joe said we wouldn't get caught... We went through them people's pockets for money for gas... I didn't think they was dead. I didn't want to kill no one. I didn't want them kids dead. Joe said we had to kill them all."

Mullins told Ferrell that Risner made him do it. "Joe killed them people. I had a gun, but I didn't use it."

"He said the victims were crying," Ferrell testified. "He said, 'I told them to shut up. I remember it all. I wasn't on no drugs. I wish I hadn't done that to them people.'"

Joe Risner was alone in a cell on suicide watch when Ferrell saw him sitting slumped over "with his head nearly on his knees." When he tapped on Risner's door, the suspect looked up and said, "I'm a killer," Ferrell testified. "Then he asked, 'Will they give me the death penalty for this?'"

Found in the vampire victims' stolen vehicle were Peter's safety seat, Tabitha's doll and Delfina's purse, as well as *The Book of Black Magic* and *The Complete Book of Magic and Witchcraft*. Sturgill had the keys to the family's home. Howell had Tabitha's "Hello Kitty" diary lock on a chain. Natasha Cornett was found to have dozens of cuts on her arms, and explained that she could only communicate with Satan after cutting herself and bleeding.

"It's a waking of a brand new dreadful day," begins the last entry in Cornett's diary. "It's my birthday.... Death shall finally take me... It does not matter if I enter hell, because I live my whole life in it." Another entry lamented, "Oh lucky me to rot in this Godforsaken world... I am death, look at me. I am hate, do hate me. Never love me, no, for I am the unloved, untouched and unwanted. Give me, take me, shred me away so I will not harm."

♀ Eternally,
Natasha

Cornett's habit of inviting spirits to communicate with her so that she could transcribe their messages had prompted her mother to seek help for her daughter. She had even taken her to a mental hospital. Although Natasha did visit "the local head shrinkers" several times, she stopped going after telling her estranged father, former assistant police chief Roger Burgess, "They're not doing me any good." Burgess reported that Natasha had talked recently about leaving home, and speculated that "her mother's persistent preaching" probably had something to do with that.

"She even brought preachers home to cast out demons," said Karen Howell, recalling the efforts Natasha's mother had expended in an attempt to bring the daughter of the Devil back from the hell she so persistently sought.

At trial Cornett admitted to cutting herself as a way of releasing her pain, and cutting three other members of the group in mutual consensual blood rituals intended to bind them together.

The day before the killings, Crystal Sturgill told a friend the errant teens were going to be wanted by the police because "we are going to get wild and go out and kill someone."

The six had held a seance in Room Seven at the Colley Motel in Pikeville, Kentucky, shortly before the killings, leaving black candle wax on the floor and razors strewn around the room.

"Yeah, there was blood in there. I'm not gonna lie to you," motel manager Jim Cochran told a reporter. "There was blood in there, and there was a place in the carpet burned that formed the number 6. Looked like they tried to burn 666 in the carpet. And yes, there was a lot of blood. More than you'd get if you were shaving."

Karen Howell testified that she and Natasha Cornett had planned to bleed to death at the motel. While Natasha confessed to a "special relationship" with Howell, calling her "my soul mate," both girls denied that it was of a homosexual nature. "We've kissed, but it's not like that."

Upon examination by assistant prosecutor Eric Christiansen, Howell described "sitting in a triangle" for protection while "conjuring spirits," but denied knowledge of a triangular pattern of three bullet wounds left in both Vidar and Delfina Lillelid.

Christiansen called the triangle a powerful occult symbol.

"Well, that's the way it looks," Howell responded. "But it seems you know more about the occult than I do."

"I've studied it," deadpanned Christiansen.

Right after the murders, B.J. Harris, 19, told reporters that Howell had expressed a desire for self-destruction. "Karen has cut herself. She made plans to commit suicide and set a date for it," she said. "It was this past weekend."

"Natasha basically said they were going to conjure some people and hold a seance and start the Armageddon," said Harris, who was part of their antisocial circle.

Shortly after their arrest, in a response to written questions from the Associated Press, a court stenographer recorded Cornett's statements that "Satan will aid me." She boasted of being sent to incite youth to rebel against the Christian establishment, and sent out a summons to "the children of America and the world to rise up against their parents and cast off their bondage."

Cornett, a diagnosed manic-depressive, urged the youth to "raise hell while they can" before the end of the world. Though hinting at the imminence of the apocalypse, hedging, "I can't give out the exact date," the year 2012 was mentioned. Cornett said she and two other antichrists would re-form the world into a new shape. "Evil will become greater than it already is and will rule everything," she prophesied.

"The word apocalypse comes from a Greek word that literally means 'lifting of the veil,'" Walter Russell Mead of the Council on Foreign Relations explained to *Time* magazine. "In an apocalyptic age, people feel that the veil of normal, secular reality is lifting, and we can see behind the scenes, see where God and the Devil, Good and Evil are fighting to control the future."

Claiming that she had been in touch with the forces of evil since her earliest memories, the twisted teen said, "The spirits or demons started talking to me when I was two years old, and they raised me to be an occultist." Though she had been baptized in a Methodist church, she complained, "When I had a lot of rough times, I looked to God, and he didn't help. And the demons did."

Though she admitted to responding to demonic voices, she claimed they never told her to hurt anybody but herself. "They kind of gave it to me to deal with things that were going on—a way of relief. And sometimes the relief would end up in suicide attempts and stuff like that."

Though like Manuela Ruda, Natasha Cornett has been known to lead men around by a chain, she denied being a leader of anything. "I don't have any followers," she demurred.

She described visual hallucinations that started at age 13 and included visions of "snakes, spirits, demons and little balls of light."

After a year of that, she "got into Celtic magic, invoking power from nature, kind of like white magic, not evil magic." But before long it was "black magic for a little while... invoking spirits."

However, she blamed not her own invocations of evil, but "someone else's foolish actions" for the vicious crimes that "caused them to die."

While dozens of the young vampires back home sympathized with the disaffected youth to a certain extent, they hastened to point out that they drew the line at criminal violence. "We all see a fucking mess when we look around us and it makes us mad that we're expected to clean it up. I'm sick of living in a world where the baby's born to, what, so many thousands of dollars worth of debt," said Reynolds. "What do we get for it? Poison air, poison water. We're all mad at the world, but not all of us are killing kids, see?"

Reynolds scoffed at the idea that the teen killers were influenced by the antisocial sentiments expressed by the vampire community. "That didn't influence them, they didn't let anything influence them. That was their whole point," he said. "They didn't want to be taught anything by anyone. They wanted to figure their own thing out. We all do. They figured out the wrong thing. They figured out how to be the stupidest people I've ever known, and now the entire nation hates them."

Like Vampire Mom Sondra Gibson, Cornett's mother Madonna Wallen testified to their dismal home environment—a single-wide trailer in a cluster of hamlets in eastern Kentucky with quaint names like Paintsville, Marrowbone, and Betsy Layne. There was the physical and sexual abuse, the multiple suicide attempts, the self-mutilation and mental illness. And again like Ferrell's Vampire Mom, after testifying, this young vampire's maternal unit fainted, and had to be revived.

Wallen, who was twice divorced and on disability following her latest nervous breakdown, also testified that she had let her daughter have other minors over for drinks because "at least she was at home and not out running around."

Just as Ferrell's mother had described her son's bedroom as decorated with Baphomets, pentagrams, and candles, Cornett's mother related that when Natasha and her five cohorts spent the night at their single-wide trailer, they had all slept together in Natasha's tiny room, which was festooned with graffiti: "*The truth is a lie*," "*Grandma is a Satanist*," "*Death is God's way of showing he cares!*" and "*I HATE EVERYONE!*" And again echoing the Ferrell case, Natasha's mother admitted her daughter used *The Necronomicon* in rituals.

The mother reminisced about her daughter's wedding the year before. The bride had worn a black dress, a burgundy cape and army boots. The bridesmaids had worn black and were chained together. "It was like a game," Wallen recalled. "She was in this little fantasy world. They were giggly and pushing each other with a wheelchair. Just having a ball. She even had a black wedding cake." The cake wound up on the floor that night and the marriage suffered the same fate shortly thereafter.

"Natasha was into the demon part of it... I feel like the demons took over," she speculated. "They're not natural born killers."

When her daughter called her after being taken into custody, "She was crying, and the first thing she said was, 'Mommy, I'm so scared. Mommy, I love you.' She just said she'd love to be home."

"I know you don't want to hear this, but all you have to do is turn to God," Wallen told her daughter. "He can give you that peace you're looking for."

Though the six nooses dangling from a gallows outside a Knoxville convenience store spoke eloquently of the public sentiment, Prosecutor Berkeley Bell agreed not to seek the death penalty in return for guilty pleas from all six, and Judge James Beckner sentenced them all to life without parole.

Bell approved. "They've all been treated the same—justly," he said. "Still we did not get the truth. We feel very strongly this was an occult killing."

Natasha Cornett told reporters she had agreed to plead guilty only if she could take the stand so she could "show people we're not all monsters." Though portrayed by prosecutors as the ringleader, she denied it and denied that she believed she was the daughter of Satan.

While Judge Beckner agreed Cornett was not necessarily a ringleader, he called her an instigator and an organizer. "You had killing on your mind when you left Kentucky," he said.

"I'm not going to be free again," grieved the young vampire, contemplating her own lost innocence. "I'm never going to get to have kids. I'm never going to see the beach again. But then," she sobbed, remembering her victims, "neither are they."

All six defendants pleaded guilty to three counts of first-degree murder, one count of attempted first-degree murder, two counts of especially aggravated kidnapping, two counts of aggravated kidnapping and one count of theft over $1,000. The Tennessee Court of Criminal Appeals affirmed their sentences. All but Howell appealed to the Tennessee Supreme Court, which refused to hear the case in 2001.

 Natasha Cornett

THE ULTIMATE VAMPIRE

A true vampire is not a role-playing fantasist; it is a bloodthirsty predator who feeds on the vital essence of his own kind. All who cross that bloody line are true vampires, yet retired satanic slayer Nicolas Claux has emerged to carry the flag of this criminal paradigm; he is the ultimate vampire of our times. In interviews with the worldwide press he has made some of the most shocking and sobering social commentaries in print anywhere, and in his "Vampire Manifesto," published in *Apocalypse Culture II*, he proudly proclaims his grim ethic:

> I am aware and proud of my heritage as a superpredator. I am aware and proud of the Neanderthal DNA in my veins. I am aware and proud of my place in the ecosystem. I do not believe that the things I did were wrong or "evil"... My task, our task, is to regulate the human race. We have the same purpose as the ebola virus. My genetic programming tells me to hunt, kill, and eat human cattle. Society cannot "rehabilitate" me, because I am genetically different from your average human insect. I am Danger. I am the Enemy. You can lock me up in a cage. But others will come and restore the balance of nature. Humanity is doomed.

The Parisian mortician was 22 years old in the summer of 1994, when he was arrested for a series of five shootings. He was covered with occult tattoos, including the words "Serial Killer" spelled out in English all the way down both arms.

His apartment was located near the Moulin Rouge cabaret, in the Pigalle quarter of Paris, and with the streets full of sex-shops, prostitutes, junkies, and tourists, his lifestyle blended right in.

The apartment was searched upon his arrest, and its décor was considered by the Court to be highly vampiric. Posters on every wall displayed violent imagery from movies like *Cannibal Holocaust*, *Texas Chainsaw Massacre*, and *Ilsa She Wolf of the SS*. One called *Anthropophagus*, depicting a man eating his own bowels, shocked the detectives, and became an eloquent exhibit in court.

Scattered everywhere were over 400 horror videotapes and shockumentaries with titles like *Human Guinea Pig*, *True Gore*, *Erotic*, *Bizarre*, *Slave Sex*, *Pain*, *Death Scenes*, *Faces of Death*, *Snuff*, *The Zodiac*, *Death Files*, and *Nekromantik*, while a King James Bible full of bullet holes was nailed to one shotgun-spangled wall.

The refrigerator was stocked with bags of fresh human blood, and standing beside the phone was an urn covered with dried blood. Stolen from a Gothic cemetery, it contained the ashes of a virgin who had died young over a hundred years ago.

Describing himself as a satanic necrophile, Claux promptly confessed to skulking through the Gothic cemeteries of Paris, unearthing coffins and stabbing corpses. His shockingly explicit confessions included details of one murder. He went on to describe in revolting detail the pleasure he derived from eating the flesh of a corpse on the slab.

From his confessions:

I woke up one day, feeling this sinister urge to dig a corpse and mutilate it. I gathered a small crowbar, a pair of pliers, a screwdriver, black candles and a pair of surgical gloves in a backpack. Then I took the subway to the Trocadero station. It was nearly noon. The gates of the Passy cemetery were wide open, but nobody was inside. The undertakers were out for lunch.

Passy is a small Gothic graveyard, with plenty of huge mausoleums build during the 19th century. It is located right between two large avenues, so it is impossible to climb inside at night. But anyway, nobody could ever imagine that there was someone robbing graves at noon.

I had this special grave in mind. It was a small mausoleum, the burial site of a family of Russian immigrants from the 1917 revolution. I had already pried open the iron door a few days ago, and I had closed it so it would seem that nobody had ever touched it. All I had to do was just to kick it open. That's how I broke into the funeral chapel. At this point, my mind was in total chaos. I had flashes of death in my head. I took a deep breath, and I climbed down the steps leading to the crypt.

It was a rather small one, with damp walls, buried deep inside the cemetery ground. There was no other source of light than the candles I had brought. To begin, for more than a hour, I removed one of the heavy coffins from its stone casing. It was specially hard not to let the coffin fall all of sudden to the ground, but somehow I managed to slowly lay it down without too much noise. However, one edge of the coffin scratched my lower leg when it touched the ground. But it didn't stop me at all.

I examined the casket for a while. It was solid oak wood sealed with big screws. It look like brand new, so I expected to find a recently deceased corpse. First, I unscrewed the coffin, which took me less than 10 minutes. Then I pried it open with the crowbar, since it was also nailed shut. Once opened, a horrible stench of putrefaction came out of the box. It also smelled like thanatyl, the product embalmers use on corpse in order to delay the process of decay.

Then I saw the body inside. It was a half rotten old woman, shrouded in a white sheet, covered with brown stains. Her face seemed like smeared with oil, but it was simply the death fluids oozing from her skin. The stench was so intense that I nearly fainted. I tried to lift one side of the sheet, but it was glued to the skin. The teeth were protruding from the mouth, but the eyes were gone.

I stared into the empty eye sockets, and all of a sudden something broke into my mind. I felt like falling into a whirlwind. That's when I picked up the screwdriver. The corpse inside the coffin started to move slightly, like it had guessed what would happen next. So I began to stab the belly, the ribs area and the shoulders. I stabbed her at last 50 times. I really can't remember. All I can remember was that I woke up with my forearms covered with corpse slime.

The State's forensic psychiatrist declared Claux a "nearly psychotic sadist," the tabloid press hastened to dub him "The Vampire of Paris."

Without sufficient evidence to place him at the other scenes of the apparently related shootings, in May of 1997, the homicidal necrosadist was convicted of one count of premeditated murder and six counts of grave robbery. He was sentenced to 12 years of prison.

While he was imprisoned in Poissy, I was introduced to Nicolas Claux via correspondence in 1999, and despite his fearsome mystique, I found him charming and cooperative in answering my questions. After our first phone conversation, a jolly *ménage à trois* with his sidekick Igor Mortiis, he wrote: "I hope you understood at least half of what I said, because of my outrageous French accent and it was the first time I had an actual conversation in English since 1994! So it's hard to actually verbalize thoughts and words in a foreign language... Damn, I can't even properly maintain a decent conversation in French anymore, so trying to speak English was a true ordeal. Ha ha!"

Nico Claux displays a high intelligence, and despite his self-deprecating disclaimers, he is articulate with a good command of English. Getting down to business, he makes no attempt to avoid probing questions about his activities of a homicidal, vampiric, necrophilic, or necromantic nature.

You wonder why somebody like me with a decent childhood would develop into someone who is accused today of murder, grave robbery and cannibalism. The answer is: because I liked it! It was fun. Nobody forced me into doing it.

Nothing is more boring than speaking of one's family and childhood. I don't believe that parenting provides a major role in forming the personality of a child. Maybe it does in extreme cases like child abuse or the death of a relative, but when nothing special happens, then the personality develops into something completely unique. Nothing traumatic or exceptional happened to me when I was a kid that could explain who I am today. Nothing. I was just born that way.

This whole thing is not about social Darwinism, behaviorism or kindergarten psychology. It's about Evil. Period. I am fully responsible for my choices, and if I chose this way of life, it's because it excited me. I've always been into this, and as I grow older, my obsession with evil and darkness only becomes stronger. I am the essence of evil.

When I see people, I see complete aliens. I cannot understand their craving for social success, family, and love. I do not have the same primal needs. My needs are: dismemberment, post mortem sex, bloodlust and stalking prey. Sex and violence.

Social skills are okay if I want to pick up a girl in a bar and bring her home. Period. I control my needs. If I need to wear a mask of sanity in a given situation, I do it. But the needs are always there, lying in wait.

Most convicted killers are rather reticent about discussing their crimes. Often, the truth is not in them, or if it is, they're not about to give it up. More often, they are unable or unwilling to confront or reveal the baleful reality that put them behind bars. Not this vampire. Although he relishes his own necrophilia and phlebophilia, strangely enough, when it comes to the ultimate crime, he recites a tale of murder most calculated:

Thierry Bissonier was shot on October 3, 1994, inside his apartment. He was shot five times in the head, execution style, and one time in the back, with a .22 caliber handgun. The first shot went through his right eyeball, into the brain. The other bullets crushed against the skull. The last bullet entered the lung and pierced the heart. Then, after 15 minutes of a slow dying process, I put an end to his misery by crushing his head with a cement flower container. Then I inserted a pencil inside one of the bullet holes to see how deep the bullet had entered into the skull.

The guy was contacted one hour before on the Minitel (a kind of primitive internet network in France). I was seeking a gay victim, so I could test the effectiveness of .22 bullets on human targets. I choose this M.O. because survivors never report to the police when they're shot during what they thought would be a gay encounter. They're too ashamed of what happened. And it was like a "practice" game for me, not the real thing yet, because I just shot 'em and left 'em lying on the carpet. Later on I intended to repeat the same M.O. on female targets. But then I would not have only shot them.

I did not commit any "vampire" stuff on the people I shot. I don't like men, and I didn't want to get AIDS. It was just target practice. I did not drink their blood. There was no intimacy before, during or after the act. It was just a matter of knocking on the door, stepping inside, pulling out the gun and shooting, then sitting down and watching the death show.

Those shootings took place in a one-month period, ending October 3, 1994, All shootings involved queers shot inside their apartment, house ransacked, no motive, no fingerprints, same M.O. (people shot standing next to the main door), and all were contacted via Minitel. The files were apparently closed on these cases. This year is mentioned in *The Guinness Book of World Records* as being the year when there were the most unsolved cases of this nature in Paris.

Although Claux himself draws no connection between the murders and his interest in blood-drinking and the occult, both are important elements to his lifestyle and beliefs. Some insight into the different aspects of his ghoulish behavior may be obtained from his own analysis. On August 8, 1999, he wrote from prison in Poissy.

I have drunk blood, but it was blood stolen from the hospital's bank (no plasma in it). I believe that this specific diet helped me gain more muscle weight, especially when accompanied by a source of human protein.

I did the grave robberies as part of magic rituals (*necromancia*) and sexual thrills. When I walked the alleys of Real LaChaise Cemetery, I often visualized Sergeant Bertrand prowling at night in search of dead flesh. Sometimes I felt like his reincarnation.

The flesh-eating part was more of a hunger. I had a fantasy of doing it since I was a kid. Each time I ate animal meat, I fantasized it was human. It excited me. So when I had the opportunity of doing it, I did not hesitate.

The blood plus powdered protein was also a sexual thing. I had this blood drinking fantasy since childhood as well, but I also believe it helped me grow muscles. I used to do it before working out (I had a workout bench and barbells at my place). The blood I consumed was liquid/refrigerated blood (without plasma). I was more attracted by warm blood.

I don't change into a bat, but I do change into a wolf, or a raven. I'm Aries with Capricorn rising. Mars meets Saturn. Violence and loneliness.

I'm really into what Gothic kids like to practice. I have tried it on a few occasions and boy, it was good! I'm looking for a vampire bride with whom I would share my blood. When I worked in those hospitals I met some girls who were familiar with that practice. They used syringes. You would be surprised to know that it actually is a common practice among nurses.

When I was younger, I was deeply into vampire mysticism. I studied mediæval grimoires like the *Book of Abramelin*. This book describes a necromancy ritual that's supposed to summon the spirits of the dead. I performed this ritual during several grave robberies, and some things happened that proved that it worked.

The temperature went cold and I felt a cold hand squeezing my heart, and on two occasions, the bodies moved under the shroud. This is not a joke, this is real. It really happened down there. These were not sensory hallucinations and there was no scientific explanation to it. It just happened. It's the power of Abramelin.

Vlad Tepes belonged to the Order of the Dragon, whose leader, Sigismund, used the Abramelin book to resurrect Barbara de Silly.

I strongly believe in the power of sigils. This sigil was used in the Abramelin rituals. It must be written with blood on parchment. The parchment must be laid on the chest of the body of the Undead. This kind of ritual is called Goetia. (Invocation of Demons, Lesser Keys of Solomon, Red Dragon, etc.) It is also used on blood pacts.

When I made my pre-trial blood pact I carved this sigil into my left arm with a razor blade. I did this blood pact the night before trial, Walpurgisnacht, the first of May, 1997. This is the signature of Lucifuge Rofocale, master of satanic pacts. I am certain that it helped me have a fair trial. It did protect me from my enemies. I still have the scars on my arm.

The Abramelin sigil was used during grave robberies. I wrote it on the crypt's wall or on the coffin's lid with chalk. Its power helped me invoke the shadow that never sleeps, the Lord of the Eastern Mountain, Vlad Tepes. The spirit of Vlad Tepes entered the bodies I unearthed and made them move.

When I am released, I will have this sigil tattooed on my left breast, and this will grant my soul the power to reach the astral plane when I die. I have already succeeded to achieve journeys in the astral plane when I was a child. I lost this power during my teenage years.

I've read several books on astral projection, but this practice demands a great deal of meditation and breath control. Only somebody well trained in yoga can achieve control over his astral body. Sigils are powerful gates to the astral plane.

What a disturbing sensation it was, then, to receive in the mail a blood pact that Nico had sworn to Satan. The darkened paper is literally soaked with the blood of this modern vampire, with a full bloody handprint over the beautifully-inscribed oath made out to *"veritable Seigneur, Satan, Prince des tenebres."*

Blood Oath

Igor writes in a cheery cover letter that the oath was sworn during the solar eclipse over Paris on August 11, 1999, "so it's full of 'evil' powers!" Indeed. Holding this chilling artifact in one's hand, there is a strong sense that it is full not only of French vampire blood and satanic sigils, but of *something else*. The French might call it *je ne sais quoi*, but in English we just call it *evil*.

While Claux was incarcerated, his lifelong interest in the infamous killers known the world over developed into a unique pastime. He spent years writing to them and painting their portraits. I asked him why.

I don't consider myself a member of mankind. I belong to a worldwide brotherhood of people who decided to make a career in mass destruction. People like Báthory, Kurten, Bundy, Ramirez, Schaefer. The shootings could be viewed as a way of becoming a member of this brotherhood. I respect these people. I've always been interested in multiple murder, and I collected true crime books, even trading cards! Then, when I was identified as part of this brotherhood, I started to make mail contact with the other members. Over the past few years I have corresponded with 15 convicted serial killers. Some of them are plain boring individuals who are ashamed of who they are. But others are proud members of this brotherhood. We have media coverage, groupies, fan mail... It's like being a rock star. But at the same time, it's much, much more than that. People have told me about the mystical side of it. We're like an urban legend came true. Real-life Jasons.

Lots of killers blame their violence on their youth, etc. but some of the serial killers I've corresponded with told me that all they said to the press and justice system was bullshit, and that they were born that way. Natasha Cornett says it. David Gore says it. Lots of them say it. Of course there are exceptions like Manson, Lucas and Kemper. But take Bundy. Honestly, now, how many people were raised by their grandparents and rejected by their girlfriend in college? Many. How many of them bashed the brains out of a girl and had sex with her dying body, more than 30 times? Only Bundy. He was born that way. There's nothing more to understand. Some people are born without a leg or an arm. And some people are born without a conscience. I know it's difficult to realize, but it happens. Some people just don't give a fuck about human rights. You know, humanity is one big herd of sheep. 10% are born leaders, 10% are born rebels. Sometimes, the sheep who was born a rebel has also wolf DNA in his veins. And that makes a lethal cocktail.

As a bit of insider shop-talk, Claux updated me on the still-undead baleful influence of my murdered co-author, the literary serial killer Gerard John Schaefer.

> You will be certainly interested to hear that a guy was recently judged here for the murder of a close friend, and as a defense strategy, he said that he had seen this documentary showing Schaefer's interview the previous night, and he claimed that he had seen the same look in his friend's eyes as Schaefer's! So even after his death, Schaefer is responsible for a first degree murder! Ah!

Contemplating his new media-star status, he admitted to some uncertainty about what life might hold for him outside prison. "Honestly, I don't know how all this will evolve when I am released. I mean, it will be the first time ever that a member of this brotherhood will meet and hang out with his fans, Ah-hah!" One could almost hear the Gallic shrug as he pondered the sensation. "I wonder what will be their reactions? We'll see."

I wondered what would change for him and what would remain the same. "One thing I have now that I didn't have when I was out there: art. Maybe it will change my life after prison. Maybe I will focus on paintings, instead of doing what I used to do before. Or maybe not."

As he continued to ruminate on his career objectives, it became clear some things would never change. "I still want to get another job in a mortuary. I cannot imagine myself doing another job. So I will apply for jobs in mortuaries, funeral homes, undertakers, whatever. I'm addicted to death. I need to feel it, smell it, touch it."

And so the death addict looked forward to spending his off-hours visiting his new pen pals around the world, and hoped to distinguish himself in the arts, emulating his role model—the courtly, refined Japanese cannibal. "In terms of post-prison career, Issei Sagawa is who I'd like to equal. He's a food critic, a TV star, and a porn movie director."

> I never went to art school. I first started to draw and paint in 1996. People who had heard of my case wrote to me asking me if I did any art. So, I realized it was a good way to get free CD's and true crime books. Then after awhile, I realized that I really enjoyed to paint and draw things that I liked. I began to read art manuals to improve my techniques. It became a real pleasure, and people seem to like my paintings. So, I started to paint on a regular basis. I read lots of books on classical

paintings. I discovered that life is about discovering the aesthetics that surround us. I discovered that death is the ultimate aesthetic pleasure. The act of dying is the most extreme aesthetic experience—the growls of a man gasping for air make a sweet music. The way a body squirms on the floor is like a choreography. The way they bleed, and the patterns the blood paints on their clothing, it's art. Life is about art. I don't feel like a murderer. I feel like an artist—an aesthete.

My life is a quest for aesthetism. I love art, beauty, perfection. I hate the ugliness of modern society: cars, pollution, television. Painting is how I express my inner torment, my turmoil.

Unfortunately, here, I cannot paint all the things I would like to. There's one thing I'd like to paint: corpses on the slab. I love their colors, the post mortem lividities, the colors of a decaying flesh, gradations of gray, purple, blue, and green. It's an amazing chromatic palette. Nothing matches the beauty of dead skin. I'd also like to bring my easel in Gothic graveyards and paint all day long. Here, I mostly paint portraits of serial killers or fantasy art, like Conan the Barbarian.

On this picture you can see Andrei Chikatilo, Nikolai "Iron Teeth" Dzhumagalayev, Danny Rolling, J.W. Gacy, Ed Kemper and G.J. Schaefer.

Of all these serial killers, Dzhumagalayev is the one I prefer. He killed, dissected and ate a dozen girls near Moscow. I'm fascinated by his case. I don't know why. He looks so weird, so primitive. He could play in *Texas Chainsaw Massacre*. And his nickname, "Iron Teeth"! I had a great time painting his portrait. I could visualize him chewing red steaks right before me.

One night, lying on his bunk in his cell, after reading *Vampire's Dream*, Nico penned a fantasy he called *Mortuarian*:

Dismemberment. Post mortem sex. The taste of plasma in my mouth. I've got to calm down, open my eyes. I'm in a cell, back to reality. But the hunger is still there.

I watch TV for a while. Pictures of incredible gorgeous girls appear on the screen. Commercials. I study their neck. I can see the veins under their skins. I feel like Tantalus. It slowly increases my hunger.

But time is at hand.

So I close my eyes once again. I have flashes of slasher movies. I'm wearing a hockey mask. I'm hunting humans. Freelance gynecology with a machete. I feel like a head hunter in the Amazonian jungle.

Flashes from the past... mortuary routine.

People are so ugly inside. They have no respect for their own body. Nicotine eats their lungs away. Sugar spreads a disgusting yellow spider

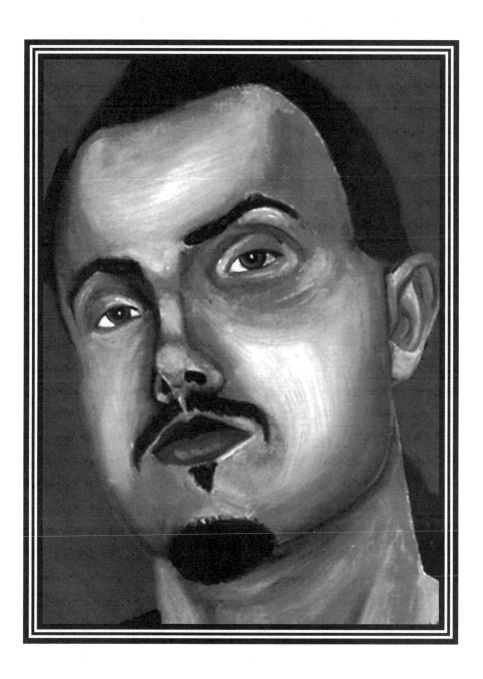

 Nicolas Claux

web of fat tissues inside their belly. Tumors. Cancers. Inside their carcass the infection breeds every day.

It takes a great deal of *abnegation* to be a mortuary attendant. There is no social honor in being a surgeon of the dead. Nobody will ever rise from the slab and thank you for having treated his carcass with respect. And their family members are too grief-stricken to even compliment you on the wonderful work you have done to make their beloved ones presentable for the afterlife.

So you end up growing a deep resentment against humanity as a whole. Hypocrites. Losers. Walking rotten carcasses. They stand up straight, stomach in, shoulders back. Proud of their apparent good looks. If only they could see under their skin. See the rot settle inside their organs. Smell the reek of decayed innards. I see the infection inside you. You turn me off.

Women's bowels are like dead snakes. They lie hidden, slimy and cold, waiting to be released by the incision of the scalpel. Handle them with care. They contain biohazardous material. Put them in the sink. Be careful not to puncture them with the tip of your blade, or feces will ooze out. Underneath lies a big bag of muscles. The uterus. Meat. Fondle it from the inside. Post mortem internal vaginal examination. Feel the rubbery consistency with the tip of your gloved fingers.

Flashes become more violent. I am now masturbating.

Dead cunt on the slab. She's so cold, and there's no tightness to her pussy anymore. Now I concentrate on her meat. I'm hungry. There's some tasty muscles on her rib cage. Nobody will ever notice it if I cut them off. I've done it before. Food. Boy, it feels so good to eat this! Refrigerated raw meat. I chew the strips slowly. I play with them with my teeth. I shred them to pieces.

Once again I've crossed the threshold. I'm no longer part of the human subrace. I'm a werewolf. I'm a ghoul. Insanity is my kingdom.

Another flash...

I'm sitting in my room, surrounded by black candles and scattered bones. A mobile made with vertebrae is hanging from the ceiling. A jawless skull is sitting on my VCR. I have drenched it with human blood. Sometimes I target shoot it with my .22 caliber.

The wall behind is spangled with bullet holes. Sometimes the bullets remain in the cranial cavity. I pick up the skull and shake it. It makes a jingling sound.

I play a videotape about a samurai who kidnaps a Japanese chick. He drugs her. Then he dissects her with nasty looking rusty knives. The FX are okay.

I watch another tape. Real autopsy footage. I squeeze the handle of my gun, hard. I aim at the skull. *BANG!!* Is this what they call psychosis?

I'm in a good mood for a graveyard trip. I take my backpack. Rubber gloves, screwdrivers, crowbar, plastic bags. I put a death metal tape in my Walkman. I enter the burial ground. I walk among the tombstones. My territory. It's noon. The undertakers are out for lunch.

I choose an old mausoleum. Smash the window, break and enter. The stairs leading to the crypt are so narrow. I feel the rush of adrenaline inside me. I make my way to a coffin. Using crowbar and screwdrivers, I pull the funeral box to the ground. I'm covered in cold sweat.

Now I break the lid open. The reek of death burns my nose. My brain is on fire. I suffocate. I contemplate the remains. Fractured bones. Locks of dead hair planted on a toothless skull. Decomposed shroud. I open a plastic bag. I pick up my trophies. I bring them home.

Back to my cell. Reality again. Caged. Caged but untamed.

Time is at hand.

Igor Mortiis has been Nico's friend since they were both teenagers, and he revealed a unique perspective on the infamous fiend.

Like you say, Nico has an evil charisma, and it's more evident when you meet him. All my friends who crossed his path before he went to jail felt uncomfortable in his presence. They all told me that he has something devilish in the eyes or something. And it was more intense with girls. They were all attracted to him like girls were to Count Dracula. He bewitches them, if I can say that. Nico practices a lot of magic and hypnotism techniques, so in a certain way it gives him this special charisma like a ghoul or magician may have.

I have not been hypnotized by Nico or anything like that, and I don't believe in what he did. After he got arrested, all his so-called friends left him. They were too shocked by what he did. My girlfriend did not like him either, saying he scared her. I am a survivor of all of this.

I talk to Nico as an old friend. We speak about the movies we like, music—like friends. I respect his beliefs because he's real through it, and he respects mine. I don't idolize him, but he's true and sincere with me because he knows that I don't judge him. It is now that he really needs a true friend—whatever he did. With me he's still what he was, a devoted friend. And so am I. I know that if I ever get in trouble he will always be on my side. We are true friends for years now, and it's not some cadaver who will break this!

To me Nico has not changed too much from the day I met him. He's still so evil and fun, that's probably why I like him. He has a great sense of black humor and I have had a lot of fun with him.

We met when we were something like 15 or 16, I can't remember exactly. My first thought was, "This guy is the Devil!" He was so mean! Then we talked about movies, music—and we became friends. I always knew that one day I would hear that Nico did some bad things. He was crazy, he loved to watch brutal SM movies, and laugh like a maniac when the girls were crying. It was unreal.

Nico has always loved to torture animals. I have a videotape where he tortures to death a living mouse with a scalpel. He was maybe 15 or 16 at that time, and he was laughing like crazy every time the mouse struck back, to the point of trying to eat the scalpel blade. Pure cruelty! As a kid, he loved to torture animals for fun. He put a little dog into a mixer for fun, put some cats into a microwave to make them explode. Then he bought a little *arbalete* and began to hunt cats in the cemetery, it was high entertainment for him. Maybe he gets the love of the hunt through this.

I didn't know what Nico was doing, but I was not surprised to know that he did it. Since I have known him he always had fantasies about murder, torture, death—he was working at the morgue, because he just wanted to be as close as possible to death. His evil ways are not fun at all, let's say scary. But he has never bothered me with his fantasies. He kept them to himself.

I hope that Nico will stay out of trouble when he gets out, that's why I try to promote his art. I hope that through painting he will find a new way to channel his fantasy—and not to exorcise it. That would be a waste of time, you can't change a wolf into a sheep. But there's so much to do with your life besides spend it in jail. So that's why I am here with him. I am trying to save a friend from the evil way.

His parents visit him and try to help him. They were really affected by his crimes and are still under shock. I often go to see them to comfort them. But Nico's "troubles" might have begun with them. Nico has no feelings for his family, according to what the psychiatrists at the trial said. He doesn't hate or love them, but just ignores them. He's "cold as life," like he says.

The thing that got him into mysticism began when he was a little child. He started talking with his grandfather about the power of spirit because of the books his grandfather owned on magical ceremonies. Then he asked his grandpa to play tennis, but he declined, saying he was too tired. But Nico insisted again and again until his mother (it was her father) told him to let his grandpa alone, because he was too old for this kind of game. But still Nico insisted. Finally the old man told him he would play. As soon as they began the game, the grandpa had a heart attack and died right there in front of him.

Nico loved his grandpa very much, so at a certain level it should have affected him, but he never expressed any sentiment for his death. Then his mother became paranoid, saying it was Nico who killed his grandfather, culpabilising him for her dad's death because of the tennis game. Then she started having nightmares, waking up at night, screaming that Nico was trying to kill her with his mind. She had been in hospital for a while after that. She believes that Nico has supernatural powers, and she's still afraid of him now. And so a demon was born!

In an interview appearing on Igor's website, Claux spoke with characteristic frankness, admitting he robbed graves "because I like to hurt people. It's the most inhuman thing you can do to a family. I like to know that one morning someone from the graveyard's office will call them and say, 'We found the remains of your grandmother impaled on a stick.' It's pure cruelty. It's like you kill them a second time."

The satanist sneered at those aspiring to identify with him through his belief system. "Most so-called satanists are *poseurs*, wimps who get beaten by other kids in school, so they pose as satanists to create an image. But then they say, 'Satanism is not about being evil and stuff, it's about criticizing society.' Ah! I personally don't give a fuck about society. I don't consider myself as human, so I won't waste my time criticizing their society. Wolves don't criticize sheep. They just bleed them to death. I worship the Devil because Satan worship is about digging up corpses, killing people for the thrill of it and spitting on their graves. It's not about dancing naked in the woods. Real satanists hate everything: yids, niggers, xians, dogs, cats... everything! So fuck the so-called satanists. They are nothing. I only respect grave robbers and killers."

When asked the worst thing about being in prison, he complained, "No red meat. They only give us boiled meat once in a while. They turned me into a fucking vegetarian."

Nicolas Claux was released from prison on March 22, 2002, after serving seven years and four months of his 12-year sentence; and after a couple of months of freedom, he gave me this interview:

SONDRA: When our readers last heard from you, you were rattling your chains & snarling, *"When parole comes, I will be a brainless Neanderthal with only one thought in mind: 'I WANT MEAT!'"* So now we are waiting to find out, what really did happen when you were released?

NICO: My mother is such a bad cook that I did not expect her to cook me any special meal when I got out. So I just went to a butcher and bought minced steak, and I did myself a nice steak Tartare. The rush of adrenaline was beyond words. Later on this year I started to learn cooking. I have learned to use spices and herbs, and different methods of cooking. Those who have tasted my preparations say I am getting very good. I am specially good at meatballs. Maybe one day I will work in a restaurant.

SONDRA: Was it hard to get used to being free again?

NICO: During the first days, I tried to get accustomed to the outside world again, dealing with noise, pollution, mobile phones ringing everywhere, people walking by fast in the streets. At first, it was too much stimulation for my brain. But I adapted to it well, I think. Just the fact of having my own key and a bit of money in my pockets was a taste of freedom. It was like being born again. At the same time, I had to struggle with all the rage that I had built up in jail. And the feeling of being so different, so removed from this outside world.

SONDRA: Where did you live?

NICO: I lived at my parents' place during the first five months, on the crack side of Paris, then I moved to live with my girlfriend. It was a hard decision, because I had the choice of staying in a familiar environment, with my friends, in my town, in a place where I was well-known, or go to live anonymously to a foreign country, learn a new language and struggle with very little money to survive. But I made the right decision, and it is well worth the sacrifices I have made.

SONDRA: How did prison change you?

NICO: I am smarter, I am stronger, and I am spiritually more aware of the world than I was. Sometimes I feel like Max Cady. Prison made me aware of my weaknesses, and it also gave me the tools to destroy them. I have read philosophy in prison, I've read Greek tragedies and anthropology, I learned art, I became physically stronger, I learned to be manipulative and to give people what they expect. I learned to stay quiet and to listen. To be cool and to control my urges. I learned burglary and street life tactics. Before prison, I was totally out of control. I learned discipline in prison. I think that now I am superior to 99% of the general population.

SONDRA: Are you still a vampire?

NICO: Yes I am, but I have won the fight over the beast inside me.

SONDRA: Have your tastes changed?

NICO: I still read the same books, watch the same movies and enjoy the same lifestyle, except that now I have the responsibilities of a family man. So I have drawn boundaries that I will never break. I think I have found the right balance between my cravings and the limits imposed by society. I have learned how to satisfy them without getting into trouble. Murdering people causes too much paperwork anyway.

SONDRA: Do you keep bags of blood in the refrigerator and drink blood?

NICO: There are bags of blood in the freezer, but they are not human. I still enjoy the taste of blood very much, but it is no longer an obsession.

SONDRA: Do you still wish to torture small animals?

NICO: No.

SONDRA: Do you have any new tattoos?

NICO: I try to collect new tattoo art on my body, but I have not much money so the process is slower than I would like. My new tattoos are very much fixated on mass murder. I have pictures of dead bodies, flames, guns, things like that.

SONDRA: Tell us about your plans to support yourself.

NICO: I am ready to take any job. I have learned filming and editing on a professional level, and I am also good at putting up websites. Of course, I am skilled at art and design. I try to make a living by selling paintings online, but I don't make enough to allow me to travel right now.

SONDRA: How have you found the World Wide Web?

NICO: I have a website. It is not about my case, it is only about the paintings I have for sale. I use it as a tool to help me sell my artwork on a worldwide level. I also include some of my correspondence and exclusive interviews with other vampire killers.

SONDRA: How have you been received at the "vampire" sites?

NICO: I have received emails from people who claim to be "High Priest of Vampire Cults," "Real Life Vampires" and so on. Usually they say the same line: "You give vampires a bad name." How ironic! We now live in a society where vampirism is considered as glamorous, because of all these silly TV shows. They have completely put aside the organic essence of vampirism, which is the craving for warm plasma. They think vampires are people who wear Armani long coats and ask to use needles to drink blood. Of course I understand that I do not fit this fantasy image. But I really do not care about that. Vampires will be remembered in history as real life monsters who kill and drink and eat their victims like ordinary people feed on beef. Wearing fake fangs won't make you a true vampire. Only the intimate experience of eating another being's soul might give you this status.

SONDRA: Have any cults tried to recruit you?

NICO: Mostly people who say they are the "High Priest of The Raven Clan of Abaddon" or something even sillier. Right after I got out of prison, I got an instant message from a European woman who suggested I might be "useful to certain people" and that I "would get a big reward." There are cults who want someone like me to do the dirty deeds.

SONDRA: Yes, I would think so.

NICO: But I'm not interested in obeying orders from people I don't respect. They are just using satanism for drug dealing and pornography.

SONDRA: Using the mystique to get people involved, but they don't even believe it themselves.

NICO: Right. The woman who spoke to me said "the most powerful clans are the one that have a perfectly legal cover." They have lawyers, congressmen, police officers, people in high places. She kept saying that they worked in anonymity. These kind of people try to trick me with promises but I don't buy it. Once you're part of the org, you are their tool. That's why I stay very far from the "scene" in Europe.

SONDRA: Rumor has it that your days of wild rampages are over, that you've found love and settled down. True or false?

NICO: Yes, I have found my immortal bride, but we have both decided to keep our private life a secret. So I do not wish to share her identity. However I can tell you that she is a gorgeous, sophisticated and very clever woman. I am very lucky to have her.

SONDRA: Do you still practice ritual blood magic? Have your magical goals, or beliefs, changed?

NICO: Yes I do, but I have learned much from my girlfriend, who is much more gifted and learned in magic than I am. But I have been reading all her books on the left-hand path and trying to understand them in a deep level. We have an altar devoted to our Lord. We both share the same beliefs. We just want to live peacefully, practice our sex and blood magic, and travel a bit to meet our friends.`

SONDRA: I understand you get quite a lot of email. Would you mind sharing some with our readers?

NICO: Sure, here's one that just came in:

> Nico Claux, I don't mean to be offensive, but firstly I'm afraid that your criminal acts don't classify you as a real vampire. You are an insult to the vampire world—people like you give vampires a bad name. Real vampires DON'T kill people, and they drink their donors (we don't like to call them victims) blood using safe methods (syringe blood withdrawals, sanitized razor blades etc), not by killing their victims. Secondly, your website may arouse suspicions with the real vampires out there. People will start looking for other vampires, and may come across the real vampire websites, and think they are all the killers that you are. I'm afraid that you're giving a bad name to the vampire nation. As a real vampire myself and member of a local vampire group, I believe you're no vampire, just a sick necrophiliac murderer. I'm not saying there's anything wrong with that—I wouldn't mind trying my hand at a murder myself, but have never (and probably never will) do it. I just find it quite insulting you refer to yourself as a "Vampire." I'm afraid you've got that bit wrong. Best regards, and good luck in your future, Arnold

SONDRA: So Arnold criticizes you but he admits he wouldn't mind trying murder himself! How can you possibly respond to something like that?

NICO: I used to write back to them personally but there got to be so many, I developed this standard form letter. I send it out and then I check off the items when I reply:

> Greetings, You have just made a fool of yourself by sending "hate mail" or just plain lame mail to Mr. Nicolas Claux. The only answer you'll ever get from him is this standard reply, so no need to try to get his attention any further.

Nicolas Claux

☐ *You claim to be a "true vampire."*

+ Hey kid, wake up! Vampires do not exist. It's not because you wear fake fangs that you have the right to decide who is a true vampire and who is not. The press called me a vampire. Send your complaints to them.

☐ *You are the high priest of "the mighty knights of Satan," or some other stupid coven.*

+ There's nothing I despise more than coven mentality. You claim to be a true believer but you will run your mouth to the cops after one hour of custody. My devotion to My Lord is genuine, I've been His Servant for decades, and prison has only strengthened my Faith. I don't give a fuck what you & your coven think of me. I serve My Lord in better ways than you'll ever dream of.

☐ *You are a Christian cunt.*

+ Why don't you send this type of email to Muslim websites? Scared of the consequences?

☐ *You are under 18 and you want to prove to yourself that you are strong by sending threats to an ex-con.*

+ Kid, get laid, you really need it.

☐ *You are a journalist.*

+ No, I don't want to be on your show, and no, I won't send you Issei Sagawa's address.

☐ *You claim to be a serial killer.*

+ Yeah, yeah, yeah... Big deal.

☐ *You want free drawings and artworks.*

+ AHAHAHAHAHAHAH!

☐ *You claim revenge for my victim's family.*

+ They don't need your help, Superman. They're still dealing with the shame of a public trial that exposed their son's homosexuality to the public. They seemed more concerned about this than by the fact that I killed him. Mind your own business and find yourself a real cause, like "Save the whales."

☐ *You are a groupie.*

+ I have a girlfriend, and I love her to death. You are starting to step on my private life by all this amount of mail. You are making a fool of yourself.

SONDRA: And what message do you have for those who aspire to be a vampire like you?

NICO: The only message I would tell them is, mind your own business and leave me alone. I do not claim anything. They claim to be something. I am a 31-year-old ex-convict who just wants to live happily and have the same lifestyle that I have always had. I do not seek the company of people who claim to be "like-minded," as I have my own family now. They can claim whatever they want, I just do not care.

SONDRA: Tell us about your plans to support yourself.

NICO: I am ready to take any job. I have learned filming and editing on a professional level, and I am also good at putting up websites. Of course, I am skilled at art and design. I try to make a living by selling paintings online, but I don?t make enough to allow me to travel right now.

SONDRA: Have you thought about starting your own business?

NICO: Yes, I am looking for a sponsor to finance a Cannibal Café. I would be the chef.

SONDRA: How have you found the World Wide Web?

NICO: I have a website. It is not about my case, it is only about the paintings I have for sale. I use it as a tool to help me sell my artwork on a worldwide level. I also include some of my correspondence and exclusive interviews with other vampire killers.

BLOOD TRAUMA

Kathleen Sullivan, a survivor of satanic ritual abuse who is undergoing therapy for post-traumatic stress disorder and dissociative identity disorder, related the following family history in a telephone interview with this author in April of 1999:

My father died in 1990. He was really into drinking blood. He was raised by his father, who was a Welsh Druid, who came to the United States when he was young. I know from personal experience that dad's father had killed children in rituals. I saw that at least once. I still have no memory of seeing his father drink blood. My dad was raised in the Druid tradition, but he broke away and chose to become a Satanist. Somewhere along the line, he also became a member of the Nazi Golden Dawn.

When I was young, my grandfather wanted me to be a Druid, and my dad wanted me to be a Satanist. So there was a real conflict in the family over that, because I was the eldest grandchild, and the eldest child in my dad's family. This was from as early as I can remember.

Somewhere along the line, my dad had developed a real need for human blood. Dad believed drinking it would extend his life span and would give him energy. He particularly preferred the blood of infants. He believed that the life-force was in the blood and that pure infants had the strongest life-force in the blood. He would torture them as they were dying and terrorize them, because he believed that would intensify the life-force somehow.

By the time I was four years old, he made me cut the veins in the baby's neck. We would hold a chalice underneath and the blood would flow into the chalice. As soon as it did, he would have me and him and other cult members drink it.

The child sacrifices started out with him putting my hand within his hand, but pretty soon I learned to do it on my own. If I didn't, I could imagine I'd be the next one he'd do.

He was trying to convince me that he was having to kill them because I existed, and it was like if they didn't exist, I would be next. So I kept being grateful that he was killing other children, because so long as he was killing them, I wouldn't die myself.

Sometimes he mixed opium in with the blood, which made it more bearable. I liked the opium. Now I have a real hard time remembering how it all tasted, and I think that's a benefit.

He talked about Aleister Crowley, and I don't care to read Crowley's material, but that's what his belief system was about. The life force being in the blood, and in the semen of animals and humans, he got that from Crowley.

Dad never did get along with authority figures. He worked for a company that had connections to the CIA, but he liked to do his own thing. Up until I was 14, he had his own cult in Reading, Pennsylvania. He considered himself more of a Luciferian than a Satanist, but he did say "Hail, Satan!" Maybe he said it to psych us children out. I'm not sure how much he really believed in the rituals he performed and how much of it was done to psych us out.

Sometimes they did the dedication and the sacrifice and all that. There were times they would do the baby on an altar. See, when I was that little, four or five, I didn't really pay attention to my surroundings. It's like I had tunnel vision—all I could see was what was right in front of me. The baby's neck, the blood, dad's hands, the chalice, the black cloth on his arms, what was right in front of my face.

As I got older, a lot of times they would do a victim right on the floor. They had a black-painted floor, and then they had what they called a hexagram. They didn't do pentagrams, they had a hexagram. And they'd have the victim in the middle. They'd have a big white candle on each point of the star in the circle.

For a long time, they wore black robes with hoods while I stayed naked. When I was 13, I was finally allowed to wear a robe, and got to officiate a couple of rituals. I guess dad was testing me to see what I'd do when I thought I was in charge. I just kept doing like he trained me to do all along. But it was so awful that by the time I got home, I didn't remember any of it; I just thought I was having another nightmare. He encouraged me to believe that, I guess so I wouldn't tell anyone.

They had some rituals they would do ceremonially. They usually did them in English. They usually didn't do runes and all that kind of stuff. That was for special occasions, special rituals. My dad's mother had a big old leatherbound book that they'd read strange words from, then. They tried to teach me to read and write the runes, but I got too upset. I guess they gave up.

I used to think my dad was evil, but the more I learned about his childhood, and the more I looked back at what I can remember about his behavior, I think he was a severely wounded little boy in an adult body, and terrified of people.

He might not have done that particular thing, had he not been exposed to rituals as a child. He might have tried to meet his psychological needs in another form. But by believing that by killing children and drinking their blood, that he would receive an extended life span, he thought they were the fountain of youth to him. Like he was a battery and he needed to be recharged. He believed he would die if he didn't have blood.

From what I heard, he was under investigation once for some crime or another in Pennsylvania, and we moved to another state, then to Georgia where he hooked up with satanists there. Mostly family generational. Then in 1989, before he died, he was under investigation for child molestation in DeKalb County, Georgia. I was 34 then, but I was still under his control. I didn't know yet that I had DID, but he knew it and he used it to keep me under control.

His youngest child was two when he died and she showed evidence of molestation; she is still a bit autistic. The youngest boy is two years older than her and at first he was diagnosed with Tourette's syndrome, but now they say he has dissociative identity disorder like I do. For years, he was really into knives and blood and killing. They had to watch the family cat for a while. He's doing better now.

Their older sibling, a brother, has blocked everything out. I was privy to some stuff that dad did to him and he doesn't remember any of it. Since I knew some of what had been done to them, it makes me very uncomfortable to be around them. Which is real sad. I'm afraid if they see me it might trigger something. Because dad made me be present in controlled alter-states when he hurt kids.

My own daughter is into drinking blood. She is 23 now and she was ritually abused also. I was forced to watch some of that too. It about killed me. She thinks vampires are very cool, but she won't tell me if she is one or not. She mutilates herself and drinks her own blood a lot, but she drinks other people's blood too. She has piercings all over and hardcore tattoos everywhere.

When she was living with us we were constantly finding pins and razor blades everywhere. I couldn't even walk in her room without shoes on because I knew I might get stuck by something in the carpet. One time, she took a razor blade and cut an inverted cross in the skin on her chest. She told me she was flashing back on a ritual and thought she belonged to Satan.

Now, she's incredibly angry. But she doesn't remember what was done to her. It's really strange to me, the way she is acting it out, even though she doesn't remember. Because she doesn't remember, she thinks it's all her own idea to do this. And it makes her feel different from everybody else, because she doesn't see anybody else doing it. So she thinks she is weird. And that's really sad because it seriously messes up her self-esteem. It makes her feel like, well, if I'm weird, then I might as well go ahead and live weird and do weird things, because that's what I am. It's really sad, because she's not weird, she's severely traumatized, she doesn't remember it, and she is reliving it.

Kathleen's daughter unknowingly reenacts her grandfather's vampiric behavior both symbolically and literally, because her memories are submerged in her unconsciousness, where she cannot identify, understand, or come to terms with them. The same mechanism seen in the individual psyche may be operative in the mass psyche as well. The bloodthirsty beliefs and customs of our forebears have been repressed as we have collectively moved up Maslow's hierarchy of needs toward world self-realization. That part of our nature and history which we repress into the area of unacceptable reality gains more power from the darkness which thus enshrouds it. The more the vampires and criminals are exiled from the happy, shiny people, the more their Outsider status creates its own fuel-injected, combustible potential energy. Inexplicable eruptions of bloody primitive violence force us to remember our submerged past, which we are thus condemned to repeat, whether we realize what we are doing or not.

PART 3

MOLDY OLDIES

Throughout the vast shadowy world of ghosts and demons there is no figure so terrible, no figure so dreaded and abhorred, yet dight with such fearful fascination, as the vampire, who is himself neither ghost nor demon, but yet who partakes the dark natures and possesses the mysterious and terrible qualities of both.

+Montague Summers

POWER OF THE BLOOD

The up-and-coming spiritual leader had just drawn a crowd of five thousand, whom he wowed by feeding them all with a paltry five loaves of barley and two fish. Right after that, when he was actually seen walking on water, people started talking about making this remarkable man their king.

But when he broached the preposterous idea of the attainment of eternal life via the quaffing of his blood and mastication of his flesh, the thousands who had eagerly dined on his miraculous loaves abruptly reneged on him, and all but a dozen of his horrified followers abandoned the nascent religious movement.

> Jesus said to them, "I tell you the truth, unless you eat the flesh of the Son of Man and drink his blood, you have no life in you. Whoever eats my flesh and drinks my blood has eternal life, and I will raise him up at the last day. For my flesh is real food and my blood is real drink... Your forefathers ate manna and died; but he who feeds on this bread will live forever." He said this while teaching in the synagogue in Capernaum.
>
> On hearing it, many of his disciples said, "This is a hard teaching. Who can accept it?" ...From this time many of his disciples turned back and no longer followed him.
>
> +John 6:53-66

The shocking idea that outraged so many of the disciples who heard it from Jesus Christ himself went on to become the cornerstone of the doctrine of the Roman Catholic Church. Transubstantiation via the Sacrament of the Eucharist provides an objective correlative for the incorporation of the teachings of the spiritual master into the belief system, and thence the behavior, of the believer.

The attainment of endless life via the literal consumption of the living substance of flesh and blood is among the most primitive beliefs found worldwide, but a more sinister twist on the same beguiling concept is involved in phenomena of a vampiric nature.

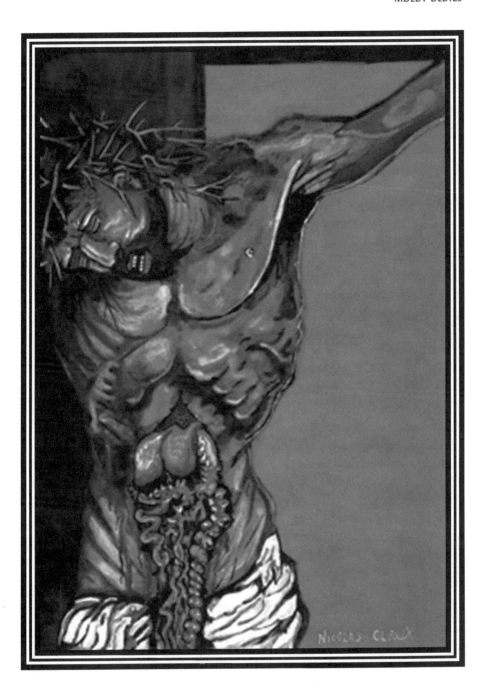

 Jesus on the Cross

THE ORIGINAL DRACULA

By the late Eighteenth century, the vampire was a stock character in penny-dreadfuls, and by the early 1800s, vampires had hit the European stage in comedies by Alexandre Dumas. In 1847, a novel called *Varney the Vampire, or the Feast of Blood* was a bestseller in London.

Finally, in 1897, Bram Stoker published his watershed novel introducing the eponymic character of Count Dracula. Stoker explained that his character was based on a combination of historical figures. He never cited his sources, but a survey of European history reveals three bloody progenitors of the fictional Count. They were not vampires, but their crimes were so villainous, they left bloodstained prints on those whose vampire dreams have shaped our own.

The first character whose crimes might have contributed to the blood-thirsty fearsomeness of the legendary vampire was the French war hero, Gilles de Rais, who embodied "the religious greatness of the damned; genius as disease, disease as genius, the type of the afflicted and possessed, where saint and criminal become one," according to Thomas Mann.

Born in 1404 in the Château of Machécoul, at the age of nine his father died; his mother remarried and sent Gilles and his younger brother René to live with their grandfather.

As the sole heir to the family fortune, Gilles loved music and was learned in Latin, early on developing a taste for the pornographic writings of Suetonius, which stimulated his sexually deviant fantasies.

The French had been at war with the English since 1338, and Gilles was born and bred to a family of mediæval knights. It would be his glory and honor to carry on that distinguished tradition. Gilles de Rais was already one of the wealthiest nobles in Europe, then in 1420 he doubled his fortunes by marrying Catherine de Thouars, heiress to a vast fortune.

In 1429 he was at the court of the Dauphin, the uncrowned heir to the throne, when a young girl named Jeanne demanded to see the Dauphin, and told him that God had instructed her to defeat the English. The Dauphin ordered Gilles to accompany "the Maid," and he fought by her side, defeating the English at Orléans, and again at Patay. By the age of 24, he had so distinguished himself in battle that he was a national hero, and at the coronation of the Dauphin, it was Gilles de Rais who collected the holy oil for the new king's anointment. After the coronation, the king declared him the Marshal of France.

After his glory years, he retired from the wars, and began to enjoy his privileged lifestyle. He built a fine library, including a copy of Augustine's *City of God*. He developed his ancestral estates in Machecoul, Malemort, La Suze, Champtoce and Tiffauges, and had sumptuous chapels built at each castle where magnificent masses were held. Yet he was bored; there was still something missing. And so he started indulging his sick sexual appetite by preying upon children.

Gilles maintained a retinue of courtiers eager to assist him in sating his most depraved urges. A boy would be kidnapped or lured to his castle, taken down to the dungeon and hanged from the ceiling, released and reassured, then hoisted and tortured again, stripped and raped, and finally decapitated. Even that was not enough. Gilles would sexually assault the remains, slicing open new orifices, until he would swoon in a perverted ecstasy, and be carried off to his chambers to sleep it off while the remains were dismembered and burned. He was wily enough to stick to peasants, so nobody ever complained when the young ones disappeared.

In 1435, the city of Orléans commemorated its deliverance by Jeanne d'Arc. Gilles de Rais sponsored the occasion, producing a play featuring a cast of hundreds, with himself grandstanding in the leading role, and providing a sumptuous feast, free food and wine for all.

With all his spending, he squandered his fortune, and started dreaming of making money the old-fashioned way: alchemy. He consulted a priest and had him inquire after the services of a magician. The priest brought him one who conjured up a flock of crows, but warned he'd have to cooperate with demons to get the gold. So he locked himself in a dungeon in his castle at Tiffauges, together with his cousin Gilles de Sille and the magician, who warned them solemnly *not to make the sign of the cross*. Whatever really happened there has never been told, but as the story has it, that effort ended abruptly with an explosion and the dungeon collapsing on the magician, though the two cousins managed to escape alive.

In 1437, when he tried to put the castle at Champtoce on the market, his family intervened and seized it. Gilles was a bit nonplussed, as he had buried dozens of children there, and had hoped to dispose of their remains before vacating the premises.

Then he started to worry about the castle at Machécoul, and put his crew to work, removing the remains of about 40 children he had thrown into a locked tower there. A year later he regained control of the estate at Champtoce and hastened back to remove those corpses, which had gone unnoticed.

Meanwhile, the Duke of Brittany ordered an investigation into the disappearance of hundreds of children, and levied a huge lien on Gilles that he was unable to satisfy.

In 1439, the priest Blanchet returned from Italy with a skilled magician named François Prelati, a young homosexual Gilles found irresistible. The magician prescribed a sacrifice to the Devil—the blood of a child and parts of his body. Gilles was happy to sodomize and slaughter another child, but as a lifelong Catholic, he still balked at closing the transaction by selling his soul to The Evil One.

Prelati doubted that gold could be produced without the soul sacrifice, but he pressed on. One day he summoned Gilles excitedly, claiming he had actually produced the gold. But when they came to the door, the magician peeked in then shrieked that there was a huge green serpent guarding it. By the time Gilles got a look, the serpent had vanished and so, apparently, had the ever-elusive gold.

In 1440, he turned over an estate called Mermorte to the Duke of Brittany, and then before it had been occupied, Gilles inexplicably decided that he was entitled to repossess the castle, and launched an invasion, entering the chapel during mass, dragging the priest outside and beating him. Murdering peasants was one thing, but this was a sacrilege; Gilles had committed a capital offense.

He was thrown into a dungeon, and all of his property was turned over to the Duke of Brittany. He stood accused of being a "heretic, apostate, conjurer of demons... accused of the crimes and vices against nature, sodomy, sacrilege and violation of the immunities of Holy Church." The indictment was 49 paragraphs long, and there were 47 charges, including abuse of clerical privilege, sexual perversions against children, human sacrifice and multiple charges of child murder.

On September 13, 1440, Gilles appeared before the court, arrogant and defiant as ever, and 110 witnesses testified against him. After six torture sessions, he admitted everything "voluntarily and freely" on October 21, and one week later Gilles de Rais was hanged and his body interred in the church. Two of his most faithful servants were burned alive.

The seductive mystique that appeals to an audience calls for the vampire to display a certain aristocratic èlan, not always perceptible in those benighted creatures disturbed enough to kill for the taste of blood. For this requisite flair, Stoker drew on the legendary Vlad Tepes, King of Wallachia, a Fifteenth-century warrior who earned the honorific title of Dracula for the ostentatious torturing and slaying of an estimated 100,000 victims of war.

The name Dracula signifies Son of the Dragon, otherwise known as Son of the Devil. Also known as Vlad the Impaler, his unique form of warfare went far beyond the mere extermination of enemy troops. An especially perverse strain of sexual sadism required driving a stake into the ground and inserting the point of it into the victim's anus or vagina, so that their demise would be excruciatingly slow. Leaving the corpses thus impaled for all to contemplate served to put the survivors in the occupied territory on notice that they would wind up the same way if they failed to submit to his bloody rule.

In a 1499 woodcut, Vlad is seated at a wooden table set for dinner, smiling ever so slightly, his hollow eyes feasting on a scene of horror as described by Anna Szigethy and Anne Graves in *Vampires: From Vlad Drakul to the Vampire Lestat:* "a writhing mass of impaled men and women, their eyes bulging, their mouths gaping open. Most have been run through from front to back, some through their spines. In front of Dracula there is a man in tunic and hat, dismembering a body. Dracula is gesturing toward this spectacle, as if giving instruction. Heads and arms lie all around, causing speculation as to what kind of meat he is dining on."

Above the scene is inscribed in German: "Here begins the very cruel and frightening story about a wild bloodthirsty man, *voivod Dracula.* How he impaled people, roasted them and boiled them in a kettle, and how he skinned them and hacked them into pieces. He also roasted the children and their mothers had to eat their children themselves. And many other horrible things are written in this tract and also in which land he had ruled."

The commander of the expedition that helped Vlad regain his throne in 1476 was Prince Steven Báthory of Transylvania, whose family crest, like that of the Tepes, displayed the Dragon. A hundred years later the devilish Báthory clan produced the second major source of imagery in Stoker's contribution to the vampiric mythos.

Countess Erzsébet Báthory was one of the most prolific sex-slayers of all time, with the sadistic torture murders of 612 women detailed in her diary.

Inbred Magyar royalty, the Báthory line was highlighted by kings and princes, and even the low lights were magistrates, civil and ecclesiastical dignitaries—but more than a few had turned out bad—*real* bad. This one would turn out so bad she would be walled into her own torture chamber and die after three years of imprisonment, in 1614. For more than a century, in Hungary it was forbidden to even speak her name, and the records on her case remained sealed.

In 1585 at the age of 15 the Countess was married to Count Ferenc Nas-

 Vlad "The Impaler" Tepes

dasdy AKA the Black Hero of Hungary, who spent most of his time off fashionably fighting the Turks, leaving the Countess to fight the crashing boredom of life in an isolated mediæval castle. Perhaps it was the boredom that drove the Countess mad. Or perhaps it was just bad blood.

As brilliant as she was beautiful, at a time when her cousin the Crown Prince of Transylvania was an illiterate lout, Erzsébet Báthory could read and write in four languages and required a higher level of stimulation than your average blueblood. Her *ennui* was eased, however, by her patronage of the black arts, as she assembled an in-house entourage of sorcerers, witches, and sexual deviates of increasingly sinister tastes as pansexual orgies degenerated into gross torture parties and worse.

Cruelty to servants was commonplace, but Elizabeth was uncommonly cruel. Light torture of young servant girls like the use of branding irons, molten wax and pins under their nails soon progressed to the most ghoulish of executions. Dungeon killings were *de rigeur*. But eventually even the bloodiest of horrors becomes routine, and to keep up the interest level, innovations were required. So in the winter, a maid might be stripped and taken out into the icy Carpathians, where water would be poured over her until she froze, to Her Ladyship's delight.

The Count shared in her perverted pleasures when he was home, and contributed several novelties of his own, such as the summer version of the outdoor execution, which called for stripping the victim, covering her naked flesh with honey, and restraining her to be bitten and stung to death by insects.

He even gave the Countess a set of custom-made silver pincers, a pernicious enhancement to the information-delivery system he applied to prisoners of war.

In 1604 the Black Hero was stabbed to death in Bucharest by a harlot who complained he had taken his pleasure with her and walked out on the tab. The widowed Countess did not grieve unduly. At the advanced age of 50, she had become a commodity on the marriage market again, and vain about her creamy complexion, she was concerned about her ability to make a favorable match. The awareness of her fading beauty exacerbated her incipient psychosis.

When the blood of a servant girl fell upon her hand, she declared that the skin touched by the blood took on a younger, brighter appearance, which led her to conclude that bathing in fresh blood was the only way she could rejuvenate her complexion.

Majordomo Johannes Ujvary, the dwarf who became her chief torturer, and Thorko, the manservant who introduced her to the occult, were ordered to strip the unfortunate maid, flay her and drain the blood into a huge vat, where the Countess bathed in it, the better to beautify her skin.

Her Ladyship's nurse Iloona Joo and two lesbian witches named Darvulia and Dorka made up the rest of the grim crew who would bring a batch of young girls to the castle, take them down into the torture chamber, strip them and hang them upside down. When the Countess was ready for her bloodbath, the batch would all have their throats cut and the blood drained quickly enough for Her Ladyship to enjoy its warmth.

But five years of bloodbaths were not good enough. Her skin was still show- ing persistent signs of age. Clearly a better grade of blood was required. And that's where the Countess made her big mistake. She could have gone on bathing in the blood of peasants unmolested, because the disappearance of the disenfranchised was as much of a non-event in those days as it is in our own. But no, her sadistic machinations escalated further and further out of control until the madness had to end.

In 1609 Countess Báthory established a charm school for aristocrats at the castle, purportedly to groom young ladies and train them in proper behavior. As soon the first batch of two dozen blueblood maidens disap- peared, word reached the Hungarian Emperor, who demanded the Countess be taken into custody by her own cousin, Count Thurzo, gover- nor of the province. When his troops raided the castle on December 30, 1610, in the main room they found a dead body and a living victim pierced with holes. Several more victims were liberated from the dungeon, and 50 bodies were eventually exhumed.

The trial was held in 1611 and the original transcript has been preserved in Hungary to this day. The Countess never appeared in court and refused to enter a plea. Her henchmen confessed and were executed by impalement. Though Erzsébet Báthory was never convicted of any crime, her torture cham- ber was walled up with her inside, and it was thus this real monster behind the legend of the modern vampire expired, proven that all too mortal at last.

The literary serial killer Gerard John Schaefer was fascinated with the Countess, and his commentary on the reality behind her myth was pub- lished in 1980 in *Coin World*, the journal of the American Numismatic Association:

> I would like to take this opportunity to comment on the preposterous alle- gation that Erzsébet Báthory, niece of King Stefan Báthory of Poland, was a "true vampire," as well as the inference that this poor deranged woman may have been a "werewolf." This is, of course, foolishness, and I would

appreciate the opportunity to speak in defense of the Countess Báthory.

There is no question but that the Countess was a monumental mass murderer who was, in all likelihood, completely insane. Court documents, depositions and testimony surviving to this day confirm that she did indeed bathe in the warm blood of exsanguinated virgins who were ignominiously hanged by their heels over her bathtub and slaughtered like cattle. Such a practice is indicative of insanity, hardly vampirism or lycanthropy.

It is a myth generated by Hollywood horror writers that a vampire suckles at the throat of a virgin. This is not to say that a vampire would turn down such an opportunity but, in general, anyone will do nicely when a vampire succumbs to the urge to satisfy its abnormal cravings. The true vampire requires human blood for nourishment, and would be dismayed at the prospect of wasting a good meal for the purpose of a bathing experience. There is no evidence that vampires concern themselves with bathing at all.

Werewolves are known for attacking and devouring people. These extraordinary creatures are compelled by demonic influences that are not clearly understood to modern man and cause a great deal of local terror in some parts of the world. It may be said with reasonable certainty that the Countess Báthory was surely mad. It was no ordinary madness that drove her to her horrible deeds, but it was neither vampirism or lycanthropy that compelled her. The Countess was tried by the criminal courts of her day; witches, vampires and werewolves were tried by ecclesiastical courts.

Certainly Erzsébet's noble family position helped to prevent her from joining her accessories on the stake, but it was more probably that her obvious insanity played a major part in the sparing of her life. Most cultures are loath to execute the insane, and consider them "touched" by the gods.

In closing it is fair to say that had the Countess Báthory possessed the vampiric qualities attributed to her, she would have simply turned herself into a bat and flown out through the feeding hole in the door. Any sensible vampire would!

G. J. Schaffer

VERY WELL FOR A DEVIL

The connection between the vampire and the devil of mediæval literature is highlighted in Bram Stoker's *Dracula*, when Dr. Van Helsing reflects:

> The Draculas were, says Arminius, a great and noble race, though now and again were scions who were held by their coevals to have dealings with The Evil One. They learned his secrets in the Scholomance, amongst the mountains over Lake Hermannstadt, where the Devil claims the tenth scholar as his due.

Like a vampire, Satan is said to be a deceiver who lurks in the darkness, lying in wait to steal the soul of the innocent wayfarer. In Hebrew, the root word *s'tn* means the Enemy, as it does in the Greek *satana*, and Arabic *shaitan*. Or to turn the phrase another way, in the words of Aleister Crowley: "The devil is your enemy's god." The ritual evocation of the evil impulse means to draw evil energy towards oneself until one is filled with it, until the Enemy becomes all that one can be. In ceremonial, spiritual or philosophical circumstances satanism can be approached as a rather abstract discipline, and in fact most satanists effortlessly refrain from killing their own kind and eating or drinking their vital substance. But then there are those for whom the ritual invocation of the Enemy is inextricably bound up in their voracious crimes.

> Your enemy the devil prowls around like a roaring lion looking for someone to devour.
> +I Peter 5:8

Confessions obtained during the Inquisition provide a rich record of folk beliefs about the ritual consumption of human blood and flesh, under the alleged auspices of The Evil One. On April 28, 1600, for example, Councilor Johann Simon Wangereck obtained the confession of Anna Pappenheimer, the matriarch of a family of vagabonds who were all under torture in Munich's Falcon Tower. Whether or not confessions coerced by torture can ever be taken as evidence of events that actually transpired, they do reveal common folkways in that they must provide details convincing enough for the torturers to accept them.

According to Anna Pappenheimer, as summarized from official records by Michael Kunze, nine days after her first night ride on a fire iron magically fueled by "a powder made from the crushed hand of an unbaptized child," the original Man in Black accosted her. "I am none other than Lucifer, whom you human beings call The Evil One," he announced, and then raped her until she swooned.

"That's the way," she recalled the demon murmuring over her as she awoke. "You submitted to my will just now, and so it shall always be. What we still must do is a pure formality. You must renounce Almighty God, the Virgin Mary, all the saints, and the whole world. You must acknowledge me as your one and only Lord, and deny the Christian faith. I will give you money so that you will know no more poverty, and you will serve me. What I order you to do henceforth, you will do, even if it should harm your fellow men, even if it be repugnant to you."

As the confessed witch described it to her inquisitors, the dark man ripped the flesh of her left shoulder and smeared her lips with the blood, inside and out. "Let us take a solemn oath," he commanded, then dipped a quill in the blood flowing from her fresh wound and handed it to the ravished woman, who protested that she could not write. Nevertheless, her hand was guided to inscribe the blood oath testifying that she, "Anna Pamb, otherwise called Pappenheimer, would henceforth be a disciple of the Devil, be loyal to Lucifer forevermore, do nothing good, but only evil."

"You have black hair, at any rate," the Devil concluded in a timelessly appropriate fashion note. "You will do very well for a devil."

J. Gordon Melton writes in *The Vampire Book: The Encyclopedia of the Undead* that vampirism poses a challenge to the dominance of the Church, which explains the employment of the Crucifix, Holy Water and Eucharist in struggles with vampire kind. "It also includes a protest," he writes, "against the authority of any particular religion and its claims of truth in a religiously pluralistic world."

DEATH, BE NOT PROUD

We have not always been as certain as we are today of what, exactly, constitutes the final visitation by the Angel of Death, and it is quite possible that the fear of those who have passed through the dark kingdom might have arisen from the primitive state of the fine art of determination of actual death.

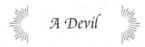

A Devil

Although the signs of death have been known from earliest times, none of them are reliable indicators. Rigor mortis, pallor and discoloration, fixed pupils, absence of detectable respiration and heartbeat—some or all of these indicators of death can be present, and yet the putative corpse may rise again.

"Centuries ago if two or more members of the same family died of the same disease the first body would be exhumed," said German vampire researcher Professor Thomas Crozier. "The corpse would be found with rosy cheeks and blood-red fluid in its mouth, which are natural signs of decomposition, but in those days people believed the person was not altogether dead." Crozier told the *Frankfurter Rundschau* that people developed ideas about vampires because they didn't understand death and disease.

In 1890 the Prix Dusgate and 2500 francs were awarded to a Doctor Maze in France for his assertion that the only reliable sign of death was frank putrefaction. One 1890 textbook probing the difference between apparent death and the real thing listed no less than 418 sources, and in 1905 the Royal College of Surgeons published a study documenting 219 narrow escapes from premature burial and 149 cases of actual interment of the living, as well as several autopsies and embalming procedures interrupted by the revivification of the corpse.

In the Nineteenth century, the fear of premature burial was epidemic. Fyodor Dostoyevski insisted that his burial be delayed five days after his apparent death. Hans Christian Andersen carried a note in his pocket at all times with a detailed death protocol, and so did English novelist Wilkie Collins. Others provided instructions that their body be definitively mutilated to prevent their interment from being premature. British antiquary Francis Douce and socialite Harriet Martineau each specified that their heads be severed by a surgeon. First lady of the British stage, Ada Cavendish, wanted her jugular pierced upon her death, and the widow of Sir Richard Burton left orders that she be stabbed in the heart. Bishop Berkeley, Lord Lytton, and Daniel O'Connell ordered their burials delayed, and their veins opened, so that they might bleed out before interment.

In March of 1896, the *London Echo* published a report on the passing of a Greek Orthodox cleric on the island of Lesbos, who was pronounced dead at the age of 80. The body of Nicephorus Glycas was garbed in ceremonial robes and placed on a throne, guarded by priests, and visited by legions of the faithful. On the second night of the wake, the mournful scene was suddenly enlivened by a gasp from the guest of honor, who turned and stared about him at the ceremony commemorating his own demise. Horrified, the priests rushed to his assistance and thus the antiquated cleric was returned to the land of the living. What if he had been a commoner? No doubt he would have been buried unceremoniously and stirred from his trance in a tomb.

Another case was published about the same time, relating the tale of one Reverend Schwartz, a beloved missionary who was aroused from his grim somnolence when the congregation at his funeral sang his favorite hymn, only to hear the voice from the coffin joining in at the chorus.

In the 1880s, a Russian nobleman and chamberlain to the czar was attending the funeral of a young girl in Belgium, when she screamed weakly from her coffin, causing several of the mourners to swoon and staggering the priest. That pitiful cry haunted the Count Karnice-Karnicki, who became obsessed by the spectre of being trapped helplessly below the ground.

He contrived a marvelous device and made it widely available for purchase by the aristocracy, and for rent by commoners. The coffin was enclosed in a hermetically sealed vault affixed with a long tube. Inside the coffin, a glass globe attached to a spring rested on the chest of the decedent. Should the least movement of the chest occur, the spring would cause the box to fly open, admitting light and air to the coffin, while a complex system of alarms would be deployed. A flag would be hoisted four feet above the ground, a bell would ring for a half hour, and a lamp would be illuminated. The long tube would not only admit oxygen, but would serve as a megaphone, to amplify the weak voice of the victim. Thousands of Europeans employed this ingenious device, and it was so popular in the United States that societies were formed to promote its use.

This atmosphere of hysterical concern was exacerbated by a demonstration performed by a Colonel Townsend, and witnessed by a panel of physicians. Using techniques similar to those perfected by yogis, the officer entered into a self-induced trance, progressively suppressing his heart rate and respirations until his entire body assumed the icy chill and rigor of death. The color drained from his face, his pupils became fixed and dilated. After he continued in this state of suspended animation for over a half-hour, the physicians actually certified him dead and were preparing to depart, when he reversed the procedure, gradually returning to his normal lively status so effectively that by the next day he was able to repeat the remarkable performance.

These, then, were some of the very real cases that have fueled the superstitious fear of the undead down through the ages, and contributed to the body of belief that shapes our idea of the vampire.

While some of the vampire myths might have had their seeds in incidents of living people being prematurely interred, there are also fertile circumstances on the other side of the veil, with signs of life coming from the other side. It can seem that the dead are belching, chewing, suckling, thrashing about, reaching out from the grave, and even giving birth, says Paul Barber in *Vampires, Burial and Death.*

"When a corpse bursts as a result of bloating, the emission of gases, body fluids and maggots—present in astonishing numbers—may be audible."

Were a stake to be driven into the heart, the unfortunate corpse might even shriek—not because it is a vampire, but because of the burst of air forced through the vocal cords.

EVIL REVENANTS

The Greeks had a word for it, and they weren't the only ones. Reports of *lamias*, or predatory ghosts, date back to ancient Libya. Philostratus provided a traditional account of one in his biography of the magus Apollonius of Tyana, and Keats recycled the story in his famous poem *Lamia.*

These are some of the names given to legendary vampire-like creatures by indigenous peoples the world over.

Adze	Ghana	Danag	Philippines
Afrit	Arabia	Dearg-due	Ireland
Alp	Germany	Doppelsauger	Germany
Asanbosam	Togo	Duppy	West Indies
Aswang	Philippines	Ekimmu	Assyria
Bajang	Malaysia	Empusas	Greece
Baobhan-sith	Scotland	Eretik	Russia
Bebarlangs	Philippines	Estrie	Hebrew
Bhuta	India	Gayal	India
Brahmaparush	India	Impundulu	South Africa
Bruxsa	Portugal	Jaracacas	Brazil
Chordewa	India	Jigarkhwar	India
Churel	India	Kasha	Japan
Civatateo	Mexico	Kozlak	Croatia

Krasyy	Thailand	Pontianak	Indonesia
Kuang-shi	China	Preta	Tibet
Lamia	Libya	Raksasa	India
Lampir	Poland	Ramanga	Madagascar
Langsuir	Malaysia	Sarcomenos	Crete
Leanhaum-shee	Ireland	Stregoni	Italy
Lobishomen	Brazil	Striges	Greece
Loogaroo	West Indies	Strigoii	Romania
Lugat	Albania	Talamaur	Australia
Mara	Slavic	Tanggal	Indonesia
Masan	India	Tengu	Japan
Masani	India	Tlaciques	Mexico
Mormo	Greece	Uber	Turkey
Moroii	Romania	Ubour	Bulgaria
Mullo	Gypsy	Upier	Poland
Nadilla	Iraq	Upiribi	Ukraine
Nachzehrer	Poland	Upirina	Serbo-Croatia
Nelapsi	Slavic	Upyr	Russia
Neuntoter	Germany	Ustrel	Bulgaria
Nosferatu	Romania	Utukku	Iraq
Obayifo	Ghana	Vampir	Magyar
Ohyn	Poland	Varacolaci	Romania
Opji	Poland	Vepir	Bulgaria
Oupir	Hungary	Vetala	India
Pacu Pati	India	Vukodlak	Slovenia
Pelesit	Malaysia	Vourdalak	Russia
Penanggalan	Malaysia	Vrykolakas	Greece
Pijavica	Croatia	Wampyr	Germany
Pisaca	India	Xiang shi	China
Polong	Malaysia	Zmeu	Moldavia

World literature is full of chronicles of the dead who return to drain the vitality of the living. Jean Marigny, a French expert on vampires, observes, "The oldest of these chronicles date from the 12th and 13th centuries, and, contrary to what one might expect, are not set in remote parts of Europe, but in England and Scotland."

William of Newburgh wrote of several English cases in the Twelfth century, citing the "unimpeachable testimony of responsible persons." His investigations had revealed "that bodies of the dead may arise from their tombs and that vitalized by some supernatural power, they speed hither and thither, either greatly alarming or in some cases actually slaying the living."

One of the most memorable tales was that of the Dog Priest of the Abbey of Melrose. This young, vigorous monk had been assigned to the post of chaplain to a voluptuous widow, and had taken up the dissolute lifestyle of her courtiers including the "hunting with horses and hounds" that earned him the scathing sobriquet *Hundepriest*.

When the high-living monk was dead and buried in the Abbey graveyard, his restless spirit prowled the countryside, fouling the waters, withering the crops, abducting and slaying the livestock. This in itself was not so bad, but his hijinks persisted until he made an unwelcome appearance at the manor home of the great lady he had counseled. Shrieking and moaning, he carried on most frightfully, until the distraught gentlewoman complained to the abbot and begged him to intervene.

Four monks set up a vigil at the chaplain's graveside, but as the hours wore on uneventfully, the three senior monks went back inside to sit by the fire, leaving a lonely novitiate to keep watch.

William supposed that "the devil, thinking that he had found a fine opportunity to break down that pious man's courage and constancy, aroused from his grave that instrument of his which apparently he had for once allowed to slumber a longer time than usual."

But as the demon emerged from its dissociated hell, the brave monk was undeterred. "As the horrible creature rushed at him with the most hideous yell, he firmly stood his ground, dealing it a terrific blow with a battle axe."

The dusty corpse staggered from the blow, and reeled back towards its grave. Miraculously, the ground opened up to receive the fetid creature and folded back in place behind it.

Astonished, the novitiate summoned the senior monks, who decided the best course of action would be to call off the vigil for the night, get some rest, and then in the morning, dig up the corpse of the *Hundepriest* and remove it from the consecrated ground of the Abbey.

When the accursed corpse was disinterred, it was found to be "marked by a terrible wound, whilst the black blood that had flowed from this seemed to swamp the whole tomb." The monks hauled the hideous execration out onto unhallowed ground, immolated it in a huge bonfire, and scattered the ashes to the wind. Thus the *Hundepriest* would ride to his hellhounds on this earthly plane no more.

Another story related by William of Newburgh involves a man who had been buried in Buckinghamshire. He persisted in returning night after night, attacking his wife, until she asked several neighbors to stay with her. When the hungry ghost reappeared, he was driven off by their angry shouts.

Bishop Hugh of Lincoln was consulted. He wrote out a charter of absolution, and the tomb was opened, revealing the corpse to be as fresh as the day it was interred. Although the archdeacon urged immolation, the symbolic power of the Bishop's absolution charter was apparently sufficient. Placed on the corpse's chest when the tomb was sealed again, in this case, it was powerful enough to prevent any more trouble from the reluctant dead.

In other cases, the rituals of the Church were less efficacious. Walter Map, the Archdeacon of Oxford, recorded an interesting tale involving an English soldier named William Laudun, who had appealed to the Bishop of Hereford for assistance with an unruly spirit.

It seems that one of the townsfolk had died and been buried, yet time after time someone recognizable as the dead man would come around the boardinghouse where Laudun was staying. In sepulchral tones, he would thrice chant the name of one of the boarders, who invariably would fall dead within three days of the spectral summons.

Upon consideration, the Bishop declared the culprit was "an evil angel of that accursed wretch, so that he is able to rouse himself and walk abroad in his dead body."

The ritual decreed by the Bishop required that "the corpse be exhumed, and then do you cut through its neck, sprinkling both the body and the grave throughout with Holy Water, and so rebury it."

This ceremony was performed, but apparently the ghost still had some unresolved issues with Laudun, because not long afterwards, his sleep was broken again by the sound of his own name as it was droned out three times by the same familiar voice.

That did it. The Bishop be damned, Laudun wasn't going to take the abuse any longer. He sprang from his bed and burst from the door brandishing his sword and swearing vengeance on the unfortunate soul of his tormentor. Impressed by this sudden show of resistance, the corpse took off running towards the graveyard, with the outraged peasant in close pursuit. Finally catching up with the creature right at the very gravesite, Laudun unceremoniously "clave its head clean through from the neck," and that was the end of that vampire.

The story of the Shoemaker of Breslau appeared in 1653 in Henry Moore's *Antidote Against Atheism*. It seems a wealthy Silesian cobbler named Weinrichius had cut his throat and died. It is unclear whether it was a suicide, but his wife tried to conceal the circumstances in any case, since suicide was considered a mortal sin that would have tainted her as well. Thus the wound was concealed, and the body hastily interred on the very next day,

September 22, 1591. Soon the ghost of Weinrichius was climbing into bed with various women and molesting them.

Finally on April 18, 1592, his grave was opened to reveal a body undamaged by decay, but "blown up like a drum." The skin of his feet was peeled away, and another skin "much purer and stronger than the first" had grown, along with a mole "like a rose" on his big toe. This "witch's mark" was taken as proof positive of demonization, and the corpse was interred under a gallows. Nevertheless, the spirit was still restless enough to visit his neighbors by night, and on May 7 of the same year, the corpse was disinterred once again, this time having grown "much fuller of flesh." The heart was deemed "as good as that of a freshly slaughtered calf." Finally, after the unnatural flesh was burnt in a huge bonfire, and the ashes thrown into the river, the hauntings ceased.

Moore relates another story of a Silesian revenant from 1592. After sustaining a kick in the head from a horse, Johannes Cuntius, an alderman in the village of Pentsch, began to complain that his entire body was afire. Although raving of being a great sinner, he refused to see a priest, and his irrational behavior had townsfolk muttering that he must have made a pact with the Devil. Sinister events multiplied, seeming to confirm their suspicions. As the confused and disoriented man lay dying, a black cat leapt onto the bed, scratching his face viciously. During the wake, before the body was interred, a woman complained that Cuntius forced his way into her home and tried to rape her.

On February 8, 1592, as he was laid to rest beside the altar of the local church, "a great tempest arose," during which doors were opened and slammed, objects were thrown about, and the entire house was shaken violently. The next morning, hoofmarks were found in the snow around the house.

His terrified wife summoned a maid spend the night with her, but the ghost appeared and frightened her off. The parson too was haunted by an evil stench and a nocturnal sensation of being squeezed and drained of energy. Finally, five months later, the corpse was disinterred and found to be undecayed. As the remains were dismembered, fresh red blood was said to flow freely. Only after the corpse was chopped up and immolated, was peace restored to the village.

An encounter with a Greek vampire, or *vrykolakas*, was described in 1701 by Pitton de Tornefort, a French botanist who was visiting Mykonos when the ghost of a murder victim was found creeping about at night and "playing a thousand roguish tricks."

Though mass was said ten days after his burial to "drive out the demon," nothing availed until the corpse was disinterred. A butcher trying to tear out the heart of the unquiet dead instead ripped open his intestines. Incense was burned to quell the stench, and the scented smoke seemed to the hysterical villagers to be pouring from the corpse itself. Even though the heart was removed and burnt, the ghost continued to disturb the village until finally the entire corpse was immolated.

In 1727, a Serbian farmer named Arnold Paole returning home from war in Greece complained to his fiancèe of being attacked by a *vrykolakas*. Five years later, an official report on the matter ordered by the Honorable Supreme Command quoted an Austrian military officer in *Visum et Repertum (Seen and Discovered)*. "He had eaten from the earth of the vampire's grave and had smeared himself with the vampire's blood, in order to be free of the vexation he had suffered."

However, Paole soon fell from a cart and broke his neck. He was buried at once, but then neighbors noticed him entering their homes at night. The ones he visited became inexplicably weakened, and four of them died. Finally, after ten weeks, Paole's body was exhumed by two army surgeons with the assistance of the sexton. "They found that he was quite complete and undecayed, and that fresh blood had flowed from his eyes, nose, mouth and ears; that the shirt, the covering and the coffin were blood-soaked; that the old nails on his hands and feet, along with the skin, had fallen off, and that new ones had grown. And since they saw from this that he was a true vampire, they drove a stake through his heart—according to their custom—whereupon he gave an audible groan and bled copiously. Thereupon they burned the body to ashes the same day and threw these into the grave."

Although the four people who had died after visits from Arnold Paole were disinterred and their corpses ritually extinguished in the accepted manner, still over a period of three months, a total of 17 villagers died mysteriously.

In 1746, Augustian Calmet's *History of Apparitions* was published, containing some of the best-known tales of suspected vampires in European history. A classic begins one night in the 1720s, as a young soldier named Joachim Hubner was having dinner with a farmer's family in the Austro-Hungarian village of Haidam. The door opened and an elderly stranger entered, touched the farmer, and departed, leaving the family wide-eyed and speechless. The next morning, the farmer was found dead in his bed, and his teenage son told Hubner their wordless nocturnal visitor had been his grandfather—who had been dead for ten years.

When the soldier reported the tale to his commanding officer, an investigation was ordered. The Count de Cadreras took sworn depositions from every member of the farmer's family, and then had the old man's body exhumed. When it was found to be in a fresh condition, the head was severed. After that, the animated corpse of the paterfamilias never troubled his family again.

The concerned Emperor Charles VI empaneled a second commission to investigate the case. After the circumstances were again verified, Cadreras recorded his findings at the University of Friborg.

Then in 1732, a vampire epidemic near Belgrade in the village of Medvegia was investigated by a team of physicians and military officials. According to a medical report dated January 7, 1732 and co-signed by doctors Johannes Flickinger, Isaac Seidel and Johann Baumgartner along with a lieutenant colonel from Belgrade, 17 corpses were exhumed, including a week-old infant, and meticulous descriptions were provided demonstrating that a dozen of them were evidently vampires. "After the examination had taken place, the heads of the vampires were cut off by the local Gypsies, and then burned along with the bodies, after which the ashes were thrown into the river Morava."

In most cases, the identity of the suspected vampire would be quite clear. But if the nocturnal hauntings were an unsolved mystery, a ritual could be held to identify the resting place of the undead predator. A virgin boy would sit astride a virgin stallion, and the horse would be led into the graveyard. It was believed that, unguided, he would proceed directly to the grave of the vampire and stop.

Most of these cases involve earthbound spirits known as "hungry ghosts" or *pretas* by Tibetan Buddhists. Arthur E. Powell observes in *The Astral Body*, "Such spooks are conscienceless, devoid of good impulses, tending towards disintegration, and consequently can work for evil only." Because they either do not realize they are dead, or are not prepared to relinquish their attachment to earthly matters, they were thought to remain trapped on the lower planes and wander restlessly as lost souls, unless ritually hastened on their way.

Some believed a hole could be found near the vampire's grave, and pouring boiling water into the hole would quell the nocturnal disturbance. Eventually, the definitive combination of methods of putting a hungry ghost to rest evolved—pounding a stake into the heart, chopping off the head, stuffing the mouth with garlic, burning the remains and casting them into a river.

Throughout recorded history, the factual would continue to become entwined with the symbolic, and a constellation of imagery would feed bloodthirsty fantasies, thus providing a pattern for a range of sexualized, nocturnal predatory behavior not only by the aggrieved spirits of the undead, but by hungry and rebellious spirits yet amongst the living. Thus an ancient myth of possession or penetration by a disembodied spirit becomes a contemporary fantasy of rape, murder and mutilation, often fueled by superstition or magical thinking.

But the traces of mediæval superstition remain alive and well to this very day. In January of 2002, *La Cuarta* reported that in Lautaro, Chile, villagers were suffering from nocturnal visitations by sexually aggressive demons. The wild erotic dreams usually began some time after midnight and often lasted all night. One woman, Olga Venegas, complained of being molested by these demons for more than eight years. The villagers held a day of prayer to persuade the demons to settle down and rest easy. When this failed, they decided to call in a team of exorcists, who worked on the theory that the demons were harassing the villagers because they had built their homes on an old graveyard.

KING JAMES AND THE CAVEMEN

It wasn't a long time ago—in the late '70s—that we were skeptical cannibalism ever went on at all. But now there's evidence it was a widespread practice. It happened in Stone Age and Iron Age Britain and all over the world.

+ Dr. Timothy Taylor

In the earliest case of multiple murder recorded in the history of England, the primitive elements of the crimes emanate from the same repository of imagery that still permeates the collective unconscious, so much so that a well-known rock band sports the name of the patriarch and progenitor of this incestuous clan of 48 bloodthirsty cave-dwelling predators.

In 1400, word reached King James I of Scotland of disappearances in Galloway that had been going on for a generation. Travelers had been disappearing without a trace. So many had vanished for so many years, that sinister forces of the supernatural were suspected. People would head down the Galloway Road and just never come back.

One day a young couple riding double on horseback were attacked by a ragged man who leapt at the horse, seizing its bridle. The horseman fired his pistol, the wild man shouted, and suddenly a swarm of savages descended upon them. The woman was pulled off the horse and her throat was slashed. The man was pulled to the ground.

It was then that a group of travelers rounded the bend and came upon a hideous spectacle. The savages had rent the woman's clothes from her body and disemboweled her. They were tearing at her flesh with their teeth and eating her live on the spot, while her husband managed to fend them off momentarily with his cutlass.

At a shout from the newcomers, the savages all vanished instantly into the wilderness. The man and his horse were the first victims to survive such an attack in 25 years.

King James brought 400 men to Galloway four days after the attack. Starting where it had occurred, they spread out over the moors in the direction the savages had reportedly run. The moors gave way to cliffs, plunging down a sheer precipice to the pounding waves of the sea. Discouraged, the scouts were ready to turn back when the dogs alerted them to a disgusting smell emanating from a narrow crack in the face of the cliff.

Following the hounds with torches, they squeezed through the narrow crack and followed a long winding tunnel into the heart of the mountain, until all at once it opened up into a pavilion of living death. Feral creatures crouched in the shadows, shielding their eyes from the glare of the torches. Money and jewels were heaped up here and there. And hanging from above throughout the cavern were human arms, legs, and torsos.

These primitive cannibals were taken into custody by the King's troops. The human remains were buried nearby and the inbred clan were taken to Edinburgh, and thence to Leith, where they were summarily executed without a trial, "It being thought needless to try creatures who were even professed enemies to mankind." Official chronicler John Nicholson went on to report that the hands and feet of the men were chopped off and they were left to bleed to death. After that, three women were burned alive on funereal pyres.

Clan leader Sawney Bean had been born not far from Edinburgh. At a young age, he had run off with a like-minded lass and moved into the cave behind the crack in the cliff to breed and feed. Eight sons and six daughters had produced 18 grandsons and 14 granddaughters, all living upon the flesh of wayfaring strangers unfortunate enough to pass down the Galloway Road.

But despite the sheer horror of these revolting crimes, people have inevitably succumbed to a delicious shudder over these tales that have become legendary down through the ages. And as we have seen in other parts of the world, there is always room for the ingenious entrepreneur who stands ready to serve the public's curiosity and recreational delight in these primitive horrors. And so it was in Edinburgh, where in mid-August of 2002, the Witchfinder ride at the Edinburgh Dungeons had to be toned down after an all-too-ghastly debut.

The boat ride carried visitors on a mediæval witch-hunt featuring a Sawney Bean re-enactment. For five minutes they would glide through underground caves, in pitch-black darkness lit only by the occasional bolt of lightning, and fraught with spooky effects like witches flying overhead and dismembered corpses in the water. Suddenly Sawney Bean himself would jump out at them. That's when the tourists were dropping dead away for fright.

"A lot of people were genuinely scared," Manager Scott Williamson told the *Daily Record*, "so we closed the ride down and made it a bit less frightening."

He added a coy proviso: "Some tourists are still coming off looking pale, but that's what they're paying for."

Two weeks later the reality TV series Scream Team announced that six participants would spend 24 hours in the cave outside Edinburgh where the Bean Clan were arrested. More than 1000 people had competed for the fearsome challenge of facing down the curse Bean was said to have put on his cave as the King's men hauled him away.

UNSPEAKABLE DELIGHT

The romantic allure of the vampire mythos is one thing, but the reality of bloodsucking crime is, more often than not, quite another. For example, take the case of what Richard van Krafft-Ebing called, in 1886, a "modern vampire" in *Psychopathia Sexualis*. In 1872, it seems an Italian serial killer was convicted of strangling, disemboweling, and drinking the blood of 14-year-old Johanna Motta, who had been walking down a road alone on her way to nearby village, when he set upon her.

"I had an unspeakable delight in strangling women, experiencing during the act erections and real sexual pleasure," Vincent Verzeni told the Court, before being sentenced to life for murdering three women and strangling several more. "The feeling of pleasure while strangling them was much greater than that which I experienced while masturbating. I took great delight in drinking Motta's blood... It also gave me great pleasure to pull the hairpins out of the hair of my victims. It never occurred to me to touch or look at the genitals... It satisfied me to seize the women by the neck and suck their blood."

The immediate cause of Verzeni's arrest was when he inexplicably attacked his own 19-year-old cousin, Maria Privitali, knocking her down and strangling her nearly to death, before she was able to fight him off and escape from his clutches. Maria and her shocked family went directly to the prefect, and Verzeni was picked up posthaste. He made a full confession to the assault of his cousin, and the murder of Johanna Motta. He then went on to detail the murder of Anna Frigeni, who had kissed her husband goodbye in the morning and left to work in the fields. When Signora Frigeni failed to return home on time in the evening, her husband went looking, only to find his young wife's despoiled body, naked and strangled with a leather thong, with the flesh of her belly flayed and her genitalia gone. Evidence revealed Verzeni's form of vampirism consisted of savagely attacking a woman by the throat, choking her and tearing at her neck with his teeth, then sucking the blood from the raw wounds.

Though he gleefully expounded upon the gory details of his crimes, the doctors who examined Verzeni for the purposes of sentencing reportedly found "no evidence of psychosis."

Krafft-Ebing related a number of other case histories ascribing a sexual motivation to blood-drinking, and defined *lustmord* itself as "lust potentiated as cruelty, murderous lust extending to anthropophagy," or the ingestion of human substance. He briefly describes one case, identifying this vampire as a 19-year-old vinedresser named Leger:

Case 19... From youth moody, silent, shy of people. He starts out in search of a situation. He wanders about eight days in the forest, there catches a girl twelve years old, violates her, mutilates her genitals, tears out her heart, eats of it, drinks the blood, and buries the remains.

PARISIAN CEMETERIES

The Gothic cemeteries of Paris were first haunted by vampires in early 1849. At Père-Lachaise, the groundskeeper set up watch after finding desecrated tombs and mutilated corpses, but the elusive ghoul kept moving, striking one cemetery after another, robbing graves and violating corpses with impunity. Montparnasse, the public cemetery where unclaimed bodies have traditionally been interred, was hit time and again, but the spectral invader was never seen.

Finally public outrage was sparked when a seven-year-old girl was found dismembered and abandoned the day after her burial, and attempts to capture the fiend escalated. Traps were set, and dogs brought in to guard the graves.

Finally alert police patrolling the Montparnasse cemetery caught a glimpse of a shadowy figure skulking about in the moonlight and opened fire. The figure jumped over the wall and disappeared. But this time something was left behind to prove this was a creature of flesh and blood, and no supernatural ephemera. A trail of blood led investigators to the wall, where a scrap of clothing was caught up in the iron spikes. The distinctive fabric proved to be from a military uniform.

That night, a soldier with the 74th Infantry Regiment was taken to Val-de-Grâce, the military hospital, with a gunshot wound to the leg. And thus the identity of the original Vampire of Paris was finally revealed to be an all-too-human handsome young blond sergeant named Francois Bertrand. After he recovered from his wounds, a hearing was held on July 10, 1849, drawing crowds of aristocratic spectators, fascinated to see such an unregenerate necrophile with their own eyes, and to watch him tell his story. They expected a sensation, and they were not disappointed.

Sergeant Bertrand described a lifelong passion for haunting cemeteries so compelling that he once swam an icy moat to enter the one at Douai. But impassioned though he may be, he was neither reckless nor foolish. When casing out a new graveyard, he would carefully examine the entrance for security devices, and dismantle any he found.

The dogs patrolling the graveyards never bothered him. He had no fear of them. Ornella Volta, a vampirologist who has studied this case, concluded that Bertrand's very presence must have had such animal magnetism that it placed them in a hypnotic trance, "because like Dracula's, it made animals lower their eyes and tails, and slink away in silence."

But although he loved cemeteries, it wasn't the landscaping or architecture he was interested in; it wasn't the sense of history or spirituality; it was the dead bodies. Bertrand testified as to the peculiarities of his predilection for the mutilation of corpses.

"I would never have taken the risk of violating a corpse if I had not had the possibility of cutting it up afterwards," he testified. "I threw their limbs in every direction after having cut them off from the body, playing with them like a cat with a mouse, whether they were men or women."

The study of abnormal psychology being in its infancy, and taking their clue from such primitive texts as *Psychopathia Sexualis*, the judges suggested that Sergeant Bertrand's paraphilia might simply be a form of homosexuality. He was offended at the very idea.

"If I have sometimes cut some male corpses into pieces, it was only out of rage at not finding one of the female sex."

Although on a bad night he might have to dig up as many as a dozen men before finding a woman, Bertrand would persist until he could find some body to love. In one romantic tryst, "I squeezed her so strongly against me that I almost broke her in two," he fondly reminisced as spectators gasped in dismay.

Bertrand did more than embrace the lifeless objects of his lust, though. His orgasmic delight was to slit the belly and plunge his hands inside to fondle the viscera. "I put my hands in their bellies in order to pull out their insides, and sometimes pushed up even higher inside them to take out the liver."

Although most observers believed the corpse-loving soldier to be insane, he was nevertheless found guilty of the violation of graves, and sentenced to one year in prison, where he penned his revolting memoirs. After release, Francois Bertrand vanished from the public eye and was never caught haunting another graveyard.

He confessed:

The first victim of my fury was a young girl whose limbs I scattered after having mutilated her. This desecration took place on July 25, 1848. Ever since then, I only came back twice to that cemetery. The first time, at midnight, under a bright moon, I saw a guard walking down an alley, a pistol in his hand. I was perched on a tree, near the surrounding wall, ready to climb down into the graveyard; he walked by me, but did not see me. When he was far enough from me, I left without even trying to do a thing. The second time, I dug up the remains of an old woman and a child; I treated them the same way as my other victims. I cannot remember when this happened. The other cases happened in a cemetery where only suicide victims and people who died in hospitals are buried.

The first individual that I dug up in this place was a drowned corpse that I disemboweled. It was on July 30. You must notice that I seldom mutilated men. I did not take pleasure from it, whereas I had a great time mutilating the corpses of women. I do not know why... You could believe that I was also prone to assault living persons, but on the contrary, I was extremely kind to everybody. I wouldn't hurt a child. So I am sure that I have no enemies. All the non-commissioned officers appreciated my frankness and my cheerfulness.

Sergeant Bertrand was gone, perhaps, but he has never been long-forgotten. Eight years later the memoirs of Monsieur Claude, the French Inspector of Public Security, related a strange tale of serial crypt-kicking that confirms the suspicion that the French Sergeant's spirit continues the obverse of life in the Undead Zone, inspiring and perhaps even animating Parisian ghouls and vampires to this day, including Monsieur Claux.

In the summer of 1854, Parisians found that even with the infamous vampire safely out of the way, once again graves in the cemeteries of Montmartre were being found opened and desecrated; the break of dawn would reveal bodies disinterred, dismantled and strewn carelessly about the grounds.

M. Claude's investigation led him to suspect a soldier whose uncle lived nearby. However, Claude's assistant, M. Col-de-Zinc, suspected a spooky old man who lived right next to the cemetery. Night after night, he could be heard playing his violin "in a lugubrious, lamenting sound which seemed, in that hour of the night, like an invitation for the dead to take part in a *danse macabre*."

M. Claude's interest in the soldier was heightened when he determined that the young man took a keen interest in all local funerals. It was hard for the Inspector to reconcile the depraved vampiric activity at Montmartre with "this youth, as gentle as a girl, so respectable, so shy, and so timid." And coming from a family that was prominent in the community, his uncle being an eminent brigadier, how could it be possible?

"I was paid to find out what lay hidden beneath the innocuous appearance of these ferocious creatures who only hold out their arm to you to strangle you, and only kiss you to bite you."

And so the Inspector and his assistant staked out the cemetery. Lurking in the shadows of the crypts, finally through enshrouding mists they saw a figure approach. Sure enough he was wearing a uniform. But he wasn't entering the graveyard. The young soldier was going to the old violinist's house.

After a while, the lone figure of the young soldier emerged from the house, but now he was wearing overalls. And as he crossed into the graveyard the doleful music began. The Inspector and his assistant watched spellbound as the ghoul prowled the cemetery, shovel in hand, until he found his heart's desire—the grave of a freshly-interred young woman.

He dug down and unearthed the coffin. Wrenching off the lid, he reached down into the coffin and drew the unresisting maid into his fervent embrace. Enraptured, he was sinking his teeth into her cheek when the officers rushed him. Hearing their shouts as they dashed at him, "the vampire started like a sleepwalker suddenly awakened on the brink of a window ledge, dropped the corpse, and allowed himself to be taken without any resistance."

It turns out the unprincipled necrophile had taken advantage of the senile old man, who had been persuaded that the nocturnal visitor was his own son who had been killed in the war. The pitiful old man told the Inspector that the mournful music was how he summoned his son from the grave.

 Parisian Cemetery

CADAVEROUS PASSIONS

"Each of us has our passions. As for me, the cadaver is mine!" So proclaimed Victor Ardisson, who became known as *"Le Vampire de Muy."* Ardisson was born to a poor family in 1872, and dropped out of school early. When drafted into the army, he repeatedly deserted, and eventually found work as a mortician. After being tried for his crimes, he was declared insane and committed to an asylum.

As described by Dr. Magnus Hirschfeld in his book *Sexual Anomalies*, Ardisson's sexuality was primarily oral. When women urinated on the ground, he would lick it up. When he masturbated, he would drink his own semen. He accepted money for performing fellatio upon anyone in his native village in southern France, and he slaughtered cats and rats to drink their blood.

In 1901, after a 13-year-old girl named Gabrielle died, Ardisson exhumed her body and cut off her head, brought it home, embalmed it, kept it ensconced in a closet, made love to it, and called it "my little fiancée." He remained faithful to his impassive inamorata for five months, until a three-year-old girl named Louise died.

From his confessions:

I dug up the body of the little girl you found at my home the day after her burial. September 12, 1901, after midnight, I opened the coffin closed by two dowels, then, after I removed the body, I closed it and I covered it up again with earth, like it was before. When I came back home, I laid the corpse on loose straw, where you found it. Then I indulged myself in disgraceful practices on her. Each time I slept next to her, I assuaged my lust. I always have done it all alone, and my father doesn't know that I do such things. To get into the cemetery, I climbed the north wall and I did the same when I had to leave.

Some time ago, I heard that a young woman I had noticed earlier was seriously ill. I was pleased to hear that, and I promised myself to have sex with her corpse. I had to wait patiently for several days, each day and night I fantasized over her and this always gave me a erection.

When she died, I planned to dig up her body the night following her burial. I went to the graveyard at 8 o'clock in the evening. I took my time to dig the body up. When she was exposed, I kissed and fondled her. I noticed that there was no hair on her pubic area, and her breasts were small. I satisfied my urges on this corpse, then I decided to bring it in my home. I did not think about the dangers I could face while doing this.

 Victor Ardisson

It was nearly midnight when I left the graveyard, carrying the body under my left arm and pressing her against my face with my right arm. On my way home, I kissed my burden and told her, "I am bringing you back home, you will be fine, I will not hurt you." Quite luckily, I met no one. Back home, I laid down next to the corpse, telling her, "I love you, Sweetie." I slept well.

When I woke up in the morning, I satisfied my lust once more, and before I left, I told her, "I'm going to work, I will come back soon. If you want something to eat, just ask." She did not answer, so I guessed that she was not hungry. I even told her, "If you're thirsty, I'll bring you a drink."

During the day at work, I often fantasized on this young girl. At noon, I came back to see her, and asked her if she was yearning for me. In the morning, I went to meet her again. Until my arrest, I spent all my nights with her, and every night, I satisfied my lust on her. In the meantime, no other girls died. If another girl had died, I would have also brought it home, I would have laid it next to the other one, and I would have fondled them both.

But I did not forget the severed head, and sometimes I kissed her too.

HIGHGATE VAMPIRE

The Cemetery of the Parish of St. James Highgate was founded in England in 1836, and the late Poet Laureate Sir John Betjemann, whose father was buried there, called it "The Victorian Valhalla." By the end of the First World War, its once proudly manicured avenues had fallen into disrepair. Many of the classic Dracula films starring Christopher Lee were filmed in its crumbling catacombs. But there are legends that the scenes made famous in vampire films were haunted by a true vampire.

In December of 1969, occultists prowled its verdant pathways, spray-painting satanic symbols and chanting incantations, in hopes of raising the dead. According to urban legend, the necromancers broke into a tomb and unearthed a towering Man in Black that sent them fleeing in fear, and as they dashed down Swains Lane, one turned back and caught sight of a bony arm reaching out for them through the railings.

One month later in January of 1970, a man from nearby Milton Park was driving his car along Swains Lane, when his engine began to clatter. He stopped by the entrance to the Highgate Cemetery and got out to investigate.

Just as he lifted the hood, he looked up to see, peering right back at him from the overgrown graveyard, a shadowy figure he described as abnormally elongated. The traveler was so frightened he jumped back in his car and drove off with the hood still open.

Then an Essex school teacher, whose name was actually Alan Blood, called for a mass vampire hunt to be held on Friday the Thirteenth of March, 1970. Blood appeared on TV explaining his thesis that the Highgate Vampire had been driven from his lair by the crowds of thrill-seekers keeping vigil near the crypt where the lanky apparition had been sighted. He told the *London Evening News* that his plan was to keep vigil until dawn, then as the first rays of the rising sun forced the vampire to return to the catacombs, Blood would fall upon him and slay him in the time-honored tradition, by driving a stake through his heart.

The crowd that flocked to Highgate Cemetery to join Alan Blood on Friday the Thirteenth numbered in the hundreds. Intoxicated with fear of vampires, bearing garlic cloves and crucifixes, brandishing torches and sharp wooden stakes, they managed to do £9,000 worth of damage to the grounds. By dawn, they had trampled the plantings, exhumed a corpse from a tomb, stolen lead from coffins, and defaced sepulchres with mindless graffiti. Of course, in the midst of all the madness, there was no sign of any true vampire.

Nevertheless, in June of 1970, Sean Manchester, the president of the British Psychic and Occult Society and author of *The Highgate Vampire*, told the *Daily Express*, "I am convinced that a vampire exists in Highgate Cemetery. Local residents and passers-by have reported seeing a ghost-like figure of massive proportions near the north gate."

David Farrant is Manchester's chief rival as a vampire hunter. He has also served as President of the British Psychic and Occult Society, and has written a book called *Beyond the Highgate Vampire*. In September of 1974, when 24-year-old Farrant was charged with entering a cemetery for unlawful purposes, he explained to the Court why he had been caught prowling amongst the tombstones brandishing his crucifix and wooden stake. "My intention was to search out the supernatural being and destroy it by plunging the stake in its heart."

Though charges were dropped and he was released on a technicality, the vampire hunter got in the last word in court: "The Highgate Vampire has to be destroyed. He is evil."

After his release, Farrant told reporters that he had spotted the Highgate Vampire himself more than once, describing him as a gangly figure about eight feet tall. He speculated that the vampire slept by day in the catacombs beneath Highgate, and came out to rove the city by night.

Today, though Highgate Cemetery has been somewhat restored, it still provides a tangled wilderness where the old-growth trees, underbrush and wildflowers offer a haven for birds and animals, and the famous philosopher, Karl Marx, resides in perpetual propinquity to the famous Sex Pistol, Sid Vicious.

As for the famous Highgate Vampire, he has managed to elude capture, but perhaps his consort has made an unacknowledged appearance. In Soho pubs in during the summer of 1988, word spread of a gorgeous, seductive blonde vampire in her early twenties, wearing tight black jeans and a silky black blouse, who would offer to go home with a guy for a little fun. Six of the men who took her up on her offer reported that when she went home with a guy, she would knock him out by dosing his drink, and then disappear into the night, leaving a wound on his arm which she had apparently used to feed.

DUSSELDORF VAMPIRE

In 1930, a reward was offered for the apprehension of a serial killer who had held the German city of Dusseldorf in terror for over a year. The killer finally urged his wife to be the one to turn him in, the better to survive the loss of her bread-winner.

"He is the king of sexual delinquents; he unites nearly all perversions in one person." These were the words used to describe Peter Kurten at trial—by his own lawyer, who went on to elucidate the range of his client's homicidal malice. "He killed men, women, children and animals, killed anything he found." He was hoping for mercy, but no mercy would be found, and justice would prove fatal.

Two movies have immortalized the legend of the Dusseldorf Vampire: *M*, made in 1931, and *Le Vampire de Dusseldorf*, in 1964.

Born in Mulheim, Germany, on May 26, 1883, the fifth child of an incestuous clan of 13, Kurten learned early to mimic the violence demonstrated by his alcoholic father. After his father was arrested for sexually assaulting one of his own daughters, young Peter repeated the attack on the girl himself.

After his father was incarcerated, a dog-catcher joined the household and introduced the boy to sadistic bestial sex, which became a lifelong practice. Between the ages of 13 and 15, he committed countless acts of bestiality with dogs, pigs, goats, and sheep—the sexual assault escalating to climax with stabbing the animals to death and violating their corpses. He especially enjoyed bathing in the blood of swans he would decapitate.

The degenerate youth also enjoyed arson, and admitted torching numerous buildings for sexual pleasure. "The sight of the flames delighted me, but above all it was the excitement of the attempts to extinguish the fire and the agitation of those who saw their property being destroyed."

As a teenager, Kurten was arrested and imprisoned for theft. After spending more than half of his life behind bars, he later blamed the inhumanity of his incarceration for his ultimate descent into criminal madness. Unproven allegations later surfaced that he had poisoned other prisoners. He admitted wreaking havoc behind bars in a bid to be put in solitary confinement, the better to enjoy his malignant fantasies. As he told the Court:

> I thought of myself causing accidents affecting thousands of people. I invented a number of crazy fantasies such as smashing bridges and boring through bridge piers. Then I spun a number of fantasies with regard to bacilli, which I might be able to introduce into drinking water and so cause a great calamity. I imagined myself using schools and orphanages for the purpose, where I could carry out murders by giving away chocolate samples containing arsenic. I derived the sort of pleasure from these visions that other people would get from thinking about a naked woman.

When he was not incarcerated, Kurten kept busy satisfying his twisted sex drive. By the age of 16, he was playing the sadist in a *ménage à trois* with a 16-year-old girl and her masochistic mother, who enjoyed being beaten and half-strangled.

Before his execution by guillotine in 1931, Kurten confessed to a grim litany of murder starting at the tender age of five, with the drowning of two playmates.

By his own account, eight years later, he strangled a woman while having sex in the Grafenburg woods and left her for dead, although she may have survived, as no body was ever found.

At 20, Kurten sexually assaulted eight-year-old Christine Klein and afterwards, slit her throat. Leaving the scene of his first documented murder, he dropped his embroidered handkerchief.

He confessed:

It was on 25 May, 1913. I had been stealing, specializing in public bars or inns where the owners lived on the floor above. In a room above an inn at Cologne-Mulheim, I discovered a child asleep. Her head was facing the window. I seized it with my left hand and strangled her for about a minute and a half. The child woke up and struggled, but lost consciousness. I had a small but sharp pocketknife with me, and I held the child's head and cut her throat. I heard the blood spurt and drip on the mat beside the bed. The whole thing lasted about three minutes, then I locked the door again and went home to Dusseldorf. Next day I went back to Mulheim. There is a cafe opposite the Klein's place, and I sat there and drank a glass of beer and read all about the murder in the papers. People were talking about it all around me. All this amount of horror and indignation did me good.

That same year, Kurten attacked two strangers with an axe, and later described the sexual pleasure he derived from watching the blood flow.

However, he was not inclined to exercise his sadistic inclinations in the service of the Kaiser. He lasted exactly one day before deserting and spent the rest of his military career in the stockade.

In 1921, Kurten took a wife, threatening to kill her if she refused. Like many of his kind, while pursuing a secret life of violence and perversion, he also managed to carry on a seemingly "normal" life, as an active trade unionist and respectful pillar of society. He was proper, polite and charming, meticulous and even vain about his appearance. His wife later stated that she never imagined someone she knew so well could commit such hideous crimes.

Kurten and his wife moved to Dusseldorf in 1925, and between then and 1929, an unknown number of victims in the area were strangled to death. Once again, Kurten described his motivations as sexual in nature.

By 1929, Kurten was indulging his sexually sadistic crimes at a torrid pace, racking up a total of 29 murders. On February 3, he stabbed a woman 24 times with a pair of scissors. Ten days later he stabbed 45-year-old Rudolf Scheer repeatedly about the head and neck. On March 9, he dragged eight-year-old Rosa Ohliger behind a hedge and stabbed her to death, returning to the scene later to burn her body.

In early August, two women and a man were attacked on their way home late at night; however, they survived. Luise Lenzen, 13, and Gertrud

Hamacher, five, were not so fortunate. On the 24th of August, Kurten lured the two girls to an open field, where he stabbed and strangled the older girl, and slit the younger one's throat.

Later on that same day, he attacked Gertrud Schulte, attempting to rape her and then stabbing her in a frenzy, before the knife broke off in her back and he left her for dead. Though grievously injured, the servant girl survived, giving police their first good description of the serial assailant.

In late autumn, the remains of a servant girl who had been stabbed 20 times were found buried on the banks of the Rhine. Kurten later confessed that he had slain Maria Hahn, 20, and had attempted to crucify her body to create terror and fear, but abandoned the effort because of the weight of the body.

At the end of September, Ida Reuter, a 31-year-old servant, was raped and battered to death with a hammer in the woods just outside Dusseldorf. The following week, another servant, Elizabeth Dorrier, suffered the same fate.

On November 7 of the same year, five-year-old Gertrud Albermann was stabbed 36 times. Emulating his hero, Jack the Ripper, Kurten sent a taunting letter to the authorities, revealing the location of her body, as well as the remains of other victims.

Finally, on May 14, 1930, 21-year-old Maria Budlick came to Dusseldorf from Cologne looking for work. When she stepped off the train, a man appeared, offering to accompany her to a girls' hostel. Though the unemployed maid had read in the papers about the Dusseldorf Vampire, she was confident that she would not fall prey to him, so she joined the stranger on a carefree stroll through the streets—until he took a wrong turn and she balked. He urged, she refused, they argued, and a soft voice spoke up from the shadows: "Is everything all right?" The sinister stranger abruptly split the scene, and Peter Kurten stepped forth to take his place, reassuring the unsuspecting maid and offering his hospitality.

So she went home with the most wanted man in the country and enjoyed a ham sandwich and a glass of milk. Then he offered to go along with her to the hostel, but steered her instead into Grafenburg Woods, where he strangled her to near-unconsciousness, demanding, "Do you remember where I live, in case you ever need my help again?" Terrified, she caught the threat and gasped, "No!" But she lied.

Kurten released the traumatized girl, but instead of reporting her ordeal to the police, she wrote a letter to a friend back home in Cologne. Through an incredibly fortuitous circumstance, she misaddressed the letter, and it wound up being examined by a postal inspector, who duly alerted law enforcement.

Three days after the attack, police escorted Maria Budlick back to Mettmannerstrasse, and she pointed out No. 71. The fugitive caught a glimpse of his latest victim fingering him, and realized the implications. Thus he paid a call on his wife at work, and urged her to be the one to turn in the Dusseldorf Vampire, so she could collect the reward.

The police had tried everything, questioning more then a thousand suspects, without breaking the case. Now the fearsome predator who had terrorized the city for four years was taken into custody without resistance, telling the officers, "There is no need to be afraid." Calmly confessing to everything, he revealed that he enjoyed drinking the blood of his victims. His wife, who was sitting next to him, promptly fainted. Peter continued his confessions, finally giving police a detailed accounting of 77 separate crimes. While his wife was too nauseated to eat, his appetite was unaffected by the shocking crimes he related, and he scoffed up her dinner as well as the one provided for him.

The first murderer ever to be interviewed by a police psychiatrist, he was diagnosed as a narcissistic psychopath. Dr. Karl Berg went on to characterize him more colorfully as "a king of sexual perverts."

"I have no remorse," Kurten told the doctor. "As to whether recollection of my deeds makes me feel ashamed, I will tell you. Thinking back to all the details is not at all unpleasant. In fact, I rather enjoy it."

Upon being found guilty on all nine counts of murder and seven counts of attempted murder, and given nine sentences of death by decapitation, the infamous predator philosophized, "The real reason for my conviction is that there comes a time in the life of every criminal when he can go no further, and this spiritual collapse is what I experienced." His ruminations, however, took on a more sinister drift as he continued. "But I do feel that I must make one statement: some of my victims made things very easy for me. Manhunting on the part of women today has taken on such forms that—" And it was then that the disgusted judge brought the gavel down on this abortive attempt at victim-bashing.

On July 1, 1932, Peter Kurten enjoyed his last meal—a delicious repast including double helpings of veal, fried potatoes and white wine. Before leaving his cell for the last walk the next morning, he posed a grisly riddle: "After my head has been chopped off, will I still be able to hear at least for a moment the sound of my own blood gushing from the stump of my neck?" Stricken speechless, the prison psychiatrist watched the doomed vampire smile as he enthused, "That would be the pleasure to end all pleasures."

 Peter Kurten

ORGY OF THE VAMPIRES

On June 24, 1924, when children playing on the banks of the river Leine in Hanover, Germany, found a bag of bones topped off with a human skull, a public outcry erupted, demanding the river be dragged. Over 500 bones comprising the remains of more than 27 victims were found, but the full impact of the horror was only beginning to unfold.

Three human skulls had surfaced in the three months before the children found the bag of bones, but police had shrugged off the finds as a "practical joke." Nor had the disappearance of scores of homeless boys caused any undue concern by authorities, until a newspaper screamed of 600 youths disappearing in a single year, and called for the head of the "Hanover Vampire."

While Fritz Haarmann, a 45-year-old homosexual butcher, was in custody on a charge of public indecency, his rooms were searched. Bloodstains were everywhere, along with heaps of clothing and personal possessions. At first Haarmann airily dismissed both the blood and the personal items, protesting that since he was not only a butcher but a clothes trader, such findings were meaningless. Then a victim's mother spotted her missing son's coat on the son of Haarmann's landlady. When confronted with this new evidence, he finally confessed to a series of gruesome murders, implicating an accomplice.

The sixth child of an elderly invalid and her young, brutal husband, young Fritz had grown up playing with dolls, avoiding sports, and despising his domineering father. First detained at the age of 16 for molesting small children, he escaped after six months. After serving in the army, he was arrested repeatedly for several minor offenses, and spent four years in prison for the theft of goods from a warehouse. Upon release in 1918, he became a police informer while using his butcher shop as a cover for fencing and smuggling stolen goods. His first known murder victim disappeared that same year.

Friedel Rothe was a 17-year-old boy who was last seen by his parents going off with a man calling himself "Detective Haarmann." Prompted by the complaints of the boy's family, the guilty ghoul's quarters were searched, to no effect. Six years later Haarmann bragged: "When police examined my room, the head of the boy Friedel was lying wrapped in a newspaper behind the oven."

Before long the persistent offender was back in prison for indecency with a minor. Upon release, he joined up with 24-year-old Hans Grans.

Haarmann and his accomplice began to lure homeless boys to a busy railway station, then to ambush and abduct them. Haarmann would rape the boys and then kill them by using his teeth to savagely tear at the flesh of the neck, bleeding out the corpse in a spectacular bloodbath.

After the orgy of blood, he and his lover would then butcher the victim's lifeless remains, placing choice cuts on the shelf in the butcher shop, marketing them as beef or pork, and dropping the indigestible remains into the river Leine.

On December 4, 1924, Haarmann and Grans went to trial for the slayings of 27 teenage boys. Haarmann continually disrupted the proceedings, shouting encouragement at the prosecutors and harassing the witnesses. As one mother cried helplessly on the stand, the jaunty defendant puffed on a cigar. The next morning, he protested there were too many women present. "This is a case for men to discuss," the homicidal homosexual pouted.

Nearly 200 witnesses took the stand in what the paper called "scenes of painful intensity," as they identified the pitiful remains of their lost boys. As the photos and names of murder victims were presented, Haarmann coolly responded, "Yes, that might well be," on one, and "I'm not sure about that one," on the next. However, when the photo of young Hermann Wolf was shown, he turned to the boy's father and spat, "I should never have looked twice at such an ugly youngster as, according to his photograph, your son must have been. You say your boy had not even a shirt to his name and that his socks were tied onto his feet with string. Deuce take it, you should have been ashamed to let him go about like that. There's plenty of rubbish like him around. Think what you're saying, man! Such a fellow would have been far beneath my notice." When all was said and done, he took credit for "30 or 40" murders, demurring, "I don't remember exactly."

Throughout the trial, Haarmann remained cocky, but composed, except when it came to the role played by his accomplice. "Grans should tell you how shabbily he has treated me," he shouted in another outburst. "I did the murders. For that work he is too young." Upon being summoned to the stand for further questioning, he testified that Grans had incited him to murder some of the boys because he wanted their clothing. He would leave Haarmann alone to do the murder and then come back to claim the jacket or the trousers he coveted. However, Haarmann complained, one time "I had just cut up the body when there was a knock at the door. I shoved the body under the bed and opened the door. It was Grans. His first question was, 'Where is the suit?' I sat down on the bed and buried my face in my hands. Grans tried to console me, and said, 'Don't let a little thing like a corpse upset you.'"

 Fritz Haarmann

After a two-week trial, the courtroom was packed for the verdict, and 12 armed guards protected the despised defendant against threats that he would be shot. Hans Grans was given a life sentence for his crimes, of which he served 12 years before being paroled. Convicted of 25 murders, the Vampire of Hanover was sentenced to death.

The day before losing his head to the guillotine on April 15, 1925, Fritz Haarmann raved:

> Do you think I enjoy killing people? I was ill for eight days after the first time. Condemn me to death. I only ask for justice. I am not mad. It is true I often get into a state when I do not know what I am doing, but that is not madness. Make it short, make it soon. Deliver me from this life, which is a torment. I will not petition for mercy, nor will I appeal. I want to pass just one more merry evening in my cell, with coffee, cheese and cigars, after which I will curse my father, and go to my execution as if it were a wedding.

The mythos of the modern vampire was enriched in 1973 with the release of the German film, *Tenderness of Wolves*, based on the saga of Herr Haarmann.

SILESIAN SAUSAGE

There were other German serial slayers of the same era who butchered, devoured, and marketed the remains of their victims to their neighbors during hard times when every scrap of meat found a ready market.

Georg Karl Grossmann was a butcher who liked to get blind drunk and pick up prostitutes. Of an evening after sex, he would butcher the unfortunate *fraulein*, and peddle her flesh as fresh pork the next day.

He got into a loud altercation with his landlord in August of 1921, and when police came to break up the fracas, they found a freshly butchered victim in the house, along with remains of at least three others. Grossman was summarily arrested, tried and sentenced to die, but he just laughed, and later that night, he hanged himself in his cell.

It was December 21, 1924, when a bloodied and hysterical young man named Vincenz Olivier staggered into the local police precinct and swore that "Vatter Denke" had taken an axe to him. The officers in the small

Silesian village of Munsterberg could hardly believe that the kindly burgher could have done such a thing. He was a devout, peaceful, generally respected fellow who was always kind to poor young men, even taking hapless wayfarers into his own home when they had no place to stay. He had a small shop next to his apartment, and a license to peddle a miscellany of items.

On the complaint of Vincenz Olivier, Karl Denke was arrested, questioned briefly, locked up, and then found a few hours later in his cell, like Herr Grossman, having managed to hang himself with a handkerchief without ever telling anyone what he had done. In his only known photo, he is shown laid out in a simple pine box with a slight smile gracing his face.

It was not until Christmas Eve that police went to Denke's apartment to clear out the effects of the suicide. And it was only then that they realized they had been dealing with something much more than a common assailant. On the window sill were identification papers for dozens of men who had been released from prisons or hospitals, and in the closet was an odd assortment of bloodstained clothing. In the kitchen were two large tubs of meat, bones and fat, pickled in brine.

On the shelves of Denke's adjoining shop were jar upon jar of the sausage meat he had processed and pickled over the past three years. In the back, there was equipment for the production of human-skin belts and human-hair shoe laces, which Denke had been peddling door-to-door. All were crafted from the remains of homeless strangers who had disappeared inside the Good Vatter's home.

No indication of occultism or sexual involvement with the victims ever surfaced; apparently this was just a pragmatic matter of preying upon those who have been weakened by circumstance, and depersonalizing them to the extent that they were reduced to nothing more than a source of groceries, belts and shoelaces.

Only 20 of Karl Denke's victims were eventually identified, but police believe a total of at least 40 were slaughtered, pickled, and either eaten by Vatter Denke or sold to his neighbors.

German serial killer Joaquim Kroll preyed on the Ruhr area of Germany for over 20 years. After his sixth murder, he cooked and ate portions of his victim's corpse, as he did his next eight victims. When police finally entered his apartment on July 3, 1976, they found plastic bags full of human flesh in the refrigerator as well as a stew simmering on the stove with carrots, potatoes, and the hand of a missing four-year-old girl.

Others who crossed that slaughterous line were not so pragmatic.

WILD BLOOD DEMONS

It was not their money but their blood that I was after. The thing I am really conscious of is the cup of blood. I made a small cut, usually at the right side of the neck, and drank the blood for three to five minutes, and afterwards I felt better. Before each of the killings I have detailed in my confessions, I had a series of dreams.

From 1944 to 1949 in England, a slayer dubbed by the press a "Vampire Killer" slaughtered nine to drink their blood, giving him what he called "a warm, relaxed feeling, with calm and disappearance of the craving."

Like "The Beast" Aleister Crowley, John George Haigh was the only child of a pair of devout members of the strictly pious Plymouth Brethren. A personable and popular child, Haigh loved animals and defied the religious constraints of his parents to serve as an enthusiastic and devout choirboy and organist for the Church of England's Wakefield Cathedral Choir.

Years later it came to light that little Johnny had been sexually abused by one of the Brethren as a young child. According to his confessions, it was shortly after the abuse began that the child was first haunted by recurrent bloody dreams, and began to crave the taste of blood.

I saw a forest of crucifixes which gradually turned into trees. At first I seemed to see dew or rain running from the branches. But when I came nearer I knew it was blood. All of a sudden, the whole forest began to twist about, and the trees streamed with blood. Blood ran from the trunks. Blood ran from the branches, all red and shiny. I felt weak and seemed to faint. I saw a man going around the trees, gathering blood. When the cup he was holding in hand was full, he came up to me and said "drink." But I was paralyzed... The dream vanished, but I still felt faint and stretched out with all my strength towards the cup... I woke up. I always kept on seeing those hands holding out a cup to me that I couldn't quite reach... and that terrible thirst... never left me. For three or four days I always had the same dream, and each time I woke up, my horrible desire always became stronger.

The troubled child outgrew his nightmares to become an ambitious and resourceful entrepreneur and con-artist, leading a nonviolent and more or less productive life until 1935, when he was first imprisoned for forgery at the age of 25. He did not actually begin indulging his barbarous passions until 1944, after sustaining a head injury in an auto accident. "Blood poured from my head down my face and into my mouth. This revived in me the taste, and that night I experienced another awful dream."

His Bible studies were as morbid as his dreams. He became fascinated with the scripture instructing the true believer to "drink water out of thine own cistern and running waters out of thine own well." Haigh's twisted insights into this scriptural admonition led him to therefore ceremonially drink his own urine and blood.

As he progressed into homicide, he developed a blood ritual in which he would tap the victim's jugular and draw the blood meticulously into a glass. He invested the drinking of a victim's blood with even greater symbolism and ceremony than his own, eventually coming to believe that his faith could only be sustained by sacrificing human victims and drinking their blood.

Working occasionally at the pinball arcade in London, Haigh had befriended the owner's son, William Donald McSwan. It was September 9, 1944, when McSwan brought a broken pinball machine to Haigh's workshop for repair, unwittingly offering himself up as the first donor of the vital elixir to the fledgling vampire.

> I got the feeling I must get some blood somewhere... The idea came to me to kill him and take some blood. I hit him over the head and he was unconscious. I got a mug and took some blood from his neck, slicing it with a penknife. I poured it in the mug and drank it. Then I realized I must do something about him. I left him there dead. I had acid and sheet metal for pickling. I found a water butt [barrel] and took it on a cart and put McSwan in acid. I put the body in a tub and poured the acid on it. I did it with a bucket.

The next day he washed the pernicious sludge down a manhole he had built in his workshop, which emptied directly into the sewer.

Assuring McSwan's parents that their son was hiding out in Scotland to evade the draft until the war was over, he traveled to Scotland periodically to post forged letters, apparently signed by his victim. Meanwhile, the pinball business was booming, but Haigh knew a way to make even more of a killing.

Posted from London, the letter from William Donald McSwan announced that he was back from Scotland, and invited his elderly parents to come meet him at the home of his dear friend, John Haigh. Thus on July 10, 1945, the vampire's next victim showed up on his doorstep. His former employer, Donald McSwan, was promptly dispatched with a blow to the head, but the old man was a disappointment when it came to the climax:

"The corpse did not produce enough blood." His hunger whetted by the paltry first course, Haigh cleaned himself up and went to the McSwan home to harvest the wife, Mrs. Amy McSwan. Transported to the workshop by her son's friend, she was bludgeoned and bled, and her exsanguinated remains tossed into the acid bath to mingle with those of her husband, before being sloshed down into the sewer.

Their estate, however, remained alive and well, with five homes and a fortune in securities managed via forged documents, until eventually the greedy ghoul had them converted and placed in the name of John Haigh.

In February of 1948, he invited a young doctor and his wife to inspect his new workshop in Crawley, south of London. Thus the bodies, and the fortunes, of Dr. Archie Henderson and his wife Rosalie were transferred with all due haste to that of the vampire.

But a year later, the bloodthirsty wastrel was broke again from gambling and debauchery, so when a dowager told him about her idea for manufacturing plastic fingernails, he replied that he thought he could help her, and invited her to visit his workshop as well. Thus, Mrs. Olive Durand-Deacon, a well-endowed 69-year-old widow who lived in the same residential hotel as Haigh, came to her ignominious demise, as related by Haigh in a sworn statement to police:

> She was inveigled by me into going to Crawley in view of her interest in artificial fingernails. Having taken her into the storeroom, I shot her through the back of the head while she was examining some materials. Then I went out to the car and fetched a drinking glass and made an incision—I think it was with a penknife—in the side of her throat. I collected a glass of blood, which I drank.
>
> I removed her coat and jewelry—ring, necklace, earrings and crucifix—and put her in a 44-gallon tank. Before I put her handbag in the tank, I took from it about 30 shillings and a fountain pen. I then filled the tank with sulfuric acid by means of a stirrup pump. I then left it to react.
>
> I should have said that in between having her in the tank and pumping in the acid, I went around to the Ancient Prior's for a cup of tea.

The insanity defense was offered at trial, but the jury took only 17 minutes to find Haigh guilty and sentence him to hang. While awaiting his execution on April 6, 1949, the unregenerate vampire announced that he had been "impelled to kill by wild blood demons," and presaging similar statements by Ted Bundy, Sean Sellers, Jeffrey Dahmer, and the Son of Sam, claimed that "the spirit inside me commanded me to kill."

On August 9, 1949, the day before his execution, he gave the *News of the World* his final interview. The specter of the gallows surely must have concentrated his thoughts must wonderfully, as they were focused almost solely on the precise cut and color of the image he would leave on the minds of those contemplating his monstrous deeds. The doomed vampire's last request was that the wax figure of him displayed in Madame Tussaud's museum be dressed in his favorite outfit: a stylish suit of green hopsacking with green socks to match, worn with a cream-colored tailored shirt, a jaunty red tie, and shiny, brown brogans to complete the precisely detailed image he held of himself. Above all other earthly concerns, he was determined only to cut a striking figure among the other fiends immortalized in the wax museum.

Stafford Somerfield reported that when prodded to comment on his crimes, Haigh "still sticks to his frequently expressed view that he was not responsible for what he had done, but that he was moved and guided by some power outside himself."

RISE!

It was a midsummer's night in 1993 when the village of Pisco, Peru turned out *en masse*, hoping to see a legendary vampire rise from her grave in the local cemetery.

The corpse of Sarah Ellen Roberts had been cast out of her native England in 1913, because she was widely believed to be a witch and a vampire. Her long-suffering husband, John Roberts of Blackburn, Lancashire, had purchased a coffin with a lining of lead, and traveled the world seeking a resting place for his accursed spouse, until he finally came to Pisco, where the burial was permitted in exchange for five pounds. After a quick ceremony, Roberts set sail on a ship, never to return.

Too late to renege, the villagers later learned that Sarah Ellen Roberts had been chained and bound in her lead coffin after being convicted of vampirism, witchcraft and murder. They trembled to hear that just as the lid of her coffin was being closed, the vampire had shrieked a warning to return from the grave to seek vengeance.

It was the eighth of June, 80 years later, when visitors to the accursed grave noticed a large crack appearing in the headstone. Word passed in a flash that the vampire would arise at midnight.

Pregnant women left town, for fear that the vampire would be reincarnated in their children. Crucifixes appeared everywhere, and door after door was festooned with ropes of garlic.

As midnight approached, over a thousand thrill-seekers crammed the graveyard to witness the sight. The mob was so unruly that police had to be called to control the hysteria. Shots were fired over the crowd, and they slowly dispersed.

Police allowed a small coterie of local witch-doctors to remain at the gravesite until midnight, when they prayed and blessed the headstone with Holy Water and white rose petals. Since the dread vampire did *not* rise, the success of the ritual was credited instead, and everyone went home satisfied.

The End

Sondra London

INDEX

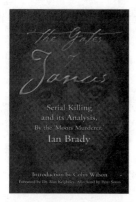

THE GATES OF JANUS

An Analysis of Serial Murder by England's Most Hated Criminal

Ian Brady

Introduction by Colin Wilson, Afterword by Peter Sotos

"...a unique moral lesson, a glimpse into the abyss of a damned soul... Like a modern-day incarnation of Milton's Satan, Brady delivers a discourse that is twisted, self-serving and strangely persuasive."
—**Stephen Lemons, Salon.com**

"...An insider's look at the criminal mind by quite possibly the most hated man in Britain." —**Anneli Rufus, Crime Magazine**

Cloth original • 5 1/2 x 8 1/2 • 305 pages • ISBN: 0-922915-73-3 • $24.95

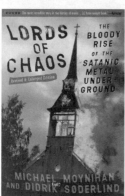

LORDS OF CHAOS

The Bloody Rise of the Satanic Metal Underground Revised and Enlarged Second Edition

By Michael Moynihan and Didrik Søderlind

Lords of Chaos tells how a peculiar variety of satanic music called Black Metal was taken to the utmost extremes and led to an astounding criminal outburst of church burnings, murder, and suicide. The 2003 edition of this bestselling and award-winning book is revised and expanded, with startling new revelations throughout.

6 x 9 • 400 pages • ISBN: 0-922915-94-6 • $18.95 • Available November 2003

DEATH SCENES

A Homicide Detective's Scrapbook

Text by Katherine Dunn

Edited by Sean Tejaratchi

"If you've ever wanted to gaze on crime-scene snaps... then this terrifying, near unbearable compilation is the book for you. Already an underground bestseller, the paradox is that *Death Scenes* is not so much a reflection of what a violent society it is that we live in, as what a safe one. For onlly in a society like ours, in which death is hidden away, would a book like this be so genuinely shocking."
— **JW, GQ Magazine**

Extremely graphic • Age statement required • 10 x 8 • 168 pages • ISBN: 0-922915-29-6 $19.95 • (Hardcover edition • limited quantity: $40)

TO ORDER FROM FERAL HOUSE:

Individuals: Send check or money order to Feral House, P.O. Box 39910, Los Angeles CA 90039, USA. For credit card orders: call (800) 967-7885 or fax your info to (323) 666-3330. CA residents please add 8.25% sales tax.

U.S. shipping: add $4.50 for first item, $2 each additional item. Shipping to Canada and Mexico: add $9 for first item, $6 each additional item. Other countries: add $11 for first item, $9 each additional item. Non-U.S. originated orders must include international money order or check for U.S. funds drawn on a U.S. bank. We are sorry, but we cannot process non-U.S. credit cards.